A SPY FOR ALL SEASONS

My Life in the CIA

Duane R. Clarridge

with Digby Diehl

A LISA DREW BOOK

SCRIBNER

SCRIBNER
Rockefeller Center
1230 Avenue of the Americas
New York, NY 10020

SCRIBNER and design are trademarks of Macmillan Library Research USA, Inc. under
license by Simon & Schuster, the publisher of this work.

Designed by Erich Hobbing
Set in Caledonia
Manufactured in the United States of America

10 9 8 7 6 5 4 3 2 1

Library of Congress Cataloging-In-Publication Data

Clarridge, Duane R.
A spy for all seasons: my life in the CIA/ Duane R. Clarridge with Digby Diehl.
p.   cm.
Includes index.
1. United States. Central Intelligence Agency. 2. Clarridge, Duane R.
3.   Spies—United States—Biography. I. Diehl, Digby. II. Title.
JK468.I6C5483   1997
327.12′ 092—dc20   96-36066
[B]
CIP

ISBN 0-7432-4536-9

For information regarding the special discounts for bulk purchases, please contact Simon &
Schuster Special Sales at 1-800-456-6798 or busi..ᴄss ⱳ sɪmonandschuster.com

For CASSI, IAN, and TARIK,
who paid a price for all of this.

Contents

Contents

PART IV: FIGHTING NEW ENEMIES

PART V: ATTACKED FROM WITHIN

Foreword

I have written this book largely for two purposes. One, to pay my most able and mostly unpaid attorney, William McDaniel, for preparing my defense after my indictment by Lawrence Walsh and his cronies. Two, I hope to establish a small foundation to be administered by a third party to provide funds to CIA officers who find themselves caught up in political intrigues as a result of their official duties, so that in the first critical days of the confrontation, they can seek legal advice without having to worry about where the money for such will come from. I noted during my own experience with the Iran-contra nonsense and from observations during the Watergate episode that during the first days officers are particularly vulnerable. Sworn depositions and the like are seldom given with perfect memory and prove to be unwise. Prosecutors failing to make indictments on the real issues fall back on these depositions and other statements to bring cases of perjury and such in order to justify their fiscal expenditures and very existence. I do not anticipate that the funds of the foundation will ever suffice for entire trials, but perhaps they will rarely come to pass if early legal advice is available.

In addition, I hope this book will provide a more fulsome and accurate description to the public of what a Clandestine Services case officer really does. This is not a book to correct the record concerning events in Latin America during 1981–84, although it will do that to some extent. A full correction would probably take a book or books. Having read a few about this period, I conclude that if the rest of the written history one reads were as distorted and full of whimsy and inaccuracies as these books, we'd really know few historical truths about anything.

I do not have to thank a lot of people for their assistance in writing this book because it is largely straight from my head. I was closer to the events about which I write than most, although I have checked some details with retired colleagues, who have my gratitude and who know who they are.

A few places, dates, and of course participants have been blurred for security reasons. An *F* in brackets after a name indicates that it is fictitious even as an alias.

Finally, I want to thank Lisa Drew, my editor, for even considering this book and for her patience with its writing, and, two others, one a delightful Democrat, the other a precious and special friend, for making the entire endeavor possible.

San Diego, California
November 26, 1995

A Life in the Shadows
of History

TWELVE HOURS IN BAGHDAD, 1986

The executive jet lifted off from an airfield somewhere in the Middle East and headed east and then southeast, into the hazy morning sun. Below, the desert appeared as through a granular, yellowish gray filter. It went on and on, interrupted occasionally by escarpments, hillocks, and black, antlike rectangles, sometimes solitary, at other times in groups and in motion. Through half-closed eyes I could almost imagine below my hero, T. E. Lawrence, rocking rhythmically in the saddle to the stride of one of the black rectangles, the camels of the bedouin Arab army of liberation he rode with on the way to 'Aqaba in the summer of 1917. My other heroes, Marcus Aurelius and Frederick Townsend Ward, would have found the climate much too oppressive. Not Lawrence of Arabia.

Taking on altitude, the plane lined up with the now closed Trans-Arabian oil pipeline, which traverses Saudi Arabia and Jordan to Lebanon. On board were just the pilots, myself, and another CIA official, alias Wallace L. Goodspeed [F]. I was Dax P. LeBaron. Most Clandestine Services officers traveled in alias those days for security reasons. Wallace and I were making a secret trip to Baghdad in the early spring of 1986, in the midst of the bloody, prolonged Iran-Iraq War, hoping to meet with the Iraqi dictator, Saddam Hussein. About thirty-five minutes into the flight, the pilot adjusted his course to the northeast, straight for Baghdad.

The genesis of this trip involved Washington policy. Concern about the radical, religiously driven foreign policy of Iran, and the possibility of Iraq's defeat, had forced the United States to quietly support Iraq with intelligence for its war effort. Iraq in return was to cease terrorist activities around the world, no longer harbor terrorists within its borders, and provide the U.S. government with information on terrorists and their activities.

Although we had given the Iraqis intelligence to improve their battle-field performance—particularly in the air—they were not fulfilling their end of the agreement. It was true that Abu Nidal and his band of murderers were gone, as were some other terrorist groups. However, Abu Ibrahim, the expert bomb maker, was still in Iraq. Ibrahim had a talent for constructing ingenious machines of death, such as refrigerator trucks whose cooling pipes were filled with liquid explosives. Perhaps the only countries in which the Iraqis engaged in terrorism those days (aside from at home) were Syria and Iran, their archenemies, who at the time were sort of allied against Iraq. The Iraqis needed Abu Ibrahim to conduct terrorism against them. Plus, some current and former Al Fatah terrorists had found safe haven in Iraq. My new area of responsibility at the CIA was counterterrorism, and I was going to Iraq to try to persuade them to cooperate to a greater degree in combating terrorism.

Wallace and I had been forced to wait almost a week for Saddam Hussein to decide when and if he would receive us. We stayed nearby in the Middle East in the event the decision was positive. Finally, we received the okay to proceed to Baghdad. In the ways of the Middle East, we were not told specifically that we would meet Saddam Hussein, but I knew that the principal point on my agenda would be decided by Saddam Hussein alone, whether we met him or not.

I had never been to Baghdad and looked forward to even a brief visit. Our aircraft began to lose altitude, and through the thick dust I could see the distant Euphrates River, and then a large city of flat-topped buildings, often within compound walls, seemingly guarded by thousands of sentinels in feathered green helmets—the famous *Phoenix dactylifera* date palms. I was diverted from this scene by the pilot's leaning back through the cockpit door, speaking to us for the first time. He advised us that he had just been vectored to land at the Baghdad city airport, rather than the new international terminal outside the city, which we had expected to be our destination. As we lined up for our final approach from east to west, I had a marvelous view of the Tigris River, whose banks Baghdad spans. Wallace began to hum; we had said little to each other during the flight, perhaps because we were both talked out from our week of waiting.

At about 12:30 P.M. we landed and taxied up to the front of a square, squat, single-story terminal with a control tower on top, a copy of those I had seen in Delhi, Patna, Rangoon, Lahore, and elsewhere the British went. These were probably the work of a single architect in the "Works Department" of the British Raj, before or during World War II. The aircraft door swung down and a blast of intense heat, mingled with chewable particles of sand, swept through the fuselage.

Standing with hands on hips in the shade of the covered porch that surrounded the terminal was a tall, dour-looking man in his early forties. Dr. Fadil Barak, chief of the Iraqi Directorate of General Intelligence (DGI), was dressed in the green khaki uniform of the ruling Baathi political party, complete with handgun in holster, and accompanied by a phalanx of bodyguards and drivers. Barak had been granted his doctorate by Lumumba University in Moscow, and like most high officials in Iraq, he was a blood relative of Saddam Hussein. He shook hands, muttered a few perfunctory words of welcome, and with a grim, unsmiling manner whisked us off in a caravan of Mercedes-Benzes.

Wallace assumed we were headed for DGI headquarters, but instead we were taken to a walled compound in an obviously affluent suburb of Baghdad, evidently a DGI safe house for VIP visitors. This was fine with me. The Iranians had been firing Scud missiles at Baghdad for some time, and DGI headquarters had to be a target. It would be my bad luck to be inside when the Iranians got lucky with one of their Scuds.

Although we were due to fly out of Baghdad at about 12:30 A.M. on an Air France flight to Paris, the Iraqis insisted on giving us each a private bedroom suite in which to freshen up. Mine had a super king-size bed and an ornate bathtub that could contain three, which made for obvious possibilities under other circumstances. I splashed some water on my face, changed my shirt, and went downstairs. Barak and two or three of his subordinates awaited us.

Perhaps because Arabs refer often to their Arab "brothers" and the Arab "nation," and the term *Arab world* is used by non-Arabs, there is the popular notion that all Arabs are rather alike, no matter from which country they come. This is incorrect. They do indeed share an overall cultural and religious heritage, but within this framework, different Arab groups, sometimes associated with a particular country, have evolved. The Iraqis are one of these distinct groups, and even within Iraq, there are major ethnic, religious, and cultural differences. For generations, other Arabs have disparaged the Iraqis as uncouth, ignorant plodders, but they have also feared them as tough and ruthless, frequently referring to them as "thugs."

Wallace and I did not know what the intermediary who had arranged our visit to Baghdad had conveyed to the Iraqi authorities about the two purposes of our trip. He thought we were out of our minds when he learned of my mission, which was the principal one; Wallace had other matters, connected with intelligence support, to discuss.

The previous year, a Palestinian terrorist offshoot of Arafat's Al Fatah led by Mohammed Abul Abbas, aka Abu Abbas, had hijacked an Italian cruise ship, the *Achille Lauro*. They murdered a wheelchair-bound American passenger named Leon Klinghoffer and subsequently threw him overboard off the Syrian coast. Eventually, the ship and the terrorists returned to Egypt. The Egyptians refused to hand over the murderers, including Abu Abbas, and prepared to dispatch them to Tunis by air. Lt. Col. Oliver North and other National Security Council staff members had devised a plan to capture Abbas and his team of terrorists by forcing down their Egyptair flight as it was en route to Tunis. Aircraft from the U.S. Navy's Sixth Fleet in the Mediterranean accomplished the task, and the Egyptian aircraft landed at Sigonella, the NATO base in Sicily. The plan had worked, but the Italians refused to arrest Abu Abbas and in fact assisted his departure to Belgrade, Yugoslavia, whence he proceeded to Baghdad. Abbas had been sheltered there by the Iraqi authorities ever since, in clear violation of our agreement.

I was in Iraq for the explicit purpose of returning Abu Abbas to the United States to stand trial for murder. I was not naive enough to expect that Saddam Hussein would hand over Abbas directly to us. In the Arab tradition, that simply was not done. Instead, I had formulated a plan to extract and capture Abu Abbas in a way that would not implicate the Iraqi government, but would require its connivance, involving our forcing down an Iraqi plane headed for Yemen with Abu Abbas aboard. Yemen was one of the few places left in the world where Abu Abbas would be welcome. It was not the greatest plan, but we had ruled out other options after extensive analysis. Perhaps the Iraqis could come up with a better solution.

As I explained the purpose of our visit and sketched the outlines of the plan, Barak's cold eyes grew wider and wider. By the time I was finished, his demeanor clearly signaled that he, too, thought I was insane. In a bizarre way, Barak took it almost personally. He seemed insulted that we would dare ask such a thing. He began to sulk.

Aside from the issue of turning over an Arab "brother" (actually other Arabs don't like Palestinians, equating them with Jews and envying their intelligence, commercial know-how, and work ethic), I suppose the act of murdering a single American tourist (and a Jew at that) and the risk of turning over the murderer simply didn't compute for a man who had witnessed and been associated with the killing of thousands on the battlefront with Iran, not to mention Iraq's internal bloodbaths, as Saddam Hussein liquidated his real and imagined opponents and failed military officers. On the other hand, Barak and the others had to consider the effect of a negative reply on the intelligence support we were providing.

Immediately Barak launched into a harangue about the inadequacy of America's intelligence support. This was not a new complaint and was, in fact, another of the reasons for our trip to Baghdad. At that point, the Iraqis were being pressed very heavily and rather successfully by Iranian forces in the Al Faw peninsula, which lay south of the large and important

Iraqi city of Basra. If the Iranians broke the Iraqis at Al Faw, they could sweep into Basra and the fate of the Iraqi regime would be in question.

Barak complained about our intelligence on this front, and in particular about the Iraqi Air Force's inability to hit Iranian oil facilities and military targets in the Iranian hinterland. Although he steadfastly maintained that it was our fault, the real problem was that the Iraqis didn't know how to use intelligence and get it to the shooter who needed it. Moreover, out of fear of the Iranians' missile defense, Iraqi pilots were loath to make their bomb and rocket runs under forty thousand feet. From that altitude, a "dumb" bomb—as distinct from a "smart" or guided one, which the Iraqis didn't have—will not hit the target, except for pure luck. Naturally, the pilots would not admit their apprehensions and thus their failure to make their attacks at lower, more effective altitudes, and their superiors had no way of checking on them. Ergo, the Americans' intelligence was faulty, and given the Iraqis' paranoia, they probably argued that it was intentionally so. Throughout our stay, Goodspeed spent much time closeted with intelligence analysts on this issue.

Even though Barak was head of Iraqi intelligence, I knew that he would not be the one to decide on the Abbas matter. Saddam Hussein alone would make that decision—with or without input from Barak. As we continued to press for our meeting to discuss the issue with Saddam Hussein, our host became frigid. While we were forced to linger over a huge midafternoon lunch, Barak engaged in a series of intense telephone calls. It became clear that the Iraqis were stalling for time. On arrival, we had made a fundamental mistake when we told Barak that we had a flight twelve hours hence. They could wait us out. Eventually, we corrected this by indicating we would stay as long as required. I suspect that the Iraqis hoped we would just go away, but when we seemed determined to stay until we got a decision, they had to do something more.

The "more" turned out to be a meeting with Iraqi spokesman and foreign minister Tariq Aziz at his office. The Foreign Ministry was a modern building with low ceilings, rather dimly lit probably because of the war, and furnished with an abundance of tasteful leather furniture. It was about 9 P.M. and after a brief wait we were ushered into Aziz's office. With his short, tubby appearance and fluent English, Aziz, the token Christian and a real survivor in the Baathi leadership, appeared almost urbane—except he, too, was decked out in the green khaki uniform of the Baathi party and armed with a handgun, which seemed odd for a foreign minister.

Aziz gave us no more cause for optimism than had Barak. We went around and around with our arguments, but to no avail. What we were asking was impossible, he said, and he indicated that his response had been cleared with Saddam Hussein. There was still some dancing around on whether we would meet him. Despite that, Aziz's attitude all but clinched it for me. I figured it was a no-go on Abu Abbas—we might as well gather up our baggage and head for the airport. It was about 10 P.M. and it had been a long, unrewarding day.

Returning to the safe house, Barak insisted on further conversation about intelligence support while we awaited dinner, which was forever in coming. When we pointed out the long drive to the international airport and the lateness of the hour, Barak brushed our concerns aside. Shortly thereafter, he left to take a telephone call and returned to say that Saddam Hussein would be unable to see us because he was preoccupied with events at Al Faw.

With a few additions and substitutions, Wallace and I were treated to another gastronomic excess, with more or less the same food we'd had for lunch. I had never seen so much beef and lamb in various forms on one table for so few people; moreover, there was a large assortment of Arab meze or appetizers, and mountains of fruit and luscious dates, probably the Barhi and Halawy varieties from Basra. Alas, there was no alcohol, and I could have used a drink. Everyone was on edge, but we continued to eat and talk. However, the pauses between the sentences grew longer and longer. There was a definite undercurrent of hostility on both sides. Barak pouted like a petulant child. Every so often we mentioned to him that it was becoming increasingly urgent that we head for the plane.

Goodspeed, one of the lightest travelers I've ever known, and I retired briefly upstairs to bring our bags down. We assumed we'd be leaving directly, but even after dinner, Barak continued to delay our departure. There was a look of increasing concern on his face. Perhaps there was behind-the-scenes maneuvering that was out of his hands; perhaps Saddam Hussein was still mulling over the idea of receiving us. Perhaps they were wondering if in refusing to meet with us they risked cutting off the flow of U.S. intelligence about Iran. They might even have been weighing the possibility of letting us have Abbas after all, but I doubted it. Perhaps it was nothing more than gamesmanship and deliberate provocation on Barak's part.

By now it was nearly midnight, and we were still sitting around the villa. It turned out that we were waiting for the phone to ring. When it did, Barak had a brief conversation with someone on the other end and finally decided it was time to go to the airport. Although I hadn't given this venture a high probability of success, I was aggravated by the way it had failed. Above all I was annoyed at Barak's unnecessarily nasty attitude and downright rude behavior. Because of his stalling, there was no way we were going to make the flight to Paris. The Arabs' characterization of the Iraqis as uncivilized thugs was correct, I thought.

A very large, new black Mercedes pulled into the drive. I assumed that the chauffeur would take us to the plane, but Barak opened the driver's door, literally yanked him out of the seat, and got behind the wheel. I sat in the passenger seat beside him, and Goodspeed climbed in back with the bags and what was to have been our chauffeur. We roared out through the gate and into the suburban Baghdad night on the way to the airport. Rarely have I had a high-speed drive like that. Barak appeared to be taking out his hostility toward us by driving at breakneck pace, and it was not because he was trying to get to the airport in time for us to catch our plane. By my watch, we were about to miss it. It was well after 12 A.M.

We were a land rocket. The speedometer read two hundred plus kilometers per hour. Fortunately, we eventually found ourselves on a four-lane highway. Careening down the road, I felt the Iraqis had acted in bad faith, that they had suckered the U.S. government into a deal with no intention of fulfilling their end of the bargain. I felt frustrated that the American government was helping them at all and enraged that Iraq was getting away with harboring criminals who murdered innocent people in acts of terror. I suspected that my government, and this was what really pissed me off, would uphold our part of the agreement. Undoubtedly, I was also angry because I had failed and I don't like to fail. Good tries don't count as far as I'm concerned.

Finally, about halfway through the journey, I turned in my seat toward Barak and said, "Tell Abu Abbas I am coming after him, and when I find him, and I will, I am going to kill him." I repeated myself to make sure Barak got it. Then, for the first and only time during our visit, the grim-faced Fadil Barak smiled, and broadly so. I had finally said something he understood.

There was an audible gasp from Wallace in the backseat. Both of us knew that a presidential executive order forbade killing anyone. I knew my remark was bluster born out of frustration, but did Barak? I doubt it, for it fit with his view of the world and I hope he conveyed it to Abu Abbas.

The moment we arrived at the terminal, guards rushed out from everywhere to take our luggage and our tickets and escort us. Barak strode through the beautiful, recently completed airport as though he owned the place. Groups of people parted in front of us as they recognized Barak or his green uniform.

We were already half an hour past the departure time for the Air France flight, but the plane was still there. It couldn't go anywhere because an Iraqi Army armored personnel carrier had been parked crosswise at its tail. We assumed that we were heading straight for the departure gate, but that was not what Barak had in mind. He ushered us into the VIP lounge and proceeded to have tea served. Arab hospitality at its best. To be polite, you really have to have two cups. Goodspeed and I looked at each other and settled back on the comfortable leather couches, drank tea, and made small talk. Barak kept us there for about twenty minutes. Finally, one of his minions produced two nicely wrapped boxes of dates, one for each of us. With that, Barak accompanied us to the gate and said an unsmiling farewell.

I am absolutely sure of one thing. He was delighted to be rid of us. However, the hostile stares of the sweating passengers and crew when we entered the aircraft indicated that we were not particularly welcome there either. We should have been; the armored personnel carrier coughed to life and clanked away; the plane could depart.

It was probably about a quarter to two in the morning when we lifted off. All I could think was that I needed a stiff drink. I asked the stewardess for a double whiskey and soda. As the plane gained altitude and the other passengers dozed in the darkened cabin, I tried to put the past fourteen hours of frustrations in perspective.

Goodspeed was already asleep in the seat behind me when the man across the aisle asked what line of work I was in. I told him I sold wholesale funerary supplies. He smiled grimly and went back to his book. My cover story was designed to be a conversation stopper, and it worked every time, on this occasion better than most, for my would-be interlocutor surely knew there were a lot of war dead in Iraq and probably thought I had filled up my order book. That Muslims don't make much use of mortuary supplies, he probably didn't know.

We had not gotten Abu Abbas, but we had signaled that we were on the offensive against terrorists and their supporters. This and the near miss of Abu Abbas at Sigonella would trickle into the consciousnesses of some of these murderers and their potential followers and perhaps give some of them pause. Meanwhile we could continue our pursuit. Maybe I was just putting the best face on a failure; time would tell. I ordered another double whiskey and reminded myself that my great friend Chuck Cogan, in Paris, had made dinner reservations for us and his wife at Brasserie Flo for that evening.

Postscript: Fadil Barak was removed as the head of the DGI not long after our trip. I doubt that our visit had anything to do with his departure. My experience in Baghdad indicated that he was a dim bulb. In October 1996, an Iraqui opposition leader informed me that Barak was liquidated by Saddam Hussein in 1991.

PART I

THE MAKING
OF A SPY

CHAPTER 1

Formative Years

After all this time, you can still hear my hometown in my voice. The clipped Yankee tones of Nashua, New Hampshire, have stayed with me—as have many of the values and traditions that were instilled in me there.

I was born Duane Ramsdell Clarridge on April 16, 1932. The following year, my parents and I moved into a house on the corner of Webster and Elliot Streets that had been built for my father by my grandfather, a contractor. It was brick, and it was double layered to keep out the New England winter. My father, a dentist, was very proud of that. The house was also an ingenious example of recycling: those two tiers of bricks had been scavenged from a church in southern Nashua that had burned down.

My father, Duane Herbert Clarridge, was the fifth of six children born into a family of some means in Milford, Massachusetts. Grandfather Clarridge's hundred-acre farm was situated on a knoll, and the wood-framed house was reached by a graceful, long gravel driveway, which wound around past the barn, garages, gas pumps, dynamite storehouse, and various outbuildings.

The main house was large and spacious. The huge living room had an impressive brick fireplace; the dining room could seat thirty-five people comfortably. Upstairs were innumerable bedrooms. In addition to his contracting business, Grandfather was a sort of gentleman farmer. A few token cows, pigs, horses, and chickens were always around. The property also contained some heavily wooded areas and a stream. In the middle of the woods was a log cabin that my father and his older brother Lee had built as a hideaway.

Grandfather's name was Arthur Preston Clarridge, but everyone, including his children, and his wife, Myrtle, called him the Boss. To some extent all of his children were intimidated by him. I don't think that my father's childhood was particularly happy. Grandmother Clarridge came from old New England stock of near-*Mayflower* vintage. Her maiden name was LeBaron, and she traced her lineage back to a French doctor of the same name who arrived in the Massachusetts Bay Colony before

1630. She ran her home like a tight ship, and she was always busy with the domestic details of managing the large establishment. She was a great cook, but not particularly warm or affectionate. Being the next-to-last kid, my father was almost a nonentity within the family. His great refuge was school and books, which were, apparently, provided in some profusion. He attended a one-room schoolhouse and always did very well academically.

In the long run, a lack of attention from Grandfather may not have been such a bad thing for my father. The Boss ran the family establishment somewhat along baronial lines, basically indenturing his two oldest sons, Fred and Lee, to his construction business and building them nice houses at the bottom of the knoll. His daughters Hazel and Sybil and their husbands had homes on another side of the knoll, but not on the family property. Hazel's husband also frequently worked for the Boss. The only two children who really became independent were my father and his oldest sister, Frances, a teacher, who escaped Milford. She was instrumental in getting the Boss to agree that my father should go to college. He went to Tufts for a year and then transferred to Harvard, graduating from Harvard Dental School in 1927.

My mother, Alice Scott Ramsdell, was educated beyond high school, completing her studies in Boston in 1929. She met my father when he came to Nashua to join another dentist in his practice and married him shortly thereafter. She was a good-looking woman with a gorgeous figure. I came to know that in great detail because when I was about thirteen, I ran across a picture album in her secretary. The entire album consisted of nude pictures of her that my father had taken in the forest on Grandfather Clarridge's farm in Milford. Serious photography was one of my father's hobbies.

Like those of many women of her day, my mother's interests were centered around family and community. Besides caring for my sister and me, she was active in a Nashua ladies' organization called Good Cheer, which supported a number of visiting practical nurses, and she spent a lot of time on her own going around and helping the elderly.

My parents were active Republican Party stalwarts and campaigners. When Wendell Willkie was running for president in 1940, they gave a party for him. I remember being introduced to him and shaking his hand. This was a special event, but political gatherings at our home were not all that unusual. My maternal grandmother, Alice McQuesten, had married George Ramsdell, the son of a former governor of New Hampshire (Republican, of course), during the 1898 Spanish-American War.

My maternal grandmother was widowed at an early age, but never remarried. She lived about a block away from us in a fine turn-of-the-century cottage with a slate roof. Grandmother Ramsdell, whom we called Nana, was by any measure a formidable woman. She had white hair, and one of the family myths was that her hair had turned white overnight after a fall down the steps leading to her front door. Educated as a teacher, she was born in the tiny hamlet of Litchfield, New Hampshire. She attended school in nearby Merrimack, a feat that required her to row across the Merrimack River, even in winter, twice daily. Moreover, she never learned how to swim.

Grandmother's son, my uncle George, lived with and took care of her. He did odd jobs for my father and worked as a deliveryman for his uncle, who was a successful grocer and butcher in Nashua.

Nana doted on me, and we spent a lot of time together. I remember her staying with me in the hospital when I had my tonsils taken out at age three. She slept in a chair at my side, held my hand, and fed me ice cream to soothe my sore throat. Of course, one reason why my mother didn't perform this duty may have been that my sister, Cynthia Delight (Delight because my father was delighted to have the daughter he wanted), was just a newborn at the time. She was born in 1935, and I remember being profoundly disappointed at her homecoming. I expected a playmate and here was this squiggly little baby.

In the 1930s most children didn't go to preschool, but stayed home until they went to elementary school. In Nashua at that time, kindergartens were just being organized. After some kind of evaluation, I began first grade in 1937, a year earlier than my peers, at Mount Pleasant Elementary School. Being a year ahead had its pluses and minuses throughout my childhood and adolescence. There was no question that I could do the schoolwork, but I didn't do nearly as well with the social "work" of growing up. I was a rather shy and withdrawn child—I played with other kids, but never formed the great boyhood friendships that other children did. Years later, my father described me as a "late bloomer."

I was a great reader—as was my father—and a self-reliant child. I was happy playing with my electric train, my soldiers (that I had molded out of lead), my Erector set, my blocks, and, of course, my books.

As I grew, the nearby woods changed from frightening to inviting—they were marvelous places for adventures, both by myself and with neighbor children. When the United States entered World War II, we started playing soldier, and the woods and fields near Grandmother's were great for acting out our fantasy battles. We dug foxholes and put up tents. Slowly I developed my own little team of soldiers from the children in the neighborhood—you might say I "recruited" them. In that respect it was an idyllic youth. I had fields and forests to play in, and time to daydream and invent games in a safe environment.

My father followed World War II and events in Europe closely. I knew as much as a seven-year-old could grasp of the Russo-Finnish War, which began in 1939. Our family was pro-Finland, and we children donned white sheets over our ski parkas and pretended to be the Finnish soldiers we admired. To this end, my father made me a copy of a French machine gun from wood. One of his hobbies was building fine American colonial furniture. I grew up with a fondness for wood, which has remained with me throughout my life. I attempt wood sculpting when I have the time.

My father had been all for entering the war on the side of the British, even before Pearl Harbor. The family across the street, the Carters, shared this activist viewpoint and were involved in the Bundles for Britain campaign, and in helping to resettle English children who had been sent to Canada and America to escape the bombing. One day in June of 1940, I was digging a hole in the driveway and suddenly Johnnie and Dickie Carter ran over to say that France had fallen to the Germans. They were five and six years older than I was and had a much clearer understanding of what was going on, but it must have made some impression on me. Late that summer, I was sent with my uncle Lee and his family to the New York World's Fair. I recall seeing the French pavilion and wondering why it was there since I had been told France had "ceased to exist."

In early December 1941, while visiting the home of friends, my father called me into the drawing room to listen to the radio report of the Japanese attack on Pearl Harbor. After the broadcast was over, he explained what the attack meant and why it was so important.

Because my father was a dentist, there was always the possibility that he would be called into military service. The youngest medical and dental personnel were being drafted, with older doctors and dentists being taken as needed. I think my father wanted to enlist before he got the "greetings" letter, but a lot of local pressure was on him to wait his turn and not leave Nashua short of dentists. As it turned out, he was never called. I think he regretted not serving.

It was Dickie Carter who gave me my nickname, Dewey. My parents had named me Duane, not only in honor of my father, but to give me a name that couldn't be made into a nickname. Dickie Carter was determined to give me a nickname. In 1944, New York governor Thomas E. Dewey ran for president against Franklin Roosevelt. Dickie borrowed the governor's last name and slapped it on me. It stuck. A lot of people think it doesn't really suit me, but attempts to do away with it have never really worked. By mistake, it even became part of my alias in the CIA. For a time I was known as Dewey Marone, but after that pseudonym surfaced in the press, I chose another drawn from the oldest branches of the family tree—Dax Preston LeBaron.

With the war came gas rationing, but we still managed to spend summers at the vacation home my grandfather had built for my father on Governor's Island at Lake Winnipesaukee. It was a time when neighbors knew one another and helped each other out. My father had to keep up his practice in Nashua, but on weekends he would take the train, together with other men who were coming up from the city. One family would go pick up all the men and bring them to the island, which was connected to the mainland by a bridge. To do the grocery shopping, each week a different family went into town and brought back whatever was needed for everyone. Back in Nashua, there was our victory garden and endless canning of fruits and vegetables in the fall and, of course, the scrap-metal and paper collections for the war effort.

By and large, my sister, Cynthia, and I got along well. She was a pretty girl and most favored by my father. Because I was a boy, I was expected to learn and adhere to a special set of male requirements or standards. My chores were to be accomplished correctly, the first time around, and on time. Punctuality, truthfulness, and self-discipline were insisted upon. Hard work came before play. One did not complain or make excuses for failures. I was taught that few things in life are important. Although not stated, it was made clear that emotional gestures and speech were signs of weakness and to be avoided. Very little pocket money was dispensed, and when it was, I was expected to have earned it for accomplishments outside my regular chores; there was no weekly allowance. All of this affected many parts of my adult life.

Back then, there were even better adventures to be had at Lake Winnipesaukee than in the woods of Nashua. There was a beach with tennis courts and a raft, and friends like the Beattie brothers, Bob and Jack, Paul Kopperl, and Bruce Langmuir. My father made me a diving helmet out of an old hot-water boiler hooked up to a garden hose. We connected a bicycle pump to the garden hose, and I walked around on the bottom of the lake (about ten to twelve feet down). This inspired my lifelong interest in diving.

The fact that Grandmother and Uncle George lived up the street from us was a boon to my parents, because they functioned as built-in baby-sitters for Cynthia and me. They joined us frequently for Sunday dinner, and of course for all the holiday celebrations. I grew up listening to heated political debates, but even when the arguments were volatile and tempers flared, it was all great fun. One came to understand that we weren't going to kill one another over the issues. This understanding served me quite well when I got to Washington and began appearing regularly in front of hostile audiences in Congress.

Most of the discussion was not about world affairs but about various factions within the New Hampshire Republican Party, which ran the gamut from conservative to moderate—and stopped right there. Nobody talked about the Democrats—in New Hampshire, they just didn't matter. (That may have been an attitude I brought with me to Washington as well.) References to the Democrats were always in the context of the "corrupt" Boston Democratic machine, and Franklin Roosevelt's destruction of the middle class with his taxation policies. It was one topic on which everyone would agree.

I must have been about eight when Grandmother Ramsdell ran for the state legislature, just before the beginning of World War II. She was elected and served nine two-year terms, which covered the entire period of the war. The legislative season was not long—they had a fall session that lasted through Christmas, and a second session in the spring. Normally the legislature met every other year unless called into special session. Representatives were reimbursed for their transportation expenses to Concord, and not much else. When the House was in session, I remember Nana commuting by bus to the capital every morning. She waited for it at the corner of Concord Street, right near her home.

At a fairly early age, I became aware of Nana's ambition for me to enter politics. Within the family, she was virtually alone in this desire. Nevertheless, every spring she would bribe me to go sit with her in the legislature with the promise of a fried-clam lunch in Concord. On several occasions I heard her give speeches. Sherman Adams was then the Speaker of the House in Concord, and a rising star in the Republican Party. He was the apple of my grandmother's eye—until he became embroiled in the great vicuña-coat scandal after he became President Eisenhower's chief of staff and was forced to resign.

In the fall of 1943, I went off to the junior high school in the center of Nashua. It was a fairly good walk, but I used the time to invent all kinds of imaginary, wonderful dramas for myself, playing out elaborate scenarios on the route between home and school. The capacity to amuse myself that I developed as a little boy never left me.

My parents were not particularly religious, but they did send me to Sunday school. One of the biggest attractions of the Congregational Church was its fine library, particularly of books for young adults. I read books about foreign countries, the adventures of deep-sea divers, and exploration of air routes in Latin America. At home, I had a whole series of adventure stories built around children my age, each one taking place in a different country.

While in junior high school I started to adopt a contrary opinion about the capabilities of Germany. Most children had the jingoistic view that everything the United States made or did was wonderful and everything from Germany was no good, and I remember arguing with my school-mates over the quality of German equipment versus Allied equipment, particularly the battleship *Bismarck*. I was beginning to realize that propaganda wasn't necessarily correct and that the Germans did indeed have a lot of military equipment that was superior to our own. My classmates, needless to say, were appalled.

This opinion was a result of my reading, but until now I had not gone out of my way to express my opinions. I think I did it to make myself stand out, which I'd never been able to do before.

Sometime in 1945, my father decided that I would go away to prep school to finish my high school education. The Carters were pressing my parents to send me to Andover, where their sons had gone. Finally it was decided to send me to Peddie, in Hightstown, New Jersey, to "broaden" me. Today it might not seem that there would be much broadening to be gained by going to New Jersey, but in those days the Garden State seemed a lot farther away from New Hampshire than it does today.

Although I was going to Peddie for prep school, my father made it clear that I was to return to New England, preferably to an Ivy League university, for college. I understood that this was not a matter I had much choice in; I was to do everything possible at Peddie to get myself into a good university. My father was not a tyrant, but he was a disciplinarian. His children (and his wife, for that matter) followed instructions; it was important not just to do well but to do your best.

Then as now, most young people arrived at prep school with their parents, who helped them settle in. Not me. In the summer of 1946, when I was fourteen, my mother sewed name labels into my clothes, packed them in a steamer trunk, and took me to the train station in Boston. There wasn't a lot of kissing and hugging at my departure. Nevertheless, I remember looking out the window as the train started to pull away and seeing the tears in my mother's eyes.

I got off the train at Trenton and was met by a ruddy-faced, corpulent fellow, driving a brand-new Hudson Hornet, who I believe was the financial officer of the school. On the drive from the depot to the campus, he drilled me with stories of how tough it was going to be at prep school. Not surprisingly, he scared the life out of me, which has to be one of the dumber things to do to a young man on his first real outing away from home.

School was exacting and a grind. I had no problem with the discipline; I knew all about that already. We had classes five and a half days a week, including Saturday mornings. The purpose of all this was to reduce the exuberance of young boys—even then there was talk about putting salt-peter in the food. There was virtually no social interaction with girls—I think there were dances twice a year.

I was quite withdrawn in dealing with the opposite sex. Sally Winters, the girl who lived next door to us at Lake Winnipesaukee, took me into a tent (a leftover from the war games back in Nashua), and more or less indoctrinated me into the kissing business. But that was the end of it. Although I was becoming aware of girls, I was much too shy to make any moves, and in any event at Peddie they just weren't around.

I spent a lot of time studying. At prep school I really learned how to study, so much so that when I got to college and wasn't forced to hit the books, it bothered me. Peddie was a tough environment. There were endless examinations, done in blue books, just as they were done in college. I didn't take examinations well, even though I was able to master the material. For whatever reason, I froze.

At Peddie as in Nashua, I was not part of the in-group, at least in part because I was younger than the other boys in my class. A few young World War II veterans were in the school, but most of the older boys in my class were guys who had not done particularly well in high school. They had been sent to Peddie to redo some of their education in order to get into a good college. Most of the older boys smoked, and they did so in a large room outfitted with pool and Ping-Pong tables. It was like a club. I didn't smoke, and for most of my time at Peddie, I wasn't old enough to do so, even with my parents' permission. Thus, I was never a member of the club, with all that that meant. On Saturday nights the older boys went into town for what they called "tomato pies." I never went, partially because no one asked me, and partially because I thought the idea of "tomato pies" sounded really dumb. Who knew it was pizza?

To get home from Peddie to Nashua, I had to catch a train for Boston at Grand Central Station. After getting off the bus from Hightstown, I used to perch on my father's Gladstone suitcase and just sit in that beautiful cavernous terminal and watch the people go by, letting train after train for Boston depart without me. I became a connoisseur of details, noting how people walked, what kinds of shoes they wore, whether their clothing was well or cheaply made, whether the women wore perfume. After I'd had my fill, I'd finally call my parents to let them know what outbound train I'd be on; four or five hours later, they'd meet me in Boston.

After I went to Peddie, I was never in Nashua for very long at a stretch. Other than lengthy summer vacations, holiday breaks were quite short—a week at Christmas and a few days at Thanksgiving and in the spring. On one of my trips home, I picked up a bodybuilding magazine. At that time, bodybuilding or weight lifting was an obscure pastime, but the magazine had an ad for York barbells. I probably didn't weigh more than 130 pounds when I left Nashua—as a young child I'd been slender and rather on the sickly side, prone to colds and ear infections. I was also not the least bit athletic—I had poor hand/eye coordination, which pretty much torpedoed me in all the bat-and-ball sports. Moreover, my father didn't encourage participation in group sports. He believed, or so he said, that one of the reasons for the decline and eventual fall of the Roman Empire was an excessive preoccupation with spectator sports.

The barbells I ordered from the magazine arrived in my dorm room by mail. By lifting weights, I was doing something none of my peers did. I diligently pursued my bodybuilding program, and after I'd been at it for a while, my physique started to fill out, so much so that my schoolmates began to comment on it. Other boys took up the pursuit. I had come up with an innovation, a new wrinkle, something I would do repeatedly throughout my life. Chuck Cogan would say I was the ultimate faddist.

I subsequently joined the Peddie wrestling team. I was still hopeless as an athlete, but at least I didn't look like quite such a runt in comparison to my classmates. The high point of my athletic career at Peddie was when I joined the 150-pound football team. I was the center, and all I really had to do was hike the ball to the quarterback; there wasn't much hand/eye coordination required in that. Eventually I was named captain.

Summers at Lake Winnipesaukee continued to be the time when I unwound and had a social life. The Morse family had a house near ours on the lake. Eventually I struck up a relationship with Nancy Morse; between my junior and senior years at Peddie, she became my first real girlfriend. I was sixteen. When I returned to Peddie for my senior year, we began corresponding. I think it bothered my parents that I wrote to her more often than I wrote to them. Moreover, it drove my father crazy that I frequently failed to date my letters. He and my mother wrote me every week.

As a senior, it was time to decide where I was going to college. My father was leaning on me to come back to New England to an Ivy League school, but I'd applied to some schools that he found marginally acceptable, such as Colgate, and some that he thought were useless, such as Duke. I hadn't applied to any prestigious Ivy League schools, and unbeknownst to him, I hadn't taken the SATs either. Despite being a good student, I still had this fear of exams. At some point he must have spoken with someone at Peddie and gotten wind of what was up. With his hot breath on my neck I belatedly took the SATs in May of my senior year, just before graduation, and filed an application at Brown. Brown, like Peddie, had an affiliation with the Baptist Church, and there was a long tradition of Peddie alumni attending Brown. Over the summer I was admitted to Brown (with about a dozen of my classmates), but as far as my father was concerned, my acceptance into a proper Ivy League school had been accomplished by the slimmest of margins.

The summer between my graduating from Peddie and going to Brown, Nancy Morse and I became a steady couple. My father had bought me for $75 a Model A Ford (with rumble seat) as a graduation present. I painted it orange, and Nancy and I traveled around a good bit. By coincidence, she was to attend Brown's sister school, Pembroke, the following fall. When I left for Providence, Rhode Island, in September of 1949, I was just seventeen years old, but at least I had a girlfriend.

CHAPTER 2

Higher Education, 1949–55

BROWN UNIVERSITY

My father drove me in a stuffed car to Providence, Rhode Island. I lived in Brunonia Hall on the third floor with three roommates. One of them was Howard (Howie) Foster, who became a lifelong friend. We took to each other immediately. He was as outgoing as I was reticent. Unlike Howie, I still found it hard to go out and party during the week. The regimen I'd developed at Peddie stood me in good stead at Brown; I was disciplined to get the work done before going out to play. I taught Howie how to study (or tried to); he taught me how to drink. Up until the time I left for college, I'd had little contact with alcohol, other than an occasional beer. Howie introduced me to bourbon, and we had some interesting times over that. I had also become a pipe smoker. I was beginning to learn about sinning.

Incoming freshmen had to elect a class president. With my urging, Howie decided to run, and I was his campaign manager. We mounted a full-scale campaign, with banners made from bedsheets, posters and speeches, and glad-handing. I don't think Brown had ever seen anything like it. Of course, Howie was elected. He should have gone on to become a career politician, for he had all the talents and best of all, integrity.

The spring of freshman year was the time for fraternity rush. Each of the dozen or so fraternities on campus had a distinct personality. Howard and I decided we wanted to join Delta Phi, one of the oldest fraternities in the United States. At Brown it had a good reputation, and it was also known for its exuberant parties. I became the driving force for recruiting about a dozen of what were considered the most outstanding freshmen and getting all of them to pledge Delta Phi. As a result of my delivering this desirable pledge class, the older fraternity brothers started calling me Mr. Outstanding. Given all my shyness and insecurity, this was a huge ego boost—finally, I was one of the in-group, and a key one at that.

My nickname as Mr. Outstanding was short-lived, however. The following summer, I was working at the state park at The Weirs near our summer home. I was a ticket-taker, maintenance man, gardener, and general factotum. While my father paid for my education—the tuition, books, room and board—he made me earn my own spending money. I worked every summer during college; whatever I earned had to last me through the next academic year.

Several of my older fraternity brothers were working as counselors at a well-known and exclusive boys' camp on an island at the lake. One night we were all in the local town and a waitress was there who had been Miss New Hampshire the year before. I was eighteen by this time; I guess she was twenty, but she seemed much older. I knew her slightly.

The brothers had had a lot to drink, and they started chasing her around. It looked to me to be getting a little ugly, and she didn't have any place to stay. I wasn't trying to be Sir Galahad, but I wasn't going to stand by and let a bunch of drunken guys take advantage of her—brothers or no brothers. You can imagine how surprised my parents were when I arrived at midnight at the house on Governor's Island with this young woman in tow. I tucked her into the upper bunk in my room and I slept in the lower one. The next morning I took her back into town so she could go to work. My fraternity brothers never forgave me for spoiling their "fun." My nickname of Mr. Outstanding was out the window, and I began to get a great deal of serious harassment from two or three who had been involved in the incident.

By sophomore year in college, most young adults have solidified their relationships with their parents, and the dynamics are unlikely to change markedly. I'm somewhat unusual because during the summer after my freshman year, my relationship with my father changed dramatically—for the better, and overnight. All of a sudden the tussles of the last five years ended. We became great friends and remained so for the rest of his life. I no longer called him Dad or Father; I began calling him Clarridge. For some reason, he liked that immensely.

I think some of the change had to do with my mother. For the first time she started to assert herself with my father and even stood up to him if the situation warranted it. She began to speak up for what she wanted, including her own automobile, and my father got her a small Nash convertible.

Although they had fights as other married people do, my parents had a fundamentally good relationship. They were very modern for their time. I think they were sexually adventuresome with each other. My father's library had a secret compartment (which I eventually broke into), which had a variety of suggestive and sexually explicit books, volumes such as *Lady Chatterley's Lover*, which might seem pretty tame by today's standards, but were definitely avant-garde at the time.

When I returned to Brown in the fall of 1950, the first thing I did was take a test to determine whether I would be exempt from the draft to go to Korea. North Korea had invaded the South in June, and U.S. troops were once again at war, even if it was undeclared. My freshman grades had been merely acceptable—a jumble of B's and C's. I'd been following a premed curriculum, thinking perhaps to follow in my father's footsteps as a dentist, but science and math were clearly never going to be my strong suit. I decided to shift into history and political science, which I enjoyed much more, even though I had no idea what career they might lead to. I passed the draft deferment test. Unfortunately, Howard Foster, who was on probation because of his freshman grades, did not do well during the fall semester and had to join the Army. He became an officer and served as a forward artillery observer in Korea.

Even without Howard to coax me, I really began to break out of my shell. My run-in with the brothers over Miss New Hampshire notwithstanding, I was now very much a part of the in-group, albeit still a bit reticent. Meanwhile, my relationship with Nancy Morse faded away. There wasn't any big scene or official breakup; we both just started seeing other people.

Toward the end of the year I had to declare my major. I took a sample law entrance exam, but did poorly on it. I considered becoming an Egyptologist, but finally decided to take an interdepartmental major in American civilization. It was probably one of the brightest choices I made. I took a smorgasbord of courses having to do with the United States—history, economics, political science, literature, and even art. I loved the program, and my grades showed it. There were no more C's, just A's and B's, and more A's with each passing semester.

During this time I developed a memory that decides what is important and what is not and discards the latter. The courses I chose required a great deal of memorization, and I was able to master and retain names, dates, and facts and their interrelationships and meaning and could regurgitate them back on tests, as required. I also became proficient at psyching out what material was most likely to show up on exams. This capacity to anticipate questions, to commit facts to memory, and to keep them at my disposal stayed with me throughout my career in the CIA; eventually I became somewhat notorious both at Langley and in Congress for these abilities.

I also became interested in Russian studies. I took a Russian language course during my senior year, as well as a couple of Russian history courses, but I still hadn't made up my mind about what I was going to do once I graduated from Brown. I did particularly well in Russian, and with my father's blessing finally decided to apply to graduate school in international relations, with an emphasis on Soviet studies. I applied to the Johns Hopkins School of Advanced International Studies and the School of International Affairs at Columbia and the Russian Institute there. I was accepted by both schools, but rejected (at least temporarily) by the Russian Institute. They told me that if I did well in my first year of graduate school, I would be admitted to the Institute for the following year. I decided to go to Columbia.

By this time I was going steady with Margaret Reynard. I'd met Maggie in the fall of my junior year. She'd just transferred to Pembroke College from Oberlin, in Ohio. As frequently happens, however, Pembroke did not accept all her Oberlin credits, and she had lost half a year with the move. Technically, then, she was a second-semester sophomore as I began my junior year. From the time we first started dating, we were very much a couple and our relationship deepened from there. By my senior year, we'd already begun to talk about marriage.

It must be hard for contemporary college students to understand the haste to marry that most of us felt back then, but the political and social climate on campus in the early 1950s was very different from today's environment. The passage of the GI Bill enabled returning servicemen to get a university education, and much of my generation went to college with World War II veterans, who were considerably older than we. Many vets felt that the war had taken a big chunk out of their lives and that they were "behind schedule" in life. They were determined to make up for lost time, so when they came to college, they had only three things in mind—to get a degree, to get married, and to get a job.

They were very focused, and when we less worldly, less focused underclassmen came to school, we fell in with their aspirations and their timetable. We, too, were driven to get the degree, get a job, get married, and get on with life. It was a process—a track, if you will—that we followed largely without a great deal of self-examination. In my opinion, this is why there was no distinctive "fifties generation" as sociologists today lament.

The summer after I graduated I didn't work. Instead, I went to Boston and took a tutorial in Russian, trying to bring up my language skills to give me a better chance of eventually being accepted by the Russian Institute. But, immersing myself in Russian grammar that summer did nothing to ease my concern about my mother's health. She was diagnosed with breast cancer and underwent a double mastectomy. Aunt Frances, my father's favorite sister, had died about a year earlier, not long after my mother's brother, Uncle George, passed away. Happily, Mother bounced back well from surgery, and the doctors were optimistic about her prognosis, but to me it seemed that death was circling ever nearer our immediate family.

COLUMBIA UNIVERSITY

My first year at Columbia is a blur, largely because all I did was study. I took courses in international law and the workings of the United Nations, as well as classes in Soviet economics, literature, and foreign policy. The faculty was outstanding, a collection of people genuinely preeminent in their field.

It's somewhat daunting to think back on how little the United States really knew about the Soviet Union. Together with another handful of Russian specialists at Harvard, these men (and they were all men) were about the only "experts" in the United States. The head of the Russian Institute was Philip Mosley, who had been at Yalta as an adviser to Roosevelt and later served in the same capacity with Truman at Potsdam.

In my studies I even met Alexander Kerensky, who was quite elderly. Kerensky had been the head of the first nominally democratic Russian government after the downfall of Czar Nicholas, but the Bolsheviks had overthrown him as well. Kerensky fled first to Paris, then to the United States early in World War II, when France fell to the Nazis. I remember having tea and red caviar with him after his lecture. I enjoyed talking with him, and he helped make the Russians real to me. I could see how, politics aside, there were a great many affinities between the American and the Russian character. It was something that I would remember later in my CIA career—for relationships in the espionage business are made on a person-to-person basis.

Between my first and second years at Columbia, I worked in Washington in the State Department's Passport Office, a job that I got largely through family connections with Republican Party stalwart Sherman Adams. While in Washington I found myself living in a rooming house in what seemed to be a broom closet, with nothing more than a small portable fan for ventilation. I sweltered. At State I worked in the filing department, using a system primitive even by the standards of the day. The office was full of wooden file cases stuffed with three-by-five cards— like a library card catalog. Unbelievably, this was how the U.S. government kept track of passport applicants and recipients. At the end of the summer I drove all the way to Indiana to see Maggie, who was now formally my fiancée, then headed back to New York for my second year of graduate school. My grades during the first year had been good, and I'd finally been accepted into the Russian Institute.

I did well academically during my second year and wrote my master's thesis on what seemed an esoteric subject—"The World Federation of Trade Unions in Asia." The main premise of my work was the increasing competition between the Soviets and the Chinese for control of WFTU units within Asia. Although I didn't realize it then, this competition was a precursor to the big 1959 split between the Russians and the Chinese. If only I had had the wit or the courage to predict it in 1955!

My thesis adviser was Philip Mosley. Having the head of the Institute as my adviser was something of an advantage, but Mosley was quite demanding. My first draft was returned covered in red ink. He must have spent hours writing all over it. Mosley objected not so much to my premise, but to my writing style, and he worked with me until I finally beat it into some sort of acceptable shape.

At this point I was faced with two divergent paths: either I was going to continue with my studies and become an academic, or I would join the government in some capacity, probably in the Foreign Service. I was fed up with the textbooks. I'd been studying for hours on end ever since I left Nashua for Peddie nine years earlier, and there would be more books and papers to come before I got my Ph.D. and started teaching. Enough was enough. I was about to become a husband; I no longer wanted to be a student.

That left government service. Rumor around Columbia had it that the Foreign Service exam was rigorous. Although I was reasonably confident that I could pass it, a part of me still seized up at the prospect of a do-or-die exam, and in any event I was reluctant to keep at the books long enough to take the test. I wanted very badly to get out into the world. The test was several months off, and spending time in employment limbo waiting for the Foreign Service test and then for the test results was not what I had in mind. Added to all this, my previous experience working in the State Department Passport Office had not exactly left me overjoyed at the prospect of reentering that bureaucracy in any capacity.

I also had a strong desire to do whatever I could to defend our country against communism and the threat from the Soviet Union. There had been some speculation that with Stalin's death in 1953, the tensions between East and West would ease, but it soon became clear that this was not to be. Many who had watched the shadow of the Soviet Union lengthen after World War II felt a patriotic duty to defend our country. Those who didn't live through this period may find it hard to grasp, but war with Russia, either conventional or nuclear, was always considered a very real possibility.

I felt the way those in the OSS had felt in defending the United States against the Nazis in World War II. I believed that I had a calling, a duty, to protect our way of life from the Soviets, and I was hardly alone in my belief. Mine was a strongly activist point of view, and it was not at all clear to me what contribution I might make within the State Department.

It was February when the CIA recruiters came to Columbia. The organization was relatively new—certainly the initials CIA were not on everyone's lips. What little I did know about the Agency, however, was all good: I knew there was no entrance exam. I knew that CIA employment meant deployment and travel abroad. Most importantly, I knew that the purpose of the CIA was to advance the interests of the American people against our foreign enemies.

What I did not know was that they were looking at me as hard as I was looking at them. To recruit case officers, the CIA had spotters in the universities, professors who provided leads to the Agency about promising students. Many upper-echelon CIA men were from Brown, and the Russian Institute was an obvious place for them to be trolling for prospectives. For any number of reasons, I came to their attention; my Ivy League schooling at Brown and Columbia and my chosen field of specialized education targeted me as someone who might make a good CIA man. When the chance came to interview for a job with the CIA, I took it. The interview itself was uneventful, even perfunctory. The interviewer probably knew a lot about me already and told me virtually nothing about the CIA. I was too inexperienced to press him for details. I can't say that I clearly understood what the Agency did, except that it was in the business of espionage.

I discussed the prospect of joining the CIA with Maggie. She knew as little about the Agency as I, but she liked the idea of going abroad, and the idea of doing something constructive to fight communism.

We were married in Columbus, Indiana, on April 2, 1955, during Easter break of my last term at the Russian Institute. My parents, my sister, Nana, and I drove out for the ceremony; Howard Foster was my best man. After the wedding, the new Mrs. Clarridge and I returned by train to New York to live in what had been my bachelor flat in Astoria, Queens. At the end of spring break, I resumed the long subway commute to Morningside Heights to finish my schooling, and Maggie went to work as a ticketing agent for American Airlines.

Shortly thereafter, the CIA paid for a trip down to Washington where I was given a battery of aptitude tests. The ink on my diploma announcing that I now had a master's in international affairs had hardly dried when the Agency offered me a job in May. Clarridge—my father—was pleased at the prospect, as was my mother. After another brief discussion with Maggie, I accepted. I knew nothing about health plans, pay scale, or retirement plans. It never occurred to me to ask. Seldom has such an important—and a correct—life decision been made on so little information.

CHAPTER 3

Apprentice Spy,
1955–57

Maggie and I had been married for a little less than two months when I left her working in New York City and took off for Washington with the other love of my life—a 1953 Austin-Healey. It was a two-seater convertible, with an aluminum body and blue metallic paint. The top leaked in a heavy rain and the ignition was balky, but who cares when you are twenty-three and the world is before you?

The Headquarters at Langley was not yet constructed, and CIA functions were scattered all over Washington. I reported to a cluster of wooden buildings on Ohio Drive along the Potomac, not far from the Lincoln Memorial Reflecting Pool. Little more than shacks, they were completely anonymous, each designated by a letter of the alphabet. The buildings had formerly been used as barracks by the OSS during World War II, and they looked their age. They are long gone now; the Lincoln Memorial Polo Fields are where they used to be.

After the inevitable forms and processing, I joined a group of other candidates for our preliminary orientation, which, for security reasons, was largely focused on the functions of the Directorate of Intelligence— in other words, the analytical process. I suspect that it was a holding exercise while the CIA administration decided to which directorates we would be assigned. However, a few of us had not yet fulfilled our military obligation. My compatriots in this holding tank, about twenty in all, were as green as I was, but many seemed more worldly to me, perhaps because they were older and had already had some other career. As we got to know one another, we spent considerable time discussing which directorate to join. Some members of my class of recruits were headed for the Directorate of Operations (DO), or the Directorate of Plans, as it was then called. However, the majority, including almost all the few women, were going to the Directorate of Intelligence (DI).

This decision would shape one's CIA career from then on. Sometimes called the Clandestine Services, the Directorate of Operations is responsible for collection of foreign intelligence (generally from human sources), pursuing counterintelligence targets, and covert action. Covert action entails special activities, such as political action and paramilitary operations, to advance U.S. foreign policy objectives by influencing events in foreign countries. I believe I concluded at this time that my purpose in life and the reason I was in the CIA was to advance the interests of the U.S. government and the American people abroad. In real terms, this meant taking on the Soviet empire, Communist China, and their satellites, and preventing their domination of the world with their grotesque, inhuman, and corrupt ideology.

This view of mine had antecedents. Although my father and mother could probably be described as agnostics in a religious sense, they and Nana believed strongly in moral absolutes: put simply, there is good and there is evil. They inculcated in me an abhorrence of the moral relativism that infected the world around the turn of the century, represented, for example, by hidden and flagrant totalitarianism in all its forms—fascism, communism, and even America's liberal left. This does not mean that I was encouraged to believe that the end justifies the use of any means. The means must be proportionate, focused, and morally defensible as a solution.

In contrast to the DO, the Directorate of Intelligence takes information gathered from a wide variety of sources (including from the Directorate of Operations) and amalgamates the data, integrates it, and analyzes it. It then forms assessments and conclusions about political, economic, and military trends around the world. This evaluation gives the president and other decision makers a complete picture, so that policies and actions can be shaped based on the fullest possible information.

All of this discussion about "which directorate" was really for naught, because the decision on where to assign us had already been made—largely on the basis of the initial battery of tests we had taken, our academic background, and our desires. In my case, although nothing was ever said to me directly, the decision had been made that I should go to the Clandestine Services; otherwise, the Agency would not have wasted the Army's time by allowing me to go to OCS. The Agency also probably wanted to see how well I did in the Army to confirm its decision.

I was polygraphed a month or so after entering on duty, in a building in the Navy Annex area, probably South Building; the DCI had his office in East Building in the same complex. For me, the polygraph was a nonevent.

By the standards or demands of the last twenty years or so, one lecture or briefing was clearly missing from this orientation. Even at this relatively advanced point in the Agency's personnel processing, nothing was explained about the benefits—that is, retirement plan, health care, insurance, etc.—a major difference from today, when it is the first question a prospective employee asks. But mine was a different era, with different values, when personal interests were subordinated to the national good or survival. We did know that if you had a BA, you came to the CIA as a GS-5 (second-lieutenant equivalent)—an MA got you a GS-7 and a Ph.D., a GS-9—and that promotions up to GS-11 jumped two grades at a time. I remember learning with considerable surprise some three years later in Kathmandu that the Agency had retirement and health plans!

During these orientation weeks, we were often herded into an auditorium in one of the barracks buildings and given a series of dry lectures, most of which were boring, country-specific profiles. All the information was from the Directorate of Intelligence, and it was all quite perfunctory. We were given little assignments or projects. We learned how to give a mini–intelligence briefing. Meanwhile the Agency was sorting us out by directorate and by area of geographic expertise. Most weekends I drove the Healey back to New York to be with Maggie.

As far as I was concerned, this CIA indoctrination was just marking time. In the mid-1950s, every young man had an obligation to serve in the military, so before I could work for the CIA, I had to fulfill a two-year commitment to the armed forces. I was envious of those in my group who had already completed their service requirement. At least while they listened to someone drone on about the intelligence analytical process, they were waiting for a directorate assignment and getting on with their careers. As for me, listening to someone recite the almanac on Switzerland and the Sudan was pointless because I was headed for the Army.

The CIA gave us a choice of fulfilling our military obligation in the Army or the Air Force. The Air Force program was considered the easy way to go. After basic training, you went to officer candidate school (OCS) and then served for two years before returning to the Agency. The Army program was by reputation much more rigorous than the Air Force, but had the advantage that after successfully completing OCS, you did only six months of troop duty and then returned to the Agency, albeit still in the Army, until you finished your two-year obligation as an officer. The whole process began by enlisting in the Army and going to basic training. Then you had to go through advanced basic training, and it had to be in the infantry. After that, you had to get yourself into officer candidate school at the Infantry School at Fort Benning.

Up until this point, you were completely on your own, like any other Army recruit. If you passed the OCS exam, the Agency stepped in for the first time. The CIA ensured that you were admitted into the first available officer candidate course that came up. The Korean War had ended, and the Army was shrinking in both manpower and budget. Courses at Fort Benning were infrequent because the Army didn't need as many new officers.

It was up to me to get through officer candidate school successfully, and that was the big catch. If I washed out of OCS, I also washed out of the CIA. But I was still in the Army. I would still have to finish my two years of military service—as an enlisted man.

Four of us were the last of the Agency recruits to opt for Army training. The Army/CIA program was phasing down—perhaps because of a glut of junior officers or because of the general downsizing of the military. One of the other Army candidates was John Stein, a Yale graduate from Rhode Island, and a Whiffenpoof. He was a superb athlete, particularly at base-ball, and a genuinely fine human being. During orientation we struck up a friendship that endures to this day. He ended up buying my beloved Austin-Healey after OCS, when Maggie decided we needed a Volks-wagen Beetle, perhaps foreseeing an expanded family.

That August, after three months in the Agency's indoctrination course, Stein and I went down to the Army recruiting office in Alexandria, Vir-ginia, to enlist, and in doing so we nearly gave the recruiting sergeant a coronary. He didn't quite know what to make of two young men looking and dressed like a couple of college kids who came in to join up. Once we had filled out the forms, the suspicious look on his face suggested that he believed something fishy was going on. In 1955, college students weren't enlisting in the Army even for two years; being drafted was something else. He probably assumed that we were undercover plants by the Army's CIC, to be infiltrated into some outfit of the Army for investiga-tive purposes.

After a cursory medical examination, Stein and I left on a commercial flight to South Carolina that very afternoon. We reported immediately to Fort Jackson.

Stein and I were assigned to the same basic training unit, an artillery bat-talion of the famous 101st Airborne Division, which had been reduced to a basic training role. The captain in charge was rather long in the tooth, and obviously a veteran who had come up through the ranks. He was imme-diately suspicious of us. It was almost as if he had received a warning phone call from the sergeant in the recruiting office about those two spies, Private Clarridge and Private Stein. From the day I enlisted until I mustered out, no one I worked with or reported to in the Army knew of my CIA affilia-tion; but somewhere in the Army Staff, the truth was known.

They cut off my hair and gave me a uniform. They even had triple-E-width boots that fit me perfectly—the first such size I had encountered. I was in the Army now. Strangely enough, I liked it. I felt comfortable. At

Fort Jackson, I was thrown in with a wider cross section of America than I'd ever seen before, including a large contingent of good ole boys from the South.

We slept in large tents that held about twenty-plus men. Coal-stoked fires heated everything, including the occasional hot water for showering and shaving. The preponderance of Southerners meant that conversations with my fellow recruits often took on a decidedly regional bias; periodically we refought the Civil War. Despite my background as a Yankee and a product of private schools, I didn't have much trouble relating to them. In fact, I found these people attractive in many ways.

One reason was that they were different, yet "real"—light-years away from the ivory-tower intellectuals at Columbia. In mid-September about halfway through boot camp, however, my former life reached out to me. Maggie forwarded me a letter from Professor Mosley. The gist of it was, "The semester has started. Where the hell are you? You are supposed to be getting on with your Ph.D. dissertation." When I left the previous spring, I'd neglected to tell Mosley that I would not be back. I quickly wrote him, saying that my career plans had changed.

The eight weeks of initial basic training passed quickly, but our captain never got over his suspicions about us. Word must have gotten around, because when Stein and I changed units—still at Fort Jackson—for advanced basic training in light infantry, our reception from the new officers was the same.

One of the indicators that I was adapting well to Army life was that I was often named Private of the Week and received other honors. One of these laurels was my selection by my new company commander to march our basic training company, about 160 troops, past a reviewing stand, parade style, sixteen men abreast on a Saturday afternoon. It was a competition among the five or six companies then undergoing advanced infantry basic training, and the company commanders had wagers on the outcome.

Taking a company, even an experienced one, from a column of four to a column of eight and finally to a sixteen-man front is no easy trick—even for a drill sergeant. The real challenge, however, is the timing of your commands when you bring the sixteen-man columns into and out of the final turn, before you proceed in front of the reviewing stand. I had been doing well in practice, and I am sure my company commander thought he had his bet locked up. On the day of the event, however, I screwed up. Something went wrong coming out of the last turn. I gave the command for forward march too early and before those troops farthest from the pivoting men could come on line. We were most assuredly a ragged-looking bunch as we passed the reviewing stand. The rows and columns were not straight; no one was in step. The company commander was quite beside himself with humiliation as he took the salute. I didn't have to bear the brunt of his ire for long. Both Stein and I had passed the OCS exam and were transferred to Fort Benning.

I was still a private when I arrived in Georgia in April of 1956, but was promoted shortly thereafter to the rank of sergeant for pay purposes. After living in tents through basic training and advanced basic training, I landed in the lap of luxury—relatively speaking. At OCS we were billeted two to a room in brand-new barracks with hot running water. The relatively comfortable facilities were in sharp contrast with the purpose of OCS, since there was nothing comforting about our training. Officer candidate school was tough in order to build leadership.

Leadership is not something you can teach directly, certainly not in a classroom or on one of those touchy-feely excursions of the Outward Bound variety. All you can do is set up conditions under which people learn by experience. Leadership consists of becoming a person others are willing to follow, even when they know it may not be in their personal interest to do so. Thus, the motto of the infantry school at Fort Benning is Follow Me.

Part of leadership training was the drive to develop hardiness and discipline, and the ability to cope with a great deal of stress. That was accomplished at OCS by pressuring the aspiring officers as much as possible to see if we could take it. We did everything at attention except sleep. We marched or ran everywhere. Everything was done on the double. We were rousted from our beds in the middle of the night. We were pressed into making decisions with little or no sleep. Our uniforms were specifically cut down to be tight-fitting and uncomfortable. They were also starched to the point of petrification. I can still recall the crunching, tearing sound the shirts made as I struggled to drive my arms through sleeves that had quite literally been starched shut. It was all harassment, and it was all quite deliberate.

I didn't have a problem with it. I'd grown up with discipline. What the Army was doing was demanding, but it was nothing I couldn't handle; in a way, I thrived on it. However, I don't think John Stein shared my feeling that being in the Army and particularly at OCS was a wonderful leadership- and character-building adventure.

The two of us established a strong tie with each other, perhaps because we were the two recent college graduates in the group, shared the same values and New England heritage, and above all had our CIA link. A third CIA recruit had joined our OCS company but was dismissed at some point for cheating. A fourth arrived and was in an OCS company behind Stein's and mine. He was an absolutely sterling individual but had a physical disability; his completion of basic training and acceptance to OCS can be ascribed only to his courage and willpower. He was eventually mustered out.

The officers running the program still thought Stein and I suspect and different from the two hundred others. This didn't afford us any special dispensation from the hazing, however.

At OCS we were all sergeants, but except for Stein and me, the others were already staff sergeants and master sergeants with Korean War experience. This gave them an early performance edge in tasks such as marching troops and giving commands. I recall the hours, those few free ones, that I spent on the parade ground across the street from my barracks yelling into the wind to improve my "command voice." However, when it came to map reading, navigating by compass, laying heavy weapons such as the 81-mm and 4.2-inch mortars, and, above all, infantry tactics, Stein and I had our turn to shine. When senior officers came on several different occasions to inspect our progress near the end of the six-month course, we were in a large segment devoted to tactics, and I was always called upon to provide the solution to the particular problem. Because these inspections were surprise visits, the instructors couldn't prime me beforehand. Invariably, I could come up with the so-called school solution. It seemed just common sense.

As graduation neared, the company commander asked Stein and me to lecture the rest of our compatriots on etiquette. I guess he thought that because we were to be commissioned shortly—and thus become "officers and gentlemen"—we needed our edges polished. This was to be accomplished in a single morning session. We found Emily Post's book and then had to bone up on it big time. I had wanted to put Stein in a dress so that he could play the female role opposite me, but he refused! Our seminar covered everything we thought meaningful for "new gentlemen," such as protocol, decorum, table settings, and introductions, much to the amusement of the rest of our OCS class.

At commencement, I received my commission as a second lieutenant in the U.S. Army Reserve. I also was named a distinguished graduate—number two in my class. The three top graduates could opt for a regular Army commission, the same received by graduates of West Point. In six months I'd gone from a rather introverted, bookworm sort of fellow to one who could say "Follow Me" and get followed. Although I did not realize it until much later, perhaps around 1969, what I'd learned in the Army, particularly about leadership, was at least as valuable for my Agency career as all the years I'd spent in the university. The Marine Corps and the Army can teach leadership. The Navy and the Air Force offer a different type of leadership. What the former instill has great relevance for a career as a case officer in the Directorate of Operations, as I will explain later.

Stein and I were given a choice of five U.S. military posts to complete our six months of troop duty. We both selected the Basic Training Center at Fort Dix, New Jersey. Stein wanted to be assigned to Dix to be near his attractive fiancée, Charlie. The proximity to Washington, D.C., brought me closer to my goal. Stein was assigned as a deputy company commander of a training company. I was luckier; my first job was teaching basic tactics for troops in the early weeks of training.

Once I got to Fort Dix, the rest of life became a great deal more normal. Maggie had quit her job at American Airlines to come to Georgia to live during my last few weeks at OCS; occasionally we were given a Saturday pass. After graduation, we drove the Volkswagen to her parents' home in Indiana and then on to mine in New Hampshire, then ended up finding an apartment in Mt. Holly near the base. For the first time in a long time, I could spend evenings with my wife. Except when there were night exercises, my day was over by five in the afternoon. We had some semblance of a social life through the officers' club. Although it was de rigueur to put in an appearance there on Friday evening, I had weekends free. I think Maggie detected that the Army had changed me; I am not sure she liked the difference.

Eventually, I taught tactics in advanced basic training. The troops I instructed were going to go be the shooters. These were live-fire exercises with the infantry, the armor, and the artillery.

An example of a mundane principle that I learned in the military that stood me in good stead in the CIA was that the troops always eat first and if anything is left, the officer eats. I tried to follow this rule with my subordinates in the Agency, in the sense of taking a real interest in their professional and personal ups and downs and their aspirations.

As my tour at Fort Dix was concluding, the colonel who was the regimental commander began pressuring me to stay in the Army and become a regular officer. In a way I was tempted. I had gotten a lot out of my military experience and knew that I would be a successful officer. But the Army was at a low point in 1957 and I turned him down. I was still bent on joining the CIA.

In February 1957, regular military orders came to report to a certain unit in Washington, which was really a paper unit. I reported to the CIA, but still a second lieutenant in the Army, albeit in mufti.

Maggie and I took a small house in Falls Church, Virginia. Stein lived with us, but that was not the only reason we needed an extra bedroom. I was going to become a father.

Stein and I reported for our real beginning in the CIA. We were classified as JOTs—junior officer trainees—now called career trainees (CTs), apparently a more uplifting designation for today's sensitive youth. When we checked into the JOT office, I came to a pair of startling realizations. The first was that the entire place was staffed with people from Brown. The second was that I was somewhat famous before I got there, because of my performance in the Army. At Headquarters much was made of the fact that I'd been a distinguished graduate from OCS. Perhaps it was something not expected of an overeducated Ivy League twit.

I confirmed that I wanted to be assigned to the Directorate of Operations. I also told the Agency that I did not want to join the DO in the Soviet Division. This may have come as a surprise to them, given my studies of Soviet affairs at Columbia.

Although my choice may have been unexpected, the Agency didn't have a real problem with it. Their approach to the Cold War was that we were locked in a battle with the Soviet Union on a global front. My knowledge of the Soviets wasn't useless to me, or useless to the Agency, just because I'd opted for the Near East and South Asia Division, or the Near East Division as it was usually called. The Russians were everywhere, and I'd have plenty of opportunity to use my background wherever I was stationed.

I wanted to join the Near East Division, specifically that part of the Near East Division that dealt with some portions of Central Asia such as Tibet and Nepal. This interest of mine dated back to graduate school at Columbia. I was fortunate to have been able to audit courses by the famous Altaic (Turkic) scholar Prof. Karl H. Menges. I was later to work with the professor's controversial son, Constantine Menges.

I was specifically interested in Nepal. It had been a long-standing desire of mine to become the world's expert on something. That something became Nepal. With more spare time than I'd had since I was an undergraduate at Brown, and with the vast library resources of Washington at my disposal, I was able to indulge my ambition. I read everything I could get my hands on. I knew the succession of rulers and politics as well as I knew our own. I learned enough to know that what little information the CIA was getting out of Nepal was not very accurate nor sufficient. The Agency had no permanent presence up there. Case officers working elsewhere visited Kathmandu, the capital, and reported back. It's difficult to get a good stream of information flowing when there is contact only on an irregular basis.

I also began reading about the espionage business. One book that especially interested me was *A Handbook for Spies*, written by an Englishman named Alexander Foote. As a radio operator working out of Switzerland, Foote was a member of the Rota Capella (Red Orchestra), the famed Russian espionage network inside Germany during World War

II. Foote was part of the Dora network run by Sandor Rado, which had sources within the German military, and was one of several persons who transmitted information to Moscow that the Germans were going to invade in June of 1941.

Foote's volume wasn't very long, but it was informative, and at the time, there was very little written material about espionage. His manual had a lot of good information about what is called tradecraft—the way espionage is conducted. He discussed how to compartment an agent, how to use a principal agent to run subagents, clandestine radio communications, and cipher techniques.

These were among the skills that the CIA was supposed to teach me. I was scheduled to take the standard Operations Course, or Ops Course, in January of 1958. Formalized training for CIA case officers was still in its earliest stages, and the Ops Course was intended to give the basics—rather like Spying 101.

The Farm is a facility near Williamsburg, Virginia, where CIA operations training takes place. I was at work in the Near East Division when I was sent to the Farm for the one-month Ops Familiarization course. Normally, JOTs don't take Ops Familiarization, which was intended for support staff. However, they had to do something with me until January 1958. They taught us a bit on recruitment—the "spotting process," how to determine who has access to the information you want; how to "develop" a person toward recruitment; and then the "recruitment" itself. This was not just theoretical—instructors would enact different roles and students tried to recruit them. The problem, although I certainly didn't know it at the time, is that you can't teach recruitment. You can provide some guidelines, scenarios, and the like, but not much more. It is a subtle issue involving the personality, background, and character of the case officer making the recruitment of the agent.

At this course I met Charles "Chuck" Cogan, a JOT like myself but a year or more ahead in the process. He was assisting with this course while awaiting his first foreign posting.

They also gave me the Escape and Evasion course. This course did not teach case officers how to avoid capture; presumably, short of war, that was an unlikely eventuality. It taught basic techniques in organizing escape and evasion networks for others trying to make their way to safety, such as agents who have been betrayed or fliers downed while on a clandestine mission over a communist country. This was pretty esoteric training for someone who had not yet been to the Ops Course.

John Waller was my branch chief in the Near East Division. He shared my interest in Central Asia and was getting ready to establish a more permanent CIA presence in Nepal. His plan was to set up a base that reported to New Delhi. The American ambassador to India at that time was the brilliant Ellsworth Bunker, who was concurrently ambassador to Nepal. That summer of 1957, Waller selected a man named Ernie Fox to be chief. Fox was a geologist and a surveyor, and a bit of a Hemingwayesque adventurer. He'd spent a lot of time as a big-game hunter and geologist in the Rhodesias before World War II and, during that war, had been military attaché in Afghanistan. Everyone called him Colonel Fox.

I became aware that Waller was going to send Ernie Fox an assistant. Ordinarily, the second person at a base would not even be a case officer. It was more likely that he would be a support officer, doing the base finances, reports, and communications. In short, he would be a high-powered clerk, but most assuredly no case officer. It was exactly the kind of assignment that any promising CIA case officer should go out of his way to avoid.

Without knowing the potentially dire career implications of what I was doing, I volunteered for the Kathmandu position, indicating just how ignorant I was about the DO and its culture. If I had had a rabbi or a mentor in the Agency, he would have told me to wait for my January Ops Course and take a regular assignment. But never in my years with the Agency did a senior officer take me under his wing, show me the ropes, and/or pull strings to advance my career. I didn't know I wasn't supposed to want to go, and nobody told me any differently. As incredible as it was that I wanted to go, it was even more amazing that Waller and other superiors agreed to let me do it.

I never made it to my January Ops Course. To my knowledge I am the only Clandestine Services officer—certainly the only one since the mid-1950s—who never took it. Once the decision was made that I was leaving, they did recognize that I needed a bit more training. I took a communications course—a two-week tutorial—and learned how to send and receive enciphered messages.

I also was given a course in Flaps and Seals, or how to surreptitiously open and reclose envelopes and diplomatic pouches. Diplomatic pouches in more primitive countries were often closed with a wax seal. We learned to duplicate them by making an impression, then reapplying the new one after the old one had been broken when the contents were examined. We were not issued tools for opening envelopes. Instead we were taught to make our own. Each officer fashioned his own implements, using ivory that came from piano keys. Ivory was the material of choice because it is very smooth and could be crafted to get underneath a flap, whether or not you were using steam.

Why my superiors thought this training would be of use to me in

Nepal of all places has eluded me over the years, but perhaps they thought any training was good. I would put my "skill" to use once, several years later.

Meanwhile I was still in the Army with nine months more to go on my commissioned obligation, and because I could not be assigned overseas while still an Army officer, I received what is known as a "good of the government discharge" and mustered out as a second lieutenant.

Maggie was as enthusiastic about going to Nepal as I was, despite the fact that Cassi was still an infant. Cassandra, our daughter, had been born in July. We were young and adventuresome, and the prospective rigors of life in the third world didn't faze us. Besides, we didn't know any better. We were permitted to take three hundred pounds air freight in addition to the normal weight afforded plane passengers. There was no safe source of milk in the kingdom, so we obviously needed to take some powdered milk for Cassi. This is not a lightweight item when one anticipates no resupply for a year. I applied for an extra baggage allowance and after some haggling was accorded another two hundred pounds.

We left for Nepal just after Christmas 1957. It was the beginning of a great adventure. From a career point of view, this tour in Nepal had all the makings of a certain catastrophe. However, the outcome was very different. Yes, very different indeed.

CHAPTER 4

Nepal:
Opportunity Creates the Man,
1958–60

Leaving the United States for the first time is usually challenging. But leaving with my new family for Nepal in pursuit of a new career was a journey filled with portent. Even today, Nepal is not particularly easy to reach, but in 1958 the trip had a seemingly unending number of stops for refueling and transfer of passengers.

After arriving in New York, we boarded a Pan American DC-6 at Idlewild International Airport (later named John F. Kennedy Airport), and following a refueling in Gander, Newfoundland, flew to Frankfurt. The government still flew its personnel first-class as a way of subsidizing the airlines and ensuring that they maintained some unprofitable routes. In those days, first class was in the back of the aircraft. For an additional fee, we could sleep in railroad-style Pullman bunks, which were built into the luggage space above the passenger seats. Maggie and Cassi took one, and I had another. But, I was much too excited by the prospects before me to sleep.

We disembarked at Frankfurt and spent the night in a hotel, a respite that afforded us a break from the noise of the whirring props and gave me a chance to purchase a German Minox camera, the first of my collection. Though the Minox is famed as the "spy camera" and has been used as such by a number of American traitors, mine was for personal use. That night we slept in proper European feather beds or eiderdowns. These were my first clues that the world beyond our shores held surprises and delights, both large and small.

The next day we got back on the plane and flew to Istanbul, on to Beirut and Dhahran, and finally to Karachi. About two and one-half days had elapsed since our departure from New York. Maggie and little Cassi were real troupers, but the trip was fatiguing, and we all became increasingly appreciative of the bunks as the flight dragged on. At one point, however, what little CIA training I'd had kicked in and I struck up a conversation with one of my fellow passengers, Prime Minister U Nu of Burma. When I learned that the premier did not have a place to rest, I offered him my bunk. He was most polite, but declined my offer. I was secretly relieved.

The teeming airport at Karachi, Pakistan, was my introduction to the third world. There were flies everywhere. The odor was astounding. We waited several hours for the Pakistani Airlines flight to take us to New Delhi, where we landed late in the afternoon and were met by Jim Burns. He was our "shepherd" for our stay in New Delhi for orientation. The tradition in the CIA is that you look after your own. Newly arrived colleagues, even if they are just passing through on TDY (temporary duty), always have someone to take care of them and, frequently, put them up in their homes. We were grateful for this attention, being exhausted and by no means sophisticated travelers. Remembering how well we were treated in New Delhi, I was always more than happy to honor this tradition of looking after our own throughout my career.

We spent two weeks in New Delhi at the Claridge Hotel. India sort of fell in around us. We were heady with the bougainvillea, the diverse population, the colors, tastes, and smells. It was an overwhelming time. Though the term had not been coined, we were in culture shock. Our feelings were not in any way negative—we were simply bowled over by how different it was from the world we'd left behind.

India and the subcontinent in general is a region about which a foreigner is never neutral. You either love it or you detest it. There are many radical factors—the poverty, the smells, the weather, and the different ethnic types that make up the quilt of the country. It can be difficult, for instance, to like a Bengali, but then there are so many other agreeable groups—the Madrasis, Punjabis, Jats. For me, it was love at first sight and this only grew stronger with time.

The British influence in India was still quite pronounced. When Maggie and I went to lunch in the hotel dining room for our first meal in India, we found ourselves served by turban-clad waiters in spotless white gloves. The service was formal and attentive, and in a way relentless. The waiters seated you, held your chair, placed your perfectly starched napkin on your lap, and attended to your every whim. About the only thing you could do for yourself was pick up your fork.

Burns and others showed us the sights of the Indian capital. The women took Maggie to buy some beautiful silk while I got to meet my boss, Harry Rositzke. Rositzke was chief in New Delhi and was the man to whom my chief, Ernie Fox, reported. Harry had been in the OSS during World War II and had transitioned into the CIA when it was formed. He was an intellectual immersed in the study of Hindu philosophy as a hobby. He had a wonderful, simpatico wife, Barbara.

Harry had personally been selected for the assignment by Richard Helms, who realized that the Soviet Union had targeted India for expansion. Indeed, prospects looked good for the Soviets, given the presence of a powerful pro-Soviet Indian Communist Party and an Indian government ruled by an elite of British-educated leftist lawyers, many of whom were pro-Soviet "fellow travelers." Rositzke had been sent out to stem the tide, so to speak, and to kick-start our then moribund activities in India. Nepal was a part of this equation, given its strategic location between India and Tibet (often a province of China throughout history and at that moment in revolt against the Chinese Communist military offensive in its eastern enclave, Kham).

I don't recall that Rositzke gave me any particular instructions for Kathmandu, probably because I was still viewed as a "clerk," although he did arrange for me to associate with the case officers and not the support personnel. In any event, I knew what Headquarters wanted to collect in Nepal: everything. We knew very little about the country's political parties, its military and police, the activities of the king, the machinations of the Chinese and the Soviets, the intentions of the Indians, or the fate of the Tibetan resistance that the CIA was supporting from afar. Almost every shred of information I could find would be welcome.

It was time to get on with the adventure. Maggie, Cassi, and I boarded a venerable Indian Airlines DC-3, one of the surplus veterans from the Hump flights in World War II. We flew along the Ganges River to Lucknow, to Allahabad, to Benares, the holy city of the Hindus, and then on to Patna, the capital of the state of Bihar. At Patna we had to change planes and board yet another DC-3 for the trip to Kathmandu.

The flight was a white-knuckler from start to finish. I worried about the plane's mechanical condition. (Later when I had my own modest fleet of these wonderful aircraft, I would know that these fears were unfounded.) The plane was fully loaded, including squawking and flapping chickens and at least one very unhappy goat. The change in scenery was astonishing as we gained altitude to fly into the Himalayas. Occasionally we glimpsed Mount Everest at 29,000-plus feet. The Indian pilot had to weave between the crests of the Himalayas. He kindly invited me to the door of the cockpit for a fuller view of the magnificent peaks and valleys.

Located in a bowl-shaped valley, Kathmandu is often enveloped by cloud cover. Tall peaks stuck up through the thick white blanketlike tent poles supporting the big top at the circus. The pilot repeatedly circled above the bowl, navigating on this two-mile-high obstacle course. Finally there was a small tear in the shroud and he quickly swooped down through it to land. It was a feat that only someone who had done it many times before could pull off.

We were met by a couple from the mission who had been assigned to help us get settled. We quickly passed through immigration control and customs. Thankfully, as foreigners, we got priority, as the airport was total bedlam with people pushing and shoving baggage and one another. Arrival of the once-a-day flight from India was still a special event for a country that had been "opened up" to the outside world only in 1950.

While waiting for our luggage, the couple who had met us ran into a Nepali whom they clearly knew. He had come to the airport to collect a new bedroll that a relative had sent him from India and which our plane had brought. We were introduced to Bhim Bahadur [F], a typical round-faced Gurkha of sturdy physique. The couple explained that Bhim Bahadur had recently retired from the police force and they had met him when he handled a small accident they had had with a bicycle ricksha. Now, my antenna was up. Here, perhaps, was a source who could educate me about the Nepalese police force. But, Ernie Fox, my chief, had possibly already acquired such an asset.

In fact, Fox had no recruited sources. He tended to send cables that were filled with acute observations on topology and the inhabitants of the country, but were short on real insights about political matters. In short, his reports were similar to those he had done as a military attaché in Afghanistan fifteen years before. Since he hadn't been to the Ops Course either, it was the blind leading the blind.

What saved the situation was that there is nothing mysterious and complicated about the spy business. The requirements are a lot of common sense, a reasonably broad education, a modicum of brains, and above all the will and motivation to accomplish the tasks. I was extremely pleased when the couple offered Bhim Bahadur a ride to Kathmandu; at the time there were few vehicles at all in the city and almost no public transport except for bicycle rickshas. Through all of this Cassi maintained her aplomb in her portable cradle; she was a delight to travel with.

We crammed into one of those Jeep station wagons of the period; the baggage was brought by another vehicle. On the way, I asked Bhim Bahadur how he had learned his English. The answer was auspicious; he had served with OSS Detachment 101 in the Arakan Peninsula of Burma against the Japanese in World War II. The couple dropped us off at the Snow View Hotel. While we sorted ourselves out at the entrance, I took Bhim Bahadur aside and asked if he would be willing to come by on the following Saturday and show me around the town. He readily agreed, and I was immensely pleased.

Sooner than I had expected, we were ensconced in our new home, the downstairs unit in a duplex about a mile from Kathmandu proper. I realized I didn't know how to contact Bhim Bahadur to tell him of my new address, and the couple who had met us didn't know either. My mistake was rectified by waiting at the hotel at the appointed hour. It was a lesson about planning that registered with me.

Ernie Fox had arrived in June of 1957, and in the six months he'd been in Nepal, he hadn't done anything to further the objectives of the Agency. I think he pretty much knew that this would be his last overseas tour, and he was determined to enjoy it.

Ernie was in his fifties and was getting a divorce. He spent his time trekking through the Himalayas and riding his horse. A very decent man, he may not have taught me anything about espionage, but he did teach me how to ride and rudiments of polo.

My cover job was both menial and administrative. I had the lowest possible position in the hierarchy: I handled communications.

Communications were primitive. All of our messages had to be encoded, or in our terminology, encrypted or enciphered, on onetime pads. This is a secure means of communications, but painfully slow until you become proficient with the system. Once you encrypted the message, you typed up the scrambled text, then took it to the Indian Post and Telegraph station in Kathmandu for transmission to the New Delhi embassy, where it was forwarded by landlines to London, then by submarine cable to the United States.

The CIA has four levels of urgency for cables: Flash, Immediate, Priority, and Routine in descending order of importance. Flash is supposedly used only in emergencies, such as when war is imminent. Immediate is sometimes accompanied by the term *Niact*, meaning "night action." No matter what time an Immediate message hit Washington or a station overseas, the communicator had to be called to come in and break the message. He would then call the chief of station to come in and take a look at it. When I arrived in Nepal, the time from transmission to receipt of an Immediate cable between Kathmandu and Washington, D.C., was forty-eight hours. Today the same message would reach its destination in seconds. Nepal's isolation meant that there was a certain do-it-yourself independence to operating as a CIA case officer. Washington was not looking over your shoulder every minute. Advice and instructions were sometimes forthcoming from New Delhi, but often decisions were made on your own. This was regarded in some quarters of the Agency as the "Lawrence of Arabia school of management": you select the best person, assign the tasks, give him the appropriate resources in terms of personnel and money, then stay out of his way while he does the job. No looking over his shoulder.

Isolation meant we had to invent our own recreation. There was a great deal of party-giving and party-going in Kathmandu, and we saw the same people at each gathering. It wasn't just Americans entertaining Americans. There were people from the Indian and British embassies and from the Swiss group that was running a dairy near the Tibetan border. There was interplay with the rest of the foreign contingent and a variety of Nepalis as well. From an intelligence standpoint, these were the people whom you wanted to be in touch with, since they had access to the information you needed.

Although I had been an active fraternity member at Brown, I'd never given a party or even been to one with the range of guests with whom I now associated. Spying is a highly social activity, involving meeting people, winning them over, pursuing relationships, and coaxing your contacts to part with confidences—exactly the kinds of activities shy people go out of their way to avoid. Small wonder that shy case officers are not usually successful. And though I'd developed a measure of self-confidence in the Army, I realized I still had to work on my social skills to be a successful case officer. I had some trouble with the cocktail party art of walking up to complete strangers and introducing myself. To avoid having to do that, I made a practice of arriving early at parties. In that way, I was already in place and people had to approach me and introduce themselves, which I found to be a lot easier. A little alcohol was also of help.

I was particularly interested in meeting the Nepalis, who were by no means a homogeneous group. There were two primary ethnic divisions, the Newars and the Gurkhas. Although a minority, the Newars exert an influence on events in Nepal far beyond their numbers—they are the traders, shopkeepers, and bureaucrats, and the original inhabitants, of Nepal. The Gurkhas had made a separate reputation for themselves fighting in the British and Indian Armies, but they were Nepalis. The famed Gurkha regiments, drawn from a number of Nepali hill tribes, earned 10 percent of all the Victoria Crosses awarded by the British during World War II. As a people, however, they were less sophisticated and less educated than the Newars.

The political climate of the country was unsettled. Nepal had been ruled by the Rana family for just over a hundred years. The Ranas were descended from Jang Bahadur Rana, a general who had staged a coup in the mid–nineteenth century, proclaimed himself prime minister, and made the post hereditary. Although there continued to be a Nepali king throughout this period, he was just a figurehead, and at times, almost a prisoner.

The Ranas and their very extended family controlled the country rather like Japanese shoguns. They built "magnificent palaces" for themselves and generally ignored the welfare of other citizens. These palaces were still very much in evidence in 1958, but for the most part they were a Hollywood set designer's invention, with ornate facades, impressive entryways, and huge reception halls with marble floors. Once you got past the front public rooms, the rest of the "palace" had dirt floors. Often there was no electricity or plumbing.

The British had left India in 1947, after which the Indians pulled the plug on the Rana regime. The Indians saw Nepal as a critical buffer state between themselves and the neighboring emerging communist power, China. They feared that with the ineffective, anti-Indian Ranas in control, Nepal was vulnerable to a Chinese takeover, especially after Mao's forces invaded Tibet in 1950.

That same year, with Indian complicity, the Nepali king was reinstalled as an authority figure. At the same time, Indian-style democratic political parties began forming, and there was pressure for the restored king to hold elections. When I arrived in 1958, King Mahendra, son of the first restored king, was still resisting that pressure. Nevertheless, there was a great deal of political activity, as supporters of the monarchy and the various political groups rallied in towns and villages all over the country.

The recently deposed Ranas were still an important part of the political scene. They were abundant and had heavily intermarried within the upper levels of society; they also had heavy representation in the officer corps of the Nepali Army. In the event of unrest, this could become a factor.

None of this was news to me. As an expert on Nepal, I didn't need a scorecard to know the major players on the Kathmandu political scene. What I needed was inside information on what they were up to. Bhim Bahadur seemed to be a possible conduit to police officers all over Nepal. The policemen would in turn feed me information about activities of political groups. It was a great way to find out what was really going on.

I wanted to recruit Bhim Bahadur, which I did after appropriate name checks with Headquarters, which confirmed his Detachment 101 service. The recruitment was easy; he needed me as a source of income in his retirement. He not only became my first recruitment but also a friend—to the extent you can allow that in espionage.

In Nepal I acquired one of the habits of a lifetime that eventually became a trademark—my passion for cigars. I'd started smoking a pipe at the age of seventeen or eighteen, but pipe tobacco was hard to come by in Kathmandu. In India, where we got many of our supplies, you could buy a large box of inexpensive "Burmah" cheroots. They came a hundred to a box and were straight tobacco, with no other ingredients. The real cheroots from Burma were greenish and were rolled in seawater and tended to give off sparks and burn holes in your pants unless you cupped the burning end of the cigar in a bowl.

Holey pants, however, were one of the few domestic difficulties with which my wife had to cope. In the curious balancing equation by which Westerners weigh the positives and negatives of living in the third world, the lack of everyday amenities in Nepal, such as running water, regular mail service, and reliable electrical power, was offset not only by the beauty of the Himalayas but by an abundance of household help.

I was astounded to realize that we had a total of seven servants, both full- and part-time. The full-time staff was headed up by the bearer, or butler, who ran the household and supervised the rest of the help. There was an *ayah*, or nanny, for Cassi, who was with her day and night. Then there was the sweeper. The butler and the sweeper had an absolute geographic division of duties. The butler handled all the polishing of the silver, the glassware, in short, everything down to the chair rail. That chair rail was the Mason-Dixon Line, and everything below it—including of course the "thunder box" or toilet—was the domain of the sweeper.

Part-time help included a dressmaker or *derzi*, and a laundryman or *dhobi*. The *derzi* did not have a shop. He would come to the house, squat on the veranda with his hand-operated Singer, and run up clothing to order. The *dhobi* would periodically come to do the washing and ironing. All this help was very inexpensive—we could afford it even on my entry-level salary. Enough was left in the budget to buy both a horse and a pony, and to retain a *zayc* or groom to take care of them.

Nepali cooks were not as accomplished as Indian cooks, in part because they had less promising stuff to work with, and because the British had never been in Nepal to develop the requirement for cooks with varied repertoires. Dal, or lentils, was a staple. Animal protein came from goats, chickens, and water buffalo. The goats were scraggly and the chickens were scrawny, but the water buffalo was the worst.

The vegetables were another story. They were gargantuan. Kathmandu was situated on a dry lake bed, with rich soil that went down many feet. Cabbages were twice the size of bowling balls. Carrots and turnips were two feet long. Vegetables were cooked for a very long time. No one with any brains ate them raw because amoebic dysentery was so prevalent.

We had four primary objectives for collection of intelligence and initially no covert action tasks—it had not entered anyone's mind that there could be such in Nepal at that time. The first and most basic objective was to provide Washington with accurate and complete information about the social, political, and military climate in Nepal. As the Agency's Nepal expert while in Washington, I knew that much of our knowledge was not current and was possibly erroneous. We sorely lacked a reliable and up-to-date database. It was almost as if I were starting from scratch. What was the strength of the Army? How was it distributed? Where were its loyalties? With the king or the Ranas? Same for the police force? The political parties—what were their ideologies, loyalties, intentions?

Second, what were the Soviets and the Chinese up to? We knew that they were trying to establish a presence by means of an embassy in the country. What about the Indians? They seemed to resent our presence in Nepal. They saw us as competitors for influence with the Nepalis, when in fact our aim was to shore up the Indian position to resist Chinese pressure on the fragile Nepali government. The British were concerned with maintaining the recruitment of Gurkhas into their regiments heavily engaged in the Malaysian Communist insurgency.

The third objective was to monitor the establishment of a democratic, representational government in the country. While the restored king was fending off pressure to hold free elections, fledgling political parties were flexing their muscles and demanding a voice. The situation was inherently unstable and potentially volatile.

The fourth objective came later, in March of 1959, with the collapse of the Tibetan resistance to the Chinese and the withdrawal of the Dalai Lama from Lhasa to India. There was a need to fill the vacuum and cover the Chinese occupation of Tibet proper.

To accomplish these objectives (principally one and three for starters), I set up a network of agents, building upon Bhim Bahadur's varied access to specific individuals of interest and the relatively abundant other opportunities that presented themselves. It wasn't exceptionally difficult, but it also came terribly naturally to me. Some people are born with perfect pitch; others have an ear for languages; I guess I had a natural affinity for espionage.

Within four months of recruiting Bhim Bahadur, I had additional sources, some of whom were paid agents producing what passed for "secret information," in Nepal. I had others in government institutions who were more akin to an official liaison between the Nepalese official entity and me. And who was "me"? Given my lowly rank and youth, I must have been an enigma to many of these officials, but I could produce results when requested. Although none ever queried me directly, they surely believed I was with the CIA, despite the fact that CIA was hardly the household term it has since become.

Coverage of the base's first objective was coming along; most of this intelligence reporting went to Headquarters by the once-a-week classified pouch; it hardly merited cabling, not being urgent. It complemented the reporting being done by the New Delhi embassy's officer responsible for Nepal, Doug Heck, who averaged about ten days a month in the country.

Heck's father was a member of the Foreign Service in Turkey around the time of World War I. Doug had just enrolled at Yale when World War II broke out, but a physical disability had prevented him from serving in the armed forces. Eventually, he followed in his father's footsteps and became a Foreign Service officer. Unlike many State Department officials, Heck was positively inclined toward the CIA and was friendly with several current and past personnel in New Delhi. We developed a good rapport, then a friendship. Heck was smart, and early on he figured out that he had much more to gain by cooperating with and using CIA personnel rather than ostracizing, bad-mouthing, and competing with them. He was not alone in this attitude, but unfortunately, he was one of only a handful I've known over the years. It was a rewarding experience for us both and I learned a lot from him. This first good experience gave me a positive attitude toward State Department officers throughout my career.

In April, four months after I'd arrived, I got a visit from Harry Rositzke, the chief in New Delhi. He was clearly pleased with my efforts to date, realizing that I was a regular one-man band. I kept Colonel Fox apprised of my activities and he signed all appropriate documents, but he wasn't really a part of the base's effort. I was the one recruiting sources and collecting information. I typed up all my own operational and intelligence reports, did the base's finances, made up the pouch, encrypted and decrypted the cables. Within a few months of Rositzke's first visit, the volume of base activity—and accordingly its administrative requirements—had reached a point where a legitimate case could be made that I needed a clerk. Harry knew this, and because one was unlikely to be forthcoming from Headquarters, he succeeded in reducing some of my communications responsibilities.

Meanwhile, I had become a communications virtuoso of sorts. It wasn't a complicated process, but it was laborious. When the material was my own, I had to write the report, encipher it on the onetime pad, then transcribe the letters—which by now were gibberish—on the typewriter. In regular typing, you are reproducing familiar words and letter combinations, so that mistakes are easy to spot. With coded text, it's akin to typing an eye chart. I checked often to make sure that I wasn't screwing up the encipherment with typographic errors; if I did, my messages would still read like an eye chart after they were decoded in Washington. The message traffic in and out was so heavy, however, that I became proficient.

One warm summer morning, I sat in my airless little cubbyhole of an office on the ground floor. The usual sheaf of incoming cable traffic from the previous night was before me. Near the bottom of the base's stack, I broke out a cable from Headquarters that was addressed to me personally—"Eyes Only." It said Headquarters had been contacted by my father with the news that my mother had died. New Delhi followed up with its own cable shortly thereafter, asking me to travel immediately to New Delhi. (They, of course, had been an "info" addressee on the Headquarters cable, as they were on all of the base's incoming and outgoing traffic.) New Delhi also asked me to try to telephone them that night to attempt to patch me through to my father. In those days telephoning from Kathmandu to New Delhi was nearly impossible, and the only semireliable phone line was at the Indian embassy. In the early evening, I asked to see an acquaintance, an official of the Indian embassy. When I arrived at his home and explained my problem, he was most gracious and persistent in putting my call through to New Delhi over the erratic phone line. It was for naught, as New Delhi could not make a successful patch through to the United States. I had a ticket to New Delhi the next morning.

In New Delhi, after hours of effort, I finally spoke with my father, who urged me not to come home. There was nothing I could do, and besides, as the funeral was two days off, I wouldn't make it in time. He probably also thought he was being financially prudent, in the Yankee tradition. A few years later, our government instituted a policy of paying for compassionate travel.

My mother had had surgery for breast cancer about five years earlier, and they believed they had gotten it all. Five years was the magic number for survivorship, and she had fallen just short. She would have been fifty within a few months of her death.

I felt remorse that my own carelessness had caused my father some trouble in trying to get me the news. I had neglected to leave him any information about how to get in touch with me through Headquarters, which, in those days, had unlisted numbers. He had had an arduous time making contact with the Agency, particularly because he didn't want to do anything wrong from a security standpoint.

There was nothing I could do about any of that now. I had my work. Maggie occupied her time as many of the wives did, with tours of temples, shrines, and other historic sights, playing bridge, and reading books. Although some of the women found life in Nepal confining, Maggie never complained of being bored. In the Jeep, she was at least mobile—though the lack of roads limited her adventures to the Kathmandu valley.

My one regret about the tour in Nepal is that I did not take more time off to see the country, despite my interest in mountaineering. We did take one trek with another family with a son a little younger than Cassi to a rather run-down British embassy summer facility. It was some miles by foot from Kathmandu and at an elevation of about eight thousand feet—

about four thousand feet above the floor of the Kathmandu valley. This trek was carried out in the grand style of old, with Cassi's screened crib, Cassi, and the other baby ensconced in baskets on porters' backs; and cooks and supplies for a long weekend. The line of porters winding up the narrow path probably was in excess of ten.

Our last excursion in Nepal was a trip with another couple down the Indian-built dirt road from Kathmandu to the Terai, the narrow strip of lowland jungle that runs the length of Nepal's border with India. The forest is mainly hardwood, with little overhead canopy; it is home to Bengal tigers, leopards, one-horned Asian rhinoceroses, gharial crocodiles, and all kinds of deer.

These rare outings aside, I'm sorry to admit that Maggie single-handedly carried most of the burden of raising Cassi. Part of it was the times: fathers were not nearly so involved in parenting as they are today; part of it was just me: I was not particularly child-oriented and was immersed in my work, trying to prove that although I'd arrived in Kathmandu as a clerk, I wasn't going to leave as one.

King Mahendra finally consented to hold the first national parliamentary elections in the summer of 1959, and all of the parties started gearing up for them. There had been diverse political parties in Nepal since the early 1950s, when the Ranas were thrown out, ranging from the Communist Party of Nepal to the rightist party of the Ranas.

The party that seemed to have the most popular backing was the NCP, the Nepali Congress Party, run by a fellow named B. P. Koirala, who was quite active in the international socialist movement. He was especially close to the leadership of the Histadrut, the coalition of labor unions in Israel. Koirala borrowed the Congress Party name from Prime Minister Nehru's party in India, which had controlled the government in New Delhi since the British pulled out.

From my point of view, Koirala was far and away the best choice for prime minister in the upcoming election. He had good support from the people and was an effective leader. The king's game seemed to be to play off the parties against one another, hoping to end up with a fragmented parliament that would let him rule as before. What the Indians were up to I never did fathom for sure. One could conclude that they would have supported the Nepali Congress Party on ideological and fraternal grounds; however, they seemed to have considered Koirala too independent of mind and therefore supported the king. The British came at it from a different and more "imperial" angle: they arranged to provide the crown prince with a young Englishman as a tutor and then bundled him off to Eton. The Nepali Communist Party was financed by its Indian counterpart, which may in turn have been the recipient of Soviet largess.

By this time, I was rather well plugged in to the principal political parties, including that of the enigmatic Dr. K. I. Singh, who seemed to be playing closely with the king.

By the early spring of 1959, Koirala had become worried about the Nepali Congress Party's ability to win a majority in the elections; the king's activities were not ineffectual. Meanwhile, the U.S. government had no policy on the election issue, but we were about to get one; I had been in touch with Koirala for some time.

In early March of 1959, Koirala signaled that he needed to meet with me on an urgent basis. Arriving at his modest home, I ascended ladder-like stairs to the second floor, where most Nepali homes had their sitting areas–cum-bedrooms. As usual, Koirala was seated cross-legged on a mattress that served both as his bed and a divan, dressed in the Nepali national costume of jodhpur-shaped pants, a tunic with cross ties to keep it together descending over the pants, a vest, and finally the Nepali hat or cap. The scar on Koirala's neck, the result of radiation treatment for throat cancer, seemed particularly vivid. Immediately, but in a round-about way, he asked me for my prognosis for the upcoming elections. When I evidenced uncertainty about the NCP's ability to win a majority, he concurred with my analysis and asked me to consider means to bolster the Nepali democratic process as embodied in the elections. I agreed to do this and to make my views known to Washington. I put together a cable to Harry Rositzke in New Delhi and to Headquarters, outlining the current political situation, the problems the NCP was encountering, and the king's machinations. It was really a summation of all of the intelligence I had already sent them, concluding that we should prefer a clear-cut NCP victory to ensure stability and a solid start at building democratic institutions in the country. And, asking, would they consider authorizing the rather benign support that I suggested?

At this point, I am not sure I knew the words *covert action*, which was what I was proposing. I was so ignorant of the Agency's history that I did not know that up until the early 1950s, the Directorate of Operations had had two very separate parts, one for espionage and the other for covert action.

Unbeknownst to me, Rositzke and Ambassador Bunker endorsed my recommendation in separate messages to their respective superiors. I had sent my cable by Immediate Precedence, not because the elections were imminent, but because if my request was approved, it would take literally weeks by foot for couriers to reach most of the villages in the country; there was only one road from Kathmandu to India and the beginnings of an east-west road in the Terai.

About a week later I got an Eyes Only cable from the legendary director of central intelligence (DCI) himself, Allen Dulles. My request had been approved.

A courier was dispatched from New Delhi. Koirala was pleased and my relationship with him strengthened and broadened; he became even more frank with me about intra-NCP matters and his tactics for the election. About six weeks later, Koirala came to me with additional thoughts on electoral problems. They seemed reasonable, and I made the case to New Delhi and Headquarters. Again I received approval.

I learned much later that both Headquarters and New Delhi were bemused and at the same time pleased by all of these sudden activities in Nepal. By early 1959, at the age of twenty-seven, I'd become a power broker on the Nepali political scene, in effect the number one American in Kathmandu. I'd been in Nepal slightly over a year and was playing a significant role in the country's first national election. More than that, I had several good intelligence collection operations going and more to come. It was all rather heady for a young man with no training on his first tour of duty, but I never stopped telling myself that all of this was happening in Kathmandu, Nepal, and not Paris, France. This tended to keep my ego under control.

Years later, I would realize I'd had the finest and broadest first tour of duty of any Agency officer up to that point and probably ever. I had indeed been lucky.

No one objected when I had a better office built. My new setup was basically a vault, with a secure, bank-style vault door. But it had a window and was on the less damp second floor of a former Rana palace.

There was still great concern in Washington over the fate of Tibet, which bordered Nepal to the north. In 1951, the Chinese Communists had forced Tibet to accept a treaty of surrender, providing for Chinese rule, but including an understanding that the People's Republic would not interfere with Tibetan government or culture.

The Chinese did not keep their part of the bargain. The Communists had been making incursions ever since, devouring Tibet piecemeal, beginning in the east. Chinese Army forces were an increasing presence in Lhasa, the capital. Though the Tibetans looked upon this as an invasion, the Chinese believed it was their suzerainty: Tibet was and always had been an integral part of the Celestial Empire.

The Dalai Lama, both the spiritual and temporal leader of Tibet, was determined to resist the Chinese. The U.S. government saw it was in its interest to support this resistance in the wake of the 1949 Communist takeover of China.

In 1957–58, the CIA had run operations to provide support to the Tibetan resistance. Tibetans were brought to the United States and given training in communications and guerrilla warfare techniques in Colorado at high altitudes to mirror the environment of the Tibetan plateau, then air-dropped back into Tibet. The idea was for them to provide us with intelligence on the Chinese Communists' activities, to train the nascent Tibetan force of freedom fighters in how to use the weapons we were supplying, and to instruct the force in guerrilla tactics.

It was a disaster. Despite our indoctrination of the Tibetan intelligence/training teams, the Tibetan freedom fighters were not inclined to conduct guerrilla warfare against the Chinese Army, but pursued conventional set-piece battles, perhaps because many of them carried amulets that they believed made them impervious to bullets. They were quickly decimated. In March 1959, a full-scale uprising in Lhasa was brutally quashed by Beijing. At the end of March, the Dalai Lama secretly left Lhasa for India through Sikkim and established a government-in-exile in Dharmsala, India. A wave of about one hundred thousand of his followers straggled out of the Himalayas and joined him in exile. He is still there. The Chinese formally annexed Tibet and installed the Panchen Lama as their puppet head of government.

With the flight of the Dalai Lama and his disciples, the United States lost its source of information on Tibet. Even before this development, I had been looking at ways to provide information on Tibet and the Chinese Communists there. I had recruited a Nepalese, Raj Bahadur Thapa [F], who traded with Tibet. He and his several employees made frequent trips by foot with porters carrying their goods to Shigatse (the second-largest town in Tibet and headquarters of the Panchen Lama) and Lhasa. These trips took about two weeks one way, for there were no roads from Nepal to Tibet and few in Tibet itself. At the time, only Nepal and India had representation in Lhasa. But, Thapa had good contacts among the personnel assigned to the Nepalese Trade Mission in Lhasa, whom I wished to recruit. I encouraged him to enhance his relationships with people inside the Tibetan capital, and at the Nepalese Trade Mission in particular, to gather intelligence. I wanted to know what the Chinese were up to, and what if anything was left of the Tibetan resistance. Little by little, Thapa began to recruit subagents, who supplied him with information. They, too, made occasional two-week treks over the mountains from Lhasa to Kathmandu, bringing snippets of information out of Tibet, or furnishing it to Thapa or his employees during their forays north.

I ran this as a compartmented operation for security reasons; the subagents brought the information to Thapa, who in turn passed it on to me. Given the relative sensitivity of this operation, I had acquired an appropriate safe house for my meetings with Thapa. I was providing one of the few U.S. "windows" on Tibet, and the only human sources.

With the fall of Tibet to the Chinese, the approaching Nepalese national election took on added significance. Although relations between India and China were amicable enough on the surface, the Indians were casting a very wary eye on their northern frontier. The possibility of a fight was already festering. The Chinese had started making forays into the mountainous parts of northwest India. They had cut off strategic little pieces and claimed them for their own, showing a particular predilection for the real estate around mountain passes. It didn't take a genius to realize that it could get a lot worse. A weak Kathmandu government could be susceptible to Chinese pressure, greatly multiplying the number of potential access points for a Chinese invasion, and making the northern Indian border much harder to defend.

Thus, the outcome of the election was of interest to Washington. This was evidenced by the increasingly frequent visits to Kathmandu by Amb. Ellsworth Bunker. Trying to cover all the bases, Bunker met with a number of the more prominent politicians, but he almost always called on the ruling head of state, King Mahendra. On one of these visits, the king let it be known that he, too, wanted some election assistance. Bunker never told me what reason Mahendra gave him for needing the help. I suspect he didn't say and Bunker didn't ask. In any event, the ambassador thought it prudent to comply and Washington agreed. Bunker was a shrewd operator with a good understanding of covert action from his days in Italy as ambassador. I opined at the time that Mahendra probably wanted to dispense some largess to politicians he considered inimical to his interests and that rumors of my activities with the NCP had reached his ears. One could argue that we were in effect canceling out our efforts with the NCP. However, by this time both Doug Heck and I were convinced that the NCP had developed enough mass to win the election with a reasonable majority. Besides, Bunker's reputation and stature was such in Washington that what Bunker wanted, Bunker got.

I requested an audience with the king through General Thapa, the king's military aide and my chief contact at the Royal Palace. At the appointed hour late in the evening, the king stepped into the parlor of a small cottagelike structure beside the palace, which he used for informal audiences, where I was already ensconced. We sat down and made a modicum of small talk. The room was extremely dim, lit by one tiny lamp with an opaque shade. Even the king could get only forty watts of power out of a hundred-watt bulb. Electricity in Nepal came from a hydroelectric generating plant, and in summer before the arrival of the monsoon rains, there was very little water to drive the turbines so power was particularly weak.

King Mahendra, as was his custom, day or night, wore sunglasses. He was clearly uncomfortable. Realizing that further attempts at conversation would only embarrass us both, I put an envelope on the small table between us. The king made no move to pick it up. I said good-bye and left.

The election was held on schedule, and it took nearly a week for all the results to come in from the mountaintops and valleys of the country. As predicted, the NCP won enough of the votes to form a government by itself. B. P. Koirala would be the first elected prime minister of his country. It seemed to me that the celebration of the NCP's election victory was muted in Kathmandu valley. Perhaps this was purposeful to avoid rubbing the king's nose in the results, for it was rather well known that the NCP and Koirala in particular were anathema to him. However, any government that diminished his power was unacceptable.

After the elections but before the seating of the new government and parliament, there was a late-night knock on my door. It was B. P. Koirala and his principal aide, bearing a small suitcase. Fortunately the *chokidar* or guard at the gate of the compound had had the wit to pass the future prime minister through without asking me. Koirala was visibly upset. In staccatolike sentences, he explained that he had received what he regarded as reliable information that the king intended to arrest, if not kill, him and the leadership of the NCP and thus negate the elections and return to autocratic rule—a preemptive coup d'état by the palace. With this, the aide opened the suitcase and displayed two British Sten submachine guns and ammunition, which appeared to have spent a lot of time in the ground. Koirala said the weapons were for his protection, but he needed more for the NCP leadership; thus his visit to me. He wanted me to provide him with additional weapons. I questioned both men at length about the information on the king's intentions; they assured me that it came from within the palace, and I could believe Koirala had such sources on the basis of family ties alone. I promised to query Washington, and it was agreed that I would contact the aide when I had an answer.

After they departed, I climbed into my Jeep and went to my office, where I prepared an Immediate Niact cable for Headquarters and New Delhi, then enciphered and typed up that text, and dispatched it by the duty driver to the Indian Post and Telegraph. My cable was factual and straightforward, but I did cite the meager available intelligence that supported Koirala's contention, as well as that which didn't, which was more persuasive.

As expected, I got a cable back from Washington indicating that they did not want to get involved. I met with the aide and delivered the decision. There were no outward recriminations on either his or Koirala's part. The aide had always troubled me, for reasons I could never verbalize. He did later take the "king's coin" and turn on Koirala. Perhaps, he had already gone over at this time; he was immensely ambitious and the king eventually satisfied this appetite.

The king did not make his move at this time. The government was formed and parliament seated. There was a reception to commemorate the event and I was invited. I shook hands with the prime minister and he quietly murmured some words of appreciation. I never saw him again.

With Colonel Fox's departure in the summer of 1959, I became acting chief. Changes were in the wind, driven by the Nepali elections. The State Department was sending a full-fledged ambassador to Nepal. In preparation for this grand event, I received a radio operator. Finally, I was free of my onetime pads—but not forever!

Except for occasional trips to New Delhi and the two within Nepal, I hadn't been anywhere else. In the fall of 1959, we were notified that CIA personnel assigned to hardship posts would be given one R&R (rest and relaxation) trip per two-year tour of duty. The transportation would be paid for by the U.S. government and the destinations were limited. There were various grades of hardship posts; Nepal was at the high end, which meant that you received 25 percent more than your base salary for serving there. By this time I had been promoted to GS-11, the equivalent of a first lieutenant. I left for Hong Kong via Calcutta. Maggie didn't want to go. From Calcutta to Hong Kong I rode in my first jet, a British Overseas Airways Comet. On the return leg, I flew on the maiden sortie of Pan American Airline's flight #1 with a Boeing 707. We blew a tire in Bangkok.

In early January of 1960, my tour in Nepal ended. I was assigned to New Delhi under Harry Rositzke. However, my slot there wouldn't be available until May. Thus, I would spend about five months in the United States in a combination of home leave and consultations at Headquarters. Maggie decided to delay her arrival in New Delhi until July in order to spend more time with her family.

In January, Maggie, Cassi, and I made our last flight on the old DC-3 from Kathmandu to New Delhi, then went on via Teheran and Beirut to Cyprus, where Doug Heck had just been named deputy chief of mission in our new embassy. Cyprus would become independent in August of 1960, and the embassy was still being set up. We spent a week with Doug and his wife, Libby, on that marvelous island, then flew to Brussels via Athens and Vienna.

There were distinguished passengers on the flight from Nicosia to Athens—Archbishop Makarios, who was to be the first president of Cyprus, and his entire shadow cabinet. One of the Greek flight attendants, upon learning that Cassi's given name was Greek, Cassandra, took Cassi from her seat and placed her on the archbishop's lap. Makarios gave her a blessing, a somewhat dubious honor considering what a nasty blackguard he turned out to be.

I was seated next to one of Makarios's henchmen, Polykarpos Georkatzis, who eventually became his minister of the interior. A known ruffian and murderer, he was properly, if not elegantly, cut down by gunfire some time later. I am, however, indebted to this charming thug for instructing me in the technique of peeling a thick-skinned Mediterranean orange.

In Brussels, we joined up again with John Stein and for the first time met his lovely wife, Charlie. They were newly married and had recently arrived in Belgium. John's fluency in French pointed him toward a European assignment. He'd attended the January '58 Ops Course that I would also have taken had I not gone to Nepal. After that he had worked at Headquarters awaiting assignment to Brussels.

As a junior case officer, John paid the price of being assigned to Europe, performing many of the station's mundane tasks, such as managing safe houses, surveillance teams, and the like. Stein's fate was typical, but he made up for it later.

We left Brussels for Paris, where I met up with Chuck Cogan, who was on his way back to Delhi for a second tour. I looked forward to working with him when I got there in May.

From Paris we took the train to Le Havre, where we boarded the liner *United States* for the trip home to New York. There my father would be waiting—with his new wife, Norma. Earlier, my father had asked my permission to marry her; it seemed a bizarre request at the time. I knew her well and liked her immensely. She was a widow; her husband had died on the first day of the Normandy Beach landings, and she was a part of my parents' circle. More importantly, my mother had always told me that if she should die, my father should marry Norma. When we left port, it was late January, the dead of winter, and after leaving the English Channel we steamed through heavy seas for most of the voyage to New York. So severe were the conditions that the liner had to reduce speed, a hitherto unknown event. Most of the passengers were confined to their staterooms with grievous cases of mal de mer. Nevertheless, three people were virtually alone in the stately dining room, eating as if they hadn't eaten before in their lives. I think I was trying to make up for two years of lentils and stringy water-buffalo meat in one transatlantic crossing.

As the tugboats met the *United States* and the Statue of Liberty came into view, I reflected on my time in Kathmandu. It seemed as if everything I'd tried to do had worked out—and rather well at that. I'd been lucky; Nepal had been a benign environment. Until near the end of my tour, there was no Soviet presence and never an effective internal security service to contend with. The young CIA officer who had left the States in 1957 as a "clerk" was returning a bit over two years later as an uncontestable case officer, albeit self-taught. Opportunity does indeed create the man.

CHAPTER 5

India:
No Tomorrow,
1960–64

NEW DELHI, 1960–62

When I checked in at CIA Headquarters upon returning in January 1960, it was in much the same condition as I had left it in 1957; the new building was still under construction up the Potomac River from Washington. I sensed a certain respect for me, despite the fact that I was a lowly case officer who had just completed his first tour. Perhaps my new branch chief, Angus Thuermer—a wonderful human being, bright and articulate—was not so much impressed by my accomplishments in Nepal as by a report he had received that I had returned to the States carrying my polo mallets. Angus himself went on to learn polo in Ghana and later played with considerable distinction in India at an age when most prefer a reclining chair in the shade with a gin and tonic.

After considerable searching, Maggie and I bought a charming house with five acres south of Leesburg, Virginia. It was a two-story log cabin about a century old with additions on either side—the guest cottage of an estate that had been broken up.

I didn't know anyone at Headquarters, and thus I spent minimal time there. I was still so naive in the ways of a bureaucracy that it didn't occur to me to network with my peers and superiors. In any event, my administrative processing was time-consuming because I was changing cover agencies.

I felt as if I were marking time, but my enforced home leave was alleviated by an opportunity few junior case officers are afforded. I accompanied one of my Nepalese contacts on a visit to see the DCI, Allen Dulles. Before I'd left Kathmandu, I'd made arrangements for the king's military secretary and close adviser, General Thapa, to visit Washington. He ran

73

the Palace Intelligence Service, perhaps too sophisticated a name for what was really a rustic and untrained entity, and had asked for our assistance in improving his service's capabilities to counter subversion. Who was doing the subverting was not altogether clear. In the interest of precluding his seeking aid elsewhere and of influencing the service's activities to some extent, Headquarters acquiesced.

Thapa arrived in the States, his first visit, in early February 1960, shortly after my return. As part of his official itinerary, we scheduled a brief meeting with the DCI. We were ushered into Dulles's office, which was decorated like a private study, in Central Building in the naval complex west of the new State Department building. Dulles, sitting in his reclining leather armchair, smoked a pipe and wore donnish tweed.

At the meeting, there were just the general, the DCI, the division chief, and me. It was all a bit too much for General Thapa, who was apparently intimidated in the presence of one of the legends of the intelligence business. We met with Dulles for about twenty minutes, roughly eighteen minutes too long. The general was brutally inarticulate. I was greatly embarrassed, but Dulles graciously carried the conversation. Of course, I later realized, he had been through many scenes like this before.

I didn't know it at the time, but shortly after Thapa's visit I realized there may have been another reason for his reticence. Thapa's boss, King Mahendra, had decided he just couldn't live with Nepal's "experiment with democracy." In early spring the king dissolved the parliament, did away with the cabinet, and banned political parties. B. P. Koirala and the other leaders of the Nepali Congress Party were thrown in jail. I was incensed; Koirala had been correct all along about the king's intentions. Curiously, the king's coup elicited little overt displeasure from Washington. Within Nepal, there was sporadic but ineffectual resistance.

Finally, the time came to leave the United States again. I made the trip to New Delhi solo via London (where I purchased a car), Zurich, and Rome; Maggie and Cassi would come later. My sole reason for the stop in Zurich was to acquire a particularly accurate target pistol made by Hammerli. Target shooting had long been a hobby of mine. I carried the weapon legally on the plane with me to New Delhi, which is a far cry from the situation today. We tend to forget how our lives have been changed by terrorism! Compared to my first trip to the subcontinent, this one was remarkably quick, even with the stops. Jet aircraft made all the difference.

To realize the importance of India, you must understand where we were in our relationships to the Soviet Union and Red China. Francis Gary Powers and his U-2 had just been shot down over Russia, and Khrushchev had scuttled the Paris summit over the incident. Castro had taken control of Cuba, just ninety miles off the coast of Florida, the year before. The Chinese had crushed the Tibetan revolt and the Dalai Lama had fled. From Washington, it surely looked as though communism was on the offensive worldwide.

The Cold War was at its height and the world was divided into two armed camps, with the nonaligned third world nations in between. Few people in Washington believed that nonalignment was viable as a long-term strategy. Eventually the third world would have to choose one side or the other. The widely held "domino theory" postulated that the fall of one third world nation to communism made the collapse of its neighbors more likely.

India was on the fence. Prime Minister Jawaharlal Nehru maintained a precarious neutrality, coquettishly soliciting favors from both the United States and the Soviet Union, and steadfastly avoiding permanent alignment with either camp. However, the Soviets were beginning to supply arms to India, and Washington greatly feared the implications of a communist government in New Delhi. India already had a large and vociferous Communist Party, which had taken over in the southwestern state of Kerala, three years earlier. Although it was turned out of power in an election two years later, Washington saw this as a harbinger of more serious events at the national level. Trumpeted as "the world's largest democracy," India was also the world's biggest domino, a great prize if the imperial Soviets were successful where their czarist predecessors had failed. Moreover, the Chinese were lurking in the north. India seemed to bend over backward to mollify them, but they couldn't ignore Chinese incursions in the border areas, even as they went about putting the best face on them.

Because my flat would not be available for occupancy for about a month, Chuck Cogan offered to let me stay with him until it was ready. Cogan had returned to New Delhi as a bachelor, having just been through a divorce. Chuck and I became great friends and were frequently referred to as the Bobbsey Twins by some of our compatriots. Cogan, a graduate of Harvard, was brilliant, intensely hardworking, and probably more stressed than I. I introduced him to polo and he quickly outstripped me; I could never get the hand-and-eye thing right. In later years, Cogan, who attained almost native fluency in French, went on to become a scholar and author of note on French political history, particularly de Gaulle and his times. Recently, he wrote a poem about me, which I had engraved on my funerary urn.

New Delhi was very different from Kathmandu. First of all, as a city, it had more amenities. There were telephones, real hotels, and some restaurants. There was no feeling of being cut off from the rest of the world.

There were vast possibilities for sight-seeing both near and at some distance from Delhi. I was fascinated with India in general and Hindu architecture in particular from my brief trips there from Nepal, so opportunity abounded for me. There was also horseback riding, polo, and in the winters, "fox" hunting—with jackals as the pursuit. And then there were the women—in some cases very different from what I knew, almost exotic.

Many Westerners who serve there get hung up on the bone-crunching poverty of India, the filth and the flies and the begging. After a short time, I was uncritical of what I saw and felt no compulsion to change anything. To me there was so much beauty and fascination in the people and the country that the squalor paled. Although even today I cannot account for it, I never felt like an outsider during my stay in the subcontinent.

Our CIA objectives in New Delhi were several. The overarching one was to keep India out of the Soviets' imperial clutches, whether the Indians liked it or not. (Nehru, of course, thought he could take care of himself; at least, that is what he maintained until the Chinese descended upon him two years later.) To do this required good intelligence on Soviet activity in India; coverage of the Soviet toady, the Communist Party of India (CPI); and some understanding of Indian interaction with the Soviets and its portents. Much of this was protected, secret information; neither the Soviets nor the Indians handed it out, despite what some State Department colleagues might claim. It required the penetration of institutions with clandestine agents. We continued to hope that a Soviet in India could be recruited locally to provide his side of the equation.

The recruitment of Soviets, Chinese, Eastern Europeans, Cubans, Mongolians, North Koreans, and Vietnamese, particularly those with known or suspected intelligence duties, was high priority, not only for what they would know about their local activities but, more importantly, to return eventually to their own countries as intelligence agents reporting secrets. Much effort went into this endeavor, with rather mediocre returns. Individuals of this ilk are often not likely to be the ones you believe are vulnerable, and thus you do not pursue them, only to have them "walk in," offering their services. Still, you keep trying, so that at least the "volunteer" will know whom he can safely contact.

In 1961, the State Department became enthusiastic about establishing diplomatic relations with Mongolia. Headquarters sent out a cable to various stations worldwide with a request to develop contacts and if possible recruit Mongols in connection with this initiative. India was one of the handful of countries outside of the Communist world where the Mongols had official representation. I had become acquainted with a young Mongolian diplomat. In addition to my professional concern, I had more than a passing intellectual interest in his country's history; however, he was so furtive and jumpy when we met that the relationship was not going any-where. Anyway, an American diplomat is not supposed to have in-depth relationships with diplomats of a country with which we have no rela-tions. As a CIA officer, my situation was different; I could pursue him. I knew that this fellow was about to rotate home to Ulan Bator. Headquar-ters decided I should have a crack at him anyway, even on the basis of our "nonrelationship."

In the espionage trade, this is known as a "gangplank" recruitment attempt. It wouldn't be my last, and I have never heard of one succeed-ing. It is a fool's game. I knew that this Mongol would not accept lunch or dinner with me; thus the challenge was how to meet him. Clearly the only choice was to invite myself to his embassy to say good-bye and hope that he would agree. The thought of making even a veiled recruitment pitch inside the Mongolian embassy, with the possibilities of their audio devices picking it up for later use or worse, was considered rather sporty by the "old hands" in the station.

Headquarters pressed me. I telephoned and the Mongol agreed to see me. When I arrived, I was ushered into a parlorlike room on the ground floor of a large home that had been converted to an embassy. The furni-ture was neo-Stalinist in design and garish in color. As instructed by Headquarters, I spoke about the possibility of diplomatic relations between our countries—a fact that had surfaced in the press. Then, as casually as I could muster, I asked him if he was willing to consider taking several questions that I had back to Ulan Bator, determine their answers, and provide me with same when he next exited his country. He had already told me that he would be in Rome for a United Nations confer-ence. Mongols are rather inscrutable! He simply said what I asked was impossible, and I saw little point in arguing with him. I said good-bye, that I hoped to meet him again someday, and walked out into the swirling dust and 112-degree heat of a New Delhi midday in May. It felt refresh-ing compared to the tense situation I had departed.

Another objective in India was generic in nature—the recruitment of third nationals. Because India was one of the leaders of the third world, other countries embracing its political line of neutrality between the superpowers found it expedient to have diplomatic representation in New Delhi, staffing their installations with some of their more talented and up-and-coming officials. Thus, Delhi was an attractive locale to recruit third nationals for dispatch back to their homelands as agents where they could be of more use. It was often less risky for us to recruit these indi-viduals outside their own country in a place like India where the atmo-sphere was also more conducive to success. Thus, Headquarters seemed to have an endless number of these targets on its requirements list.

There were other objectives, counterintelligence for example. We were probably one of the first operations in the third world to have a full-time counterintelligence officer, an indication that Rositzke was ahead of his time, or that Jim Angleton, chief of counterintelligence at Headquarters, prevailed upon him.

Covert action was also in our operating directive, but was rather benign in its goals. The major thrust was to thwart Soviet and later Chinese influence through propaganda activities and countering similar Soviet efforts, such as their effective tabloid "rag" of propaganda and disinformation published in Bombay called *Blitz*, which had influence beyond India, and introducing wrenches into its wheels preoccupied us considerably. The Communist Party of India was just beginning to split into pro-Soviet and pro-Chinese factions, largely as the result of the overall Sino-Soviet confrontation; we sought to weaken the party even further.

My position in India was quite different from that in Nepal. I was no longer a lone ranger; I had to mesh with a diverse group of case officers, most of whom were older and more experienced. I already had good rapport with Harry Rositzke from my time in Kathmandu. His enlightened approach to management was one that I tried to follow in later years.

Rositzke didn't care how much time you spent at the office, as long as you got the job done. In fact, Harry didn't much like it if you spent a lot of time at your desk. He wanted us roaming around the city, getting to know India, and meeting individuals with access to secret information whom we might recruit. On occasion, some senior visitor from Headquarters would ask him why he had no case officers who spoke Hindi, Tamil, or Hindustani. Harry would caustically reply that if he ever found one of his case officers dealing with an Indian who required knowledge of an Indian language, the officer would be sent back to the States forthwith. When the ignorant Headquarters type asked why, Harry explained with feigned patience that the Indians with information of interest to the CIA all spoke English.

Rositzke did expect us all to show up for his morning staff meetings. A Rositzke staff meeting had a certain Dickensian quality, like a colloquy between Fagin and his young pickpockets. At these sessions, Rositzke went right around the room at us case officers, one by one, relentlessly interrogating us about our results from the day before. What intelligence had our agents produced? Whom new had we met? When were we going to see him again? Better still, whom did we recruit? On and on.

I was a self-starter, but a couple of my colleagues constantly needed a kick in the ass, and Rositzke was certainly prepared to provide that. Woe to the fellow who was trying to conceal a lack of development activity behind a flurry of paper shuffling. There were enough officers who tried to make their careers that way, but they didn't do it under Harry. He acknowledged our successes, making a fuss over the case officer who had had a "score" the night before. Rositzke deliberately encouraged a certain amount of competition among his case officers—a useful leadership tool, if not overdone.

This suited me fine. My self-taught approach to recruiting meshed perfectly with Rositzke's. I'd learned that a case officer has to get out on the street and meet people, develop them, and then recruit them if they've got the information you need. "On the street" does not mean wandering around looking for somebody. Much of the development of potential agents happens at evening events, and in that respect, New Delhi was a smorgasbord of social occasions.

Because of the large foreign community and our location in India's capital city, there were lots of diplomatic functions and private entertaining. We tried to get invited to everything; if we didn't, we'd attempt to crash the parties.

The social whirl meant a great deal of drinking. Scotch was the drink of choice, particularly in the evening, and the cocktail time usually lasted about two hours. On top of that, just before you went in to dinner, you were served what was called a rammer, which was a martini, straight up. The name comes from the pole used to ram the gunpowder and ball into a cannon, and the analogy was highly appropriate. Dinner was usually an assortment of curries, served buffet style, accompanied by more alcohol, usually beer. When dinner was finished, you tucked your plate under the buffet table, bid your host good-night, and went home.

It may sound debauched, but this was how the real work of the Clandestine Services got done. In any post I've ever been stationed, meeting and developing an individual is more often than not a very social business in which alcohol plays a major part. The trouble is you can't ply your target with alcohol while you sit there and take notes over an iced tea. What you do is excuse yourself to go to the bathroom, go into the privacy of the stall, and write notes like crazy. Next morning you tend to your hangover, go to the office, and write up what you can decipher of your notes from the night before.

Generally it didn't take more than the morning and early afternoon to have your meetings and do the paperwork. Not much developmental work was done over lunch, largely because there were few restaurants in New Delhi at the time. Most offices, not ours, worked straight through until about 2 P.M. and then quit—particularly when it was hot, which was most of the time. Thus, evening events at homes were when most entertaining occurred. This meant some real downtime in the afternoons, and thus the Wednesday Club was born. The godfather of the Wednesday Club was an astute seat-of-the-pants case officer named Howard Bane, who'd had previous experience in Korea and Bangkok. He was the antithesis in some ways of the clean-cut Ivy League case officer characterized in books and the media. He was dedicated with great persuasive power, which made him a successful recruiter. Bane also had no patience for management of which he was not a part, even the hands-off management of Harry Rositzke. I think he saw the Wednesday Club as a means of securing his own power base. Rositzke probably understood this, but was astute enough to let it ride—as long as he was getting results from the participants, which, by and large, he was.

The Wednesday Club consisted of about five case officers who were not "management"; that seemed to be the only criterion for inclusion. Chuck Cogan and I qualified. The meeting site rotated among our homes, and the agenda basically consisted of an elaborate lunch followed by a protracted skull session. We dissected personalities in and out of the office and batted around ideas and theories about the spy business, both in general and in specific.

The food was always superb. All of us had cooks as part of the domestic retinue, and there arose a none-too-subtle game of one-upmanship among the chefs and the wives to see who could put on the best Wednesday Club luncheon. When it was your turn to host the group, the occasion called for the best china and linen and the real silver and crystal. Sometimes we managed to return to work in the late afternoon. Sometimes we didn't.

On the whole, I think the Wednesday Club was useful for exchanging experiences that might benefit another officer in his pursuits. Perhaps it was more useful to me because I had been alone on my first tour and had had no opportunity to exchange "war stories" with other case officers; or perhaps I was finally attending the Ops Course. It was on one of these Wednesdays that I made the observation that successfully making a difficult recruitment is very much akin to the sensations of a sexual orgasm. No one said very much. Those with the experience were perhaps recalling their successful, hard recruitments. Near the end of his tour, Harry hinted to me that he wanted to become an honorary member. We, of course, agreed. In reality, Rositzke was much admired. Like other departing members, he received a metal beer mug with the names of the current Wednesday Club members engraved upon it. Four of the eight or so Club members who participated at various times went on to become Clandestine Services division chiefs and/or major station chiefs.

Since its inception, the Clandestine Services has pondered why one officer can make significant recruitments and another cannot—the emphasis being on significant producers of secret information, not safe-house keepers or members of a surveillance team. Solving this puzzle would allow the Agency to draw up a profile of the individual who will make a successful recruiter and then apply it in recruiting case-officer candidates into the Clandestine Services. Over the years, studies were initiated and batteries of psychologists interviewed successful and unsuccessful recruiters, without significant results.

Near the end of my career, at a dinner Bill Casey gave for a visiting foreign service chief, I was seated next to Gen. Bill Odom, then head of NSA and a very acute observer. Somehow we got on the subject of the different cultures of the American military services, and how they affect the attitudes and styles of leadership of their leaders or flag officers. For some reason, this conversation led me to the solution of the recruitment conundrum and explained to me why I always valued my training at infantry officer candidate school at Fort Benning and my brief stint of troop duty.

I realized that although my time in the university gave me a certain confidence in my intellectual abilities, the military provided me with an opportunity to develop self-confidence in my capacity to handle people. This is leadership and centers on certitude in oneself. While it took me some time to realize development of myself (others saw it before I did), this delay probably allowed me avoid the trap of cocksureness.

When the lieutenant of a thirty-man infantry platoon is told to take a hill—without supporting fire—that is defended by a number of the enemy with, say, two machine guns, and he so briefs his men, the latter regard him as out of his mind. Does he think they are so stupid as to risk their lives on such an enterprise? However, in most instances, they do indeed put in the assault. Why? The threat of court-martial for disobeying orders or a general desperate situation aside, they do so because of his leadership and manifest confidence in the success of the operation. To be blunt, leadership is the ability to dominate and get your way. To do that requires the ability to inspire and provide trust, self-confidence, recognizable professional skills, caring, and many other qualities.

I submit that you need these same skills when recruiting an agent, whose cooperation with you, if exposed, holds risk of death, imprisonment, or at a minimum dishonor. As you move into the recruitment "pitch" and the full dimensions of what you are asking dawns on the prospective agent, he or she looks at you with consummate disbelief, even when he or she more or less expects something is coming. Although perhaps not articulated, their eyes scream that what you want is the most ludicrous thing ever requested of them. In the end you succeed through leadership, for through the development of the agent you have brought yourself into a position of dominance and trust.

For this reason, I have long found the proclivity of the Directorate of Operations to say that an agent "accepted" recruitment to be nonsense. A target doesn't "accept" recruitment—you recruit him. "Accepting" recruitment implies an act of volition on the part of the target, but the act of will in the relationship belongs to the recruiter. You pull your target into a relationship with you—often against his better judgment—by the force of your personality and leadership. The motto of the OCS at Fort Benning applies—Follow Me. That few case officers today have had any military leadership experience is a serious limitation.

Although there have always been too few recruiters, you can make the argument that if every case officer made one intelligence-producing agent recruitment during every two- or three-year tour of duty abroad, the Clandestine Services would be awash in agents to handle. For this reason alone, it is probably acceptable on the margin that most case officers succeed only at agent handling. Many accomplish this task far better than the initial recruiters of the agent, and there is some evidence that women are better at handling than men. In my own case, I must admit that I always preferred recruiting to handling. Recruiting is addictive.

Maggie and Cassi had arrived in July 1960, and I had already moved into a pleasant apartment above the landlord in the Nizamuddin East enclave in New Delhi. We had the usual retinue of servants—Cassi's *ayah* from Nepal had joined us, and we had one of the best cooks in New Delhi, a Muslim from Allahabad, as well as a sweeper and a bearer. Every Christmas, the cook produced a large cake in the shape of some Indian architectural triumph; I vividly remember the Taj Mahal. His repertoire of dishes made eating at home like dining in a restaurant: Indian, English, Chinese, and French. Moreover, he could cook a many-course meal on short notice. More than once, I telephoned from some party at 10 P.M. to say I was bringing a dozen or more guests home in an hour for dinner. All the cooks borrowed from one another's households; at 11 P.M., Mohammed would be ready for the guests with a sit-down dinner of several courses.

About six months into my tour, largely on the basis of information from an operation run by a fellow case officer and some analytical work of my own, I concluded that a diplomat at a Middle East embassy named Omar Habib [F] seemed to have extraordinary insights into the activities of the Soviets in India. I also suspected that he was an intelligence officer, although Headquarters traces on him were inconclusive. Habib was a handsome, dapper man, about thirty-seven years old, married, with two rather young children.

I decided he was worth cultivating, but he was rarely seen on the diplomatic party circuit, so I phoned him at his embassy and invited him to lunch. This was a somewhat brazen approach. Habib countered with an invitation to lunch at his home the following Sunday. On the appointed day, a big party had sprung up at my house, one of those spontaneous boozy gatherings. I eventually excused myself from the festivities to make my meeting. My non–air-conditioned car was hot, and stupidly I drove with my forearm slightly extended out the open window. I never saw the bus that passed traveling in the opposite direction until after it had left a sizable hole in my arm. It bled a lot and hurt like hell, but I didn't want to blow off the meeting, so I wrapped something around it and kept my appointment. It was worth it. As two professionals, we quickly got down to cases and agreed to meet again on a more clandestine basis. Only then did I go get sewn up—you can still see the scar.

A working relationship emerged out of subsequent meetings. Habib insisted that for our first operation together we open a sealed diplomatic pouch from a country to which he had access and in which he, not I, had an interest. I expected little result from the effort, but was all set to dust off my set of honed ivory piano keys and display what I'd learned in Flaps and Seals. However, Headquarters decided to send out an expert to help us. We opened the pouch and examined its contents. As expected, there wasn't much in it, and what was there was practically worthless. I alone opened subsequent pouches and became rather adept at handling and replicating wax seals. It was all for naught in terms of useful intelligence, but it showed our good faith to Habib, which turned out to be the real payoff for us. A short time later, Habib left India for personal reasons and was not replaced. This might have been a loss for us but for the fact that Habib's subordinate, Hakim [F], had actually handled the pouch operation. I maintained contact with Hakim, assuming, in a way, Habib's supervisory role. Gradually, I developed and recruited him as a unilateral agent. By "unilateral," I mean that Hakim's intelligence service was still receiving the information he gathered, but that agency was not aware that I was receiving the same data and that Hakim was being paid by me for his efforts. No intelligence service can tolerate such a situation. Moreover, Hakim's service was also still paying the agents that Hakim so skillfully ran. We got a free ride.

The intelligence from this operation was startling in both quality and quantity. Hakim ran a principal agent who worked for the Soviets and who, in turn, controlled a network of subagents with a variety of access. From the intelligence requirements with which the Soviets tasked their principal agent, we gained a rather good idea about their priorities and modus operandi in India. Hakim was not this principal agent's first case officer from his service and had only a sketchy idea about how this operation originated. However, there were hints that the principal agent had come to the unfavorable attention of the authorities in Hakim's country when there on a special mission for the Soviets.

The operation reinforced for me what I had read in Alexander Foote's book and tried with considerable success in Nepal. Specifically, that a network of subagents run by a principal agent is not only more secure than a case officer's handling several agents by himself, but it is also more economical. The principal agent recruits the subagents under him. In the best of tradecraft practices, the subagents are not know to one another. In other words, you might have three or four subagents, but they're all reporting to the principal agent. That insulates them—and you—and provides protection. If one goes bad or is rolled up, the others are not necessarily all going to go up in smoke. The case officer only has to control one agent, the principal one, which saves time. The Soviets knew what they were doing.

The election of John Kennedy in November of 1960 brought us John Kenneth Galbraith as ambassador to India. Galbraith was basically anti-CIA. The ambassadorship was a booby prize as far as Galbraith was concerned. Having been part of the Harvard brain trust that helped get Kennedy elected, Galbraith had set his sights on becoming secretary of state. Instead, that plum had gone to Dean Rusk. Kennedy was no dummy when it came to reading people; he knew he didn't need an ego-tistical know-it-all for his secretary of state.

Ambassador Galbraith hadn't been in New Delhi very long when he was apparently handed a ticklish diplomatic problem. Her name was Angie Dickinson. I suspect she had been dispatched from Washington because of her alleged affair with the president. Perhaps Kennedy's staff had ordered up this gold-plated tour of India to get her out of town. She was outfitted with a State Department escort officer; the military attaché's plane was put at her disposal for sight-seeing. Later Jacqueline herself showed up for an extended visit. Galbraith had become a "baby-sitter" of sorts.

Sometime in 1961, I developed a rather intense intellectual interest in the phenomenon of terrorism. I read rather extensively on the Assassins, the Irish and Italian terrorists of the nineteenth and early twentieth centuries, and the writings of the Russian Mikhail Bakunin. I actually accumulated a modest library on the subject. In undertaking this study, I claim no prescience for the reemergence of terrorism worldwide in the late 1960s. But, interestingly, these books and only these books failed to arrive with our household shipment when we were transferred from New Delhi to Madras.

Meanwhile, action with the Soviets was pretty much toe-to-toe. India was considered a major battleground, and the Russians were campaign-ing hard to expand their influence. India became a favorite venue for showcase conventions and conferences of Soviet-controlled organiza-tions such as the World Youth Organization and the World Federation of Trade Unions.

We used all kinds of techniques to disrupt or nullify the positive impact of these events, some juvenile, but they were effective. In this cat-egory, there was this stuff called Who Me? that came in glass vials directly from Washington. Its intense fecal odor was more concentrated than an acre of outhouses. The plan was to break one of these containers inside Delhi's big conference hall during a showcase convention, but before we could do that, one of the vials cracked open inside our embassy due to the idle curiosity and slippery hands of one of the officers. Because the air-conditioning was always working, the excremental aroma wafted throughout the building. It almost seemed as if a Delhi *nullah,* or open sewer, had found its way into the embassy. There was much scurrying around to find the offending cause, with no success. Eventually, the embassy aired out. Other effective activities included counterdemonstra-tions outside the convention, and the suborning of attending delegations or individual delegates to raise issues or move resolutions embarrassing for or contrary to the goals of the Communist front organization.

At a later point, I conceived the idea of creating an alternate Commu-nist Party of India based on Indian nationalism rather than pro-Soviet ideology and subservience. I implemented the plan using defectors from the pro-Soviet CPI. Though it was never a major force, it was a useful platform for alternative ideas and was a bit of a thorn to the regular Com-munist toadies.

Meanwhile the Soviets were trying to recruit us and vice versa. On one occasion, at a diplomatic function, one of my fellow case officers, Ernie Wiedel, invited a number of us back to his house for dinner. Included in the entourage were two Soviet "diplomats" and their wives.

We sat down to a fine meal at Wiedel's bungalow at about 11 P.M., after admiring his wife's marvelous portrait paintings. The first course was mulligatawny soup, a rich, creamy curried chicken stew that had been a favorite of the British. By now all of us had had a bit to drink, and one of the Soviets fell facedown into his soup. Wiedel didn't miss a beat. With solemnity, he silently rose from his place at the other end of the table, walked around behind the Soviet, grabbed him by the hair, and pulled up his head. His features were barely visible beneath the pale yellow cream coating—he looked a bit like the man in the moon. Ernie then removed the man's napkin (which he had tucked under his chin) and polished his face. The fellow came around and conversation resumed as if nothing had happened. The Soviet's wife appeared a bit bewildered but said nothing. With an absolutely straight face, the butler offered the Russian sahib a fresh napkin.

At the end of the meal, the time came to drive home. Two cars were employed, a Soviet couple in each. I was in the front seat with Ernie, who was driving, and Maggie and the Russian husband and wife were in back. As we came to the traffic circle on one side of which Prime Minister Nehru's residence was located, I started to smell smoke. Pretty soon the car was full of it. We were all bouncing around trying to figure out where the smoke was coming from; it was a scenario with Marxian overtones—not Karl, but Groucho.

Finally we found the source. When we'd started our journey, the Soviet had been puffing on one of those acrid unfiltered cigarettes that smelled like Stalin's old socks. In his stupor, the Soviet had let his cigarette butt fall from his lips. It had lodged behind his own butt and set the rear seat cushion on fire. Most resourceful, Ernie stopped the car in front of a peddler selling ice cream bars from a pushcart and bought two of them, one banana, one coconut. I thought he was loony until with great aplomb he stuck them down into the smoldering upholstery. Problem solved, we proceeded to deliver the couple to their home.

Farcical episodes like this aside, life in New Delhi had a patina of British elegance left to it. Some Indians maintained some of the British traditions that still made sense to them. I played polo, which was coming back in India twice a week during the "cooler" months—November to March.

I also went tent pegging, a British Indian sporting event if ever there was one. A row of wooden tent pegs was placed along a track at regular intervals. A rider armed with a lance rode off at high speed toward the pegs. The object was to pick up as many pegs, one at a time, as you could.

Tent pegging was, in a sense, practice for the sport of pigsticking. The Brits had developed pigsticking into a fine art. The hunter carried a spear or lance, which was actually a long bamboo pole with a particularly sharp, double-edged, steel spear tip. A lead ball was fastened to the other end of the shaft to give one more penetrating thrust. In the days of the Raj, the English were pigsticking all over India and had horses trained to the quick turns of the boar, in a dancing type of movement known as jinking.

The Indian cavalry-regiment pigsticking weekend was held at Meerut about 70 km northeast of Delhi in the spring of each year. It was considered an honor to be invited, and Chuck Cogan accompanied me on the outing. The weekend began in a big encampment set up by the Indian Army. We were billeted two participants to a tent, with a potty tent to the rear and an Indian Army private as batman. Following a hearty curry dinner preceded by a lot of beer, we drew lots for horses. The horses were known as Australian Whalers. They were huge battle horses, almost the size of draft animals—seventeen, even eighteen hands and used as such by the Indian Army's cavalry regiment. Most of these horses hadn't been ridden in weeks and they had mouths as hard as steel.

We were awakened in our tents at 4 A.M. the next morning to begin the hunt. After an hour's ride out of the camp, we reached the "kadir," situated on the wide alluvial plain of the Ganges and covered with five-foot-high elephant grass, which grows in clumps close together and is rather treacherous for a horse's footing. By this time of year, the farmers had usually cut the grass for their thatched roofs, but in some areas it still struck riders at waist level. By this time, dawn was breaking. We were joined by a group of villagers on foot who were to flush out the wild boar. The villagers were strung out on a long front that stretched for perhaps half a mile or more. At the starting point, the riders were formed up in five-man teams, or "heats." About eight heats were lined up behind the beaters, so that there were about forty to fifty riders in the hunt. Behind the "lancers" was the "field," the non–spear-carrying riders, mostly ladies.

If the boar broke in front of your heat, all five of you went for it, and the boar belonged to the first fellow in your heat who drew blood. The rest of the heats rode on at a normal gait awaiting the results.

Thanks to regular riding, polo, and in part to my lessons from Ernie Fox back in Nepal, I was a competent rider by this time; I could stay on the horse under most circumstances. Nevertheless, I can't say I was the picture of confidence as I sat there on the starting line, lance in hand.

It wasn't long before the first boar broke, as luck would have it, right in front of my heat. Cogan was in a different heat, but it didn't matter. As soon as the boar broke, all of the horses bolted in pursuit. Everyone was off to the goddamned races because no one could control his mount. It was like a cavalry charge, forty or so of us roaring across the plain, elephant grass whipping chest-high, spears waving dangerously. At one point, an Indian Army subahdar major was riding stirrup-to-stirrup with me. Suddenly, at full gallop, his horse stumbled on one of the clumps of elephant grass and hit the ground head-on. The horse died instantly. The subahdar major, complete with spear, was launched like a projectile into the air on a rather flat arc. Shortly thereafter, another Indian rider was thrown to the ground. Both of them suffered broken collarbones, and the "ambulance"—an elephant—was summoned. It lumbered up and the two men were placed in stretchers, one on each flank.

Eventually, one fellow in my heat drew first blood on the boar and it was finished off. The beaters flushed a second boar farther down the line, and this one was dispatched as well. By this time it was noon and getting hot. The cooks made a fine feast of the boars for our evening meal, but

Cogan and I were more interested in nursing our aches and pains over beer and cognac. Most of all I longed to soothe my muscles in a hot bath. This was only day one. Cogan went again the next year; I didn't.

Maggie and I made a number of friends, mostly Indians, the odd foreigner, and a few Americans, some of whom I still keep in touch with. There were Bhim and John Bissell as well as Bhim's sister Padma, and her husband, Sami Deogin. And there was Surendra Singh, the raja of Nalagarh, a former small principality in the Punjab. Surendra was now a rupee-a-year official with the Indian government's Agricultural Ministry. A rose fancier, he gave me a beer mug made from a silver-coated, cut-down 75-mm artillery shell, with half a stirrup as a handle. It is now my funerary urn and is adorned with another gift, a crystal eagle, as the cap. Then, there were two delightful British ladies, the advance party of the first all-woman mountaineering expedition to the Himalayas in Nepal. Before their arrival, Maggie and I, together with another couple, had climbed an eighteen-thousand-foot mountain northeast of the Dalai Lama's retreat at Dharmsala and spent a few minutes with His Holiness afterward. That winter, the two British climbers and I tried the same peak again, only to become snowed in for two days. We aborted the effort, but during our enforced incarceration, I taught them American history, about which they were woefully ignorant; Oxford began to offer courses in Americana only in the mid-1960s.

Part of the inimitable experience of India is the escapist mind-set that all of us had about being stationed in India. We lived a "no tomorrow" existence, suspending in some ways the social conventions that governed behavior back home. Like sexual dalliance during Mardi Gras revelry, it was as if you wouldn't be held accountable for whatever you did during your time in India. This outlook affected not just those of us in the CIA, but Americans in the Foreign Service and others in the expatriate community as well. I'm not saying that I'm proud of it, but that's what happened.

I was becoming a "short timer" about to depart New Delhi for home leave and then onward to assignment to Madras as I had requested. I had few competitors for the position; Madras was regarded by most as a backwater. I had heard that before and knew better—any post is what you make out of it, as long as the intelligence targets are there, and they were. Cogan and Rositzke had left. We had a new chief named Dave Blee. Like Rositzke he was an alumnus of OSS, but this time with service in the South Asian and Southeast Asian theaters during World War II. Blee was an interesting, shy man with a thorough understanding of operations. Though he had a different personality from Rositzke, they were alike in many of the aspects of running an office. Although they probably didn't realize it, they were both practitioners of the Lawrence of Arabia school of management—give the right officer clear tasks and adequate resources; then stand back and await the all-important results.

Among the many duties one must undertake upon leaving a post, none is more important than the turnover of your agents and contacts to your successor. This is sometimes harder than it might appear, for agents establish personal bonding relationships with their case officers over shared risk and the like and resist turnover. My successor, Theodore Wrangel [F], was designated to take over Hakim, whom I judged the most difficult of all my agent assets to turn over. I believed that the chemistry between them would be excellent once we hurdled the change.

Wrangel and I discussed the Hakim turnover at length. We couldn't make a mistake, for the operation was too valuable and the Soviets were seemingly more and more influential in Delhi. Then Theo had a most imaginative, almost inspirational, thought: "Let's give Hakim a medal at the turnover." By this time, I knew that Hakim was a military noncommissioned officer, and the military appreciates medals more than civilians; it is part of the culture. The CIA did not then give medals to its employees, let alone agents, but ever resourceful, Theo said that he had a medal that his late father had received from the Haitian dictator Papa Doc Duvalier. To firm up their relationship, I thought it was important that Theo, rather than I, give Hakim the medal. So, the two of us staged a small ceremony.

At the turnover Hakim was edgy. After some small talk and much praise of Hakim's accomplishments, Theo with great dignity removed the accolade from its velvet box and explained his intention. Hakim almost elevated from his chair and stood at attention as Theo pinned the medal on his chest, saying, "To recognize your service to the United States, this has come for you from CIA Headquarters in Washington." Hakim remained ramrod straight with his eyes staring ahead; he didn't even look down at the honor, but I saw the tears well up in his eyes as he saluted. As soon as Wrangel took the salute, he removed the medal and put it back in its box, explaining that for security reasons, both ours and his own, Hakim could not keep the medal. He said he understood perfectly.

Hakim never knew how unusual his "honor" really was. Some might claim that we were crass and exploitative with the ceremony, but we truly admired this deserving man.

I completed my other turnovers without incident, said my farewells, and left New Delhi. I spent a week in Istanbul and then a few days in Munich to purchase mountaineering equipment, then flew home to New Hampshire. I reunited with Maggie and Cassi, who had left New Delhi a month or so before me, at my parents' summer house at Lake Winnipesaukee. Chuck Cogan and his daughters came up to visit, as did Howard Bane and his family. We spent several weeks there on the lake, boating, swimming, and tippling. For my father, this was probably one of his most memorable events; he enjoyed our "war stories."

MADRAS, 1962–64

At the end of the summer of 1962 I was posted back to India as chief in Madras. I was excited to be officially in command of something. Located in southern India, Madras is the capital of Tamil Nadu State and the most "Indian" of the major Indian cities. Unlike the north, there was little historic Muslim incursion into many of the areas around Madras, so all the ancient Hindu shrines and temples were still largely intact. This was a mecca for one interested in Hindu architecture, as I was.

Madras in 1962 was a village of two million people, most of them Tamils. The Tamils guarded their culture avidly, considering themselves the true descendants of the original inhabitants of the Indian subcontinent. They have fine features and coal black skin—coloration that put them at a social disadvantage in their own culture. Though the Indians were often sharply critical of Americans and Europeans for our racial prejudices, they were the most color-conscious people I've ever met. The caste system was attuned to skin tone—the lightest people were on the top and the darkest people were on the bottom, but not necessarily so within an overall darker ethnic group such as the Tamils. To have a child who turned out dark was considered a disaster, particularly if a daughter. She would be difficult to find a husband for unless you could come up with a sizable dowry.

The same prejudice exists today. Indian newspapers still carry a lot of advertising by young men and women looking for prospective spouses. Skin tone is one of the first attributes mentioned: "looking for light-colored groom" or "seeking wheat-complexioned bride." It's well-known that a groom's mother, on meeting the prospective bride, would take a wet towel to her face to make sure she hadn't been lightened up with any powder or Pan-Cake makeup.

The Tamils are generally considered a passive people, though recent events in Sri Lanka open this to question. The British never recruited them for the Indian Army's combat units after encountering the more warlike groups in the north such as the Jats, Punjabis, Sikhs, and Marathas; instead they used the Tamils for administrative duties. Because the Tamils tended to congregate around their extended families, Maggie's and my Indian friends were largely from the north, such as Jai and Shub Pal, Sat and Prakash Singh, and Rudy and Odette Singh, with all of whom we are still in touch.

The Madras CIA presence was small, and we were back to onetime pads. My ciphering technique was a little rusty when I first arrived, but after a couple of weeks I could still break out a cable faster than most. We had to cover a large area that extended far beyond the city limits of Madras. Besides Madras State (now Tamil Nadu), our territory encompassed almost all of southern India, from Andhra Pradesh across to Mysore, renamed Karnataka, and down through Kerala on the western or Malabar coast.

Madras is a large port on the Bay of Bengal, hot and humid year-round, and mosquito netting over the bed was useful in those days. We were allowed one air conditioner per bedroom and another for a study. Madras, with a growing industrial base and a movie industry second only to Bombay's, featured lovely white sand beaches and a soft, almost sensuous sea. Unfortunately the sea was occasionally infested with poisonous water snakes drawn to the area by garbage dumped by the ships in the nearby port. Snakes aside, Madras was a good post for a family. Cassi, an active, beautiful little girl, began first grade at an international school run by Catholic nuns.

The Madras consular community consisted of the French, British, West German, and American consulates general and no practice of a consular party circuit in which to trawl for interesting targets. Besides the consulates, which eventually included a Soviet one, there were a number of foreign trade missions. The Eastern European Communist regimes were represented by the Czechs, Poles, and East Germans.

One can reasonably ask why the CIA thought it useful to have a presence in the area. Again, the answer is the Cold War. Monitoring the activities of our adversaries and trying to recruit them were the rationales, along with our preoccupation with the threat posed by the now-split Communist Party of India (one faction pro-Soviet, the other pro-Chinese). The Kerala and Andhra Pradesh Communist Parties of whatever persuasion were particularly strong. Our focus on the local Communists probably appears bizarre now, but Washington in general, not just the CIA, viewed the CPI, even with its fissiparous tendencies, as a serious potential threat to India's nonaligned status. This view was shared by some of the American press, in particular the *New York Times,* whose representative in New Delhi monitored the political situation carefully, with his articles frequently on page one.

Kerala had elected a Communist state government in 1957, but Nehru's Congress Party had taken the government back. By 1962 the situation was again shaky, with the Communists making serious inroads, and it remained tenuous through the end of my tour in 1964. However, the situation was different from that in 1957, principally because Nehru's Congress Party had learned its lesson and was taking steps to cauterize the situation. That would have been apparent to an embassy political officer, intelligence officer, or even a journalist with some reasonable sources and periodic investigative visits to Kerala. However, the *New York Times* correspondent rarely visited the state and depended heavily upon a local stringer to feed him information. I noted that his articles on the politics of Kerala were alarmist and didn't comport with what was going on there, almost as if he were writing about some other place. I began for the first time to question the accuracy and motives of U.S. journalists. It would not be the last.

When I arrived, I took over an agent named Vijay [F], who looked like a termination case, and learned another lesson. This agent had been invaluable at one point, but time had passed and so had his apparent usefulness. I was quite prepared to sever our connection with him, albeit as gently and graciously as possible. The more I talked with Vijay, however, the more it appeared that the CIA had another opportunity with him that had not yet been exploited. He turned out eventually to be a gold mine. Because of his background, he made contacts that were remarkable in their breadth. Apparently, this access had been overlooked by previous case officers, or deemed not to be of sufficient importance to his other mission. Through Vijay I was able to create an elaborate network of sub-agents, not just in the south around Madras, but in various locations throughout the country. This network monitored the activities of the splintered Communist Party factions through a web of clerks in the various party bureaucracies. They had marvelous access to paper, the documents that all bureaucracies live by and suffer with.

In time, Vijay became almost another case officer for the base. On one occasion, I mentioned to him that I wanted to meet a particular fellow from Eastern Europe, who was on temporary duty in Madras. Vijay found a way to meet him and actually delivered him to my house so I could begin to work on him.

On another occasion, I urgently needed a location where I could maintain regular track of the comings and goings of the personnel and vehicles of one of our adversaries. No suitable buildings or apartments were available. I finally suggested that he have constructed a shantylike vendor stall like those frequently seen on the no-man's-land between the street and the compound walls of buildings throughout India. Vijay decided that we should hawk bananas; the street was well traveled; perhaps we would turn a profit. Although our target would not like its presence, there was nothing it could legally do to stop our squatting.

Nevertheless, to soothe them somewhat, we decided that the structure should be as architecturally pleasing as possible, allowing for security concerns. In due time, probably the nicest banana stall in all of India was built and staffed with a trusted subagent. The surveillance was a success—although I don't recall any profits.

At one point in my tour of duty, I became Chinese—or, at least, I convinced a newspaper that I was. By 1963, the pro-Soviet Indian Communists were supporting Nehru's Congress Party government. This support came on instructions from Moscow because Nehru leaned toward the Soviet Union. The pro-Chinese Indian Communist faction was centered in Bengal, specifically in Calcutta. It had become quite virulent, especially after the Chinese attacked India's northern frontier in 1962. They were pretty much biding their time, believing that eventually India would fall into their hands.

In south India, I became aware of a minor weekly newspaper that, if not an official organ of the pro-Chinese faction, supported it completely. I devised a plan to push this newspaper further and further to the left—so far into Bolshevik extremism that two things would happen. One, the Indian government would be forced to come down on the newspaper and hopefully take the leadership of the pro-Chinese Communists with it; and two, its vitriol would add to the already serious tensions between the pro-Chinese and the pro-Soviet Communists.

The publisher was a Tamil, and to get in touch with him I borrowed a support agent named Petros [F] from outside India. Petros didn't look Chinese, but on the other hand, he didn't look Indian either. "Eurasian" might fit. I brought him to Madras and gave him specific instructions: "Go see the pro-Chinese publisher. Tell him you have come from Beijing, or 'the Center,' as they call it. Offer him this stipend that he can't refuse, and recruit him on behalf of Beijing."

This would be a "false flag" recruitment—when an intelligence service recruits a target while pretending to represent another nation—a common piece of tradecraft. When you finally recruit the target, he believes he is providing information to some other nation. The Israelis have often used this technique by impersonating CIA officers when trying to recruit Arabs.

Petros brought off the charade brilliantly. The pro-Chinese publisher eagerly took the bait and was proud that his work had come to Beijing's attention. Petros told him that he would soon begin receiving instructions on what party line the Center wanted him to take in his newspaper. The plan was for me to write up the bogus instructions, orders from "the Centre," which would form the basis for the newspaper's editorial policy. In some ways the key to the operation was communication with the publisher.

I had to have a secure way of communicating with him, that kept me entirely separate so that our linkage was in no way detectable. In alias, I recruited a fellow who worked for a foreign Communist installation (I thought this was a nice touch) to serve as our go-between, or cutout as it is called in the trade, and then ensured that both men had matching bicycles.

Every two weeks, the publisher came to Madras by train. He had his bicycle in tow, which was not unusual on an Indian train. Upon arrival, he cycled to a specific location identified in the previous orders from the Centre—a location that was changed each time for security reasons. There, he would find a matching bicycle with instructions and funds concealed in the seat. Earlier, I would have passed these to the cutout, who placed the bicycle at the location only shortly before the designated time to reduce the likelihood of theft. I always ran the risk that the curiosity of one or both of these fellows would cause them to stake out the location to determine who was involved. However, I was insulated from the publisher by the cutout, which was my main concern. I cautioned them severely about the dire consequences of such curiosity: the drying up of remuneration and cessation of contact with the Centre. After a suitable time, the cutout would retrieve the publisher's bicycle to repeat the scenario the next time. I felt the operation was compartmented about as well as possible.

My secretary and support officer and I had an amusing time composing these instructions from the Centre. I was pretty well versed in Communist jargon and was able to run off a credible approximation of Red Chinese prose. I always ended my messages with the Chinese Communist saying "Revolution is the locomotive of history. Signed, The Centre."

The editor/publisher ate it up. As far as he was concerned, I was Chinese. Slowly and deliberately, I began to move this newspaper further and further to the left. I could tell from the reaction in the major newspapers of the pro-Chinese Communist Party that they were getting concerned about how radical this fellow was becoming. They actually commented on it in print, but it was difficult for them to be too critical. I knew my Communist orthodoxy well and stayed within the gospel according to Chairman Mao. Because none of it was quite heretical, they really couldn't find fault with it. To a certain extent, the rest of the pro-Chinese found themselves compelled to fall into line and sidestepped further left as well.

The denouement to this operation happened after I left Madras. I remember being shown a press report early in 1965 from New Delhi. It reported that the Home Ministry (which is like the Ministry of the Interior) had arrested and imprisoned the entire leadership of the Communist Party of India Pro-China. When the head of the ministry rose in the parliament to defend his actions, one of the first justifications out of his mouth was the radical position the newspaper in south India was taking.

I enjoyed my tour in Madras immensely. The work was productive and satisfying, but the pace of life was much slower than it had been in New Delhi. Although the Cold War was still being waged here, we were insulated from the press of world affairs, so much so that Kennedy's assassination did not have nearly the impact here that it had elsewhere. It didn't affect my work in the slightest.

There were endless rounds of parties in Madras—not of the diplomatic variety as in New Delhi, but smaller, more intimate affairs. Most of them were not particularly useful from a professional point of view, because the number of targets was so small. But you could meet personnel from the Soviet consulate and invite them to your home. They would come; they had little else to do for amusement, and better still, you had something to drink besides vodka.

On arrival in Madras, I was intent on studying Sanskrit and, to that end, engaged an elderly, jovial Brahman to tutor me. Eventually, he came to despair at my inability to get the complicated verb forms right, and my busy schedule forced me to give up the pursuit. However, my tutor had introduced me to another scholar from a neighboring country. This gentleman, who was about twice my age, was in some form of exile from his own country. He had been active in its independence movement from the British, but was now on the outs with the current ruling political party. He was researching some obscure form of tantric Buddhism on an international fellowship, but I knew he had a skimpy existence.

What made this fellow interesting from the professional point of view was that he was a regular contributor of articles on political topics for the leading newspaper in his country. Headquarters wanted access to that newspaper to insert material countering blatant Soviet disinformation against the United States in other journals in that country. The development of this gentleman proceeded rapidly. Although following a nonaligned position in his writings, he was fundamentally anti-Soviet and fearful about their intentions in his homeland; thus I had a basis for my recruitment, which went smoothly. By this time, I had so much experience I could almost "smell" the correct moment to make the approach.

There was a problem, however. I recognized that this gentleman was much too proud to take any remuneration for his efforts, despite his and his family's real need. After a bit of pondering, I told him that I realized that he would not take any assistance from me for his help. He acknowledged this. But, said I, "you must have a favorite charity in your country." After considering this for a while, he said he did, and it was the library in the village where he was born. I then said that I would like to contribute a monthly amount to the library, and because I obviously couldn't do so directly, I suggested that I pass the funds through him. He agreed. Thus, face was saved on all sides and the operation proceeded smoothly.

The British were still present in Madras and the surrounding area, such as the tea estates in the hills between Madras and Kerala States. The British may have pulled out of India in 1947, but they left behind many traditions, one of which was their social clubs. Eventually, I joined the Adyar Club; it did take in "colonials"—unlike the Madras Club, which had blackballed Winston Churchill twice—and held marvelous word games on Sunday evenings at which the British excel. Somehow, unlike America, the British have found a way to teach the English language to the young.

Outside of the clubs, the British were less snobbish and more gregarious. They were frequently the instigators of social gatherings and hosted several types of parties from the "small eats" and "big eats" variety through the formal sit-down event. Formal attire in Madras made an accommodation with the tropical climate, but was still rather narrowly defined. Men wore what was known as the Red Sea kit, which consisted of tuxedo pants and a short-sleeved dress shirt with cummerbund and bow tie. In two years I went through two Red Sea outfits. Indian women, of course, came in saris, British ladies were outfitted in long gowns, and other foreigners usually in cocktail dresses.

Late in my stay in Madras, for a period my telephone rang almost daily at about four in the morning. Each time, it was an Immediate Night Action cable from Headquarters. These cables were not about life or death or imminence of war, but over my Soviet case, and whether the target was controlled or not by his side.

The exchange of long messages (all on onetime pads on my end) had several interesting facets. At no point was I told to drop the operation; Headquarters seemed more intent on intellectualizing why the case was no good and why my contrary opinions were invalid, than with getting on with testing the operation or killing it outright. Moreover, I sensed that my own division, the Near Eastern, had no hand whatsoever in drafting the messages, although issues of interest to them or their local area knowledge was often germane. I realized, of course, that the Soviet Division had primacy in such cases, but the overall atmosphere was strange. New Delhi seemed to be neutral. In time, a Soviet Division officer took over the case; he had been sent to kill it and he did.

Upon my return to Headquarters, I learned that frequently my correspondent at Headquarters had been none other than the Soviet Division chief himself, David Murphy. Much later, I really understood what had happened. Jim Angleton, chief of counterintelligence, was in search of traitors within the CIA, and his belief that there was no such thing as a "good" Soviet case had surfaced. Clearly, my Soviet case had been caught up in that fiasco. Later, a task force of which I was a member was convened to examine some of the problems of Soviet operations. One of that task force's recommendations was that the geographic area division in which there was a developmental Soviet case would have prime responsibility, with the Soviet Division providing it staff support until after recruitment.

Normally, DO officers begin thinking about what they want to do for their next tour early on in their current one. Some begin to maneuver mightily in this regard; however, this is accomplished more easily and effectively at Headquarters than abroad. Washington was not on my list as an assignment. I still did not understand that I had much to learn at Headquarters that was essential for advancement to senior positions. What I had in mind for myself was not career enhancing, but frankly, I'd come to love the subcontinent and my work there, and I didn't want to go home. I even volunteered to go to Calcutta, an assignment that no one in his right mind wanted.

Fortunately, I was not the only one thinking about my future. Dave Blee in New Delhi had other ideas for me. He knew that having good support at Headquarters was important, and in the case of India at this time, it was crucial. He wanted to have someone backstopping him in Washington who understood India firsthand, and he wanted me to be that person. Thus, he quickly disabused me of any notion of re-upping for a fourth tour overseas.

Maggie, Cassi, and I packed up in October 1964 and headed home. It was a marvelous trip: by air to Bombay, then aboard the SS *Marconi* of the Italian Lloyd Trestino line to Aden, a passage through the Suez Canal (where we heard of Khrushchev's overthrow), on to Palermo, and finally Genoa. After five days there, with a visit to the Italian Riviera, we boarded the SS *America* for New York. In those days, ship travel was still a privilege of the American foreign service.

Leaning on the rail of the SS *Marconi* as it slowly made its way out of the Bombay harbor en route to the Indian Ocean, I wondered whether my activities during almost seven years in the subcontinent had mattered a whit, and if I had really contributed to my goal of advancing American interests abroad and protecting the homeland. I think I came down on the positive side. However, I always tended to be optimistic.

PART II

POLICING THE GLOBAL VILLAGE

CHAPTER 6

Washington, 1964–68

Dave Blee sent me back to Washington in 1964 for his purposes, but for my own good as well. Although he truly needed someone in Headquarters who knew India, Blee also knew that case officers who stay out in the field too long tend to go native and lose touch with reality. "Reality," for a career DO officer, *was* Washington. I returned to the new headquarters building at Langley, Virginia. Before I took over my branch, the administration decided that I should take the six-week "midcareer" course. This was a new course for up-and-coming officers, and I attended its second session. It included an evening with Allen Dulles, who by this time was no longer DCI. Our small group had dinner with him in the director's conference room; then we all sat around and asked him questions. It had been just four years since the meeting with him on my return from Nepal, but Dulles, not surprisingly, had changed. The pipe was still lit, but the fire behind his eyes had gone out. I could hear that his mind wasn't as crisp as it had been four years earlier. Nevertheless, it was a memorable occasion.

The first two weeks of the course were devoted to the Agency, and the following two weeks were spent exploring the rest of the federal structure and our relationships with other departments (such as State and Defense) and other agencies (such as the FBI). The final two weeks dealt with relationships with nongovernmental sectors, such as the business community and the press. During this segment I cemented my lifelong distaste for journalists after a seminar on dealing with the media led by Benjamin Evans [F], an editor with the *New York Times*.

Because of our success—and that of the Soviets—in planting propaganda in the "legitimate" press, I'd already acquired a healthy suspicion of journalists. The behavior of the *NYT* correspondent in New Delhi had reinforced it. The session with Evans confirmed the worst of what I already believed—that the press will print whatever they know (and a great deal of what they think they know but really don't) just to get a good story, no matter whom it compromises or who pays the consequences.

One of the issues that came up in the question-and-answer discussion with Evans concerned the "Stanleyville massacre" in the Congo the year before. There had been a great deal of unrest in the former Belgian Congo (now Zaire) since the Belgians had withdrawn in 1960, including coups, assassinations, and a U.N. peacekeeping force. A dissident group had rounded up nuns, priests, and missionaries, and a number of other foreigners, both women and children, and held them hostage in Stanleyville (now Kisangani). This group had threatened to kill all of them and appeared to be quite willing to carry out that threat.

An executive decision was made to attempt a parachute drop on Stanleyville to try to save these people. The United States was going to furnish the C-130s for the airlift; Belgian paratroopers were to go in and bring out the hostages. This operation was to be staged from tiny Ascension Island in the South Atlantic. The need for secrecy was paramount—the lives of the hostages were at stake, and parachute operations, which are risky under any circumstance, are downright suicidal when your enemy knows you're coming. However, a *New York Times* reporter got wind of the operation, filed his story, and the *Times* printed it. The crucial element of surprise was removed, but the paratroopers went in anyway. Though they saved the majority of the people, many died needlessly.

I asked Evans, "Why? Considering the humanitarian purpose of the airdrop, considering the need for surprise, why on earth didn't the journalist hold his story at least until the planes had lifted off? Even if he didn't, why didn't the editorial board of the paper sit on the story until everyone was out safely?"

Evans's smug and unprincipled answer was, "Well, he had to feed his wife and children."

That cynical response forever fixed in my mind the lack of accountability and rank opportunism that typifies so many journalists. Responsibility is not part of the profession anymore, if it ever was. That truth was probably the most important thing I got out of the midcareer course. Later in my career, I thought back from time to time to that session with Evans, especially during the war with the Sandinistas and during Iran-contra, when journalists started sounding off about the lack of "ethics" and lack of "morality" in the CIA, especially the Clandestine Services.

Maggie and I settled into our log cabin home outside of Leesburg. We had asked our realtor to rent out the house while we were in India. I guess no one checked references, because the tenants turned out to be some nut cases from the American Nazi Party who really trashed the house. It took about two months to get the place back into shape. Maggie was still putting the finishing touches on the interior when she told me I was to be a father for the second time.

On December 10, 1965, his mother's birthday, Ian Reynard Clarridge was born by cesarean section. He was a delightful and an "easy" baby. He slept through the night and never had colic. However, he could find trouble in the most unexpected places. He discovered a wing nut on a supposedly inaccessible portion of his playpen—with his nose. The wing nut split one of his nostrils completely open. Of course, it was sewn back together. Today you can hardly tell.

Late in the summer of 1965, I received a late-night phone call from Headquarters, saying that my division chief, Jim Critchfield, wanted me in his office immediately. Driving to the office, I guessed the reason for the summons. One of the most contentious issues I had to monitor as branch chief was the dispute between India and Pakistan over the province of Kashmir. Despite having a Muslim population, Kashmir had been grafted onto India when the British left in 1947, and ethnic tensions had been festering in the province ever since. It was just the kind of situation the Communists loved to exploit.

Shortly after independence, Nehru had jailed one of the leaders of the Kashmiri Muslims, a charismatic activist named Sheikh Abdullah, known as the Lion of Kashmir. In 1964, Nehru finally released him from prison, and Abdullah immediately left for Paris.

To get a handle on the situation, I had decided to meet with Sheikh Abdullah. With Dave Blee's blessing, I flew to Paris to see him. Cold approaches such as this can be difficult because you have no real entrée to the person. I didn't have any bona fides with Abdullah, meaning no one he trusted had vouched for me. At this point very little tradecraft was used. I went to his hotel, a dingy no-stars place on the Left Bank, picked up the house phone, and called him. I said, "I'm from the U.S. government. I'd like to come and speak with you."

Even though he didn't know me and had no outward reason to trust me, he had a lot of interest in talking with somebody from the U.S. government. My only shred of bona fides was my passport, which wasn't even in alias. The CIA still had a long way to go with the State Department on that issue. The United States was obviously a power in the Indo-Pakistani problem involving Kashmir. The United States and Pakistan, together with Turkey, Iran, and Britain, were allies in CENTO. We also still maintained military bases in Pakistan. Abdullah probably thought that if it came to a firefight between the Indians and the Pakistanis, the United States would side with Pakistan or at least stay out of it.

Although the years in prison had not been kind to him, I could certainly see why Nehru would have wanted him locked up and out of the way. He must have been quite formidable in his younger days. Now, however, he seemed a bit tentative, and nothing much came of the meeting, except for an agreement to meet again, this time in Jidda, Saudi Arabia, during the hajj.

Later, I flew to Jidda and contacted him. This time, Abdullah really did have something to say, and it was explosive. He had returned to India between our meetings. When he left for Saudi Arabia, he'd scrupulously avoided setting foot in Pakistan, because that would have compromised him with the Indians. However, during his pilgrimage to Mecca, Saudi Arabia, for the hajj and before my arrival in Jidda, Abdullah claimed he had been briefed on Pakistan's next moves on Kashmir, which would result in the first Indo-Pakistani War in the fall of 1965.

The Lion of Kashmir basically gave me the whole plan of the Pakistanis for Kashmir. His source for this was authoritative and was known to have been in Saudi Arabia when Abdullah claimed he was. The Pakistanis were going to begin infiltrating small guerrilla units out of Azad Kashmir, the little chunk of Kashmir that Pakistan did get, into Kashmir proper. Those units would then begin to stir things up. Once the insurrection got under way in Kashmir, regular Pakistani military forces would come to Kashmir's aid. I assumed that, anticipating Indian counterreaction in Kashmir and against Pakistan in the Punjab, the Pakistani Army would mobilize for a blocking position in the latter. The Pakistanis were clearly trying not to look like aggressors but as defenders and protectors of their beleaguered brethren in Kashmir.

The reaction at Headquarters was pretty bloody interesting. It was the first strategic intelligence report I'd ever received. I appeared to have good information that the Pakistanis were going to try to take Kashmir in late summer of 1965. The trouble was that my report received little attention at Headquarters, and I was so new and so intimidated by the chain of command that I did nothing to follow up.

One reason my report was ignored was that the Pakistanis were able to conceal their activity from outside observers—there were no apparent blips to corroborate my data until the last minute. However, the primary reason was that the analysts in the Agency simply couldn't believe that the badly overmatched Pakistanis would really take on the Indian Army. The same thing occurred again in 1973. What analyst could afford to stake his reputation on bits of intelligence indicating that Egyptian president Anwar Sadat intended to launch his Army across the Suez Canal against the proven invincible forces of Israel?

A Westerner trained in Western logic would look at the imbalance of power between India and Pakistan and say, "No one in his right mind would do that." The trouble was that whether the Pakistanis were in their "right mind" or not had nothing to do with the decision to proceed. It was my first direct Agency experience with the wog factor.

Wog stands for "worthy oriental gentleman." In the nineteenth century it was a genteel euphemism for Indians with English manners and a quasi-British social status, but it quickly became derogatory. By the time of Lawrence of Arabia, it was the British way of cursing anything and everything east of the Channel. I believe it was Alec Waugh who said, "The wogs begin in Calais," meaning that inexplicable (and inferior) non–Anglo-Saxon behaviors start to manifest themselves as soon as one crosses the Strait of Dover.

We used the term to acknowledge that the motivations that shape decision-making in North Africa, the Middle East, and the Indian subcontinent are very different from our own. With respect to Kashmir, the Pakistanis were irrational—in American terms—about the whole episode. Their efforts at provoking a confrontation with India had nothing to do with whether they had any hope of winning. They were simply going for it. Of course, the Pakistanis hoped to win, but even if they didn't, they had the reasonable expectation of moving the Kashmir issue off dead center internationally, much as Sadat succeeded in doing with the Arab-Israel dispute in 1973.

The late-night phone call to me in the summer of 1965 was because Headquarters had received information that regular Pakistani military units were moving up to Kashmir. The infiltration of guerrilla units from Azad Kashmir had begun several days before, but still apparently no one could believe the Pakistanis would be so irrational as to engage their regulars. In short, the Pakistani game plan was unfolding according to the information Sheikh Abdullah had given me—absolutely to the letter.

I was tempted to say, "I told you so." I was exasperated about what had happened. I had delivered perfectly good intelligence from a rather credible source (who, I acknowledged, had an ax to grind), and I had been ignored. With a few more years' experience in the Agency, I might have insisted that a closer, more imaginative analytical effort had been brought to bear on the issue. I learned another lesson, and in subsequent similar situations, I did considerable analytical work of my own in close collaboration with DO reports officers and DI analysts. In the end, the DO also failed because it had no sources that could provide collateral information bearing on the original report until the final minutes.

If there was ever a good time to be that particular branch chief, it was then. Not only was it enlightening bureaucratically, but operationally as well. The hours were extraordinarily long, even for the DO, and I worked most Saturdays. As a fundamental part of my responsibilities, I had to work with other components of the Agency, and often at a much more senior level than myself. I had been promoted to GS-12 in New Delhi and GS-13 (major equivalent) in Madras at age thirty-two.

On a Friday about midday, an Immediate cable was handed to me by my secretary. As I read the cable, I mused, not for the last time, that crises—flaps as we called them—always seemed to develop on Fridays. This was a serious and urgent flap; moreover, we needed help from outside the Agency. My immediate superior was not in the building, so I checked with the division chief, who told me to contact the CIA liaison officer assigned to the Pentagon and to brief him on the situation and what I needed.

I made an appointment to see the liaison officer and immediately drove over to the Pentagon. It took more time to find a legal parking place than it took to drive there. In future visits, I received a space directly in front of the river entrance.

The liaison officer listened to my tale. He quickly grasped its gravity and urgency and knew we had to begin at the highest level. He got an immediate appointment for us with Deputy Secretary Cyrus Vance.

I was enormously impressed by Cyrus Vance, whom we met in his cavernous office. With all the other international problems he had, including Vietnam, Vance was right on top of mine. After listening to what I had to say, he called in his military aide, a colonel, and told him, "You get Clarridge anything he needs. And Clarridge, you report periodically to me in person on your progress."

The military aide whisked me away to the bowels of the Pentagon to begin figuring out how to respond to the situation.

I went to work the following day, Saturday, and again no one was around. I got a call from DDO Desmond Fitzgerald, saying that the J3 of the Joint Staff was waiting downstairs in the lobby to see me. This was pretty heady; a three-star admiral had been dispatched to see me. The J3 was in charge of all operations of all services, and if he was dismayed at dealing with a junior officer, he didn't show it. I got to know him as time passed and he was a straightforward, no-nonsense officer.

At this point I was in way over my pay grade, but this was to become a hallmark of my career, especially my tours in Washington: I was frequently involved in problem-solving with people far above me in seniority. This stood me in good stead in later years in that, when by dint of my senior positions I operated at a high level within the Washington bureaucracies, I didn't have to learn the techniques in real time as did most of my contemporaries. I already knew them.

On Monday, the rest of my chain of command got briefed on what was going on. I expected that the matter would be handed from me to my immediate superior, given the level of the Pentagon with which I was dealing, but it wasn't. The CIA top brass never got in the middle of my relationship with Vance or the J3. Initially, I briefed Vance weekly on events, then it tapered off; his own staff knew enough about the situation to take over.

I suspected I was allowed to continue to run this affair because, by the time my immediate superiors heard about it, I was so far into the relationship with the officials at DOD that for my bosses to have inserted themselves would have appeared ridiculous. Besides, I knew all the nuts and bolts of the issue. To their credit, my superiors were unlike most officers in bureaucracies.

An amusing, albeit rather painful, event occurred as the situation unfolded. I needed to get to the West Coast quickly. Without my asking, the J3 made a military executive jet available to me to fly there from Andrews AFB. It was a Sabreliner, in reality a modified F-86.

The admiral sent a military liaison officer along with me, a colonel. The two of us boarded the Sabreliner for the trip to California. I was almost immediately sorry that I had drunk a lot of coffee. We were over Tennessee and I suddenly had to urinate. I looked around, and there was no likely facility to be seen. Too embarrassed to ask, I shifted uneasily in my seat as I realized that our refueling stop was Tulsa, Oklahoma.

I suffered all the way to Tulsa. Making his approach to the airfield, the pilot asked my rank. He inquired because the rank of the officer to whom the plane is assigned apparently determines how far from the terminal the plane must park. I thought the airplane had been assigned to the colonel, but, unfortunately, it was assigned to me. As I was the equivalent of a major, we were parked so far from the terminal that you could barely see it, or so it seemed, for by this time I was desperate. I somehow waddled bowlegged to the urinal just in time.

Shortly after we reboarded the Sabreliner, the crew chief announced his own onset of nature's call. He pulled up a cushion between the seats, and astonishingly enough, there was a toilet.

Through all the events, I had the privilege to see the U.S. military, particularly the Air Force, at its finest. Its rapid response was absolutely astounding, its willingness and maintenance of secrecy admirable, and above all the courage of the airmen and officers remarkable. I must have done something right, too, because I got promoted to GS-14 in 1966 just before transferring from the India Branch.

I thought I might be headed for Cyprus, but after serving as branch chief and receiving language training, I was posted to Istanbul as chief in July 1968.

CHAPTER 7

Turkey,
1968–73

ISTANBUL, 1968–71

Maggie, Cassi, Ian, and I arrived in Istanbul in June of 1968, about halfway through that violent year. Antiwar sentiment about Vietnam was running high. The United States was not losing this war, but was choosing not to win it. Vietnam would have been a win with few casualties had we had a senior military and political leadership with imagination and acceptance of innovation, rather than plodders locked in their past. Vietnam was a total nonevent in my life.

Earlier in 1968 there had been anti–Turkish-government demonstrations in Istanbul and Ankara, mainly in the universities. As yet, they had been largely devoid of anti-American content, but it was only a matter of time. The United States had a rather large (and in some locations visible) military presence in Turkey connected with the latter's participation in NATO. Besides America's role on the world stage as a force for order, in Turkey it was easy for agitators to portray the United States and even NATO as the sinister underpinnings of the Turkish government, which, if removed, would occasion its collapse. This view was fueled by Turkish politicians of the left who were out of power.

They accused the United States of exploiting Turkey—how was never really explained. (Such a notion might have surprised American taxpayers, considering the volume of their taxes that was flowing into the Turkish economy in one form or another, and the fact that we were prepared to defend Turkey against Communist Bloc aggression.) Of course, the United States supported the Turkish government, as it had supported others in the past that it probably found less agreeable, and had never interfered in the Turkish political process, despite the ever-present canards to this effect.

Shortly after we arrived, Maggie and I were invited for lunch at the home of Betty Carp, whose apartment overlooked Dolmabahçe pier. Betty had been born in Turkey, was now an American citizen, and had worked in the American consulate general for decades. A fabulous, intelligent lady, she was rumored to have been the girlfriend of Allen Dulles when he was a young consular officer at the U.S. legation in Istanbul during World War I. They were certainly good friends; numerous pictures in her living room attested to that. A group of us were enjoying the view and watching the arrival of some sailors from a carrier task force of the U.S. Sixth Fleet, which had anchored in the Bosporus opposite the Dolmabahçe Palace, heading into Istanbul for shore leave. Small tenders ferried the sailors to the pier. The sailors were milling around on the dock, waiting for buses that would take them sight-seeing in Istanbul.

Suddenly a crowd of university students (and undoubtedly others masquerading as such) surged down the hill past the stadium. Shouting anti-American slogans, they attacked the sailors. From Betty's apartment we watched helplessly as the rampaging mob rushed the pier and pushed the sailors into the gray waters of the Bosporus. Eventually the police came and dispersed the rioters. A number of sailors were injured, and the situation could easily have produced even more casualties. It was the beginning of my involvement with terrorism, an involvement that would persist throughout my CIA career.

This incident was also the bellwether for a significant change in Turkey. It signaled the beginning of a depressing time; the Turkish economy went into the doldrums, and the government instituted a ban on most imports. Average citizens became pessimistic, even fatalistic. The parks were full of rubbish; people didn't paint their houses. Istanbul became an uncharacteristically dreary place. Life for foreigners deteriorated because of a rise in anti-Western attitudes. Student unrest festered at the universities, and there were frequent demonstrations and protests. Americans were mugged and assaulted—simply because they were Americans.

Anger about Vietnam was the ostensible cause of this anti-Americanism; but most of the agitators couldn't have found Vietnam on a map. It did not help that the United States had failed to support Turkey in its efforts on behalf of Turkish Cypriots several years earlier. By the end of the year, the agitators had turned to terrorism. There were murders, and although Turks were the primary victims, Westerners and others were also targets. For example, a British group manning a communications site at a remote location on the Black Sea were gunned down; the Israeli consul general in Istanbul was murdered; the American ambassador's car was overturned and burned during his visit to a university in Ankara, but fortunately he. escaped.

Working against the local terrorists was one of our tasks, particularly because they were targeting Americans, but it was difficult to accomplish much in this environment. The odds of our penetrating a Turkish terrorist group such as the Dev Genc (Revolutionary Youth) were minuscule, short of having a walk-in from the group. We just didn't have the infrastructure to get at the target, certainly not immediately. Moreover, because the terrorist phenomenon had seemingly burst full grown overnight, we had no database—we didn't know who was who. We were in close touch with the Turkish authorities, but they made it clear they didn't want our help. Terrorist activity was a domestic issue and an embarrassment, and to seek assistance from even a close ally such as the United States would have been an admission of failure or inadequacy.

Political violence on the streets, especially near the universities, became commonplace. As a result, all of us in the foreign community became a lot more cautious. From time to time, I did carry my own weapon on the street when I thought the situation might call for it. In most official circles I was known as the CIA chief in Istanbul, and a leak to the terrorists was always a possibility.

Fortunately, we benefited from a close relationship with the U.S. State Department in the consulate general in Istanbul, which is not always the case. Shortly after my arrival, a felicitous reunion occurred when Doug Heck, my State Department colleague who had the responsibility for Nepal in the embassy in New Delhi during my tour of duty in Kathmandu, was posted to Istanbul as consul general. Unlike most Foreign Service officers at that time, Heck was pro-CIA. He was also smart enough to use the CIA presence to his advantage.

During this time, Daniel Patrick Moynihan came to Turkey. Moynihan was not yet a senator—at this point he was Nixon's domestic policy adviser. His mission was to put the issue of Turkish opium-poppy growing on the table with the Turkish government.

Most opium was grown in western Turkey on the Aegean coast. From there it was converted into morphine base and shipped to Marseilles—the so-called French connection. Nixon sent Moynihan in an effort to secure Turkish cooperation to stem the export of opium; the president was willing to support an aid program to help farmers convert to other crops.

The negotiations took place in Ankara, the capital. At their conclusion, Moynihan decided to spend three or four days in Istanbul. However, because of Vietnam, there was an austerity program at State, and the consulate was technically broke until the beginning of the next fiscal year. Consul General Heck, who was tasked to baby-sit him, was fresh out of funds to entertain Moynihan in a manner befitting his station. Doug asked me to throw a party, and I obliged him. To make it a legitimate expense for CIA budgetary purposes and to get some mileage out of Moynihan's presence, I arranged to have some Turkish and other nationals at the gathering.

Maggie and I had a handsome eleven-room apartment on the sixth floor of a vintage building called the Izmir Palas, which was ideal for entertaining. The building was located in the Maçka district of the city on the European side of the Bosporus. Built in the 1920s in response to Kemal Atatürk's request for more European-style construction, it was also one of the first attempts to combine twentieth-century conveniences with old-world craftsmanship. Even the elevator was a work of art, crafted in Italy, made of olive wood with elaborate inlays, parquetry, and beveled-glass windows. Unfortunately, it often functioned like a work of art instead of as an elevator—the craftsmanship was far better than the machinery that ran it. The elevator frequently was little more than an ornament, and on the night of the party it was, as usual, out of order.

After the party, Heck and I arranged to take Moynihan and a few others for a dinner of *lahmacun,* the Turkish version of thin-crusted pizza. Everyone had tippled a good bit, including Moynihan. With the elevator out of commission, he headed for the stairs. The winding terrazzo staircase coiled tightly all the way down to the foyer and was rather poorly lit. I was immediately behind Moynihan and I saw him peer down from the top step into relative darkness. Teetering and bending even farther over to see the next step, Moynihan was about ready to topple headfirst down the stairs. I grabbed him by the collar of his overcoat, which was fortunately buttoned, and righted him. With that we gingerly descended the stairs together and went on to an amiable dinner. I don't recall that he ever thanked me for my assistance.

The next day, Moynihan told Heck that he was interested in buying old Greek coins. One of my officers, Jamie Munson, was a numismatist and collector, and Heck asked me to have him take Moynihan to coin dealers in the Grand Bazaar on the other side of the Golden Horn. There, Moynihan was offered about sixty silver Alexandrians—a concave coin minted in the time of Alexander the Great. The coins were extremely handsome, almost the size of a silver dollar, showing Alexander with lion-skin headdress. The asking price was about $30 apiece. The price was so good that Moynihan was afraid they were fakes, so he took one with him back to the States to be authenticated and left the rest with me. At the Smithsonian, he was told that his coin was one of a hoard of over a hundred that had been found in northern Syria near Aleppo just four months prior. For less than $2,000, Mr. Moynihan got himself some museum-quality antiquities.

Before he left, Moynihan had asked if I would show his brother appropriate courtesies (i.e., take care of him and show him around) during his visit to Istanbul for a conference of the International Chambers of Commerce. Obviously, I was willing to oblige. The sibling had the same Moynihan family charm, without the pretensions; we had a marvelous time floating around the Bosporus on our boat.

Istanbul has a conspiratorial soul. The city quite literally has one foot in Europe and one foot in the Middle East. Like Vienna and Lisbon, it has long been one of the intrigue capitals of the world—a place where East and West meet and where money and secrets change hands. Perhaps as a result, the day-to-day intelligence business was tough going; victories, when they came, were small and hard won.

The Soviets maintained a large naval force in the Black Sea, and we covered the comings and goings of the warships and cargo ships with military equipment on deck, usually headed for some foreign customer. In the wake of the Soviet invasion of Czechoslovakia, we were inundated with refugees and occasional defectors with useful information from the Eastern European Communist regimes. Their debriefings took up a great deal of energy and time. Periodically, however, there was a significant score.

Whenever Soviet or Cuban ships transited the Bosporus, sailors carrying submachine guns were posted along sides of the open upper decks and in the bows and sterns of the vessels. These seamen weren't there to prevent an attack on their vessel; they were there to prevent their comrades from jumping into the water and escaping. One day, a Cuban ship was passing through the Bosporus into the Black Sea when a man leapt off his ship in the middle of the Bosporus and evaded the gunfire from the deck. Intelligently, he had chosen to jump in the middle of the ferry route between the European and Asiatic sides of the Bosporus and thus was quickly picked up by one of the many Turkish ferries that zigzag back and forth across the strait. A Cuban lieutenant and missile officer, he was returning to the Soviet Union for training on the new Soviet ground-to-air missile, the SA-3. He had previously been trained in the Soviet Union on an earlier version of this missile, the SA-2, which was bedeviling our aircraft over Vietnam. Between trips to the Soviet Union, he had commanded or at least been part of an SA-2 battery on Cuba. Now, here was a defector of real value.

With the approval of the Turkish authorities, he was quickly moved to a location elsewhere in Europe for intensive debriefing. He provided substantial and highly valuable information that allowed us to construct countermeasures against these missiles. He apparently knew the crucial mathematical equation for the intercept trajectory of one of them, but couldn't remember it. Days went by. A blackboard was set up in the apartment he was occupying, and one night he suddenly awoke, stumbled to the blackboard, and scribbled out an equation. It was correct. The young man's desire was to become an engineer, and the U.S. Air Force was only too happy to ensure that he received such an education.

I inherited a group of case officers of varied levels of ability and received replacements over the years. Many chiefs of base or station would pore over personnel dossiers and interview potential case officers trying to get the best they could, but as far as I was concerned, the dossier with its PARs (performance appraisal reports, or fitness evaluations) was near useless, because you couldn't trust them. Rarely was a PAR direct about failings; weaknesses were hidden between the lines and required agonizing decipherment. Personal interviews are hardly an improvement; almost everyone projects well or has excuses for past failings. The best data is the opinion of other officers you respect who have personal knowledge of the candidate. If you are in the field and don't get to go to Headquarters on TDY (temporary duty), you can't read personnel files or interview possible candidates, anyway. Thus, I took what candidates I was given throughout my career, unless personal experience or others' opinions strongly suggested otherwise. I figured—naively, as it turned out—that I could make something useful out of anyone.

However, I got a lesson in humility in Istanbul as I bent my pick attempting to motivate the more senior officers. Turkey is a tough place to operate, and in less exacting arenas, these officers would have done better. But inspiration, example, cajoling, and ass-kicking all failed me. Then, in a normal rotation, I received two young officers on their first tour. What I knew about them was contained in a page-and-a-half cable on each from Headquarters—largely biographic data and general comments on their performances in the Ops Course at the Farm. They were an interesting pair and very different.

When Alan Fiers arrived, you would have thought from his demeanor that he was replacing me—and down deep, he probably imagined he could. A Middle Westerner and former Marine officer with live-fire experience in the Dominican Republic in 1965, Fiers was bright, had common sense, marvelous language skills, and was politically sensitive. However, he was brash and egotistical. I have always maintained that ego can be handled, particularly if the man produces results. And he did. Over the years, Fiers proved my point about the centrality of leadership and everything that goes with it—self-confidence, a modicum of ruthlessness, ambition, for example—in the character of the successful recruiter.

The other young officer, Quill Cox [F], had also been a Marine, but an enlisted man. He had a good college education and had done reasonably well at the Ops Course. His Turkish was reasonable, but he was not assertive and I thought at first that he was a bit intimidated by Fiers. Like Fiers, he had a beautiful wife with two small children. Both Cox and his wife were Mormons.

There has always been a sizable contingent of Mormons in the CIA, in particular in the Clandestine Services. Philosophically, they have found the CIA a compatible environment in which to work, and the Agency has sought them as recruits because of, among other things, the language skills that some of them had acquired during their missionary service overseas.

I give an officer time to get established in a new post and a first-tour officer even more. But after four months or so, with our frequent one-on-one discussions in addition to our near daily operational meetings, I expected to see Cox show some movement toward development of targets. With agents who had been turned over to him, Cox did well. But I was frustrated by his lack of developmental activity. I coaxed, cajoled, and got angry. He seemed incapable of making even the first steps toward developing sources of information.

Some of the other officers noted that Quill had never entertained anyone at his home, at least not foreigners. The other officers and their wives offered to help the Coxes to organize a dinner party, to which appropriate targets for development could be invited. First of all, the team had to buy some alcoholic drinks; the Coxes had none. Then the basics of giving a dinner party of this sort had to be explained. The dinner apparently was a rather successful social event, but the Coxes never repeated it.

Toward the early spring of 1971, I had to write a PAR on young Quill Cox, and I thought about it at length. Then, one day, it all came together based on a number of facts from several sources and my own conversations with him. After the university, which was probably Mormon, Quill enlisted in the Marine Corps. In one of his conversations with Fiers, he told him that while in the Marines he'd largely associated only with other Mormons. When he eventually joined the CIA, he moved to Washington, D.C., and lived in a Mormon neighborhood; in fact, he and his wife lived in an apartment building inhabited only by Mormons. It dawned on me that Cox had spent his entire life inside a Mormon cocoon.

There is nothing wrong with a person's choosing to remain within the confines of a religious group, but it certainly made his chosen career as a Clandestine Services case officer almost impossible. When they were assigned overseas, Quill and his wife had to adjust to Turkey and its environment, as all of us did. They also had the added burden of transitioning from a near total Mormon environment to a secular American life. It was asking too much of them. I wrote the PAR, explained the problem as I saw it, and recommended that Quill seek some other line of work. He didn't like it; nobody likes to be told they have failed. But he didn't argue too much, so perhaps my analysis was correct. Later, Cox left the Agency, and got his Ph.D. in archaeology. Oddly, during my home-leave consultations at Headquarters between my Istanbul and Ankara postings, my division chief stopped me in the hallway to ask why I had written Cox out of the service. He didn't wait for my answer. Apparently, my PAR on Cox had been too frank. I reasoned that I had done Cox and the Agency a service by my honesty.

Istanbul finished off what was left of my marriage. Maggie and I had grown apart over the years. In the summer of 1970, she headed for home, taking Cassi and Ian with her. I took them to the airport, put them on the plane for the first leg of their journey back to Washington, and came home to the grand apartment in the Izmir Palas and its quirky elevator. It had never felt so empty. Sitting on the balcony that evening, I knew I was going to miss my children, but I also knew that it was dead between Maggie and me. The separation from my children was difficult, but not in the every-day, every-week sense of it. My work has always dominated—perhaps unfortunately. I moved out of the apartment in the Izmir Palas into a smaller, more centrally located flat. I hired a cook, a man from Bolu (as all good Turkish cooks are), who was an acknowledged master at calamari, one of my favorite foods.

In the early fall, I was invited to round out a quartet for several sets of mixed-doubles tennis. Our opponents were a German husband and wife, Friedrich and Helga Beier. Friedrich was an executive with Siemens, the big German electrical conglomerate, and Helga was blond and gorgeous. Unbeknownst to me on the tennis court that day, their marriage was already starting to disintegrate.

Helga and I first became friends, and then our relationship deepened through the rest of 1970. Helga's English was limited, and I spoke no German. We carried on our romance in Turkish, which both of us could speak well enough for the purpose, but most of our communication was, quite frankly, nonverbal. In December, my division chief called me to Headquarters for a series of meetings and consultations just before Christmas. My holiday visit to Washington had a legitimate Agency component, but my division chief, who abhorred divorces, was transparently hoping to muster an eleventh-hour reconciliation between Maggie and me. I started to go through some halfhearted motions to that end, but the truth was that I was now head over heels in love with Helga, and I returned to celebrate the beginning of the New Year with her in Istanbul.

In March of 1971, I received evidence of an impending military coup. The Turks called it a "coup by letter," and that was exactly what it was. The top brass of the Turkish Army sent a letter to the civilian government saying, in effect, "Step down. We are taking over." On March 12, they forced Prime Minister Suleyman Demirel and his cabinet out of office. Parliament continued to function, but the military was really running the show, and martial law was imposed in several major cities. Terrorism was out of hand and the military moved swiftly and effectively to snuff it out.

Our advance knowledge of the coup by letter was certainly an intelligence success. We were one up on our compatriots in Ankara in that regard, but that was often the case. Although Ankara was the capital, our office in Istanbul frequently had a better perspective on what was happening in Turkey. This was soon to become my problem. In the middle of 1971, I was due to rotate out of Istanbul. It was preordained that my next position was to be deputy chief in Ankara, serving under a chief whom I had worked for before during the mid-1960s at Headquarters. We'd become friends. The chief wanted me in Ankara, and I knew damned well why. My main function would be to try to jump-start operations at what had become a rather moribund installation.

In the summer of 1971, I left Istanbul for home leave in the United States before taking up my post in Ankara. Helga's divorce was finalized and mine was in process. I brought her to the United States with me. The time had come, I decided, for Helga to meet my children and my family. It's not that introducing her to Cassi and Ian was the wrong thing to do. It's just that I didn't set it up well, which is to say that I didn't set it up at all.

Helga and I picked up Cassi and Ian at Maggie's house in Leesburg, Virginia, and drove to my family's summer home on Lake Winnipesaukee in New Hampshire. Maggie knew I was taking the kids to see their grandfather, but had no idea that I was not coming alone. Cassi, then a teenager of fourteen, was in shock to see her father with another woman, who she immediately assumed had broken up her parents' marriage. Ian, just five, was too little to understand anything, but picked up on the tension that Helga's unexpected presence generated. Of course, Helga's halting English only made matters worse.

My father almost saved the day. When we got to Lake Winnipesaukee, he welcomed Helga with open arms. However, his warmth was not contagious to the children. Cassi remained aloof and resentful, Ian seemed lost, and I'm sure Helga was quite uncomfortable for most of our visit. She was undoubtedly relieved when we left for Frankfurt, where we picked up our red Opel GT and broke it in on a leisurely romantic drive through Italy and Greece back to Turkey.

DEPUTY CHIEF, ANKARA, 1971–73

The chief agreed to look the other way as Helga and I quietly set up housekeeping together in Ankara. We kept everything low-key, and I was careful not to bring her to a lot of official gatherings where tongues would have wagged and caused problems. The chief and his wonderfully warm wife took an enormous liking to her, which helped, of course. Nothing was ever said about our situation, and to this day I am not sure how much Headquarters knew. In any event, because we were to marry eventually, appropriate Agency traces were run on Helga, with negative results. In today's CIA, you couldn't get away with the premarital living arrangement we had.

Ankara is not a particularly attractive place. Situated on the Anatolian Plateau, Kemal Atatürk had made it the capital to get the seat of government away from Istanbul, which he viewed as corrupt. However, as with many purposely built capital cities—Washington, D.C., and Brasília among them—there's a sterile feeling about Ankara. Because it was put together by outsiders, it lacks a certain vitality and sense of itself as a community. It also has some of the most dismal climatic conditions in Turkey. One of my assignments was to coordinate drug interdiction efforts with the Drug Enforcement Administration (DEA), a task that was far more complex than it should have been. Moynihan's visit a few years earlier had been part of a larger effort to stem the flow of narcotics into the United States from Turkey. This was the first time, I believe, that the CIA had been tasked with working against the drug business. The DEA had a large contingent in Ankara, but for a variety of reasons the relationship between the two agencies was never good.

For starters, DEA personnel had not had any experience overseas. They didn't know how to interact with the U.S. embassy or other Americans who were part of our official presence in Turkey. That they bumbled clumsily about within the American community rubbed a lot of people the wrong way.

Worse, the institutional culture of the DEA was completely different from that of the CIA. Within the CIA, there's a long tradition of intellectual honesty and of loyalty up, loyalty down. Within the DEA, that tradition did not exist. Instead, it was common practice for DEA agents to keep a black book on the foibles, failures, and indiscretions of their colleagues. This information was, in a way, blackmail protection in case somebody was out to do you in—which happened frequently enough. At the DEA, the propensity for backstabbing was unlike any I'd seen in a government agency up to that time.

Worst of all, the official delineation of assignments between the CIA and the DEA was never clear. The CIA was required to "support" DEA operations, but did this mean operationally or analytically? Operational assistance posed a turf problem. Because DEA agents get their promotions based on the number of busts they generate, they were nervous about the prospect of having Ankara-based CIA case officers "steal" credit for "their" collars.

After much discussion with Frank Briggs, who headed up the DEA effort in Ankara, we finally decided the CIA would gather strategic intelligence but would not participate directly in seizures or busts. It had to be this way in any event, because the Agency wasn't about to have its officers appear as witnesses in courts in Turkey—or for that matter in the United States. Moreover, the CIA had to protect the methods, particularly the technical ones, by which information on criminal activity was obtained. A prosecution requires the presentation of evidence of criminal activity, which often leads to questions about how it was obtained. If it was obtained by technical means, that would have to be disclosed in open court, which would mean the end of that technical operation for the CIA and perhaps embarrassment for the foreign authorities who were assisting. The CIA cannot afford to lose these technical operations over and over again, much less the foreign support. These problems continue today and are a real impediment to Agency support to tactical drug enforcement.

This drug enforcement assignment in Ankara brought me directly in conflict with another unfortunate aspect of the DEA's institutional culture—the complete absence of record keeping. One of the chief mandates of the Clandestine Services is to have on paper a full account of your activity—a paper trail. In the DEA, there were usually no paper trails. Files, when they existed, were little more than big aggregations of papers, all lumped together. Reports to DEA headquarters were sporadic and often made only when there was something to crow about. This disorganization hampered us greatly in our efforts to gather strategic intelligence, since we had to depend on the DEA for data to get started. It was almost a hopeless situation.

It didn't have to be this way. Before the CIA was officially ordered to support the DEA, I had an excellent working relationship with DEA officer Richard Salmi. Salmi and his colleagues were very successful in infiltrating drug operations in Turkey. They had worked well with the Turkish drug enforcement authorities and with the CIA. Salmi had none of the insecurity vis-à-vis the CIA that I encountered in Ankara. In many ways, he operated like a Clandestine Services officer, and when we came across data of interest to him, we passed it on. On occasion, he asked for our specific help and we worked together effectively. But all that ended with the creation of a bureaucratic structure that forced a suspicious DEA onto the CIA in an uncomfortably formal manner.

The rest of my efforts to solve CIA problems in Ankara were only moderately more successful. I started to implement the chief's mandate to increase development activity. Alan Fiers had followed me from Istanbul, but many of the rest of the crew were indifferent. As was the case in Istanbul, I took this as a challenge. After that experience, you'd think I would have learned, but at this point in my career, I still believed that with proper leadership, instruction, and force of will, I could build myself a group of effective case officers. It wasn't that nothing was accomplished; it was simply not enough.

Part of the personnel problem was due to Turkey itself, and its difficult operating environment, particularly Ankara. Moreover, in many cases, assignment to Turkey meant learning Turkish, a moderately difficult tongue. At that time, there was no other place of assignment where Turkish or any form thereof was spoken. Given the Agency's investment in your language training, it therefore expected you to have several assignments to the country, sometimes back-to-back or with intervals. This made Turkey one of the least desired posts in the Clandestine Services. As a result, the less successful case officers often found Turkish assignments open to them, which is how I found myself saddled with a particularly sad case named Aldrich Ames.

Ames had come into the Directorate of Operations in 1962 through the back door as an analyst in RID, or Records Integration Division. He read, coded, and filed documents there, in part as a way of putting himself through college. The Clandestine Services gave a number of those who had done well in RID a chance to train as case officers in the Clandestine Services—not unlike sending talented noncoms to OCS in the military. However, many case officers who came in via this route harbored an inferiority complex. They felt they were treated as second-class citizens by those officers who had joined the Agency in the traditional manner as career trainees or CTs. I never saw evidence of this, but it might well be true, particularly in the officer's initial years.

When I arrived in Ankara, Ames had already been there for over a year on what was his first overseas assignment. He was married to a poised young lady, who was more outgoing than her husband and who provided assistance in the social milieu. Ames's supervisor had been discouraged with his performance over the prior year. I decided to have a crack at the problem and during the next twelve months had many one-on-one meetings with him to motivate a better performance. It was all for naught. To be entirely fair, he should not have been assigned to Ankara as his first tour of duty, and he had less than ideal cover to develop and recruit agents. However, others had this handicap and were successful. I finally concluded that he didn't really try, and initially this annoyed me. I can recall his sitting across from me and looking at me myopically through the thick lenses of his eyeglasses. As he did, this creepy, supercilious half-smile would come over his face. What it said to me was: "Clarridge, you are a real asshole; I'm a hell of a lot smarter than you."

However, gradually, I came to understand that he couldn't really "try" because he didn't know how. He lacked the necessary, fundamental personality skills. Once I understood this, I saw the problem in a different way: he was in the wrong business or, at least, the wrong side of the intelligence trade. He was introverted and devoid of interpersonal skills. He was never going to be effective with foreigners, as he was unable to relate to them, much less bring them along toward recruitment. Even the role of access agent was beyond his capabilities. Perhaps because of all of this and his concurrent frustration, Ames had developed an indifferent attitude toward his work.

In my final review of Ames's tour of duty in Ankara, I wrote that by temperament and personality he was not fit for operational case-officer duties and should be given an assignment involving analysis and collation "in the Counter Intelligence Staff" at Headquarters. In hindsight, that has to have been one of the stupidest recommendations anyone ever made. At the time, I thought he was totally unsuited for any intelligence work; but perhaps the Cox episode had subliminally influenced me. When I went over my reviewing comments with Ames, he didn't like them but he signed them. According to the CIA inspector general's report in the wake of Ames's treason twenty years later, he was so discouraged by my evaluation that he almost left the CIA. Now, in the dark of night, I sometimes mentally torture myself about my failure to have been more piercing in his PAR.

Helga and I were married in September 1972. My chief, who was away in the States with his wife, let us use their home for the event. Our son was born in November. We named him Tarik, after Tarik Şahingiray. Elder Tarik and his accomplished wife, Güsfent, are indomitable close friends from Istanbul. Tarik was baptized in the Catholic chapel within the Italian embassy compound in Ankara as Tarik Pedro Clarridge, with my chief and his wife as godparents. The Italian priest objected to the order of his first two names, wanting to reverse them. We refused. Unfortunately, my father died on March 21, 1973, and thus never saw his youngest grandson. In the summer of that year, I rotated back to Washington with a new wife and infant son in tow.

CHAPTER 8

The Long Pursuit

Because of the mystery that has long surrounded recruiting (even within the Clandestine Services), throughout this book I have explored the philosophical and practical aspects of the art that recruiting surely is. Among his attributes, a successful recruiter requires creativity in inventing opportunities to meet and develop targets. More often than not, he also requires patience in seemingly endless amounts, and the ability to capitalize on sheer luck. Often, this is the force multiplier of your effort.

All recruitments, particularly significant ones, are different, and not just in the details. However, certain elements are consistent. The episode that follows is illustrative of one recruitment that has all of these elements, plus its own peculiarities, one of which was the knowledge that if the operation was compromised, the penalty was death.

This chapter is a story within a story and takes place during my assignment in Turkey. The occurrences related in this chapter are real, except for changes made to protect those involved. The locales have been changed; the time sequence has been modified (but not in length); and of course, the name and nationality of the target of the recruitment attempt are fictitious—the real human being involved in this effort is still alive.

When I arrived in Turkey as the new chief in Istanbul in 1968, America's attention was still focused on the assassinations of Martin Luther King and Bobby Kennedy, and the violence at the Democratic National Convention in Chicago. However, the rest of the world—and certainly the CIA—was more interested in Czechoslovakia. In August, Soviet troops with accompanying tanks and artillery and the support of most Warsaw Pact nations rolled into Prague in force, crushing the movement that had become known as Prague Spring. Leader Alexander Dubček was ousted and replaced by a Soviet puppet regime.

Hours later in Istanbul we received a Book Cable from Headquarters. A Book Cable deals with a subject that has relevance to all, or at least many, stations abroad. In effect, a Book Cable from Langley is the equivalent of an encyclical from the pope, and all the faithful are duty-bound to follow its directives. This particular Book Cable said in effect, "Because of the gravity of the situation in Czechoslovakia and what it may portend for a general war in Europe, pull out all the stops to increase your efforts to recruit additional Soviet and Eastern Bloc personnel in your country."

No one knew what the Soviets' ultimate intentions were, and Headquarters was urgently trying to get a reading on the implications of the Soviet occupation of Czechoslovakia. They particularly wanted to know whether it was an isolated event or something that would lead to a larger confrontation in Europe between NATO and the Warsaw Pact nations. By increasing recruitment efforts, they were hoping for hints even through the grapevine—pieces of the jigsaw puzzle that they could fit together to make an assessment about Soviet designs.

The next day, my case officers and I met for the usual morning meeting. I held brief meetings the first thing every morning, as my chief, Harry Rositzke, had done when I was in New Delhi. I was interested in what my officers had accomplished in the previous twenty-four hours. Depending on what I heard, I provided guidance, encouragement, congratulations, or a kick in the ass. Of late, a lot of the latter had been the norm.

The Book Cable was the principal topic of conversation. Several of us had already been dealing with Soviet and Eastern Bloc officials in Istanbul for a number of months, but we weren't getting anywhere. The officers in those consulates that you could get to come to your home or out to lunch or dinner—the usual opening gambit in your effort to develop and recruit them—were almost invariably undercover intelligence officers themselves. They had agreed to see you because they saw your invitation as the beginning of their effort to recruit you. In short, they were trying to do the same thing to you that you were trying to do to them.

The KGB resident in Istanbul and I had sparred on a number of occasions since my arrival. He was an old KGB whore who had made the circuit from Moscow to Istanbul, back to Moscow, then to Ankara and again back to Istanbul over and over again. Yes, he was fed up with this life; he would have liked some other country of assignment, but he was not recruitable because he wasn't imaginative enough to be recruited.

Over time I came to believe that the Clandestine Services wasted a lot of emotional energy trying to recruit Soviets during the Cold War. Historically, those who really wanted to cooperate with the United States have walked in of their own volition and offered their services, usually for money. I know of no significant Soviet recruitment that was spotted, developed, and recruited from scratch by a CIA case officer. Likewise, those American traitors who went to work for the Soviets were invariably walk-ins. This doesn't mean that the CIA case officer should cease trying; he must go out on the circuit and mix it up with the Soviets and other targets because he may get lucky. Far more importantly, the Soviet will know who to "walk in" to when the time comes, as it always does.

My case officers and I sat around the table in my office trying to figure out how to respond to the cable. Nobody had any bright ideas on how we might do something better to increase the possibilities of recruiting a Soviet or Eastern Bloc official. We were all too well known to one another. We focused instead on developing access agents—individuals who had frequent contact with Soviet or satellite officials. Often these were Turkish or foreign businessmen with commercial relationships behind the Iron Curtain.

An access agent offers a number of advantages. Above all, he is usually a person a target has an interest in, perhaps from an intelligence stand-point, but more likely for cultural or business reasons. This gives him a legitimate reason to be in touch with Soviet or Eastern Bloc officials. Indeed, they often seek out and cultivate these individuals. If you can recruit an access agent—and it's usually not all that difficult—he can do a number of things for you, such as introducing you to your target and providing you with an assessment on him. Sometimes Soviet and Eastern Bloc officials are more candid with people like this because they don't perceive them to be a threat. If he's clever, an access agent can also sound out your target's thoughts about you, giving you an invaluable perspective on how your relationship is progressing.

Headquarters had asked for a return message outlining our plans for implementing the request in the Book Cable. It may not have been what Langley wanted to hear, but I felt strongly that direct contact with Soviet or satellite officials was not going to yield results. We proposed to Head-quarters that our base should increase the quantity—and the quality—of our access-agent cadre to get at Soviet and Eastern European officials who had not previously been accessible to us and who were not part of the usual cast of characters. This was not really undertaking anything new; it was rather a shift in emphasis. I turned up the heat on the case officers.

Istanbul, and Turkey in general, have been a refuge for centuries for the oppressed fleeing their homelands. The Ottoman Empire, the prede-cessor to present-day Turkey, was particularly enlightened in this respect, accepting a wide variety of peoples such as the Jews expelled from Spain in the wake of the Christians' defeat of the Moors in the fif-teenth through sixteenth centuries; Hungarian and Polish patriots of the nineteenth century; and others. The tradition has continued, and since World War II a steady stream of refugees from the Soviet Union and Eastern Europe have made their way to Turkey seeking asylum. Eventu-ally, they were put into refugee channels run by the Catholic and Protes-tant churches and settled outside of Turkey.

After the Soviets' stupidity with the Czechs in 1968, Istanbul experienced a flood of these refugees, not only from Czechoslovakia but from all over Eastern Europe. Intermingled among these refugees were a few who had enough information of significant value to the United States and its allies to merit definition as "defectors" and thus special status in handling. Usually defectors were moved rather quickly to a country of asylum of their choice, which in most cases was the United States. All of this took up time for base personnel and occasionally required us to travel across the Bosporus to the Anatolian side for meetings or a debriefing of a defector.

Istanbul has a Balkan climate, and summer can turn rapidly to fall some years. Such was the case in 1968, and the blues of the Bosporus and Marmara Sea and the skies turn a steely gray by October. The weather was certainly unrewarding, but in addition to that, the Turkish terrorist situation was spiraling out of control, the Turkish economy was floundering, and everything in the country, including the people, seemed gray. Besides, neither I nor my troops were making any progress on recruiting Soviets and their toadies. This was probably what was bothering me the most.

On a Wednesday in November 1968, I found myself on the car ferry departing Yalova, on the Asian or Anatolian side of the Bosporus, and proceeding to Sirkeci at the entrance to the Golden Horn on the European side. The skies were full of gray, dyspeptic clouds, which seemed to mirror my mood, and the ferry was full of large tractor-trailer trucks. Most seemed to carry Bulgarian registry as well as a TIR sticker, which allowed for customs-free passage through countries of transit to the truck's declared final destination. These trucks were returning to Bulgaria from runs to Iraq and Iran. The preponderance of Bulgarian trucks on these runs supported the theory that the Soviet Spetsnaz or special operating forces used these vehicles for their purposes. The Bulgarian Communists, through Kintex, their front company, used them to smuggle weapons, narcotics, and their locally manufactured, fake Marlboro cigarettes to keep their economy going. It was a problem we were closely watching.

With the wind steady from the northeast at about force 7, there was a helluva chop on the Marmara. I was standing beside my car, the Land Rover that I'd brought with me from Washington. This vehicle was useful in Istanbul because the traffic was often semiconfrontational and people tended to give way and act reasonably when they saw the half I-beam that served as my front bumper.

As I stood there with my car, I noticed a couple about my age—midthirties—emerging from a rather nondescript vehicle. Actually, the vehicle got my attention first, or rather, its license plate. The first two digits, 34, indicated that the car was registered in Istanbul Province. These digits, like the other numbers and letters of the plate, were colored green, signifying that the vehicle belonged to someone assigned to a consulate. But the letters *CK* between the 34 and the final three digits were of particular interest. These letters were those assigned to the Polish consulate general in Istanbul. Thus, I could presume that the couple standing beside the vehicle were assigned to this Polish installation.

I did not recognize the couple, but then I was not an avid student of our mug books. We had ways of acquiring photographs and biographic data on Soviet and Eastern Bloc personnel assigned to Istanbul, which we cataloged in police-style mug books. These two did not stand out.

By now the spray was heavy, breaking over the bow of the ferry. Our cars were near the front and subject to its full force. It was becoming damned unpleasant standing there, and we still had a long way to go before reaching Sirkeci. I could see that the couple was considering whether to take refuge back in their car or perhaps go up and have a cup of tea on the upper deck. Trying to be as nonchalant as I could, I moved toward them, placing myself between them and the staircase. I introduced myself, saying that I noted from their car that they were from a consulate. The couple said almost in unison that they were with the Polish consulate, which I'd already determined. We exchanged pleasantries, and I suggested that we move upstairs for a cup of tea. Since that's what they already had halfway in mind, they readily agreed.

Çay or tea is the Turkish national drink, and a great deal of tradition and ritual goes with it. It is the social lubricant of the country. Over aromatic, steaming hot çay in tulip-shaped glass cups with sugar in the bottom, we chatted amiably but innocuously about life in Istanbul. Their names were Wladyslaw [F], Slava [F] for short, he said, and Irina [F] Adamski [F]. Slava was about my height, five feet nine or ten, and good-looking. He spoke excellent English, and Turkish as well. Irina was attractive enough, but a bit frumpy, Eastern European couture at that time being what it was. Like her husband, she worked at the consulate. This was no surprise, since in many Communist installations the wives of the officers worked at some sort of job—clerical, secretarial, or even janitorial.

The Adamskis also mentioned that they had two school-age children. Consistent with Communist Bloc policy, however, they were home in Poland. It was one of the methods the Soviets invented to ensure that their personnel assigned abroad didn't defect, and a similar system was adopted by all of their satellites. In some cases, the children were sent to visit their parents once or twice a year at appropriate holiday times, or the parents went home for a visit once a year or so. The children were basically hostages for their parents' good behavior while they were assigned abroad. You never saw Communist Bloc officials abroad with babies or toddlers. Unless grandparents were willing to take over raising the baby, until the child was old enough to be placed in a child care center, the parents remained in their homeland.

The conversation was general—the usual small talk about home and family. About halfway through our conversation we exchanged business cards. According to his, Slava was a trade official, but he quickly volunteered that because his consulate was small, he was frequently dragooned into handling consular matters as well, such as visas, passports, and stranded seamen. Irina commented that they lived in an apartment within the consulate, which meant that their movements could easily be controlled. And, although not an absolute, it was also a fairly good indicator that Slava was not an intelligence officer because they frequently lived away from their official installations to facilitate their work.

I continued to keep the conversation bland and looked for an opening to suggest we get together again. This was where push always came to shove. Trying to get Communist Bloc officers to accept another meeting often didn't work because their superiors or the mission's security or counterintelligence officers forbade it—unless they were intelligence officers themselves, and even then, the decision to attend could be negative. The policy varied among countries of the Communist Bloc and frequently depended upon, among other things, who was doing the inviting. Was he a known or suspected Western intelligence officer? Other factors that might influence official approval of a meeting included the general political atmosphere in the country where the event was taking place and the degree of tension between the superpowers at the time. The latter was not in my favor on this occasion, given the recent Soviet invasion of Czechoslovakia.

The ferry was beginning to cross the Bosporus itself on the final run to its berth at Sirkeci, and I decided to make a move. Our conversation seemed to have been cordial enough to suggest future contact. Besides, in a few minutes we would dock, and it was now or never. I didn't want to telephone him at his consulate (and signal to all his colleagues that we had a connection) since he might not report our chance meeting. I told them that I'd very much enjoyed our conversation, and I was sure that my wife would enjoy meeting Irina. I casually mentioned that we were having a small group of people over for dinner on Saturday night and extended an invitation to them. In truth, I didn't have any party arranged for Saturday night, but I sure as hell knew I could arrange one in a hurry with people appropriate for the occasion if the Adamskis agreed to come.

The Adamskis looked at each other, and there was quite a long pause. Finally Slava said that they would enjoy coming to dinner, but that he needed to check his schedule. I knew that meant he was supposed to consult with his superior or with the security staff of the consulate to find out whether he would be allowed to attend. At this point he had a choice. He could report my invitation and seek clearance; if it was granted, this might mean that he was an intelligence officer, or it might mean that his consulate's intelligence personnel had decided to determine what I was up to and perhaps eventually allow me to "recruit" him so that they could run him as a double agent. I assumed the Polish intelligence service knew I was CIA, and if they had any doubt, the KGB could clear it up.

Slava's other choice was to take a flier and come without checking, which is what I hoped—but doubted—he would do, because he would have been taking an enormous risk. The Adamskis would have to fabricate where they had gone that evening, since in their system you logged in and out twenty-four hours a day. If he was caught doing this, he could be sent home immediately and perhaps never assigned abroad again.

Slava insisted on paying for the tea, and as he did so, I scribbled my home telephone number on another of my cards and gave it to Irina without comment. The ferry had slowed and was edging toward the pier. As we went out on the upper deck and started down the ladder to the lower one, a heavy, rather cold rain began. We ran for our vehicles, hardly saying good-bye. The last I saw of the Adamskis was through rapidly moving windshield wipers as their car preceded mine in exiting the ferry.

I went directly to my office and got into the safe with the mug books. Our data on the Adamskis was sparse, showing only that he was an officer of the consulate engaged in trade matters, which jibed with what he'd told me. Istanbul was apparently his first posting outside Poland. The Adamskis' dates and places of birth and passport numbers were listed, but that was it. I wrote a cable to Headquarters describing the afternoon events and asked for immediate traces on the Adamskis. My communications center was still open, so the message went out without delay.

I knew that in the scheme of things, a trade official was not an interesting target for the type of information that Langley was then looking for. Trade representative Wladyslaw Adamski in Istanbul would not likely have any knowledge about Warsaw Pact troop movements in the wake of the Czech invasion. However, trade officials often rise to more senior positions within consulates or embassies, and when they return home, they can acquire information of interest at meetings or from friends and colleagues with better access. Indeed, when you have a milestone event such as the Czech invasion, Headquarters looks upon any official as a potential source of some fragments of information. Therefore, it was no surprise to me that Headquarters' reply the following morning instructed me to pursue Adamski, even though they acknowledged that he would at best be a long shot as a source.

Headquarters' message did have an interesting bit of information on Irina Adamski. According to a recent defector, Irina's mother was Russian and had been married before to another Pole. The offspring of this union was a son who was believed to be a Polish General Staff officer with the rank of major. Now this made the Adamskis more interesting—a stepbrother in the Polish General Staff.

Thursday passed, then Friday, with no call from Adamski. In situations like this, you spend a lot of time waiting for the phone to ring, and it leads to much frustration and even despair if you're not careful. Normally I was at the office on Saturdays till about two in the afternoon, and on this particular Saturday, just as I was ready to leave, the phone rang. It was Adamski, telling me that he and his wife would be delighted to join us that evening.

I was elated he accepted, despite myself. I knew damned well that it probably didn't mean anything. In all likelihood, he'd reported the meeting on the ferry and the dinner invitation to his superiors and had received permission to come in order to check me out. The odds were that I was dealing with a probe by the opposition to see what I was up to.

In case the Adamskis accepted, Maggie had put together the dinner party for Saturday evening. The cast was chosen with great care. If Adamski was an intelligence officer, I didn't want anyone at the party who would be so attractive to him that he'd spend the evening trying to develop that individual. I wanted a group that was benign, but interesting—no Turkish officials, no other CIA case officers. I wanted a situation where I would have as much time as possible with Adamski without being totally obnoxious about it.

On Saturday evening I stationed one of my officers in a car near the entrance to the Izmir Palas, where my apartment was located, to monitor how they arrived. It was an important signal. Would they come by taxi; drive themselves; or have a chauffeur-driven consulate vehicle? Would they walk? The Polish consulate general and their quarters were within walking distance of my building.

The couple arrived very much on time in a chauffeured consulate car, which drove off immediately after unloading them, which indicated Adamski had sought and received permission from his authorities to accept my invitation. As customary in Europe, they brought a small bouquet of flowers for the hostess. Upon arrival, they spent quite a bit of time with Cassi, then eleven, and Ian, just three, perhaps because they were separated from their own children.

Throughout the evening Slava seemed to mix easily with the other guests. He was comfortable conversing in both English and Turkish. Although the party was a rather boisterous one, both he and Irina drank only moderately. It became apparent that they were devoted to their children; they intended to do everything they could to ensure their advancement. Maggie gleaned what may have been the most important piece of information of the evening. After talking at some length with Irina, she concluded that Slava was exceedingly ambitious from Irina's admission that he was anxious to get to the top of the trade hierarchy, or to move into straight diplomacy. This could be factored in further as we proceeded to develop Slava. To do that, however, we faced the next hurdle of arranging another contact.

My impression was that Adamski and I were getting along well. He was genuinely interested in me, and I think he felt the reciprocation. Although I'd learned not to be too optimistic about what such observations portend—one's eagerness to succeed can lead to reading too much into them—the chemistry seemed right. Adamski's trade speciality was in heavy machinery for milling operations, and he was basically a salesman trying to flog this equipment to various Turkish customers. I confirmed that he and Irina were living in the consulate. This meant that his home phone came through the main switchboard of the installation and was tapped. If I called to arrange a get-together, my contact would be noted. Therefore it was better to try to arrange a meeting now, and as the party was breaking up, I gingerly approached Adamski with the idea of meeting for lunch.

He paused, then said that he was terribly busy and that his schedule didn't leave him much time for daytime meetings. He didn't indicate that I should call him, either at his office or at his home. He definitely put me off, and I chose not to press. It wouldn't have done any good. Instead, I hoped to devise an alternative way to get in touch with him. He and Irina then thanked us effusively and joined the rest of our ebullient and tipsy guests making their way down the tortuous spiral staircase. Once again, our work-of-art elevator was out of order. Another guest offered to drive the Adamskis home, and they accepted.

Now, of course, I had a problem. Unless I could come up with another way to get in touch with him, I was at a dead end. I had an intelligence analyst begin to examine the various companies that Adamski might be in contact with, based on what he had told me of his trade speciality. We focused on three Turkish firms. Of these, one had real potential, because I already knew an individual working there. Sebastian Wittel [F] and I shared an interest in scuba diving, and I knew both him and his wife rather well. Both were descendants of European families that had settled in the Ottoman Empire in the nineteenth century.

I felt I could trust Wittel. From what I knew of his political feelings toward the Communists, he would probably be amenable to assisting me with Adamski, provided that it didn't put his life, his family, or his job in any jeopardy. That would not be a problem because his role would be fundamentally passive. After appropriate name checks and clearances from Headquarters, I asked Wittel to join me for lunch. He did indeed know Adamski and agreed to cooperate with me. Because we were already friends, I knew that any mention of compensation would be offensive to him. Over the ensuing months I provided him with a number of small gifts—luxury items that were scarce in Turkey at the time.

I first asked Sebastian to put down on paper any knowledge about Adamski as a human being—his personality, his family, his political attitudes, etc. I needed to know more about the *man.* Unfortunately, Wittel knew little more about Adamski than I did; their relationship was straight business and they had not socialized. He promised to be more alert about Adamski the next occasion they met, but I didn't expect much—Sebastian was a survivor and meant to stay that way. Above all, I wanted Wittel to alert me the next time Adamski made an appointment to see him, and this he agreed to do.

I gave up hope of hearing from Adamski directly. Christmas and New Year's came and went. After such a promising beginning, I waited with great frustration for something to happen. The rest of our efforts were not panning out, and Washington was still holding everyone's feet to the fire to get at more Soviet and Eastern Bloc targets. Finally, toward the end of January, Wittel let me know that he was to meet with Adamski.

At the appropriate time, I positioned myself across the street from Wittel's offices. It was pouring rain, and I sat myself by the window of a *çay* shop diagonally across from the building. Adamski arrived on time and on foot for his meeting. I did not see any consulate car. I watched him enter the offices, and after about half an hour I moved across the street. I stationed myself near the building entrance. My trench coat and umbrella were near useless in the downpour, and the wait was interminable, but eventually Adamski emerged. As he put up his umbrella, I walked by and virtually ran into him.

It wasn't subtle but it worked. He was obviously surprised to see me, but he seemed pleased. We chatted beneath our umbrellas for a few minutes, and because it was near lunchtime, I invited him to a *lahmacun* restaurant to join me for the Turkish version of pizza. He hesitated, then accepted.

Again, I kept the conversation light. He had revealed at the party that he liked to fish, so during lunch I mentioned fishing. His eyes lit up. He told me that he planned to go fishing at Küçük Çekmece in about ten days. Küçük Çekmece is a lake southwest of Istanbul known for its abundance of freshwater fish. Of course, I said I'd been out at Küçük Çekmece quite often, and that perhaps I'd see him there next week.

This was a lie. I hadn't had a fishing pole in my hands since I was about fourteen, but I damned well knew that I was going to give myself an intensive refresher course and be there when he went fishing. He didn't ask me to join him, and I didn't push for an invitation, nor did I invite him to come with me. I was hoping that he'd go alone, so I would have an opportunity to engage him in conversation for several hours and move the development forward.

I was now trying to get to see Adamski often enough to determine whether he had real recruitment potential. The stumbling block with all developments of Communist Bloc officials was having enough private contact to move the process along. Moreover, the counterintelligence issue was still very much front and center: To what extent was Adamski under control by his security personnel? If they were running him as a possible double agent, they were taking their sweet time about it by not making my contact with Adamski easy. To test the possibility that he was under control and in the interest of pushing Adamski's development forward, fishing would do quite nicely. It was those unbroken hours alone with him that I coveted.

Before heading for Küçük Çekmece, I debriefed Sebastian about his meeting. As I'd requested, he'd queried Adamski on his feelings about the Soviet invasion of Czechoslovakia. Adamski had been sorrowful. He didn't approve of how fast the Czechs were trying to liberalize, but he didn't appear to be a hard-liner. So far, so good. I borrowed some fishing gear from a friend and practiced casting into the Bosporus.

I knew I might be in for an all-day outing. Adamski hadn't said whether he was going to fish early or late. This was February, and God knows it was going to be colder than hell at dawn out there on the lake, but I didn't want to miss him. I tried not to think about the possibility that his fishing expedition might include a few of his compatriots from the consulate, but I knew from other information that they usually fished in groups.

I was on the lake by 7 A.M. Mercifully, the last few days had been quite warm. I'd already scouted the site on a previous visit and knew how the area was set up. I rented a boat and proceeded out a good way into the lake. From that vantage point, I could see both docks and the parking areas. I practiced my casting while I waited for one of those nondescript Eastern Bloc sedans.

About two hours later he arrived—or rather, they arrived. Adamski was not alone. Three men emerged from the car, collected their gear, went to the dock, and picked up a boat. I was disappointed, but now I wanted to see what his reaction to seeing me would be. I rowed fairly close to the dock and waited for them to shove off. Adamski was rowing, and as they approached, he saw me. He didn't say hello; he didn't wave, but it was obvious that he'd seen me. Clearly, he didn't want his companions to know that he knew me. This was interesting. It could imply that when he came to dinner, he had hidden from his consulate authorities that it was actually *my* home that he was visiting.

Meanwhile, luck intervened. Through a regular, routine contact in a tourist agency, we learned that the Adamskis and others from their consulate were going to Bursa for a long weekend. Bursa was the first capital of the Ottoman Empire and was known for its mosques, tile work, and hot springs. Located on the Anatolian side of the Bosporus, the picturesque medieval city was a popular weekend getaway from Istanbul. I knew where the Adamskis would be staying, and I arranged for Maggie and me to stay at another hotel nearby. The day before we were to leave, Maggie came down with the flu, so I headed off to Bursa alone. Since the Adamskis were due to arrive on Saturday, I went to Bursa Friday night to check out their hotel and the surrounding area. There was nothing particularly imaginative about what I planned to do, and I knew that my abrupt appearance in Bursa risked scaring the living shit out of Adamski. But, weighing all the factors, I saw no other course of action. My unexpected arrival in Bursa might just shake the situation enough to determine what I had or did not have with Slava.

I intended to call Slava after he'd checked in to ask him to my hotel room for a drink. In case he didn't want to come to my room, I formulated a backup location—a small open-air restaurant popular with tourists where we wouldn't be conspicuous. On Saturday morning I wanted to time my phone call to coincide with his arrival. The best way to do that was to station myself in his hotel where I could watch the front desk without attracting much attention. Figuring the Adamskis and company might get an early start out of Istanbul, at about 10 A.M. I planted myself behind a newspaper in the alcove and waited.

Shortly before noon, they showed up with two other couples. I quickly walked back to my hotel and made my phone call. As planned, I caught him in the room. I mentioned that I happened to be in Bursa and had seen him drive up to the hotel. He was surprised, to put it mildly. By now, Slava must have found it curious that I kept popping up everywhere—in front of Wittel's office, the encounter in the rowboat at Küçük Çekmece, and now this. If you believed this was all coincidence, you could make yourself believe in alien abductions and the tooth fairy. Once he recovered from the shock, he seemed genuinely glad to hear from me. I suggested that he and Irina join me for a drink. He said he was there with friends and that he would be happy to meet with me alone. I was astonished, but delighted. I told him where I was staying, and how to get there. He made a date for seven that evening. I had the hotel send up a few beers and some snacks and settled in to wait for the evening to arrive.

Again, the wait was interminable. I still had no idea whether he was under control or acting of his own volition, but at least I would have him on my turf for a while. I tortured myself, wondering whether my target would really show up, but at seven sharp there was a knock on the door. Adamski was affable and at ease. Irina had gone off with the others to take the waters at a nearby hot spring. Although he initially told me that he could spend just a few minutes with me, we bypassed the beer and settled down over a good bottle of Scotch and spent the next two hours together.

As friends would, we talked about everything under the sun, from how things were going in Poland to his hopes for his children. Initially we skirted political issues, such as Czechoslovakia. I pushed it as much as I dared, because I didn't know how many more opportunities like this I would have. We put a goodly dent in the bottle of Scotch. Hoping to capitalize on the mood when I sensed that he was about to leave, I made my move. I told him that I would really like his help in better understanding what was going on inside the Soviet Union and Eastern Europe. I was deliberately vague about Poland so as not to arouse his possible nationalist feelings. His immediate response was that he was in the trade business and couldn't help me. He didn't say he wouldn't help, just that he didn't have access to any information I might want. I didn't offer anything in return because I suspected it would be rejected. It was too early for that.

As Slava got up from his chair, I floated one more time the idea of wanting his help, but got the same response. He just couldn't imagine how he might be of assistance to me. Then, he let go a bombshell: he and Irina had completed their tour in Istanbul and were returning to Poland in May. They'd be reunited with their children, at least for a time. I asked him what his next assignment would be, and he didn't know, except that it would once again deal with heavy machinery. By now, I knew exactly which government firm he worked for and much about his ambition, which was acute. Hiding my disappointment, I asked whether it would be possible to get together with our wives for a farewell dinner. He thought that was possible and said he would call me. There was nothing I could do to push him further.

I mulled everthing over on the drive back to Istanbul. Officers in the Directorate of Operations are trained to maintain perspective and to consider all the angles. It's wise to retain a bit of skepticism about potential recruitments. The more suspicious tend to put a heavy emphasis on counterintelligence and would at this point probably see Slava as controlled—i.e., that he had told his superiors of the repeated "chance" meetings with me and was being run *into* me.

But if he were, then he was a helluva lot better actor than most. Too many things about our relationship indicated that he was not controlled. If he was, I doubted very much he would have rejected my overture in the hotel room by pleading lack of access to information—his superiors would likely have instructed him to be more responsive, as the contact with me was of little value unless they let me go through with his recruitment. Once I recruited him, I would set up a system of communication with Slava for when he returned to Poland, which would have given them a window on our techniques and perhaps the opportunity to compromise one of our officers making contact. That Slava hadn't made himself an easy target for recruitment increased the odds that he was not under control. Also, he had never probed me about myself or anything else of possible interest to an intelligence/security officer who might be running him, and there wasn't the slightest indication that he himself was an intelligence officer. By now, he had to have concluded that I was a CIA officer.

The rest of March and all of April passed. I tried not to stare at the telephone, and I considered a number of alternatives, including having Wittel host a farewell party for the Adamskis. I think Wittel would have done it, even though it would have completely blown his cover. I decided not to ask.

I settled for yet another "accidental" meeting on the street near Wittel's business. Perhaps Slava was getting used to running into me because he didn't seem surprised to see me. He apologized for not calling and agreed to come to the house for dinner with Irina a few nights later. This was all I was looking for, and you could read his acceptance a number of different ways. Either he had been authorized to come to dinner or he hadn't and had decided to do it on his own. In either event, he didn't find it necessary to hedge his acceptance by saying he had to check his schedule. He fished his diary out of his breast pocket, thumbed through it briefly, and made the date.

Maggie and I organized ourselves for the evening. We purchased a modest gift for Irina—nothing ostentatious or U.S. made—something that they could have purchased locally. We settled on a piece of Turkish embroidery.

Again, I posted a case officer on the street near the entrance to Izmir Palas to watch their arrival. They came by cab, which was an interesting sign—consistent with my tentative conclusion that Adamski was on his own. They arrived with flowers and once again made a fuss over Cassi and Ian. There was no purpose now in my pressing forward with a recruitment attempt. They were leaving so shortly that there was no time to train him even if he'd agreed. I did, however, mention again (out of earshot of our wives) that I believed he could be of assistance to me, and that I hoped we would meet again sometime. He let my remark pass.

That evening it became clear in a new way how close Irina and Slava were as a couple. They had a solid marriage and were committed to each other, but it was also apparent that she was a much stronger force in the relationship than we had thought; Maggie and I each reached that conclusion independently. During dinner, we learned that both Slava's family and Irina's family were "worker" class, but there was no mention of Irina's mother's first marriage or Irina's stepbrother in the Polish military. Shortly thereafter, in May of 1969, the Adamskis left for Poland. Frankly, I didn't give them much more thought because I was preoccupied with a number of professional and personal problems. In the summer of 1970, Maggie returned to Washington with the children to seek a divorce. The Turkish internal situation deteriorated further; the Israeli consul general was murdered in his flat just up the street from where I lived. I met and fell in love with Helga. Through it all, we were still under intense pressure from Washington to boost Soviet and Eastern Bloc recruitment. Finally, in March 1971, the Turkish military took over the government and got a handle on the terrorism. March drifted into June, and Helga and I went on home leave to the United States. We arrived in Ankara for assignment in late August 1971.

We lived in a modest apartment on the outskirts of Ankara while waiting for my divorce to come through. I had hardly settled behind my desk in my new position when we received information that the Adamskis were being assigned to Ankara. If you're of the counterintelligence bent, you could read all kinds of suspicious coincidences into his posting. What the Poles might gain by sending Slava to Ankara to resume contact with me I couldn't imagine—unless they had finally decided to run a serious double-agent operation against me. I also knew the Soviets and their Eastern European satellites had historically shuffled personnel back and forth between Istanbul and Ankara. If you spoke Turkish, there weren't many other places they could use you. Perhaps it was a double-agent operation against me; perhaps it was just a normal reassignment. Time would tell.

For an intelligence officer, Ankara was a much tougher place to do business than Istanbul, particularly in regard to tradecraft, with its labyrinth of streets and hundreds of cafés, restaurants, and out-of-the-way places. Finding safe locations to meet was easy. Because the Bosporus splits the city in two, you could always get on a ferry with someone or rendezvous on board, then debark on separate banks.

Ankara, in contrast, had a lot more in common with Kathmandu: a small bowl ringed by mountains, and a capital full of foreigners whose movements are highly visible and of interest to Turkish security. It was extremely difficult to be anonymous in Ankara.

My first problem was to reestablish contact with the Adamskis without drawing his colleagues' attention to my effort. In Ankara, trade officials tended to deal with Turkish ministries rather than private commercial firms like Wittel's in Istanbul. I had no ins with Turkish ministries with which Adamski would be in contact. Thus arranging a "chance" encounter with Adamski à la the Wittel ploy was unlikely. Furthermore, I didn't want to bring Adamski to the attention of Turkish authorities. When people's lives are at stake, even U.S. allies such as Turkey have to take a backseat to the security of the operation.

Any case officer who says luck plays no part in the intelligence business has probably never had any or has lacked the wit to make use of that he had. Luck always plays a role. While I was beating my brains out trying to figure an angle to get to Adamski, Helga and I ran into the Adamskis at a *bakkal*, the ubiquitous Turkish mini-supermarket, near our home in the Çankaya area of Ankara. They'd been in Ankara only six weeks, about the same length of time as Helga and I. They seemed overwhelmed with surprise. We didn't have a lengthy meeting, just long enough to catch up on what had happened since we'd last seen each other.

I explained about Maggie, the divorce, and my relationship with Helga. Irina's English had been good but shaky in Istanbul, and now she was out of practice. She had trouble fitting Helga into the picture, and finally Slava said he would explain later. Like us, they were not looking forward to a tour in a smoggy, charmless city. When I mentioned getting together, Slava demurred and said he would get in touch with me at some point. Headquarters was still interested in pursuing Adamski, but he controlled when and if we met. The rest of 1971 came and went, and I was still waiting. Several attempts at chance meetings failed, and at times I began to think of him as almost a phantom.

We were well into 1972 before I heard from him again. In August I received a phone call at home, just as I was leaving for the office. I found it curious that he'd called me at home, because in the confusion of our meeting at the *bakkal,* I had stupidly not given him my home number, and home numbers were not easily obtained because of the terrorist problem. Plus phone books were only infrequently issued, and the current one did not contain my name. I later learned that Adamski had acquired my number rather ingeniously. He told a somewhat inebriated Australian diplomat at some function that he hoped to get something going with my fiancée, Helga, and needed her home number. How Adamski got this conversation launched I do not know. The Australian obligingly crossed the room, I assume unsteadily, to a Pakistani diplomat with whom he knew I was close. Under some pretext, he received the number and passed it on to Adamski. Not bad for a non–intelligence officer.

Adamski's voice was a bit urgent as he asked me to meet him at the Büyük Ankara, a government-owned luxury hotel on Atatürk Boulevard, catercorner from the U.S. embassy, and almost directly across from the large Soviet trade mission building. I told him that I'd meet him there in twenty minutes.

From a tradecraft standpoint, the Büyük Ankara was not a bad place to meet, particularly on short notice. It was large, and it would be difficult to be set up there, unless it was done before the phone call was placed—but I couldn't figure out why I would be set up in the first place. The downside was there was only a front entrance. All others were reserved for tradesmen.

I dropped my car at the embassy and exited the compound, going left toward a street containing a *bakkal,* where I purchased some matches. Then I walked around the block where the Soviet trade mission was situated and eventually found myself on the same side of Atatürk Boulevard as the hotel. I noticed absolutely no interest in my meanderings. This is known in the trade as doing a surveillance detection route (SDR). Although I went through this precautionary exercise, I was well aware that the hostile coverage of our meeting could already be in place if Adamski were a double agent, or if he had been careless or naive enough to call me from a phone monitored by his security personnel. If he had, they would have had to act with more alacrity than the average security staffers.

Entering the hotel, I saw nothing suspicious, but then again I didn't expect to. It was not yet eight-thirty, and the nearby ministries and embassies were just coming to life. Going deeper into the lobby, I still didn't see him. I moved into a corridor that led to the public rooms, and there he was, dressed as if he were ready to go to work. He grasped my hand; he was profuse in his apologies for not having contacted me before. We crossed to another small section, which was like the reception area for one of the ballrooms or conference rooms. There were chairs there, but we never did sit down.

He was obviously agitated. After a bit of hemming and hawing, he told me that he had a real problem and needed my help. "Dewey," he said, looking directly into my eyes, "we think Irina is pregnant."

At first I didn't get it. Helga was pregnant, too, and we were surprised and pleased, especially because during her first marriage she'd been told by doctors in Germany that she'd never be able to conceive because she had a hooked uterus.

Before he had a chance to explain, I realized that if the Adamskis had another child, it would end any hope of overseas assignments in the near future. Their two teenage children were looked after back home, but a baby meant the Adamskis would be grounded in Poland for a number of years. Those who went abroad tended to be on the fast track for promotions, and confinement at home portended a curtailment in advancement. Finally, it meant an end to many of the luxuries they'd been able to send home to their children from their postings in Turkey.

I immediately agreed to help them. The first hurdle was to verify that Irina was indeed pregnant. Adamski asked me to help them get a frog test done, and he'd already identified a clinic where it could be performed. I knew why he or Irina didn't just go there in person: they wanted no record. In a clinic, there would be forms to fill out and questions to answer, and the Adamskis wanted none of that, particularly if the next step, an abortion, was required. Poland might be a Communist country, but it was also staunchly Roman Catholic.

I told Adamski to meet me with a specimen of Irina's urine in the men's room of the Dedeman Hotel. I scheduled the rendezvous for 8 A.M. the next day. If for some reason he could not make it, he should come the next day or the next, until we made the pass. I said I would already be there, and that he should await an opportunity to make a hand pass to me. I didn't anticipate much traffic at the urinals at that time of day.

Adamski left the Büyük Ankara, and after fiddling around for a while just to sense the atmosphere, I, too, departed. I took a roundabout route to my office, where I was acting chief. The regular chief had gone to Headquarters for a five-week promotion board.

The next morning I went to the Dedeman Hotel at about 7:40 A.M. I had a coffee in the lobby and looked around. The hotel was dead; it wasn't tourist season—if Ankara really ever had a tourist season—and besides, the turmoil and terrorism of the last few years had discouraged visitors to Turkey. I checked my watch and a few minutes before 8 A.M. went into the men's room. It was empty. I took a leak, and as I moved to the washstand, I sensed the men's room door open behind me. Turning, I saw Adamski. I completed my turn, forgetting about washing my hands, and headed for the door. As we passed shoulder to shoulder, Adamski thrust not a vial but a sizable mayonnaise jar into my hand, which I quickly inserted into a trouser pocket before exiting the men's room. It may rank as one of the more unusual hand passes in the history of the intelligence trade. Proceeding directly through the lobby to the street, I mused that the warmth of the bottle on my thigh must indicate how long he had had it in his pocket. Also, the hand pass of the jar had not been bad for an amateur. Adamski was clearly trainable.

Much to his surprise, at the same time that he gave me the mayonnaise jar, I had passed him one of those small matchboxes that are used throughout that part of the world. In the matchbox, along with a few matches, was a note. It told Adamski to call me at home at 8 A.M. three days hence, and if contact failed, every day thereafter until we connected. I already knew from Helga's pregnancy that three days were required to obtain results from frog tests. I added to my note that he should use a public phone for his calls. All of this was good preliminary training, if indeed I really had anything going here. However, the jury was still out.

I had already confirmed that the clinic he'd mentioned did indeed perform frog testing as a means of determining pregnancy, and then I needed to find someone to claim responsibility for Irina's urine sample. It had to be someone from the station or their spouse. Carol Passman [F], my most competent secretary, agreed to take the sample into the clinic and maintain that it was hers. Carol was not married; she had a boyfriend, a Marine guard, and was the epitome of the angelic girl-next-door.

Following my instructions, Adamski called me at home three days later at precisely 8 A.M. Carol had returned to the clinic the prior afternoon and received the news that she, or rather Irina, was pregnant. When I gave Slava the confirmation, there was a long silence, followed by a heavy sigh, but I don't think he was really surprised. He then requested to meet with me again. I suggested my home, so I could push the development along further. I could have used a safe house for the purpose, but concluded that it might spook him. Besides, his entry into the odd safe-house apartment building, if observed by his security personnel or others, might light him up. He agreed to come to my house, and I gave him directions. At my request, he selected the time; it was more critical to him than to me and did not affect my security. He said 4:30 P.M.; I knew that during the summer, the Polish embassy/trade mission worked special hours, and work ended at 4 P.M.

This case was now looking quite promising. I went all out to cover this particular meeting to detect any potential hostile interest. Mobile surveillance was arranged from the moment Adamski drove out of the Polish embassy compound to my house; in addition, coverage was placed at cross streets in the vicinity of my home, while officers on foot, walking dogs or children, checked for the odd static surveillant lurking near my home or the surrounding streets. If Adamski was controlled, this was for naught, but at this point I was more concerned with whether he had come to the attention of Soviet or other security services.

Adamski drove himself and parked about two blocks from my apartment building. From my living room window, I saw the signal from the officer handling our surveillance effort that Adamski seemed to be clean. I was in the foyer when he arrived on foot, a very sober man. Usually jovial and animated, today Adamski looked as though he hadn't been sleeping and his shoulders sagged. He walked in the door of our flat with a look of resignation that never really disappeared. I told him that Helga was out; actually she was in a back bedroom keeping quiet. I wanted Adamski's undivided attention. If he evidenced any emotion above apathy when he first arrived, it was the twinge of surprise in his eyes when he saw the modest surroundings in which we lived in Ankara, compared to the spaciousness of Izmir Palas in Istanbul.

I gave him the report that Carol Passman had obtained from the clinic. He looked at it and nodded his head bleakly. Then he said, "Dewey, can you help me to obtain an abortion for Irina?" Of course I would, I said as I tried with bravado to figure out how it might be accomplished. I knew up front that Irina's obtaining an abortion in a local clinic was out of the question for security reasons, and bringing in one of our own doctors to do it posed some serious logistical and security problems. However, Adamski was way ahead of me.

He produced a slip of paper on which was the name of a drug that, he said, he had on good authority induced abortions within the first four months of pregnancy. He had tried in vain to locate the drug in Ankara. Pharmacists acknowledged that it existed, and although its principal purpose was not for abortions, they agreed it would be effective for that. The drug was unavailable in Turkey and the pharmacists had no substitutes to recommend. Could I obtain it for him? he asked. I said I would try.

Adamski declined a drink, clearly wanting to get going. This was not the time to press on with recruitment. I told him to call me at the usual time two days hence. If I had the medicine, we would do another hand pass in the men's room of the Dedeman Hotel. I mentioned that I hoped he was using a public phone for these calls; Adamski didn't even deign to reply. Our surveillance tracked him back to the Polish embassy and reported nothing unusual. I went to the office.

I sent a message to our regional medical officer in Europe as well as an information copy to Headquarters. I explained the situation and asked that the medicine be immediately dispatched. The regional medical officer was my friend Robert Blunt [F], whom I had met in the Near East and South Asia Division. He was different from most of our medical officers in that he was interested in using his professional expertise to advance clandestine operations, not just to minister to CIA personnel in the field. Bringing in Blunt to examine an agent or potential one for some real or imagined malady when the agent distrusted local physicians was a remarkable tool for advancing one's operation. Having sent my message, I went home.

To my surprise, the next day about noon, an officer asked to see me; he had just arrived in Ankara on TDY and had a small package for me. It was the medicine from Blunt, with a brief note stating that although this was not the specific medicine I had asked for, it would do the trick and had no side effects.

I learned later that Blunt had received my message just as he was going home for the day. Not having the medicine I wanted or anything similar in his medicine chest, he had scoured local pharmacies for hours and finally settled on a substitute. Knowing my time line with Adamski and recalling that another officer was leaving for Ankara early the following morning, he gave him the medicine to deliver to me. This was an example of the can-do tradition of the CIA. Now, all I had to do was await Adamski's call the next day.

About 6:30 P.M., as I was about to leave the office, the communicator handed me an Immediate cable from Headquarters, which had been sent at about 11:30 A.M. Washington time. It was fairly unusual, a personal message for me from my division chief. It read, "Under no circumstances are you to pass any abortion pills to FELIX." FELIX was our cryptonym or code name for Adamski.

The message provided no reason for the decision, but knowing the party involved, I suspected that it was a moral rather than a medical issue, and now I faced a dilemma. I sensed by this time that assisting the Adamskis with the abortion was the key to Slava's recruitment. Without the abortion, the recruitment operation was definitely finished because the Adamskis would be forced to return to Poland, with no opportunity of going abroad again for several years, if ever.

I decided to be insubordinate for the first and last time. As acting chief, I was able to do it without implicating anyone else. Interestingly enough, the issue never came up again—either in correspondence or in person. It vanished without a trace.

I passed the pills to Adamski in the vacant men's room of the Dedeman Hotel. He looked at me gratefully and said he would contact me shortly to arrange a meeting to tell me the results from the pills. For several weeks, I waited expectantly and with enormous impatience for a phone call. I thought about Adamski a lot when our son Tarik was born that November. Still there was no word from him. I began kicking myself for not pressing harder for his recruitment when he was at his most vulnerable and desperate, needing the pills. But I always came back to the fact that a strong recruitment pitch at that moment would have been perceived as crass and heavy-handed and would probably have failed. Of course, staring me in the face was that my chosen route hadn't worked either. Where the hell was he, and why didn't he get in touch with me?

In April of 1973, we learned through an access agent working on another case that Irina Adamski was still at her post in the embassy. Obviously, she was no longer pregnant. It may seem surprising that we had no other way to confirm this, but the Communist Bloc personnel regarded Ankara and Turkey in general as hostile territory, Turkey being a NATO country and vehemently anticommunist. Thus the Communist Bloc community tended to be insular and self-contained, and we often found it hard to get a fix on anyone within it, particularly when we wished to avoid drawing attention to the person. Moreover, the Adamskis had never been on the diplomatic circuit.

Again chance intervened. We learned from another operation that Adamski himself had not been in Ankara for virtually the last six months. He'd been in Warsaw for consultations, and in various other parts of Turkey working on trade matters. Most disturbing was the information that the Adamskis were to be reassigned to Warsaw that summer. Helga and I were due to rotate home in the summer as well. Clearly, Adamski had not been a double agent in waiting, and time was running out for me to complete his recruitment. But, try as I might, I couldn't figure out how to get in touch securely with him.

When I'd just about given up, he called me, a few days after I'd returned from a trip to the States for my father's funeral. He offered his condolences and asked right away to get together. When he came to the house, he was his cheery old self. Surveillance again indicated that he was clean. As I brought out the Scotch and soda, he explained what we already knew—that he'd been out of Ankara consistently for the past six months. It was also true that he was to be transferred. He thanked me profusely, embarrassingly so, for the abortion medicine, but said that Irina had aborted naturally the day before she planned to take the pills. Adamski said that his transfer a year earlier than normal was occasioned by the poor market for his line of products in Turkey with no foreseeable upturn. Turkey was indeed experiencing severe economic stagnation.

After a few drinks I got around once more to the issue of his helping me. For the first time, he didn't give me the business about not knowing anything. Instead, he wanted more detail about exactly what was involved. I told him that I was interested in whatever data he might be able to provide, particularly when he went home, based on a set of requirements I would give him. I then rolled out that I knew he had a stepbrother-in-law in the Polish military. Adamski was obviously surprised by my knowledge, but he just smiled without comment. He knew full well what I was getting at by raising the issue of Irina's stepbrother. I said that knowledge of the relationship between us would be closely held to just a few people. He was most concerned about exactly how many. I told him that I couldn't give a precise number, but it would be minimal, including those who would participate in his training. That seemed to satisfy him.

I then warned him that this was a very serious business and asked if his security personnel seemed to have any suspicions about him. He said that he didn't think so. He had had the regular security interview after he returned to Poland from Istanbul, and nothing untoward had arisen. There had been no questions about me. I then told him that all CIA personnel were polygraphed, and like them, I needed to polygraph him. He said he had no problems with this.

We quickly reached a level of candor where I could discuss communications with him in Poland. I would communicate with him by radio, and he would use secret writing concealed in letters to maintain contact with me. I said that in addition to a two-hour meeting for the polygraph, I required at least two other meetings of two to three hours each, separated by a day or so to conduct the communications training. He said that he could arrange to make the meetings securely, pointing out that because he was leaving for home, he was allowed considerable freedom of movement and time to settle his affairs.

He then inquired about the radio. I asked him if he had a transistor radio with a shortwave band. No, he didn't. Could he legitimately take home a ubiquitous transistor radio, readily available in Turkey, that would be slightly modified? The modification would be undetectable unless the radio were destroyed for inspection. Yes, he could. I said we would broadcast a series of numbers to him on a regular schedule on a frequency I would give him. He would have a decipherment pad—a onetime pad like what I'd had in Nepal, only far smaller—from which he would translate the numbers into letters, which would spell out the message. We would teach him how to receive the broadcast and how to work the onetime pads. He could pick the time of the broadcast so that he'd be at home when we transmitted. To know which broadcast was for him, I asked him to select a tune he would recognize. After he heard us playing his song, he would know that the next set of numbers broadcast were for him. He thought for a moment and came up with the "Volga Boatmen's Song." I thought that a nice touch—a Russian song. I then reiterated that he would communicate to us via secret writing, or SW, and it would be necessary to train him in that as well.

This was a long meeting, with a lot for Adamski to absorb, but I still had a final matter to discuss, and I edged up on it casually. Compensation. I said that I knew Adamski was not helping me for reward, but at the same time, I wanted to do something for him and more particularly for his children. Adamski waved me off but I pressed gently. Finally, he said that he had begun collecting ancient Greek coins in Istanbul and would appreciate some additions to his collection. I asked him for specifics and he said he would bring a list to our next meeting. I didn't know whether Adamski was a real collector or not, but if coins were what he wanted, I would obtain them, providing we didn't jeopardize his security. I suspected the coins were negotiable instruments in Poland. In this context, I said that we had to agree on an item that he could have purchased in Turkey that could be modified to conceal the onetime decipherment pads and probably the coins. After much discussion, we settled on a mirror with a wooden frame inlaid with mother-of-pearl in the Syrian style, which was common in Turkey.

Finally, I told Adamski that henceforth, unless there was a real emergency, we would stay off the telephones. We established the date and time for our next meeting, which would be for the polygraph. We also established alternates in case he had to change his schedule. Adamski left and I eventually went to the office to communicate with Headquarters. Again, surveillance reported no suspicious activity.

My chief was elated with developments, but sitting in my office drafting the cable to Headquarters, I wasn't elated; I was simply pleased. There was no orgasm this time. Perhaps because this operation had been so long in gestation, I was simply emotioned out. I believed the abortion assistance was key to the recruitment, but I still pondered Adamski's basic motivation. Compensation was probably the real driver; time would tell. Hostile control still seemed unlikely, and the polygraph result would be a further indicator—but only an indicator—on this issue. In any event, there was a lot to do and not much time to do it. Helga was dispatched for the mirror; she knew every possible shop in Ankara that might have one and soon had an appropriate piece, which was pouched out for modification.

The day of the polygraph, I went over the questions with the examiner. Most had to do with counterintelligence issues—had Adamski been directed to contact us, had he told his security about contact with us, etc. When the exam was administered, I left the room, which was standard procedure. After completion, the examiner called me aside and told me that as far as he could tell from the charts, Adamski showed no signs of deception. Of course, a polygraph is not foolproof; there are ways to "beat the machine." It should be just one of the tools to authenticate an agent. Unfortunately, in subsequent years the Clandestine Services afforded polygraphs too much centrality in authentications—and paid the price. Some cultures polygraph more effectively than others. Americans, because of our puritanical tradition of right and wrong, are good subjects. Arabs and Iranians, for example, are notoriously difficult, because lying under certain circumstances is culturally acceptable. I guess it is the wog factor at work again. After all, the polygraph is a device devised by Westerners initially for use on other Westerners. Take it out of this cultural context, and you are bound to have problems. Arabs can be successfully polygraphed, but the key is the experience and education of the examiner. There is simply no substitute for experience.

Adamski continued to look like the real thing. Before he left, I turned to the matter of setting up contact with him in the event he traveled outside Poland to a new post or on a temporary assignment. We arranged that he would signal us by SW that he was departing. When we received his message, we would allow five days from the date on his letter and then try to meet him. We established a fixed time and a fixed location no matter where he was—twelve noon local time in the city's main post office. We would be there each day for the next seven days until we made contact. I also gave him a visual recognition signal and a parole—a key word or phrase to be used by the individual meeting him, because it was unlikely to be me.

I told him that we would make no contingency plans for meeting him inside Poland, for which he seemed immensely relieved. I took this as a good sign. I figured that if he were under hostile control—polygraph results notwithstanding—his handlers would have encouraged him to press for an emergency meeting capability within his homeland, enabling them to smoke out our modus operandi for dealing with agents within their country, and to set up an ambush if they wanted to. Finally, I asked Adamski for his list of coins; he gave it to me a bit sheepishly.

The list was brief. I gave it to our resident numismatist; fortunately we had an officer who was knowledgeable about Greek and Roman coins. He found the list interesting, in that all the coins were small because they were gold. Adamski knew what he was about. The officer left for Istanbul to try to buy them, having estimated their value at about $6,000.

When it came to radio broadcasts and secret writing, Adamski proved to be a quick study. His first session went smoothly. For the second session, he'd been asked to do some homework and to prepare some SW messages. There was very little to correct, and the training officer was satisfied with his performance in all respects. At the same meeting, in a most casual manner he mentioned that he'd trained Irina to receive the radio broadcasts because she would be consistently and dependably at home to receive the transmissions. Our instincts about Irina's behind-the-scenes involvement had been correct: the two were a team in everything, and she might well have been the driving force that led to their recruitment. There was no longer any question that my help with the abortion had been the decisive element.

When the time came for our final meeting, I handed Adamski the SW material, which could easily be concealed with other papers. We reviewed the contact instructions in case he was traveling outside of Poland. Once again, I went over the list of our information requirements, which he had committed well to memory. The list was not extensive, but it did contain questions that I knew only his stepbrother-in-law could answer. I cautioned him as before not to press his in-law unduly just to please us. Slava's security came first.

Finally, I gave him a small sheet containing a sketch and instructions for opening the secret compartment in the mirror, the construction of which was still under way. I told him that in addition to the onetime pads, there would be eight coins, two of which were substitutes for others he had requested, in the mirror. He looked pleased, and before I could remind him, he said he would destroy the instructions on how to open the compartment after his first try. We agreed that I would pass him the mirror six days hence in the Büyük Ankara Hotel in a corridor off the lobby. Alternative arrangements were made to ensure he had the mirror before his departure. We said our good-byes. They were warm but not emotional, since neither of us was inclined that way. Our relationship spanned almost five years. Yet in that time we'd actually seen each other on only a handful of occasions, often contrived. In a different time and a different political climate, we would probably have become close friends, for the chemistry was right.

The hand pass in the Büyük Ankara went down professionally. In the gloomy corridor, we walked in opposite directions. Adamski took the package without comment and, in fact, didn't meet my eyes. Except for the obscured exchange of the mirror, we were just a couple of strangers passing through. And maybe in totality, we really were strangers.

CHAPTER 9

Washington,
1973–79

CHIEF OF OPERATIONS
FOR THE NEAR EAST DIVISION, 1973–75

At the beginning of my second Headquarters tour, I was assigned one of those jobs with an impressive title—chief of operations for the Near East Division—and a jumble of responsibilities that had little to do with the sign on my door. It was a catchall staff position, rather than an operational position, the first and last I would ever hold.

Earlier in the history of the Agency, the chief of operations had been in charge of significant day-to-day operations in both espionage and covert action. At that time, the division was organized by geographic branches that reported to the chief of operations. Now, however, there were regional deputy division chiefs responsible for the appropriate geographic branches—South Asia and Arab Operations (AO)—and the line of responsibility went straight through them to the division chief, bypassing the chief of operations.

Jim Critchfield had introduced this concept when he took over the division beginning with AO. The responsibilities of a chief of operations had been stretched by the previous organizational structure. The countries of the regional groupings had much in common, and a deputy division chief in charge of such a unit could bring an economy of scale to his resources and more direct and concentrated management to his area's operations. Additionally, the new system mirrored the State Department's hierarchy, which made coordination with State easier.

Thus, if a task didn't clearly belong to one of the area divisional deputies, I ended up with it.

The truth of the matter is that this was a temporary assignment. Unbeknownst to me, I was slated to replace Clair George as deputy division chief for South Asia when he left to become chief in Beirut in the spring of 1975.

George was the protégé of Dave Blee, who was now the associate deputy director for operations (ADDO), and of John Waller, the officer who had sent me to Kathmandu, who was now the Near East Division chief.

In the meantime, as chief of operations, one of my principal preoccupations was to manage our intelligence support for Henry Kissinger during his "shuttle diplomacy" throughout the Middle East. Alan Wolfe, an acerbic New Yorker with a rapier wit who had recently returned from a tour as chief in Islamabad, Pakistan, had also pulled Kissinger duty. He had been heavily involved in facilitating Kissinger's initial trip to Beijing through the good offices of China's friend Pakistan.

Back in Washington, Wolfe became Near East Division deputy chief under Waller, whom he would clearly replace. This couldn't come soon enough for Alan, who constantly measured Waller's chair for size.

Despite my complaints about boredom and bureaucracy, my new job had a few redeeming features. For one, I had the time to complete the recruitment of a very senior military officer of a newly independent, important third world country where the military played a significant role. His development had spanned nearly ten years, during most of which he was in exile abroad.

I was also promoted to GS-16—in military terms the equivalent of brigadier general. Given the previous situation in the Clandestine Services, it was an important promotion. James Schlesinger had been DCI for just five months before becoming secretary of defense, but during his tenure he'd initiated a sizable reduction in force (RIF) in the senior ranks. Schlesinger believed the Agency was top-heavy, and by the time he left in mid-1973, he'd purged more than 7 percent of the staff, mostly high-ranking officers in the Clandestine Services. This opened up a lot of what we called supergrades (the ranks of GS-16 through GS-18), which were later converted to Senior Intelligence Service (SIS) grades one through four.

I'd been promoted in Ankara, fairly soon after I'd arrived, which in itself was pretty unusual. Promotions to GS-15 were extremely slow, because at that time the whole DO system was constipated. An entire division might get just one or two GS-15 promotions a year, and promotions to supergrade were almost nonexistent. Schlesinger's housecleaning in the higher echelons opened up the supergrades. Even though I was in this dumb job, I got promoted to GS-16. I was forty-two years old.

Schlesinger's hasty switch from the CIA to the Pentagon was just a minor part of the upheaval from the Watergate scandal. He was brought in after Nixon sacked DCI Richard Helms—or rather, packed him off to Iran as our ambassador—because he refused to involve the CIA in the Watergate cover-up. Schlesinger went off to head up DOD after Nixon tapped Secretary of Defense Elliot Richardson to become attorney general following the resignation of Richard Kleindienst. The Watergate hubbub was at its zenith, and the Beltway political and media hacks detesting successful powerful individuals delighted in it. Washington decries too much success; you have to be brought down. Kissinger escaped, but just barely.

When Nixon finally resigned, it didn't affect my life. If the White House changes hands, government goes on. Our task at the CIA is to advance the interests of the American people. The Clandestine Services marches for the *office* of the president, not the man in the chair at the moment. In that respect, it didn't matter who was in the Oval Office, as long as he was the rightful occupant. I always looked at it this way, and I think most of my compatriots did as well. This loyalty, however, infuriated the Congress, for the president had a resource, the Clandestine Services, that was beyond congressional reach. Power of the purse was almost meaningless because the budget of the Clandestine Services was minuscule. But Congress was lying in wait, and the ambush came with the Church and Pike investigations.

Though Watergate had no impact on my division, we had other problems to deal with. On October 6, 1973, Egyptian and Syrian forces attacked Israel as that country began the observance of Yom Kippur, a major Jewish holiday.

Before the war, there were indications that Sadat was getting ready to cross the Suez Canal and attack. We knew the Iraqis were mobilizing; we even knew that the Jordanians were determined to stay out of it. The biggest Klaxon was the shift of a bellwether unit, the Syrian Fifty-fifth Armored Brigade. Both the United States and Israel knew that the movement of this key elite unit into a strategic location was a significant indicator of imminent assault.

Chalk up another victory for the wog factor. As in the case of Kashmir and the Indo-Pakistani War in 1965, Headquarters refused to believe its own intelligence. Despite all the indications and warnings (INW), the intelligence analysts in the Agency just couldn't believe that this Yom Kippur War would really happen. They couldn't see how Sadat could cross the Suez Canal in any force, or why he would even try. He had to know that he would lose, they reasoned; therefore he wouldn't do it.

This willing disbelief that Egypt would attack was symptomatic of a wider problem in the Agency: intelligence analysts. Analysts in the Directorate of Intelligence (DI) receive information from a multitude of sources, including communications and photo reconnaissance, as well as agent reports. It's their job to take what they call "all source data," digest it, analyze it, reconcile the inconsistencies, and produce a piece of what is called "finished intelligence"—which should be a coherent and objective evaluation of what's happening and what's likely to happen. The purpose of their assessment is to give policymakers something to go on—a sound foundation on which to base a decision.

When the DI ignored indications of the Yom Kippur War, there was considerable speculation about the deterioration in the caliber of analysts. When the Agency was young, the analysts in the DI were all highly educated; many were former professors. Perhaps that was a simpler time and the problems were less complicated. Perhaps, too, there was less data. Nevertheless, the sense inside many parts of the Agency and out was that analysts were less competent than their predecessors, more cautious and sensitive about their career progression.

A lot of pressure was on analysts to be cautious, which manifested itself as a stupefying reluctance to reach a genuine conclusion. This paralysis was rooted in fear. Many analysts feared that putting forth a definitive conclusion that proved wrong would jeopardize their chances for promotion. Consequently, they hedged—the "on the one hand and then on the other hand" syndrome.

The hierarchical setup of the directorate contributed to the problem, because each layer of bureaucracy diluted the analysis, adding more and more CYA qualifiers and disclaimers. Even if the original analyst was bold enough to call it the way he saw it, above him was a boss who would review the work before passing it on. Then a third layer would repeat the process. By the time the analysis got to the policymaker, it had been so muddled and watered down that nothing was left on which to base a decision. Unfortunately, this remains an ongoing problem.

Deputy Chief of the Near East Division for Arab Operations, 1975–78

For about a year and a half I treaded water as the jack-of-all-trades chief of operations in the Near East Division. By spring of 1975, however, the Clandestine Services merry-go-round started up again. Alan Wolfe, as expected, became Near East Division chief. Clair George plucked a plum assignment as chief in Beirut. Beirut, "Paris of the East," was one of the more pleasant posts in the division, and an important intelligence-collection crossroads for the various factions in the Middle East. I was slated to become deputy chief of South Asia, but at the last minute Dave Blee decided, probably with advice from Alan Wolfe, to make me deputy chief for Arab Operations instead. The officer recently assigned to that position became the overall deputy division chief.

To say the least, I was delighted. I was back where the action was. Aside from Vietnam, Arab matters were the main concern of the Clandestine Services—the aftermath of the Yom Kippur War; our new relationship with Egypt; terrorism in the wake of the disaster at the Munich Olympics; the Arab oil embargo and the increase in crude oil prices; Libyan leader Muammar Qaddafi's games; and more.

I am sure there were those in the division who were appalled that I was given this assignment with no experience in the Arab world. (Turkey didn't count, in the opinion of these self-styled Arab experts.) What the "experts" didn't understand is that a clandestine operation is a clandestine operation, no matter where it occurs. Moreover, the sociology, the personality traits, the chemistry of interpersonal relationships, and the approach to fundamentals such as life, death, work, truth, and falsehood in the Arab world and Latin America are all based on a seminal Hellenistic cultural root, with strong overlays of various forms of Islam and Christianity. Muslim Arabs, Christians, Ottoman Turks, and others carried the components of these faiths and their accompanying cultures east to the Indus River and arguably beyond; west to the Straits of Gibraltar; and north to the gates of Vienna, Moscow, and the southern Siberian deserts. Then the Spanish and the Portuguese took it all to their part of the Western Hemisphere. In a generic sense, it's all the same.

My previous foreign assignments provided the cultural ingredients that allowed me to feel at home nearly immediately in these "questionable" assignments. My geographical knowledge came swiftly through travel and my able deputies. My first deputy was Charles Waterman; he was followed by Robert Ames, who was so tragically murdered in the Beirut embassy bombing in 1983. Each was an "Arabist," one who can read, speak, and hopefully write Arabic, an immensely difficult language, and who has spent much time in the Arab world.

My relationship with Alan Wolfe developed during this period, both personally and professionally. Though we both belonged to the same division for several years, we never met until 1974. Among other things, we shared a great interest in wine, but only of the red variety, believing few white wines have any redeeming features. One or the other of us would pick up a few experimental and inexpensive bottles (a five-dollar limit in those wonderful days) on the way home from Headquarters, and together we'd sample them at Alan's house, trying to determine whether any of them were decent enough to stock in quantity.

Perceptive and bright, Alan could be cutting, even as he mellowed in his later years. He had a low threshold for the dim-witted and made little effort to hide his opinion of those he felt lacked common sense and operational know-how. He understood espionage well and was one of the finest officers that the Clandestine Services produced during that period. From the beginning, he made no bones about his aspiration to become the deputy director for operations (DDO), a suggestion I later made twice to Bill Casey, to no avail. It may be that he was stabbed in the back by the long knives of those who felt his real or perceived slights, or he may have been just a tad too blatant with his ambition. Whatever the reason, he was never appointed to the post, which is a pity, because he would have made an excellent DDO.

We developed a warm and comfortable working relationship. Wolfe, who surely had the capacity to become a micromanager (especially if he felt that his underling was a twit), left me alone. He trusted my judgment and was not one to peer over my shoulder. I met with him daily—but never before 10 A.M. Alan didn't begin to function until the sun was well above the horizon.

One of our principal objectives was to acquire Soviet military hardware, known to us as SOVMAT. The Soviets didn't send their first-line stuff everywhere. Often their export versions were not as sophisticated as the weaponry they kept for home consumption, but they were still of interest. One goal was to obtain operating manuals for aircraft, missiles, and the like. We were after the specifications and operating instructions, but, of course, we really wanted the hardware itself.

A lot of Soviet hardware was rattling around in the Middle East. In addition to aircraft and missiles, we were curious about Soviet ground weaponry, particularly tanks. In the Yom Kippur War, the Israelis had successfully attacked Egyptian and Syrian armor, all of it Soviet made. The susceptibility of their tanks and armored personnel carriers (APCs) to the Israeli helicopter gunships had stunned the Soviets, since it put their master military strategy in Europe at risk.

In the event of a Soviet offensive against Western Europe, we knew that their battle plan called for attacking through the Fulda Gap. This thrust was to be led by masses of tank battalions—a mistake if their tanks were critically vulnerable from the air. In the aftermath of the Yom Kippur War, we were curious to see whether Soviet tanks with heavier overhead armor were being shipped to countries in the Middle East.

Though often effective, Soviet hardware was simple by U.S. standards—the AK-47 is the classic example. This was deliberate because many of the people who had to maintain it or shoot it were rather uneducated. Their aircraft engines were similarly constructed. Nevertheless, they had some sophisticated design features that made them of interest not only to the Air Force but to U.S. industry as well.

Some countries within the Middle East had a substantial inventory of Soviet aircraft, acquired when their relationship with the Soviets had been close. In an operation that seemed to go on forever, I took advantage of an opportunity developed by officers in the DI to acquire some Soviet aircraft engines, as one of our key SOVMAT objectives was a particular engine. Eventually, this involved working with senior officers in the State Department and the Defense Department. Again, I was getting experience that most officers at my level never had. The operation was completed by Alan Wolfe after I was transferred from the division, and he received a well-deserved medal for the result.

Although my work was challenging, things were not going well on the home front. Helga was having trouble adjusting to life in the United States, and a lot of it was my fault. The hours at Headquarters were long and I made frequent trips abroad. Worse, I'd picked a newly minted "town" called Montgomery Village in suburban Gaithersburg, Maryland, to live. Helga didn't want to drive a car for the time being, and here you could walk to the supermarket and many other facilities. But there was no one from the CIA "family" to look out for and support her. My father, who was her biggest fan in our family, had passed away shortly before we returned to Washington. She was not yet adept in English and made friends slowly. Thus, she was isolated with a baby and an absentee husband.

I had no illusions about any sort of friendship developing between Maggie and Helga—it was way too late for that—but initially, I did hope Cassi and Ian would accept Helga and befriend their baby brother, Tarik. It was not to be. Even though my divorce had had nothing to do with Helga, neither Cassi nor Ian understood that. Ian was too small to see Tarik as anything other than competition for my time—and my time was in short supply. He couldn't understand why he wasn't with his father, whereas this other boy was.

Meanwhile I had to deal with Clair George and his mushrooming difficulties in Beirut. What had started out to be a trophy assignment for him had turned into a nightmare. No sooner had he arrived to take command of Beirut than the Lebanese civil war erupted into a major conflagration. The various factions—Maronite Christians, Druze, Shiite Muslims, Sunni Muslims—began going at one another hammer and tongs. During the summer and fall of '75, the Syrians entered the fray as well. In a matter of months, the city was converted into a war zone with no front line and no safe rear.

Up until that time, Beirut had been an accompanied post, meaning that wives and children went with case officers to the station. By late 1975 their safety could not be guaranteed, and it was time to get the families out. The State Department and other U.S. government agencies represented in Beirut were determined to do likewise. We believed that the evacuation would be temporary, because we assumed the Lebanese were not suicidal nor bent on destroying their own country. Thus, we decided to send the CIA wives and children and many of the officers themselves to Athens for safe haven to wait out developments.

Athens had more than enough major problems of its own. Two days before Christmas 1975, just a few weeks before the Beirut evacuation, the Athens chief of station, Richard Welch, had been murdered by Greek terrorists in his driveway. Although Welch had compromised his security by taking up residence in his predecessor's house, it didn't help that both the *Athens News* and an anti-CIA publication called *CounterSpy* (which we suspected was funded by the Soviet and East German intelligence services) had published his name and affiliation. *Athens News* also printed his Athens' address, which the CIA had reason to believe was furnished to the newspaper by the Greek intelligence service (KYP). Relations between the CIA and KYP were poor at the time because of Cyprus and other issues. Still reeling from the assassination, Athens station and its able acting COS, Ron Estes, were doing their best to help the refugee dependents from Beirut settle in, but the situation was unpleasant at best.

In early 1976, I was scheduled to make an extended visit to much of the Middle East, including Beirut. Wolfe decided that since Athens was on my way, I should stop there and attempt to mollify the unhappy dependents of Arab Operations officers there. In truth, a far more serious and operational reason for my presence in Athens arose shortly after Wolfe's decision.

Upon arriving in Athens I was confronted by a group of attractive women in their early thirties. They refused to believe that the situation in Beirut had been dangerous enough to require their evacuation, and now they thought they were getting insufficient support from Athens. Separated from their husbands, they'd been sequestered with infants and toddlers too long—they were angry and getting angrier with each passing day. They wanted permanent housing; they wanted to place their older children in schools. I listened and promised to talk to our colleagues in Athens about doing more, which, eventually, they did.

Over the years, the U.S. government has not handled the safe-haven issue well. The government starts with the premise that dependents will eventually go back to the post they have left when matters quiet down; unfortunately, situations that cause such evacuation rarely ameliorate rapidly. Thus, in the interest of costs and the husbands' access to their families, the government selects a safe haven near the evacuated post. The result is that the receiving post's resources are taxed, the evacuated women are unhappy, and their husbands can rarely visit because they are dealing with the situation that caused the evacuation in the first place.

The solution is simple: evacuees should be sent to their home leave point in the United States. In the end, it will cost the taxpayers less, even allowing for the occasional spousal visit, and everyone will be more content.

The angry women may have felt a bit better believing that they were the sole reason for my visit to Athens, but in truth they had become the cover for a more serious mission. I was in Athens because of Ilich Ramirez Sanchez, much better known as Carlos the Jackal—the most wanted terrorist in the world.

His most recent atrocity had made headlines everywhere. On December 21, 1975, Carlos had led a raid on OPEC's headquarters in Vienna, kidnapping the Saudi and Iranian oil ministers and killing three people. Several months before, he had tried to destroy an El Al passenger plane at Orly airport in Paris using a shoulder-fired, Soviet-type grenade launcher; later he killed two French security officers who were trying to apprehend him. The world was appalled and security services were frustrated and under heavy pressure to corner him.

At the time we were running operations in Beirut against an alphabet soup of Palestinian terrorist groups, including the PFLP (Popular Front for the Liberation of Palestine) led by George Habash, the PFLP-GC (Popular Front for the Liberation of Palestine General Command) led by Ahmed Jibril, Al Fatah's Black September, and others. Although Carlos had associated with and drew support from a number of these Palestinian and European terrorist groups, he seemed to have his own separate organization.

Our efforts to penetrate these groups were just beginning to pay off, but we were still on the periphery. One of the conduits into these terrorist organizations was through European leftists—groupies, if you will, of these terrorists. We had recruited one who appeared to have the potential to gain access to Carlos and his inner circle. The Beirut case officer who was developing the man had arranged to meet him in Athens. I was to size him up and, if my assessment was positive, make him an offer.

It was late January 1976, and it was chilly on the open veranda of the bar on the top of an Athens hotel. I had a magnificent view of the Acropolis, which was bathed in moonlight. The case officer came in first, stating that surveillance indicated we were clean of possible hostile attention on arrival. The agent arrived a minute or so later. We were alone on the veranda; it was too cold for sensible people to be outside. After introduction in alias, I ordered a round of drinks and considered the agent. In his early thirties, medium build, he had been well educated, spoke excellent English, was articulate and looked at me directly, and just missed being handsome. Our conversation continued at great length; I was particularly interested in his motivation and access to targets of interest. As to the former, he claimed to be fed up with the terrorists, their unpredictability and paranoia, but I rather thought his real motivation was money. I liked that better; ideological conversions can be temporary. His access was promising, but hardly sure. All in all, the situation looked like a go, so I got down to it. When I finished, the agent said he understood perfectly and would do his best. We left the bar one at a time, and again the countersurveillance noted nothing untoward.

Just hours before I had left Headquarters at Langley on this trip, a very senior clandestine service officer asked to see me alone in his office on the seventh floor. He could be excruciatingly elliptical when he desired—and this was such an occasion. Referring to my meeting with this agent in Athens, he hinted that if the agent could set up Carlos to be taken by a security service, it would be a boon for mankind and worth a bonus. I recall ten thousand dollars being mentioned. If Carlos was killed in the process, so be it. I acknowledged that I understood and left for Athens.

On February 18, 1976, President Ford promulgated Executive Order 11905, which forbids U.S. government agencies from undertaking assassinations, and every president since then has reaffirmed the order. While it was perfectly okay at the time, in today's legal climate, what I asked the agent in Athens to do would probably be deemed within the strictures of the order. In the end, he was unsuccessful anyway. Despite my belief in Stoic philosophy, I find it hard to accept that occasionally God is on the side of the truly wicked. It took nearly another twenty years—and unknown numbers of murders and terrorist acts by Carlos—before he was apprehended in the Sudan on August 14, 1994.

From Athens I went on to Lebanon and soon realized that the exiled women had grievously underestimated the danger in Beirut. All it took was a taxi ride from the airport into downtown. The "taxi" was an armored personnel carrier—by this time, the only safe way to travel to the embassy from the airport. The embassy, or what was left of it, had contracted with the Lebanese Army for transportation. The embassy building itself was all shuttered up. The ambassador was still there, but the staff was minimal. Clair told me that his office was still functioning, but it was difficult to move around town. They were still running agents, albeit under dangerous circumstances. Clair was still optimistic about the future, but what was transpiring in Lebanon looked to me like the final act of the Crusades, which had begun A.D. 1095. The Crusades had established a veneer of European culture and values, support for local Christian communities, and degrees of hegemony over or influence in the Levant ever since. But the Muslims, both Shiite and Sunni, were bent on completing Sultan Saladin's goal of driving the Westerners— including now the Americans, and their local co-religious factions, such as the Maronite Christians—out of Lebanon and the Levant for good.

The rest of the Arabs had another motive as well; they stood by or aided and abetted Lebanon's disintegration out of envy of its prosperity and its skillful mercantile population.

From the turmoil of Beirut, I went on to Kuwait, Riyadh and Jidda in Saudi Arabia, and finally San'a in Yemen, then returned home to the turmoil of Washington. The furor of Watergate had passed; now the capital was embroiled in a crisis over the CIA that was largely the making of former DCI William Colby, but it would probably have happened in any event.

George Bush had been appointed DCI in January of 1976 by Gerald Ford. Colby, his predecessor, got the ax from Ford over the public disclosure of what became known as the CIA "family jewels." A longtime CIA officer and former OSS man, Colby was deputy director for operations under Schlesinger when he compiled a report of any suspected CIA violations of federal law or of the Agency charter—proven or not. Colby's iniquity was turning this list over to Congress after Schlesinger's departure—during Colby's confirmation. In what was to become an ongoing pattern, Congress couldn't maintain confidentiality. Eventually much of the information found its way into the hands of Seymour Hersh of the *New York Times*. Revelations of CIA "sins"—many in the past, many of which were never implemented—dragged the Agency through the mud in headlines across the country.

These disclosures opened the door for a congressional investigation, called the Church/Pike hearings, which eventually changed the way the Clandestine Services operated. Following so closely on the heels of Watergate, they became yet another media circus. Sen. Frank Church, who had presidential aspirations, called the CIA a "rogue elephant." Journalists failed to note that proposals for covert action don't necessarily come from the CIA; more often than not they come from the State Department or the White House, or sometimes the military.

I wasn't surprised that Congress and the press made a huge racket over the "family jewels." The person I was really upset with was Colby, and I was not alone. Officers in the Clandestine Services felt that Colby, despite having risen through the ranks to become DCI and therefore not being an Agency "outsider," had not tried to fight Congress even though he seemed to have White House support to do so. He had betrayed his own because he didn't try.

Why did he do it? Colby had a strong Jesuit background. Whether he thought he had to atone for Vietnam, or whether there were deep-seated personal reasons, he wore a hair shirt. When he became director, he tried to make the Agency more "democratic" and "egalitarian." Instead of parking in the underground garage for senior officers, he used the last lane of the farther parking lot. He did this in an effort to be one of the boys. Well, you don't expect the DCI to be one of the boys. He'd also go down to the cafeteria, sit down, and chat with the troops. This was a better idea, but Colby couldn't pull it off as a natural thing. He was too stiff, so it always seemed contrived.

Worst of all, when the hearings began, he did not do a good job of defending those boys he tried so hard to be one of. He didn't comport himself like the leader of the Agency. Perhaps, if he had had a bit more courage, he could have fended off some of the more egregious wounds that the CIA suffered during these hearings. But he didn't. As a result, legislation was passed to rein in this "rogue" agency.

Congress set up a formal procedure within the executive branch for review and approval of covert action. The CIA was required to submit a proposed covert action to a committee chaired by the president. This was not an innovation; such a committee had always existed under one name or another. If it supported the proposal, then the president signed what is known as a Presidential Finding. Barring special circumstances, Congress was to be notified of any Presidential Finding within sixty days.

In addition to the more formalized approval process for covert actions, Congress also established its right to remain informed on intelligence matters. Permanent committees in both the House and Senate were established for the oversight of intelligence: the House Permanent Select Committee on Intelligence (HPSCI) and the Senate Select Committee on Intelligence (SSCI). Henceforth, CIA officers would appear before these committees and be grilled by staffers ahead of time. In other words, we were now very much a part of the normal Washington bureaucracy or the executive bureaucracy in its relationship with Congress.

There is nothing wrong with congressional oversight. In fact, there is much to be said for it—provided that congressmen and their staff play by the rules of secrecy and have a modicum of interest in advancing the interests of the American public as a whole and not just catering to some special constituency, which may occasionally be under the influence of foreign interests. My problem with oversight is that the congressional staff are all wanna-be spies and demand access to all the secrets, yet none are trained or polygraphed—as are all employees of the CIA, NSA, and other intelligence agencies. Some congressional staffers have tried and failed to get hired by these institutions; I would bet the farm that many could not sit for a counterintelligence polygraph without exhibiting deception.

Within the Near East Division, the Church/Pike hearings did not immediately have a great impact. This was largely because the Near East Division had not been significantly involved in covert action in the areas that Congress was excavating. But, we knew that the rules of the game had changed, and that the episode had tarnished our reputation.

George Bush came in as DCI with a mandate to restore confidence in the Agency, both within and without, and did a laudable job on both counts. As a former congressman, he was in a good position to establish ground rules we could live with in our new relationship with the House and Senate. As an obvious outsider, he admitted that he hadn't had much background in intelligence. Nevertheless, he was a quick study and rapidly developed a remarkable grasp of the Agency and how it operated. He liked the intelligence business. He was also astute enough to leave the nuts and bolts of the Directorate of Operations to career officers, with William Wells as the DDO and Ted Shackley as his associate.

Shackley had become the associate deputy director for operations, or ADDO. Blee moved on in the aftermath of DDO Bill Nelson's decision to retire when Bush selected Enno Knoche rather than Nelson to replace Gen. Vernon Walters as the deputy director of the Agency. Shackley was notoriously prickly and demanding—trouble if you were on the wrong side of him. Shackley was also tough, precise, calculating, and extremely capable.

I got along fine with him, but I can't really say we were friends. I appreciated his competence, and for some reason he never showed to me the aspects others found objectionable. I could see that he had experience in dealing with the bureaucracy, and I learned some valuable lessons from him. One of his habits that I picked up was to keep a log when sensitive operations or other matters were involved. He even kept a record of his telephone conversations and the cables that he sent and received. This was CYA in a way, but it was useful to have a ready reference when a flap developed, instead of searching through files and one's memory. I followed his method once—during the Iranian arms delivery in November 1985. You could argue that it redounded to my detriment during the later furor over the Iran episode, for without it, there would have been no file of messages for the lawyers to misinterpret.

Shackley had a hostile relationship with the Near East Division chief, my friend and boss, Alan Wolfe. About the only things he and Alan had in common were a burning desire to become deputy director for operations and a mutually low opinion of each other. Alan coped with the situation by letting me handle it. Whenever Arab Operations issues came up, Wolfe sent me to deal with Shackley, despite the fact that we were often discussing matters whose gravity would ordinarily have called for the involvement of the division chief. This was my first but not my last experience with an interruption in the chain of command. Over time, Shackley and DDO William Wells (another fellow Wolfe couldn't abide) concluded that I was the only one who spoke for Near East Division on Arab affairs. They left Wolfe out of the loop entirely, assuming I would fill him in later.

Because of Wolfe's hands-off policy with Shackley and Wells, I got to see Director Bush more than most officers at my level, especially during our dealings with Libya. Lt. Col. Muammar Qaddafi had seized power in Tripoli in 1969 and sent King Idris into exile. By 1976, Qaddafi's coterie of fellow coup-making officers was breaking up, some seeking exile in Egypt or elsewhere, and at times Egypt and Libya seemed near hostilities. Qaddafi was playing the spoiler in the Middle East, and Sadat's efforts for peace with Israel were anathema to him. We were supporting Egypt, but unfortunately, we didn't have the capability to affect matters in Libya at that time, although our intelligence inside Libya was rather good.

The Libyans had by now acquired some sophisticated Soviet equipment, and the threat of open conflict with Egypt was growing. Keeping the DCI informed was essential. Usually, Shackley or Wells briefed Bush, but because I was in charge of Arab Operations, I was always brought in to explain the details of what we thought might happen.

Consequently, I spent a lot of time with Bush, and I got to know him better than any other officer of my grade level, and probably better than most of the division chiefs. Sometimes, we would talk one-on-one about the various issues, usually Libya or Beirut.

The situation in Beirut had deteriorated, and to evacuate everyone safely out of the city was going to take some real doing. Through an intermediary, we established a relationship with Ali Hassan Salameh (aka Abu Hassan) of Al Fatah. He came from a prominent Palestinian family; his father had been killed by the Israelis. In 1972, Salameh had been the architect of the Black September kidnapping and murder of Israeli athletes at the Olympic Games in Munich. PLO chairman and Al Fatah leader Yasir Arafat was both his champion and his mentor. In the three and a half years since Munich, Salameh had theoretically mellowed under Arafat's tutelage. He had married an extremely attractive Lebanese woman (and a Christian at that), a former Miss Universe named Georgina Rizk. Salameh was now one of Arafat's must trusted lieutenants, and the commander of his personal bodyguards, a unit known as Force 17.

Arafat put Salameh and Force 17 on security detail for the U.S. embassy in war-torn Beirut as a means of signaling his desire for a better relationship between Al Fatah and the United States. The CIA and Beirut embassy security officers were in touch with Salameh and his subordinates on security issues and other matters. By the summer of 1976, Washington decided to draw down the embassy staff even further and to encourage all Americans to leave the chaos. Because of possible shelling, Beirut airport could not be used for the evacuation, and thus the U.S. Navy's Sixth Fleet accomplished the task with landing craft and security provided by Force 17.

No sooner had this been accomplished than the State Department ordered another reduction in embassy personnel. Only a skeleton staff would remain; Washington urged that all Americans leave the country, though many were reluctant to do so. Although it seemed impossible, the security situation in Beirut had worsened in the interval. This time, however, the evacuation was going to be far trickier because safety considerations would not allow for the movement of the evacuees to a port facility. Landing craft from the Sixth Fleet would move up to the corniche along the seafront near the embassy and take the personnel off from there. In the meantime, we had arranged with Arafat's blessing for Salameh and his unit to provide perimeter protection around the embassy and the evacuation points.

We set up an operations center at Headquarters to keep track of the Beirut pullout and to provide all possible source intelligence on the situation to the Near East Division's unit on board the Sixth Fleet flagship, which in turn afforded intelligence support to the admiral in charge. He was most concerned about shelling or other threats to his men and the evacuees during the extraction. We were all edgy. In the middle of the night, Bush himself came from the Situation Room in the White House where senior officials were monitoring the event to join us in the operations center. Clad in a golf sweater and slacks, he unceremoniously took a seat among the rest of us. This was so like Bush, joining his troops rather than remaining remote with his White House peers in the Situation Room. And how the troops loved it!

Suddenly, we received a message from our unit with the admiral saying that the Navy was unsure of the depth of the water at high tide in the sea in front of the evacuation point. The Sixth Fleet was about ready to dispatch its landing craft toward the shore. Incredible as this must seem, the Navy apparently either had no depth charts or did not trust them. Initially, I thought of having one of our Beirut officers go out and measure it. Then, I had a better thought and certainly a safer one. I recalled that one of my officers, Henry Miller-Jones, had related to me that while assigned to Beirut in the past he had often scuba dived in the sea along the corniche. I rang Henry, finally finding him doing duty at the State Department's operation center. I asked him for his estimate of the depth and why he thought so. I knew the depth he gave me was sufficient for the landing craft. We cabled our unit with the fleet, and the landing craft moved shoreward. The evacuation went smoothly.

On January 22, 1979, Ali Hassan Salameh, exhibiting poor security by not alternating his route to and from work, was killed in his car by a blast from a bomb placed in a parked car along his usual road to work. I suppose the Israelis did it; it's the eye-for-an-eye ethic, and they have long memories. However, they also knew that he had been helpful to us and probably saved many lives during the evacuations and later, and that we owed him.

Everyone at the Agency wished that Bush's tenure as DCI had been longer, but in the fall of 1976, Ford lost his bid to become an elected president. When Jimmy Carter took office, he decided to replace George Bush with Adm. Stansfield Turner, which was not an auspicious appointment. Turner was a moralist like Carter and didn't seem entirely certain that intelligence operations, particularly covert-action ones, were ethical. Turner was certainly bright, almost intellectual. He was an example of the introspective naval officer with an all-powerful certainty in his opinions, but basically insecure.

Years later, Gen. William Odom, then head of the NSA, explained the phenomenon to me. He said that the admiral of a carrier battle group in the northwest Pacific Ocean off Siberia with nuclear weapons is a lonely man, particularly in the dark nights of winter. Depending on the man, he may worry about such issues as what he will do if he receives the order to launch a nuclear strike by his carrier aircraft. Moral issues such as this are not clear-cut, and gradually, over months of cogitation, black and white turns to gray.

Moreover, his problem is compounded by the fact that he is the only admiral in the task force. None of his subordinates are near peers, but rather captains and commanders, who, when they come aboard the flagship for professional and perhaps afterward more philosophical discussions, will answer with nothing more than "Aye, aye, sir." Thus, the admiral has no one with whom he can really debate the issues that concern him and sinks further into the certainty of his opinions and the grayness not only of the physical world that surrounds him but the intellectual one as well. By contrast, the admiral's equivalent in the Army, a corps commander, will have four or more generals in attendance when he calls in his immediate subordinates. Although they may be of lesser rank, they are unlikely to be so inhibited about voicing their opinions.

Turner appeared to be paranoid about the Agency and scared to death of those of us in Clandestine Services. He brought in associates from the Navy as his personal assistants and surrounded himself with gatekeepers. He was as aloof as Bush was approachable.

He also employed Rusty Williams as sort of a special investigator, and one of his first assignments was to compile what amounted to a Kinsey Report on the Agency. Williams seemed to function as the official Agency Peeping Tom.

Williams and Turner were always preaching about morality. They took a dim view of affairs and divorces. The divorce rate was high in the Clandestine Services, due to any number of factors: the long hours; the travel; the stress; the frequent drinking. Much activity occurs at night, and if a marriage is already rocky, a wife can get all kinds of suspicions about what's really going on. Sometimes, these suspicions had a solid foundation.

The fact that Turner and Williams were clucking about the problem didn't make it go away. Investigating "immoral personal behavior" when it has security overtones is a legitimate pursuit, but Williams seemed more interested in morals than security. Ironically, not long after Turner and Williams left the CIA, both of them divorced their wives of long standing and remarried. They'd created so much animosity and resentment within the DO with their posturing, but in the end they were just like the rest of us. I wonder if they ever came to feel that rubbing elbows with spies had somehow contaminated them.

Turner had an unfortunate tenure as DCI in many ways, but he was dead right on one essential issue and pilloried unjustly for another one. He tried to transform the office of the deputy director of operations from that of the nominal "chief spy" to that of head administrator for the directorate. He understood that the world had changed from the days of Allen Dulles. In the contemporary climate, the DDO, and his deputy, the ADDO, had three functions to perform. Instead of playing senior case officer and getting mixed up in operations, their job was to worry about budget, personnel, and Congress, not necessarily in that order.

Turner appointed John McMahon as his DDO, bringing him over from his post as deputy director of science and technology (DDS&T). McMahon's background—and the fact that he had not come up in the Clandestine Services—probably made him attractive to Turner because of the types of tasks he believed the DDO should perform. Instead, McMahon became enamored of the spy business, and Clandestine Services never functioned quite the way Turner had intended. John Stein, my compatriot from the days of officer candidate school, was yanked out of his post as chief in Brussels to become associate deputy.

Shortly after becoming DCI, Turner issued pink slips to a significant number of officers and others mainly in the Clandestine Services. Turner has always been blamed for the firings when, in fact, it was Bill Nelson, then DDO, who initiated the action many months before, understanding that the Clandestine Services had to be downsized from its inflated strength during the Vietnam War.

In the CIA, you often bring your work home with you—not on paper, but in your head. I often lay in bed ruminating on various ways to deal with the problems of the day. During these late-night seminars, I habitually got up and ate some ice cream, very fast. On two or three occasions, I had then had a powerful pain in my sternum. I didn't think too much about it; it always went away. I figured it was some sort of muscle contraction.

On July 29, 1977, I got up at about 1 A.M. and headed for the freezer. Standing in the kitchen, rapidly eating some vanilla ice milk, I got this strong pain in the sternum again. I went back to bed, but the pain didn't subside. If I stood up again, it felt better.

When I realized that the pain was spreading and that I was feeling a bit nauseous, I began to suspect that something more serious than ice cream "brain freeze" was going on. I woke Helga and suggested that I drive to the hospital. She didn't drive, but insisted that I not drive in my condition. As we headed for Bethesda by taxi, numbness was starting down my left arm, a sure sign of what was up. Fortunately, a cardiologist was on duty in emergency.

As I looked up at the ceiling from the gurney, the cardiologist, after reading the EKG, told me what I already knew: I had had a heart attack, or more specifically a cardio infarction of my right coronary artery. It had blocked up. At the age of forty-five, the long days, long nights, drinking, and stress had crashed headlong into my mortality. They wheeled me straight into intensive care. Dying didn't cross my mind; rather, I was worried about what I was going to do with the rest of my life.

Two days later, a nurse came in and told me that someone had called asking if I was well enough to receive a phone call. Up to this time, calls had been forbidden. The doctor agreed I could take it. Alan Wolfe's voice boomed across the line: "Cheer up. You've just been promoted to GS-17."

I figured GS-17—which is equivalent to a military major general—might be a nice grade for retirement. The previous year, Helga and I had purchased a vacation home in the Bahamas. Lying in my hospital bed, surrounded by tubes and meters and needles and bedpans, I thought that life in a hammock slung between two palm trees sounded a helluva lot better than a posthumous Distinguished Intelligence Medal.

During my convalescence, I was inundated with flowers, books, and cards from friends within the Agency and outside. At first I couldn't figure it out, but then it dawned on me that my wonderful secretary and friend, Joanne Judge, was orchestrating this therapy. What she used for blackmail to get me all of this attention, I will never know.

The medical authorities were baffled both by my heart attack and by my rapid recovery. When my cardiologist gave me a treadmill test about forty-five days after the event, the results confirmed his previous suspicion that my left coronary artery, the most important one, was in good shape. Later, as he looked at the results of my arteriogram with a smile, he said, "Don't go measuring for that hammock anytime soon." It turned out that I'd had only half a coronary. I wouldn't need surgery or medication. I was going to be just fine.

The doctor didn't even make me give up my cigars. The best news of all was that I was cleared to go overseas. The medical staff of the Agency, which tended to be conservative (and for good reason), didn't give the okay to be posted abroad unless you were free of significant medical problems. After a review of all the tests, they told me I could be sent anywhere.

For a while, however, it looked as if I would remain at Headquarters. Wolfe wanted me to replace him as Near East Division chief, but *career management* had become the new buzzword at the Agency, and I was one of the first in the Clandestine Services—some say the last, also—to have even a portion of his career managed. In theory, you couldn't become a division chief until you'd been chief of a large station, and that was still a hole on my résumé. Thus, when a group of senior officers met in late 1977 to do some career planning for some of their fellow senior officers, they decided that I would be assigned to Rome as chief in the summer of 1979. In the meantime, before undertaking Italian-language training in the fall of 1978, I would become deputy chief of European Division/South to "broaden" me and give me some familiarity with Italy and Europe in general.

DEPUTY CHIEF OF EUROPEAN DIVISION/SOUTH, 1978–79

I didn't know the chief of European Division, Richard Stolz, well, but I had admired his performance in his previous assignment as Soviet Division chief. Stolz, a very decent man, was somewhat timid operationally, probably because he had been almost totally in Soviet and Eastern European operations. Officers with such experience tended not to be adventurous.

While I was with European Division, we stumbled upon a French official assigned to the United States conducting industrial espionage in the South. By the time we uncovered his activities, he had completed his assignment. This was a new phenomenon, at least to us, and we pondered what to do. In the end, we decided not to accuse the French, but to save our knowledge for an occasion when they might accuse us of something untoward in France and then roll it out. This is typically how "friendly" intelligence services handle such matters among themselves. Apparently, the French forgot how the game is played when they publicly accused the CIA of industrial espionage in France in 1995.

In late 1977, a special panel of senior officers was convened to look into the cases of two significant Soviet agents who had been compromised. Participating were the chief of the Counterintelligence Staff, two former chiefs of the Soviet Division, a former COS Moscow, Rusty Williams, and me.

Leaving Williams and me aside, all of these officers had far broader, general operational experience than the titles suggest. In fact, only one could perhaps be called a Soviet specialist. None were counterintelligence experts. We met about three afternoons a week for a number of weeks, talking with officers with detailed knowledge of the cases, poring over files, and discussing the various issues among ourselves.

The question, of course, was, Why had these agents been compromised? Was it faulty tradecraft on our part? Were the agents doubled by the Soviets from the beginning? Was information provided by the agents misused by recipients outside the Agency? Was there treachery within the Agency? Was it actions or behavior of the agents themselves that brought them to the attention of the Soviet counterespionage authorities? Many agents are notoriously unstable, given their understandable emotional stress. They are also prone, despite our advice to the contrary, to do things that are insecure and that diametrically clash with their self-preservation. (Look at the traitor Ames, with his expensive car and house.)

After completing its study, the panel unanimously concluded that the agents' own actions had brought about their downfall. Frankly, it was rather clear from the beginning that this was probably the reason, but all other possibilities were examined in detail for contributory factors. In the case of these two compromises, senior management faced the situation head-on: officers of broad experience were consulted; and the problem was not placed in a closet. It did not become the domain only of counterintelligence and Soviet specialists, whose mentality and vision are frequently narrow and limited for lack of more catholic operational experience. (This situation contrasts markedly with the mismanagement of the investigation of the Soviet agents compromised by the traitor Aldrich Ames. Apparently, Stolz, who was the DDO during a portion of the flawed investigation of these compromises, forgot his experience on the 1977 panel.)

In preparation for my assignment in Rome, I was required to study Italian. My extraordinarily talented teachers have my sympathies, since I have always had a tin ear. I hope the chief instructor has finally written her Italian grammar book. Her ability to simplify and clarify Italian grammar was profound.

From a career standpoint, my Headquarters tour had been highly useful. I handled appropriate responsibilities and established relationships with people in the State Department, the Pentagon, and elsewhere that would serve me well. How well, I would learn much later. I'd gained a lifelong friend, Alan Wolfe, who, in another "career management" move, was to become European Division chief. "You can't get rid of me that easily," he said as we finished test-driving a fine bottle of Brunello di Montalcino.

CHAPTER 10

Rome,
1979–81

You know you're headed for the thick of things when Headquarters holds discussions on whether to issue you an armored vehicle for your next posting. In 1979, Rome was the mayhem capital of Europe. By official government tally, over two thousand acts of terror a year occurred in the mid to late 1970s, including up to forty murders. The Red Brigades had become quite bold. In March of '78, they'd kidnapped a former premier, Christian Democrat elder statesman Aldo Moro, despite his five body-guards. The guards were killed in the ambush, and Moro was held for almost two months before he was murdered. His body was later unceremoniously dumped in the trunk of a Renault. This really shook up the Italians. Kidnapping had long been a tradition in Italy, but now it was understood that if Moro, one of the grand old men of politics, was vulnerable, everyone was.

In addition to the Red Brigades, both Palestinian and Libyan terrorist organizations used Rome as a base of operations. The Agency, of course, took any terrorism seriously. Even though there had been no Red Brigade attacks on Americans, with the Palestinians and the Libyans at large, we were potential targets for a kidnap or ambush.

Headquarters wanted to make sure Agency personnel knew how to defend themselves. Before leaving, all of us who were newly assigned to Rome were to be sent to the Farm for a two-week defensive-driving and weapons course. Quietly, but firmly, Helga told me that she very much wanted to take the course as well. Not only were CIA officers and support staff potential terrorist targets, but their dependents were at risk, too. It took a bit of negotiation, but I got the Agency to agree that she could take the course. Other wives attended with her, and many more followed in her footsteps. I give her great credit for insisting.

The defensive-driving staff taught us by setting up possible scenarios— you are confronted by a vehicle roadblock, for example. The instructors then gave us techniques to deal with this situation—from backing up at high speed and performing a 180-degree turn to face the opposite direction, to smashing through the blockade. The cars for the course had been confiscated by law enforcement agencies and were used over and over again until they looked a bit like survivors of a demolition derby.

Of course, the ideal situation was to not get trapped by terrorists in the first place, and the other part of the course was awareness training. In the end, successful antiterrorism protection starts with you, the quarry. If you sense something out of the ordinary, that's the time to take action. By the time you see terrorists, it's often too late.

I appreciated the course, and the instructors were superb, knowledgeable and patient. It was interesting to watch the others in the group pick up on the techniques—secretaries, first- or second-tour officers, and above all, Helga. Through the course, I could see her perception and her alertness increase. She learned to continually check her mirrors, taking note of the cars on either side, as well as ahead and in the rear. By the time we left for Rome, she had learned how to run a roadblock, and how to throw her car into a 180-degree turn at high speed. She also qualified with a 9-mm Browning and a Smith & Wesson .38 at the standard level for an FBI agent. This was an astounding achievement, and I was proud of her. To my knowledge, she'd never fired a pistol before in her life.

One of the most useful things I learned at the course was that a twelve-gauge pump—repeat—*pump* shotgun loaded with buckshot is the best home defense. Nothing is more terrifying to a thief or terrorist than to hear the unmistakable sound of a pump shotgun chambering a round. It is a mind focuser for even the most hardened criminal.

As chief, I was entitled to my own car and driver in Rome. The driver would have been an Italian, but one who was cleared by the Italian security services and trained in defensive driving as well. As a driver, he might have been more proficient and might have had better reflexes than I had. But if faced with having to go through a roadblock, he most probably and understandably might hesitate—after all, he's just the driver, not the target. He would not have the same enthusiasm and motivation for crashing the barricade as I would. Therefore, I decided to be my own driver.

That left the question of the armored car. The Agency was beginning to furnish armored vehicles to the chiefs in high-risk places such as Rome. They weren't as armored as the presidential limousine, but they were substantially beefed up. You can't reinforce the coachwork in a car without making it a lot heavier, which means slower. And reinforced means bulletproof windows that don't roll down. I wasn't about to spend two or three years cooped up and suffocating in a Mercedes that was outfitted like and about as nimble as a scale-model rhinoceros. I knew there would always be a number of weapons with bullets that would go right through anything "bulletproof"—and that these would be the caliber weapons terrorists sought. I wanted a highly maneuverable car with some zip. I chose an Alfa-Romeo, four-door sedan. It was agile enough to weave through the narrow, traffic-clogged streets of Rome, and it had enough pickup that if I saw something I didn't like, I had a real chance of getting out.

Helga, Tarik, and I arrived in Rome in the dog days of August 1979, and I spent the next week in a transition period with Hugh Montgomery, the departing chief. Montgomery was one of the greatest linguists the Agency ever had, and although he may have been a perfectly charming man, he wasn't glad to see me. A senior officer who had spent most of his career in the European Division, he had tried all kinds of tricks to block my coming, and I knew it. I don't think he bore me any ill will, but he wanted desperately to extend his tour for another year. In the end, the system worked despite Montgomery's efforts to stay on, but he delayed leaving until it got to the point where I was getting nervous because I had a child to put in school. Tarik was six and would attend the International School in Rome.

Shortly after my arrival, a leftist news magazine called *Panorama* did a story on me as Rome's new CIA chief. This is exactly what you don't want, and it's part of what had led to the assassination of Station Chief Richard Welch in Athens in 1975. *Panorama* didn't identify where I lived (that came later), but this was the first of a number of news articles that came out about me over the years, even after my retirement, in the Italian press. Anybody in Rome who wanted to know who the CIA chief was could easily find out because I had extensive relationships with Italian officialdom—and there were plenty of leaks out of there.

Because CIA officers had become targets all over the world, the Agency issued weapons, mainly automatic pistols (the 9-mm Browning was the designated handgun of the Agency), to be kept in a safe. If the chief thought his officers needed to carry weapons for their safety, he asked Langley for permission to issue them firearms. With the concurrence of the ambassador and an okay from Headquarters, he could do so.

I occasionally carried a weapon in Rome, which was against regulations, but it was my own gun, not a U.S.-government-issued firearm. I preferred my own weapons, though I've always thought a handgun is a pretty useless weapon when you're dealing with terrorists, because you need a lot of practice to use it effectively, and most people don't have the time for regular practice. Carrying the weapon at times when I felt particularly vulnerable gave me a sense, albeit false, of security. In a dangerous situation, I doubt that I could have cleared the weapon from my satchel and chambered a round in time to do me any good. The best defense is always being alert and aware of your surroundings.

When I went to Rome, I was not going to move into Montgomery's accommodations for security reasons. For Helga and me, finding a place to live entailed balancing the need for security and the need for a space with some style. Because a part of the job as chief of a big European office such as Rome is entertainment, the chief's residence must have a degree of panache, what the Italians call *bella figura* or beautiful impression.

Palazzo is Italian for "palace," but the word has come to mean any substantial edifice. Our palazzo was a large flat on the third floor of an apartment building in the upscale Parioli district overlooking the gardens and buildings of the Villa Borghese, the residence of the American ambassador. The apartment was well designed for entertaining, with a balcony that ran along the entire facade that fronted on the park. Our building had two other features that recommended it. First, the lane on which it was located could be entered from two different main streets; and second, it was within walking distance of the embassy.

The owners were wealthy Romans in the insurance industry, and the patriarch of the family had been kidnapped by the Sardinian Mafia and held for ransom not long before we moved in. Because the family was determined to avoid a repeat of the kidnapping, security was tight. The building was relatively new, and it had underground parking. There was a *portiere*, who functioned as a combination concierge and superintendent, who lived in the building. For our first year, an armed guard was on duty during the night. All these measures were good, but I knew not to put too much confidence in them. If terrorists are really after you—if *anybody* really wants to kill you—they're going to kill you. At least I was doing what I could to make it harder for them.

After the departure of Hugh Montgomery, I inherited his superb cook, who was by strange coincidence a Nepali. His name was Ram Malakar, and he had become the cook for one of the Agency officers who replaced me several years down the line in Kathmandu. At a later date this same officer had become chief in Rome and had brought Ram to Italy with him. Ram had become the official cook for the Rome CIA chiefs through several rotations.

Although you might joke that Ram had more seniority than anyone else in our Rome office, the unfunny part was that this was not good security. Having any kind of long-term employee can be quite dangerous. Even if his loyalty is unswerving (as Ram's indeed was), he just gets to know too much over time. If somebody gets to him, it can be a serious breach of security. If I were a hostile intelligence officer who wanted to get an audio device into Duane Clarridge's place, Ram Malakar would certainly have been my first target.

Ram's story has a satisfactory ending. The chief who brought him to Rome was heavily involved with major Catholic organizations. Even before I left Rome, Ram had finally gotten the okay to come to the United States. He went to Suitland, Maryland, just outside Washington, to become the chief cook for a Catholic alcohol rehabilitation center.

During his years with me in Rome, Ram was always busy, since we did a great deal of entertaining. Helga used to call our apartment "the train station" because people seemed to be coming and going constantly. I often walked from the apartment to the office, which was a pleasant fifteen-minute stroll down to the Via Veneto.

I had a small but rococo office. The walls were covered with silk fabric; there was gilt and ormolu and ornate woodwork everywhere. I had my own marble fireplace. It was not unlike working in a museum. The hallway that led to my office also provided access to reception rooms, which also served as offices. Lining the walls of the corridor were hinged, framed, silk panels about five feet tall. If you opened a panel, you were treated to a marble inset in which some poignant statement of Mussolini's was engraved in gold. The panels were installed to hide Mussolini's pronouncements. Rome was like that—if you peeled away the glossy exterior, something was always hidden underneath.

I hadn't been in Rome more than two days when there was a farewell cocktail party for the deputy chief of mission, a congenial fellow named Alan Holmes. The son of a famous ambassador, Alan went on from Rome to eventually become ambassador to Portugal, but I lost track of him after that. He showed up later in the Clinton administration as assistant secretary of defense for low-intensity conflict, a role that would seem to be a waste of his talents, given that Clinton and the U.S. military have little interest in the responsibilities and goals of this office.

Early on at the party, while Holmes and I were chatting, he said, "I bet half of your staff is unhappy with life in Rome." I was dumbfounded. I'd barely met my staff, and Rome still looked pretty good to me. Before I could ask the reason for his remark, he was enticed away by the gorgeous wife of political counselor, Robert Frowick. Unfortunately, Holmes was dead right.

Many Americans assigned to Rome were less than happy—a feeling not confined to CIA personnel by any means. American government personnel returning to the United States from assignments in the Middle East, South Asia, and Africa often took a holiday in Rome. They came as tourists, stayed in good hotels, saw the sights, and fell in love with the

173

wine and food. Many vowed to seek assignment to Rome and maneuvered mightily to get one.

There was inevitably a sad awakening. When those who have spent several tours of duty in Africa or the Middle East are assigned to Rome, they quickly discover that they are back in the third world. Those from northern Europe who, when assigned to Rome, are thankful for still being posted to Europe discover they have arrived in the third world. Both groups feel deceived.

There is a tremendous difference between being a tourist in Rome and living there. Some claim there are two Italys and the line between them is drawn just south of Florence. North of Florence is "European Italy"; the south is more third-worldish. In many ways, Rome is far more like Cairo than London.

Rome's traffic is horrendous and undisciplined in the extreme. Ordinary chores such as paying your light bill are an ordeal; you must stand in lines for hours because you cannot pay by mail. Then, there is the attitude of the Romans, who are often arrogant and cliquish, based on professions, family connections, or regional origin. Shopkeepers act as if they're doing you an immense favor by waiting on you. The tourist visiting Rome sees only snippets of all this, hence Holmes's perceptive remark.

Years later, I met with an Italian admiral on terrorism. Looking out the window of his comfortable office at the handsome buildings below painted in all those marvelous earth tones for which Rome is famous, I was awed. "Rome is absolutely beautiful," I exclaimed.

"Yes," he responded, "except unfortunately it is populated by Romani." This fellow was Venetian and found the Romans arrogant and egotistical. But, on balance, I loved Italy, particularly when I could escape from Rome to the countryside.

One of the reasons why Rome may have felt like Cairo was that it was awash in Libyans. Libya had been an Italian colony from about 1911 until it fell to the Allies in World War II. After its independence in 1951, the cordial relationship between the two countries continued and became economically profitable for both. Many Libyans still spoke some Italian. Even after Qaddafi took over in 1969, a lot of business was still conducted between the countries, including military sales from the Italians to the Libyans. The Italians had always been at best rather minor-league imperialists; consequently the Libyans looked upon Italy and Rome in particular as sort of a familiar and welcoming place.

Qaddafi was becoming a real thorn in the side of American interests. He was causing problems all over the Near East, and most Arab leaders were reluctant to denounce him openly. One of the requirements in our

operating directive was to collect intelligence on Libya, Qaddafi's machinations, and the activities of Libyan groups opposed to Qaddafi. When
Qaddafi's goons attacked the American embassy in Tripoli, the entire
staff was evacuated, and Rome became more important a focal point for
intelligence collection on Libya than before.

At this time, two opposition groups appeared to have some potential
for making life difficult for Qaddafi. However, we had credibility problems with the Libyan opposition that dated back to an incident in the
early 1970s called the Hilton Affair. At that time, two former Libyan officers who were brothers had organized a coup attempt. Small ships were
readied in Italian and other ports along the Mediterranean Sea to move a
"trained" assault force to topple Qaddafi. A British Middle East adventurer, David Stirling, provided advice to the plotters, with or without the
agreement of Her Majesty's government. He was garrulous, and the CIA
got wind of it.

Some in Washington naively thought we could still deal with Qaddafi
diplomatically. Thus, the decision was made to abort the operation by
revealing it to the Italian authorities. The Italians swooped down on the
insurgents and their ships and ended it. Libyans were well aware of the
Americans' involvement in aborting that operation and thus were understandably suspicious of our claims of hostility toward Qaddafi in 1980. It
took some persuasion to convince them of our sincerity. Though serious
about modifying Qaddafi's behavior, we came to the game too late.

A second problem in dealing with the Libyan opposition was that most
Libyans are not assertive, or, at least, they are easily intimidated. The
Italians say *a loro manca il fegato,* meaning they lack guts or nerve.
(*Fegato* translates as "liver" in Italian.) I sensed this alleged lack of nerve
could be a problem. They, like other Arabs, are prone to equate talking
about action for action itself. Thus, I was not overly sanguine about the
likelihood of developing good agents.

I was in contact with an opposition leader who claimed to have adher-
ents in the Libyan leadership and, in particular, a close relationship with
a senior Libyan intelligence official. To prove this, a meeting was
arranged between this official and me in Rome, but it was a standoff. He
seemed to question the sincerity of our policy to undermine Qaddafi, and
I sensed that he might still have a foot in Qaddafi's camp. Nevertheless, I
was instructed to continue my relationship with his opposition group.

Meanwhile, the Near East Division was pursuing other possible
groups. Several exiled Libyans of some stature were in Cairo, one or
more of whom had been in the coterie with Qaddafi that had overthrown
King Idris, but they seemed a feckless lot. Before I left Rome in August
1981, I turned my contact over to the Headquarters officer responsible

for Libyan operations and, in keeping with my policy of "no legacies," lost sight of developments. In the end, however, the Near East Division decided to cast its lot with the other group. I suspect that this was because the ruler of the country in which the group was located supported it, rather than because of an objective analysis of its potential. As time passed, our efforts proved largely ineffectual. Among the Libyans, only Qaddafi appeared to have *fegato*, unfortunately.

Meeting with the Libyan opposition in Italy could be dangerous. Qaddafi had been methodically crushing opposition in any form, and being a Libyan dissident in Rome in 1980 was certainly a life-threatening occupation. Qaddafi had ordered that all Libyan "dissidents" return home. If they refused, he had decreed that they were to be shot down wherever they were found.

This campaign became bloody, and in Italy, officially sanctioned Libyan death squads gunned down eight to ten "dissidents" in cold blood. We lost Libyan agents this way, one of whom was particularly valuable. We didn't know whether they had been killed because they were in contact with us and our security had gone bad, or because they were in the opposition.

The trick was, of course, not to be in the line of fire when one of these hit teams went into action. Compounding the problem was the equivocal policy of the Italian authorities toward Qaddafi. Italy had a large economic stake in Libya including significant military sales; Libya at one point had a rather large holding of shares in Fiat, the Italian industrial giant. Thus, Qaddafi had real leverage with the Italians, and at times it appeared as if Italy looked the other way when confronted with some of Qaddafi's murderous plots.

Meanwhile, my son Tarik's Italian became more fluent as mine dissolved from lack of practice; I rarely got out of the office, for there was so much to do. No English-speaking children lived in our neighborhood, so Tarik played after school with the *portiere*'s two sons, who spoke only Italian in the Roman dialect.

At this time, the Italians were supplying nuclear technology to the Iraqis supposedly for scientific purposes, and the station was heavily and rather successfully involved in collecting intelligence on this. Using this information, we and the embassy tried to block Italian exports of equipment that could be used to make a nuclear device, often with indifferent results.

The U.S. ambassador to Italy during most of my tenure was Richard Gardner. He had been a professor at Columbia University and had served in various subposts for the State Department before Carter named him ambassador. A bright fellow, he was a liberal Democrat and a bit of a whiner. Both he and his wife were enamored of the Italian Socialist Party (PSI).

Gardner very much wanted to bring Bettino Craxi's Socialist Party into the Italian government to broaden the appeal of the various coalitions, usually led by the now flagging Christian Democrats. They'd been in power since 1948 and were wearing thin. I had nothing against the Socialists, but where Gardner and I disagreed was over my plan to yank the Italian Communist Party out of the Soviet orbit. That to him was anathema because it meant that his favorites, the Socialists, would become odd man out in Italy's political merry-go-round.

The Communist Party of Italy is usually referred to as the PCI. As a result of their major role in the fight against Mussolini and the Nazis, the PCI had emerged from World War II as a major political force. They had taken heavy casualties, especially in their partisan guerrilla units in the north. Soviet policy was for the PCI to capture power in Italy, but throughout the 1950s and 1960s, U.S. support to various other parties—the Christian Democrats in particular—blocked Communist participation in the government. In effect, Washington maintained virtual veto power over the issue, barring an overwhelming Communist victory at the polls (which was unlikely). It was all done by inference and diplomatic innuendo. Our ambassador never came flat out and said, "PCI is unacceptable," but he didn't have to. Everyone knew what the U.S. position was.

As time rolled on, Italian governments fell . . . and fell . . . and fell. The Communists remained a potent electoral force, at times pulling as much as one-third of the vote in parliamentary elections. Nevertheless, they remained frozen out of the various coalitions that were cobbled together to run the country. By the late 1960s and early 1970s, however, it became apparent that the PCI was becoming less pro-Soviet and taking a more independent position. This was particularly true after the 1968 Soviet invasion of Czechoslovakia. The PCI was shocked and dismayed and criticized the Soviets openly. Then in 1979, the Soviets invaded Afghanistan; the PCI was irate.

European Communist parties, except for the neo-Stalinist French, began to distance themselves from the Soviet Union, in part due to heavy-handed moves such as the Czech and Afghan invasions, and in part due to a greater degree of financial independence. *Eurocommunism* became the buzzword, and scholars such as Michael Ledeen wrote learned works on the phenomenon. The PCI was on the brink of political respectability, but the United States maintained its veto on PCI involvement in the Italian government. There was some suspicion in Washington that Eurocommunism was essentially a wolf in sheep's clothing—a canard by Moscow to come to power via the back door.

By the time I got to Rome, the possibility of Communist participation in a coalition government was a major issue, both in Italy and in Washington. The PCI was beginning to put out feelers to the United States and made some exploratory visits to Washington. Within the CIA, the Directorate of Intelligence tended to believe that the Communist Party had dropped enough of its allegiance to the Soviet Union that bringing the party into the Italian government was a viable option. On the other hand, Italian Communists who came calling at the State Department were uniformly rebuffed, and this position was heavily supported by Ambassador Gardner. His aim was to integrate the Socialists into the government, even though they never pulled more than 15 percent of the vote and often stood at less than 10 percent.

American support of the Socialists may have been a payback to the Socialist leader Bettino Craxi, who had been instrumental in nudging the Christian Democrats to permit installation of ground-launched cruise missiles in Sicily. A few years earlier, the Soviets had installed SS-20 missiles in Eastern Europe, and we felt it was essential to have a ready counterpunch. The deployment of our missiles in Germany and Italy was a highly sensitive political issue in Europe. The Soviets had organized an all-out effort to block them—there were "spontaneous" anti-American demonstrations and rallies by students and peaceniks all over Italy. With Craxi's support, however, the Christian Democrats finally green-lighted the installation. Hence, there was some feeling that we owed Craxi, and Gardner was playing that card.

The deployment of missiles in Eastern Europe amply demonstrated that although it was slipping, the Soviet Union was still a major political and military menace to Western Europe. Gauging the strength and independence of the PCI, I sensed an opportunity, and I devised a plan to widen the fissure between the Italian Communist Party and the Soviet Union into a full-fledged chasm.

The station could convey a message from the U.S. government directly to the secretary general of the PCI so he would know it was genuine. My plan involved three escalating gestures of good faith on both sides; each step away from Moscow by the PCI would elicit further support from us. The final step would be a complete and public break of the PCI with Moscow, and the blessing of the United States on Communist participation in the government of Italy. We were well aware that the hard-line faction within the PCI would oppose such a break, but we also knew that a sizable element of the leadership was salivating to participate in government before they died. We argued that even if our initiative failed to obtain a public break with the Soviets, we might achieve a split of some dimension in the PCI, a useful outcome in any event.

We forwarded our proposal to Headquarters and circulated it within the embassy to Political Counselor Frowick; the deputy chief of mission, Bob Paganelli; and the ambassador. Frowick was strongly opposed, not because he favored the Italian Socialists but because his previous assignments in Eastern Europe had made him leery of all Communists. Paganelli was also probably opposed, but his reaction was muted. The ambassador was in Washington.

Within the Directorate of Operations, they were a little surprised—not at the plan, but at me. Had Clarridge—of all people—gone soft on communism? My personal politics and the advancement of American interests abroad have always been separate. Nevertheless, it was always presumed—inaccurately—that I rode at the right stirrup of Attila the Hun. Hence my support of a plan to bring the PCI into legitimacy in Italy was met with some incredulity. Even people who thought they knew me well wondered how a good anticommunist activist such as I could come up with such a plan. They failed to look past the mechanics of the operation; my objective was clearly anti-Soviet and anticommunist. I wanted to publicly jerk the PCI out from underneath the Soviet Union—once and for all.

Under normal procedure in Langley, if Headquarters decided to pursue covert action, they would circulate the plan to the appropriate agencies involved—in this case State, the Pentagon, and the White House. It would eventually have to go before a special committee of the National Security Council for a Presidential Finding, if it got that far.

Ambassador Gardner, in Washington for consultations, saw my proposal at the State Department. Since all this was happening while he was gone, it probably looked to him like an end run on my part—the derailing of his efforts on behalf of the Socialists. Judging by his panic, my proposal was gathering support. That Gardner had seen the paper at State meant that it was being circulated in preparation for possible committee review leading to a Presidential Finding.

By the time he got back to Rome, Gardner was apoplectic. Paganelli had organized a lunch for Alan Wolfe, chief of European Division, who was visiting Rome, and Gardner came directly from the Rome airport to join us. He had only one thing on his mind. Four of us were present at lunch—Gardner, Paganelli, Wolfe, and me—and it was a pretty acrimonious meal. Gardner was ranting; Wolfe was defending my plan; Paganelli tried to play referee. No real conclusion was reached at lunch. In any event, Washington would decide, taking into account, of course, the ambassador's and his officers' views.

The discussion ended inconclusively late in 1980. With the run up to the 1980 U.S. elections, no one in Washington was interested in addressing so controversial a plan as we had proposed. Carter lost the election, and even if my proposal had not been quite so provocative, no one was going to recommend it for action without consulting the new administration; it was clear the new fellows had other ideas for handling communists.

In the following years, Gardner got his wish when the Socialist Party entered coalition governments and eventually formed governments of its own. I suppose I got mine when the PCI became a national Italian political party.

Several months prior to the above-mentioned events, I encountered the first, and to my knowledge only, attempt by a fellow officer to undermine me while I was with the CIA. My deputy in Rome, Don Healey, had come up in the East Asia Division. I inherited him from Montgomery, and he made little impression on me. About six months into my tenure, however, I was called back to Langley to sit on a promotion board. While I was in Washington, I ran into Jim Kelly, another officer from East Asia. We had the briefest of conversations as we passed in opposite directions through the badge readers at the northeast entrance of Headquarters. He said, "How are you doing with Healey?"

"Everything seems to be fine—I've got no complaints," I answered.

"Just watch your back," warned Kelly.

When I returned to Rome, I found out what he meant. While I had been away, Healey had tried to organize the equivalent of a palace coup. Vince Cannistraro tipped me off—not that Healey got very far. Cannistraro was one of my best officers in Rome. I'd first run into him in Washington in about 1975, when he was a Near East Division officer at Headquarters. He'd preceded me to Rome and was working primarily on issues involving the Italian Communist Party.

I suspect the catalyst for Healey's uprising was Helga. My wife was one of the many who were disenchanted with Rome and felt vulnerable to terrorism. She was repeatedly propositioned as she walked along the streets by men in passing cars—even when she had Tarik by the hand. And she was worried about Tarik, who had no place outside in which to play except in the street beside our apartment building. During my absence, Helga was hospitalized briefly with a nervous breakdown.

I guess Healey figured that I would have to go back to Washington early because of Helga's problems. He wanted to be settled as the new chief when I left and Cannistraro and others told me Healey was trying to build up support among the other officers during my absence. Armed with this information, I was able to resume command quickly, if indeed I'd ever lost it. There wasn't much point in having it out with Healey, but I made him aware that I knew what he'd tried to do.

*   *   *

In April of 1980, I received a message from Headquarters saying that an old friend had popped up in Ceylon, now called Sri Lanka. The message explained that a State Department officer named Oliver Marconi [F] had run off the road while driving in the Ceylonese backcountry. To right his vehicle, he had hooked a cable to a tree and activated his vehicle's winch. Unfortunately, the cable snapped and wrapped around his lower legs, seriously injuring him.

Marconi was lying in the road when a Polish embassy vehicle happened by. The Poles stabilized him as best they could and took him to a hospital in Kandy, a large town surrounded by tea estates in the hills of central Ceylon. A few days later, Marconi had a visitor, one of the Poles who had rescued him. It was Wladyslaw Adamski, the subject of my long recruitment. After asking after Marconi's health, Slava told him that he wanted to contact me. He used both my first and last names and gave a telephone number where he could be reached in Colombo, the capital of Ceylon. He urged Marconi to get in contact with the U.S. embassy security officer and to pass his request on. Marconi eventually did as asked when he was moved from Kandy to Colombo, and the message was conveyed to me.

Since the hand pass of the mirror with the concealment device in the corridor of the hotel in Ankara in 1973, I hadn't heard much about Adamski. In the intervening years, I had scrupulously refrained from inquiring. I did hear that he was still in contact with us, but I knew nothing of the nature of the information he was providing, or of its value. From an internal security standpoint, that was as it should be. Unless his information bore directly on my activities, I had no need to know. An officer in Headquarters had once remarked that the case had been incorporated into an informal handbook on how to do such operations.

The message from Headquarters also noted that Adamski had been out of contact for more than a year and they did not know why. Headquarters was suspicious and rightly so. They wanted me to go to Ceylon and establish contact. If the operation still looked viable, they wanted Adamski repolygraphed and, if no deception was indicated, reequipped for eventual communications to and from Poland. To help gauge the counterintelligence issues, Serge Kadinsky [F], a senior officer highly experienced in Polish operations, would participate in the meetings with Adamski. I suspect that the primary reason for Kadinsky's involvement was that Headquarters was worried about my objectivity; this was okay with me, for I respected Kadinsky's professionalism and knowledge.

When I finally reached Colombo via Bombay from Rome, Kadinsky was already there and had a polygraph examiner in tow, one of the most experienced around, I noted with relief. A safe house had been arranged on the beach south of our hotel.

Kadinsky was skeptical about the operation; he, of course, had read the complete file on Adamski. Adamski had maintained communications with us over the years, and his information, although hardly of the level that found its way into the U.S. President's Daily Brief or PDB, apparently was of enough interest that Headquarters wanted to continue the operation—if it had not been compromised. We had met Adamski on many occasions when he had been abroad on TDY, but Ceylon was his first permanent overseas posting since Ankara about which he had failed to inform us, and which we had failed to pick up through other sources.

Kadinsky's concerns were more instinctual than anything else. I respected that; he had had more than his share of doubled and compromised agents during his career, and sometimes the nose is better than the brain in these situations. Kadinsky and I had never met before; I knew him by reputation. From the start in sweltering Colombo, we got along well.

We ascertained that the telephone number that Adamski had given Marconi was in a building of flats that the Poles had leased for their personnel. We doubted that it went through a central exchange controlled by the Polish embassy, which is why Adamski had given it to Marconi. Selecting a time when we assumed Adamski would be home from work, I dialed the number and Slava answered. He had been expecting my call. With a minimum of conversation, we agreed to meet the next day. We had selected a location he would have to walk to and that we could cover with countersurveillance to see whether he was being watched.

He was punctual, as was his custom, and we had seen no indications that he was under observation. I was a little concerned about whether I'd recognize him after all these years, but I needn't have worried. He was a bit grayer—as was I—but other than that, he'd not changed.

We got into our car; I introduced Kadinsky in alias. During the ride to the safe house, both Adamski and I were restrained. We caught up on all the personal things that had happened in the intervening years, but saved the professional discussion for the safe house. We were still strangers, even more so given the intervening years. On the other hand, this dangerous link, espionage, connected us in a special way that transcended the passage of time and motivation, and we both sensed it.

The safe house was rather shabby, as they often were. I poured drinks. Without being prodded, Adamski quite freely discussed his communications lapse. He recounted in some detail how about four months or so before being assigned to Colombo, he had overreacted to a colleague's remark about their security officer's interest in him. He had panicked, gone home, and destroyed all of his communications equipment, including the radio. He'd tossed it into a river only to find out a few days later that the colleague had exaggerated. Their security officer was only doing a routine check in anticipation of Adamski's assignment to Ceylon.

I asked Adamski if he was willing to take a polygraph exam immediately. He agreed, although he was surprised that I had the capability right at hand. Many issues were tested—the circumstances of the destruction of his equipment and so on. Upon completion, the examiner joined Kadinsky and me on the porch. "No deception" was the verdict. We rejoined Adamski and made plans for the next meeting two days hence, which fit nicely with his schedule.

The next day, Kadinsky and I went over and over the operation. He concluded that it was not under hostile control and decided to reequip Adamski for communications when he was eventually reassigned to Poland. Moreover, steps were taken to handle him in Ceylon, although Headquarters recognized that he would be unlikely to be privy to any information of really significant value in such a locale.

At the next meeting, Adamski asked for some specific additions to his Greek coin collection. Apparently, over the years at meetings with him outside of Poland, additional coins had been requested or offered, often duplicates. For the first time, Adamski also asked for some cash. We had no problems with all of this, providing his security was not put in jeopardy. Adamski's motivation, or perhaps better put, Irina's, was now out in the open; it was what I had always suspected it was—and why not?—a better life for themselves and their children.

Kadinsky, Adamski, and I sat for a long time and talked about philosophy and politics; we agreed on almost everything. At times, they would lapse into Polish to express some particular thought. Kadinsky was staying on in Ceylon to debrief Adamski on a variety of topics and to redo the communications training in the event Adamski were jerked out of Ceylon unexpectedly. After a while, Adamski needed to move on to another appointment. I asked him to convey my sincere best to Irina. The farewell this time, unlike our parting in Ankara, was more emotional.

In Rome, I developed a reputation within the Agency as a risk taker. Even Alan Wolfe's fitness reports reflected this. Later, I was tagged in the media as a "buccaneer," a "shooter," or a "cowboy." These terms all connote risk taking in the gambling sense. I have gambled only once in my life. I was having lunch in Rome with a couple of gentlemen from a European embassy. In our conversation, I mentioned that the Italian government was going to fall at about noon on Sunday, two days hence. One of my foreign colleagues challenged me and asked if I would care to wager a good bottle of wine over the question. I told him I had never bet on anything in my life. He persisted, and finally I agreed. Based on a sensitive operation, I knew my information was absolutely accurate; my bet was a sure thing.

Sure enough, at noon on Sunday the government fell, right on schedule, and although it seemed to take an inordinate amount of time, eventually a nice bottle of Brunello was forthcoming from this gentleman.

I believe in calculated risk taking, which comes from weighing all the pros and cons and making an intelligent go/no-go decision, applying a large dose of common sense. There is a world of difference between this measured analysis and taking a risk that in effect is a gamble. I never felt I was reckless or irresponsible. I simply knew that excessive caution was paralyzing, and that if you waited for everything to be perfect, you'd never do anything. Moreover, from experience, I knew that my technique worked.

Several years ago, my ex-wife, Maggie, told my daughter, Cassi, that she thought the difference between me and other Clandestine Services officers was that while we all had more or less the requisite amount of intelligence, mine was coupled with an abundance of common sense. Maybe that was part of the secret to my success, but there were other reasons as well. Once, probably sometime in 1987, I was returning to Headquarters from a meeting at the National Security Council (NSC) with then acting DCI Bob Gates. For some reason the conversation turned to risk taking. Gates, too, considered himself a risk taker, and we mused that among the reasons for our willingness to take risks was that neither of us had been touched by the traumas of Vietnam or the Church/Pike investigations of the Agency during the mid-1970s—which had paralyzed many of our colleagues. In the last few years, the Agency has been infested with lawyers and second-guessed and pilloried in hindsight by doughfaces ignorant of what espionage and covert action are all about.

Reagan named William Casey to be the new director of central intelligence in January of 1981. As was the custom, the director made the rounds of the major European capitals early in his tenure. He came to Rome in March, accompanied by the chief of the European Division, Alan Wolfe. All I knew about Casey was that he had been the organizer of the Reagan campaign and could take a lot of credit for its success. Upon meeting him, my initial impression was positive. He was obviously bright; moreover, he was well read. He may have been a political appointee, but he was a political appointee who had at least been in the intelligence business. Casey was with the OSS during World War II, so he hit the ground running. Casey wasn't one to engage in a lot of small talk. I got the impression that he played his cards close to the vest.

Casey already knew a great deal about Italy in general, but he needed information about CIA relationships with specific organizations and individuals. What we did on this whirlwind tour was fill in the details. My time with Casey in Rome was nothing if not aerobic. In about a day and a half, we squeezed in meetings with most of our major Italian counterparts. Casey set a rapid pace—he wanted to absorb as much as he could. In talking with him and watching him talk to our counterparts, you could see that he had prepped himself or had been briefed to be able to do that.

Under Casey there would probably be changes in the upper echelon of the Directorate of Operations, including a new deputy director (DDO), and maybe a new associate director (ADDO). Alan Wolfe's great ambition throughout his life was to become the deputy director for operations, and I think he was hoping to impress Casey on this trip as the best candidate for the job.

Casey and I rode together as we made the rounds to visit various officials. Wolfe followed in another car. Seizing this opportunity, I launched into my salesman's pitch on behalf of my friend. "If you plan to appoint a new DDO, you should consider Alan Wolfe," I began, and I went through some of his qualifications.

Casey was absolutely noncommittal, and unfortunately my pitch didn't work. Casey had another candidate in mind, a peculiar man who had been active in Republican politics, a total outsider named Max Hugel—who turned out to be a huge fiasco.

Casey's schedule included consultations with various Italian officials and briefings by my officers. He took a keen interest and asked many questions. In the evening, I arranged some entertainment in his honor. One night, I held a cocktail party at my home for my more senior officers followed by dinner at a restaurant. Vince Cannistraro picked a pleasant place for us, but nothing ostentatious.

We, together with Casey and Wolfe, had a nice meal together and that was it. Much has been made of this dinner with Casey by imaginative writers, but it bore little resemblance to its description in the media—described by those who were not there. The fable that the journalists cooked up has me wining and dining Casey at an elaborate restaurant to cajole him into naming me chief of the Latin America Division. In fact, I was scheduled for a third year in Rome. This nonsense betrays not only a lack of understanding about the way the CIA works, but also ignorance of Casey, the man. During his time at the CIA, he only infrequently got involved with assignments. He wisely preferred to let the system work.

Casey had questioned me carefully about the terrorist Red Brigades, and what we were doing to find out more about them. The Red Brigades were a bunch of university dropouts and what has become known in latter-day parlance as Eurotrash. There may have been just as many crazy and violent people in the Brigades as there were in their northern European counterparts—the Red Army Faction (RAF) and the Baader-Meinhof gang—but even terrorist groups mirror the cultural characteristics of their homeland. Although the Italians of the Red Brigades were surely capable of carrying out an operation with some exactitude, they were in general lacking the Teutonic precision of the RAF and Baader-Meinhof. For example, in Italy, terrorism would be almost nonexistent in the August holiday season. All of Rome was *chiuso,* or closed, and even the Red Brigades were sunning themselves on the beach.

At first we attempted to work directly against the Red Brigades, but we lacked the requisite access, and we simply didn't have the manpower. Moreover, the Italian authorities, who had been working on the problem a lot longer, were way ahead of us.

Within Italy, the carabinieri and a special unit of the National Police had been taking the point against the Red Brigades because they were simply more effective than anyone else. When they made an assault on an occupied Red Brigade safe house, for political and public relations reasons they would often go easy as they went in and suffered heavy casualties as a result. After a chain of such assaults, the next time the carabinieri or the special police unit went in, they would figuratively raise the "red flag," meaning take no prisoners and blow everybody away. The result of a tough assault was that terrorism would drop off dramatically until the carabinieri reverted to their benign ways, and then it would rise again.

A key issue of concern to Langley and the Italian authorities was support provided to the Red Brigades by the Soviet Union and the Eastern Bloc, particularly Czechoslovakia. I discussed this situation with Gen. Giuseppe Santovito, head of the Italian Military Intelligence Service, or SISMI. General Santovito spoke excellent English and had gone to our Command and General Staff College at Leavenworth. Santovito was an interesting character who was fond of bourbon; he would insist that I join him in a glass even at 11 A.M. meetings. He was always sort of gruff, but beneath that demeanor was a teddy bear of a man.

In spy circles, one of the hottest books of 1980 was *The Terror Network.* It was written by an expatriate American woman writer named Claire Sterling. Sterling contended that the Soviet Union and the Eastern Bloc extensively sponsored and trained the Red Brigades and other terrorist organizations. The book also implied (without documentation) that the Italian intelligence services—people such as Santovito—knew this and were sitting on the information. Mike Ledeen, a fine journalist and scholar who had spent a lot of time in Italy and spoke good Italian, shared Sterling's views about terrorist sponsorship.

Ledeen had two connections that made life difficult for us. He and Ted

Shackley (now retired from the CIA) had gone into business together to provide war games–type training for European intelligence services in managing terrorist crises, and Santovito was a client. Shackley and Ledeen guided Santovito's officers through a series of exercises designed to familiarize them with how to handle these crises within a large bureaucracy with many competing elements. The CIA took a dim view of freelance enterprises such as this, but there was nothing we could do.

At the same time, Ledeen had also been looking into Billy Carter's involvement with Muammar Qaddafi. He discovered that the first brother had accepted a fee of $50,000 from Qaddafi, and an additional $220,000 loan. The trumpeting of the Billy/Qaddafi relationship had damaged Jimmy Carter's presidential campaign. After Reagan's victory, Ledeen was highly regarded by Alexander Haig and other prominent Republicans. Many suspected Santovito or other officers within SISMI were his source. Ledeen represented a conduit between Secretary of State Haig and General Santovito. This three-way linkage meant that the CIA, both in Washington and Rome, was in danger of being bypassed.

Shortly after Casey's visit in the spring of 1981, events reached a crescendo when Ledeen was apparently involved in organizing a trip to Washington for Santovito to meet with Secretary of State Haig. This infuriated Headquarters. When a foreign intelligence chief is invited to the United States, he is sponsored by the CIA. Inevitably, his primary contact, the CIA chief in his homeland, accompanies him back to Washington. Haig told CIA Headquarters that he wanted to meet with Santovito alone. I guess he didn't want me or anyone else from the Agency there.

Before long, I had figured out what Haig was really after. He wanted Santovito to brief him on the issue of Soviet and Eastern European support for the Red Brigades that Sterling had made so much of in *The Terror Network*. The implication was that Santovito would tell Haig things that he would not tell the CIA. Langley was really upset, but decided not to make an issue of it. Santovito was scheduled to see Casey as well, so it wasn't as if the Agency would be entirely snubbed. Within Headquarters, Casey was still an unknown factor, but everyone knew he and Haig were friends. Casey was also known to think highly of *The Terror Network*.

The Terror Network had made a huge impact on members of the incoming administration, above all Haig. His vendetta against terrorism was understandably quite personal. In June of 1978, days short of his retirement as NATO commander, a remote-control bomb had been triggered just a split second after his Mercedes passed over the detonation point, blowing a ten-foot crater in the street and demolishing the pursuit car carrying his three bodyguards. Several groups claimed responsibility, but no one was apprehended. Already highly anti-Soviet, Haig was more than willing to assume they had instigated the attempt on his life. Now Ledeen was probably telling him that Santovito had evidence that could conclusively prove that the Soviets were behind all the various terrorist groups in Europe. To become privy to this intelligence, all Haig had to do was talk to him in private, one-on-one, general-to-general.

I was specifically excluded, but Headquarters told me to come to Washington anyway. I knew from Santovito himself that he had no real evidence of Soviet, Czech, or Eastern Bloc complicity with the Red Brigades, and I had other sources who corroborated in detail Santovito's reports to me. However, I feared that in the presence of Haig, Santovito might hedge and give Haig the erroneous impression that there was something to the allegation.

Haig could keep me out of Foggy Bottom, but he couldn't keep me out of the Watergate Hotel, which is where Italian government VIPs liked to stay. I stationed myself there the morning Santovito was to meet Haig and soon found Santovito in the lobby, waiting for the State Department car to transport him to his rendezvous with Haig. Santovito knew I was in Washington, but I think he was a bit surprised to see me at the Watergate. I pulled him to one side and sat him down on a sofa. "General," I said, "I think you know why Haig wants to see you." Santovito nodded. "He believes you have evidence of Soviet or Eastern Bloc collusion in the activities of the Red Brigades."

Out of the corner of my eye I saw the State Department limo pull up in front of the lobby. I knew I had to make this fast.

I looked straight at him. "Look, General, you know as well as I do that you have absolutely no evidence of any Soviet or Eastern Bloc involvement in training or guiding the Red Brigades. Isn't that true?"

Santovito didn't flinch from my gaze and said, "Yes, that's true."

"I hope that you will make this clear—perfectly clear—to the secretary of state."

The general didn't comment and left for the State Department.

Just minutes later, he did exactly that. The director of the Intelligence and Research office of the State Department, who was present at the meeting with Haig, reported his statements to Headquarters minutes after the meeting.

The rest of Santovito's story is not so happy. Later in his career, he got into trouble at home over what became known as the P-2 scandal. P-2 was a fraternal organization with Masonic overtones. When a fellow member needed help with a promotion, one of his brothers who had the right contacts provided assistance. It was like an old-boy network. In the best Italian tradition, however, P-2 was blown up into a gigantic conspiracy by the press, and all manner of sinister intentions were read into the organization. Unfortunately, Santovito was a member, and in the early summer of 1981, he was put under house arrest. I went to see him before I left Italy, and he was kind of sad.

Haig's abrasive demeanor, his difficulty in getting along with other cabinet members, and his "I am in charge" gaffe after the assassination attempt on Reagan eventually cost him his position as secretary of state after about a year and a half. Ledeen fared much better. He became a significant fixture in the Reagan administration on foreign policy and eventually became a consultant to the National Security Council. Over the years he and I have become friends, but our relationship surely got off to a rocky start.

During this trip to Washington, I told Headquarters that I wanted to leave Rome a year before the end of my expected three-year rotation. The major burdens of living in Rome were falling on Helga, and problems that had surfaced during the lonely years in Washington and had led to her breakdown had worsened. Resources for treatment in Rome were not as good as those in the States. Her health was in danger, and help was essential.

Shortly after my return to Rome, we received a congressional delegation, or CODEL, as they were called for short. This one was from the House Permanent Select Committee on Intelligence (HPSCI), one of the Agency's oversight committees formed as a result of the Church/Pike investigations. It was the first such visit we had received, and Headquarters' guidance was sparse. Basically we were told to tell the congressmen what we were doing. How much we could reveal about sources and methods was notably absent from our instructions. Headquarters was still feeling its own way with these committees.

At the end of my briefing, a congressman from California asked me to arrange a meeting for him with Boris and Vera Solomatin. I was surprised because Solomatin was the Soviet KGB resident in Rome—my intelligence counterpart. The congressman brushed my comment aside, explaining that Boris and Vera had become good friends of his when they had served in the Soviet embassy in Washington a few years earlier. They had entertained each other in their respective homes; he had a personal relationship with this wonderful couple. The congressman became obnoxiously insistent on my arranging the meeting. I agreed to look into it to gain some time to figure out my next move.

Solomatin had been in New Delhi when I was there, but I did not know him well. We knew that he specialized in American operations, and my chief, Harry Rositzke, and his wife, Barbara, knew the Solomatins rather well. We assessed Solomatin as not overly bright, although his wife, Vera, was quite intelligent. She was attractive, vivacious, and above all, well connected in the Soviet hierarchy, which probably accounted in part for her husband's success and his several postings to the United States.

To put a United States congressman—and a member of the House Intelligence Committee—in touch with "his close, wonderful friend," who just happened to be the KGB chief in Rome, has to be one of the dumbest things I have ever been asked to do, but I figured out how to handle the problem. I told the congressman I could arrange a meeting, but that the Italian security authorities would undoubtedly pick up the phone call and would photograph the congressman's arrival at the appointed place. The photographs would undoubtedly be leaked to the press, and eventually a highly exaggerated version of the meeting would appear in the media.

All of this was true. The congressman's face whitened perceptibly and he allowed as how he could forgo the appointment. What did this ninny of a congressman think Solomatin was up to? Of course he was out to recruit him. It would have been a real hoot—perhaps even a lesson—if I had let the meeting occur.

In early June 1981, the CIA began a flurry of reassignments. At first I was to be head of International Activities Division, responsible for overseeing the rebuilding of the DO's covert action capabilities, but I could not return soon enough for Casey, who wanted to get started with this effort. Then I was slated to become chief of the European Division (EUR), replacing Alan Wolfe, who was off to become chief of station in London. This lasted until Bobby Inman, Casey's new number two, was convinced that another senior officer with more experience in Europe should have "my" seat as European Division chief. After the hasty departure of Max Hugel, John Stein was tapped as the new deputy director for operations. He and Inman suggested that I become deputy chief, which didn't thrill me.

This situation lasted until Latin America Division chief Nestor Sanchez decided to leave the CIA to take a position at the Department of Defense with responsibilities for Latin America. That left the Latin America chair vacant. Stein put me in this position. I had no experience there, but that's where I landed. The system, not Casey, made the decision, although he undoubtedly concurred in it.

I left Rome for Headquarters at the beginning of August, but Rome followed me to Washington—and from there eventually even to San Diego after my retirement from the CIA. Events that occurred during my time in Rome, such as the crash of a Libyan MiG-23 in Calabria in July 1980, seem to have lives of their own. Above all, there was the tragic midair destruction of Itavia Flight 870 with eighty-one persons aboard on the night of June 27, 1980—the so-called Ustica Affair—which still bedevils Italians more than fifteen years after the event.

PART III

BATTLE STATIONS

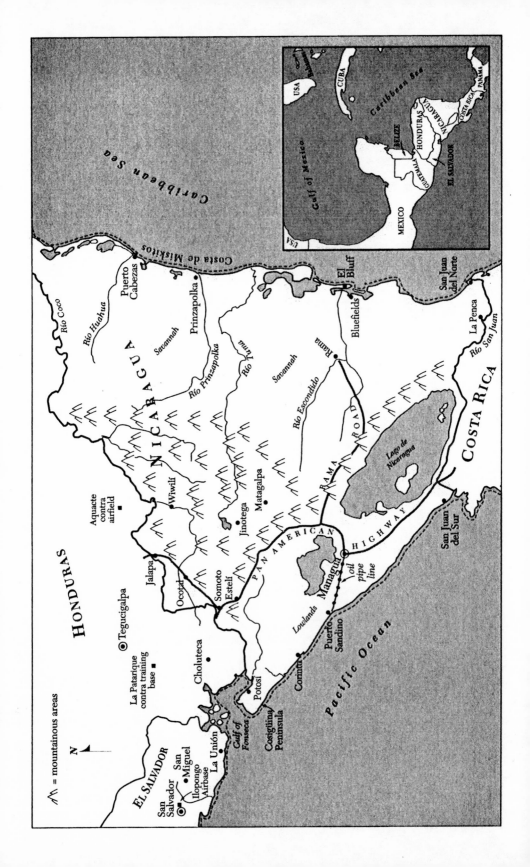

CHAPTER 11

Taking On the Sandinistas

Helga, Tarik, and I flew to Washington from Rome on a hot, muggy Saturday, August 1, 1981. My sister, Cynthia, and her husband, Gene, collected us at Dulles Airport and deposited us at a hotel in Gaithersburg while we waited to move back into our home. I reported to work rather early on Monday, August 3.

Arriving at Headquarters, I talked my way into the VIP parking lot, left of the main Headquarters entrance, retrieved my badge, and went up to the third floor, where the Latin America Division was located. I looked in astonishment at my office. It was large, tastefully decorated with paintings and artifacts from Latin America, and had a private bathroom and a pantry. It was clearly not normal division chief accommodations. I later learned that it had been the office of the deputy director of operations before that office moved to the seventh floor to be in closer proximity to the DCI.

I was very conscious of being the new kid on the block in Latin America. The division's area of responsibility stretched from Mexico to Argentina, including the Caribbean islands and Cuba. After trying out my desk and chair for size, I started walking around the hallways, opening doors, saying hello, and introducing myself. I heard much later that this had made an impact on people—apparently my propensity for "management by walking around" was unusual in this division. I've always found it to be effective because it counters the image of the chief as an imposing, distant figure.

Returning to my office, I met with my deputy, Al Wedemeyer, a man with long experience in Latin America. Not only was Al knowledgeable and unflappable, he was also a gentleman and of great professional and personal service to me during our time together. We divided up the work of the division between us; I concentrated on Central America, and he handled most of the rest.

The Latin America Division was snakebit. The CIA had been battered across the board by the Church/Pike investigations, but the Latin America Division had been hit the hardest. In 1970, an avowed Communist, Salvador Allende, was elected president of Chile. The Latin America Division, acting in response to a directive from then-President Nixon, had tried to foment a military coup to prevent him from taking office. The Chilean military did overthrow him and Allende was killed. In the coup's wake, former DCI Richard Helms had pled nolo contendere, having denied Agency involvement in testimony before Congress, and the Chilean chief of station had been pilloried. Then, among other things, came the revelations about the idiotic attempts to assassinate Cuban dictator Castro at the Kennedys' behest. The Carter years, with their generally anti-CIA attitude, hadn't helped; the entire division was still faltering and reluctant to take the initiative. In a way, who could blame them?

It was the worst possible time for Latin America Division to be in the doldrums. The Reagan administration had been in business for only about seven months, but their hit-the-ground-running attitude had already signaled a new activism in foreign policy. With the administration came a new commitment to stop further Soviet territorial gains and to reverse some of those already made, if possible. There was no doubt that Latin America and Central America in particular would now be one of the focal points of American foreign policy. Although I didn't like his meeting with Santovito without me, I did like that General Haig was an activist secretary of state who, when it came to Communist inroads in Central America, was "pushing to go to the source," in his words. He wanted to take care of "the Cuban problem" by almost any means short of invasion, and I'm not so sure that in his heart of hearts he would have ruled out just going down there and taking the whole place out.

Political realities, of course, prevented that kind of direct military action, and William Casey was surely a political realist. I don't think he had much trouble with Haig's point of view, but he realized that it wasn't going to fly. Casey wanted to define a CIA approach to Central America that would play within the new administration, complement diplomatic and other initiatives, get the job done, and yet not be as extreme as what Haig was advocating. Casey also knew that, as an outsider coming into the CIA, he now had to be extremely astute about handling his own situation. His unfortunate appointment of Max Hugel as DDO had been a disaster, and Casey now had to mend fences, above all with the veterans of the Clandestine Services. He calculated that to get the support of the career officers of Directorate of Operations, any plan of action with regard to Central America would have to be an insider's idea. That's where I came in.

I'd barely finished meeting senior division officers when the telephone rang. It was John Stein, chief of the Clandestine Services or DDO.

He welcomed me back and said we had an appointment with Casey the next day. John and I had not seen much of each other since the early 1960s, but it turned out that the glue of our relationship established in our early days in the Agency was still very much intact. The meeting with Casey the following afternoon was brief. Casey reviewed the Central American situation in general and the Nicaraguan export of its so-called revolution to El Salvador in particular. He said I should take a month or so to examine the problem and come to him with recommendations on how the Clandestine Services could contribute to fixing it.

The failure of the Cuban economy is blatantly apparent today, but in 1981 the bloom was not yet off the rose. The Cuban "experiment" was still enjoying good, if undeserved, PR. Cheery stories of Cuban progress in health, education, and industrialization made the news even in the United States, but particularly in Europe and the rest of Latin America. The Soviets continued pumping all kinds of assistance into the island, and Castro still basked in considerable respect as a world leader, derived in part from his being perceived as a thorn in the American side.

In that regard, Castro had been instrumental in carrying out or supporting Soviet aggression throughout Latin America and in Africa. Because of its location ninety miles from Florida, Cuba had become a major Soviet communications intercept site, picking up our sensitive military and governmental communications taking place on unsecured phones. Furthermore, the United States remained concerned about the possibility of a war in Europe with the Soviet Union. In that event, Cuba would have taken on enormous importance, since it was sitting strategically astride the main shipping lanes for transport of military supplies out of our Gulf ports to European battlefields. Because much of the U.S. defense industry had moved westward after World War II, unlike in that war, the Gulf ports rather than those on the Eastern seaboard would be the principal dispatch points.

In Nicaragua, Cuban support of the Sandinistas had come to fruition with the overthrow of the Somoza dictatorship in 1979. This made Nicaragua a major staging area to support Communist insurgency elsewhere in Central America, including Guatemala, Honduras, Costa Rica, and—of course—El Salvador. Nicaragua was in every sense a beachhead. It represented the first Soviet/Cuban base on the mainland of the Western Hemisphere.

Meanwhile, the Sandinistas had become the darlings of the European socialist world. The parties that belonged to the Socialist International— the Swedish party, the Spanish, German, and French, and of course the Italians—were supplying them with money and enormous moral support, giving them considerable legitimacy in the world community. The prevailing opinion within the European left was that the Sandinistas were an attractive, idealistic group of young people bravely leading their country into a new era of progress. We Americans, on the other hand, were bullying Central America by intervening where we didn't belong.

For a long time, the Carter administration had tried hard to look the other way while the Sandinistas were setting up a totalitarian government and building up the largest military establishment Central America had ever seen. They basically abdicated the whole situation. We were even supplying the Sandinistas with aid—over $120 million between 1979 and 1981. Of course, it paled by comparison in quantity with what the Communists were giving them. The Soviets sent equipment, and the East Germans were helping with security and communications intercept or communications intelligence (COMINT). Cubans were there in large numbers to help in the reeducation propaganda program and in the medical field.

Finally, to his credit, President Carter signed a series of Presidential Findings in the fall of 1980, authorizing CIA covert action, and the Central American Task Force (CATF) had been formed to implement them. What had tipped the scales was irrefutable evidence of Sandinista military, training, and financial support to the Salvadoran Communist terrorists attacking the Salvadoran government. From defectors, the CIA had both documentary and anecdotal evidence of the Nicaraguan support.

The Sandinistas hosted Cuban-run training camps for Salvadoran guerrillas. They were sending troops, guns, and other Soviet-financed supplies into El Salvador via a busy series of arms supply lines. There were four different routes to transport weapons into El Salvador. Arms were sent overland concealed in trucks and cars, in small aircraft that took advantage of the myriad landing strips in Central America, in big Indian canoes across the narrow Gulf of Fonseca, and on fishing craft and other small boats running up the Salvadoran coast. To aid this effort, the East Germans constructed a large communications-intercept facility on the Cosigüina Peninsula of Nicaragua, which juts into the Gulf of Fonseca, to monitor efforts by Salvadoran military and security forces to intercept these arms shipments. The Salvadorans were suffering all of the pain and destruction of war while the Sandinistas were splashed across the covers of glossy European magazines. They were building more bases for Cuban advisers and were gathering more political and financial support every month from anti-American European leftists and their U.S. counterparts, who saw them as popular winners.

Carter was willing to put up with a lot in honoring his doctrine of nonintervention in the internal affairs of other nations, but not the overthrow of another government in Central America. To be sure, the people then in power in El Salvador were an unsavory collection of rightist cutthroats with an abominable record on human rights, but there was no way a U.S. president could tolerate their violent overthrow—certainly not by Nicaraguan-backed Communist terrorists.

The Carter Findings specifically concerned political action in support of democratic forces and support to local security forces in interdicting the weapons flow from Nicaragua and fighting Communist terrorists—both training and equipment. When the Reagan administration came in, it affirmed the Carter Findings, but it also sensed something more was needed to stem the Nicaraguan and Cuban aggression. The Carter Findings were on the mark, but they were defensive in nature. Seriously inhibiting the flow of arms and matériel from Nicaragua to the Salvadoran Communist terrorists was proving more difficult than first imagined.

In the days following the meeting with Casey, I received innumerable briefings from the CATF on the situation and was given a copy of *The Sandino Affair* by Neil Macaulay. This is an insightful book about U.S. involvement in Nicaragua, particularly between about 1926 and 1933, when we supported the Nicaraguan government against the bands of peasants led by Augusto Sandino. It dawned on me that we needed to mimic Sandino and his tactics, and in the end our 1981–89 involvement in Nicaragua was a mirror image in its essential parts of the 1926–33 episode. One of the key questions was, of course, the availability to us of an indigenous guerrilla force. However, my briefings and study had indicated that the rudiments of one existed along the Honduran-Nicaraguan border.

I also determined during my study that the current tragedy in Nicaragua need not have happened. Somoza had to give up power and leave the country with his cronies, both within and outside of the National Guard, the equivalent of the Nicaraguan Army. What the United States government should have done was get rid of Somoza and the worst of the National Guard officers and enlisted men. The Guard should have been reorganized but kept intact as the guarantor of free elections when the democratic politicians and the Sandinistas rolled into Managua as victors. It didn't take superior intellectual ability to figure out that we needed an offensive approach to containing Nicaraguan aggression. The Central American problem did not require a month to figure out the obvious. Within a week or so, I had my recommendations ready for Casey. Someone just had to say it. Stein and I went to see Casey.

My plan was simple:

1. Take the war to Nicaragua.
2. Start killing Cubans.

I explained in detail how I intended to proceed. The advantage I saw in taking the offensive in Nicaragua was that we might more successfully interdict the arms traffic to El Salvador, cause the Sandinistas to turn inward to deal with their own guerrilla movement, and perhaps eventually consider allowing a real pluralistic form of government.

My plan, stated so bluntly, undoubtedly sounds harsh. Ask the Cuban citizens in Castro's prisons what harsh is. Ask the Salvadoran civilians who watched their villages burn and their children die what harsh is. The Sandinistas were literally getting away with murder because no one could find a politically acceptable way to stop them.

It was exactly what Casey wanted to hear. A smile broke across his rumpled countenance as he asked me to produce a Presidential Finding to cover and fund this operation. He knew as well as I did that the idea of killing Cubans was part bravado and part pandering to Haig and his supporters. I certainly didn't intend to go out of my way to find Cubans in Nicaragua to kill. The idea was to make them pay for their involvement in Nicaragua, in the hope that they'd find it too expensive and get out.

In addition to our offensive, I believed that we should maintain and augment our activities under the other Presidential Findings and significantly step up our intelligence collection efforts. That is:

- Continue to support the security forces of noncommunist Central American nations.
- Increase political action, particularly in El Salvador and Nicaragua, with the cooperation of our Latin American allies.
- Increase propaganda efforts, particularly with European socialist parties.

In later years it became popular to blame the CIA for starting the war in Nicaragua. This is media-created fiction. The Sandinistas, from the moment they took power, had the clear intention to create a Cuban/Soviet-style state and to spread their revolution within the Hemisphere. They'd begun forming an army of outrageous proportions, claiming it was for defensive purposes when in fact it was organized and equipped for offensive operations against or intimidation of Nicaragua's neighbors, Costa Rica and Honduras. They sent pilots to Bulgaria in 1980 to train on MiG-21s—a very advanced aircraft in the Central American context—at a time when Carter was still in office and the United States was sending them millions of dollars in foreign aid. They'd set up a state security apparatus. And they began clamping down on political opposition, forcing those who did not want to fall into line into exile or silence at home.

I did not "invent" the Nicaraguan guerrillas, freedom fighters, or contras, whatever you want to call them. The truth is that anti-Sandinista forces, both political and military, were in Honduras *before* we got there. We simply capitalized on the disenchantment of a sizable Nicaraguan population with the anti–Catholic Church, agricultural-collectivization, single-political-party, and generally dictatorial policies of the Sandinistas themselves to create the largest guerrilla force in Latin American history.

With Casey's decision, we could get under way with preparing a Presidential Finding for the new covert action activity and have it undergo staff review, first within and then outside the Agency, before submitting it to the National Security Planning Group (NSPG) for its approval. The NSPG was a subelement of the National Security Council, with restricted participation based on need to know. It consisted of the president, vice president, secretaries of state and defense, the chairman of the Joint Chiefs of Staff, the director of the CIA, the president's security adviser, the attorney general (by invitation), and the White House chief of staff and counsel, depending on their interests. The NSPG dealt with Presidential Findings and other sensitive foreign policy and military matters, but before we came to this august body a number things needed to be done.

First of all, I had to brief the so-called Restricted Interagency Group (RIG), chaired by Tom Enders, assistant secretary of state for inter-American affairs. I liked Enders. Bright, not one to suffer fools, he could cut through the bullshit to the main issues in seconds. He seemed to appreciate what the CIA could and could not do for the foreign policy process and supported covert action as an element of the process when appropriate. Unlike those less experienced, he knew that covert action cannot and should not stand alone as the sole element of a foreign policy.

Also in the RIG was Lt. Gen. Paul Gorman, assistant to the chairman of the JCS. I admired him greatly. He was a warrior but also erudite and thoughtful; some said he was the most intelligent general the Army had ever produced. Nestor Sanchez, my predecessor as Latin America Division chief at the CIA, represented the Office of the Secretary of Defense. Initially, Al Sapia-Bosch represented the CIA's Directorate of Intelligence. When Casey hired Constantine Menges as the national intelligence officer for Latin America, he replaced Sapia-Bosch, who went to the National Security Council as the Latin American referent and showed up in the RIG again in that capacity. Finally, Enders's principal deputy, Steve Bosworth (later Jim Michaels), Central American director Craig Johnstone, and Enders's executive officer, Tony Gillespe, were also present. All were fine professional officers and I frankly treasure my association with them.

By early October 1981, I was ready to brief the members of the RIG, who in turn would advise their principals so that fine-tuning of the Presidential Finding could take place before staffing outside the Agency. Enders had an RIG at least once a week; any participant could ask for a special one and did.

My proposal to Casey that we take the offensive in Nicaragua was based on intelligence that a force of about five hundred men was already in place in Honduras. It was primarily composed of remnants of the Nicaraguan National Guard, which had fled northward to the Nicaraguan-Honduran border after the collapse of the Guard in the wake of Somoza's departure. It was augmented by a number of local mestizo peasants, a people of mixed American Indian–Spanish blood who inhabit this border area and the chain of mountains that separates the heavily populated and rich agricultural western lowlands of Nicaragua from the sparsely inhabited savannas and swamps of the portion that stretches east of the mountains to the Caribbean Sea. The latter is the home of the Miskito Indians and Creoles. Successive Nicaraguan regimes had left these people to their own devices, but now the Sandinistas were attempting to establish their heavy-handed rule in the area, much to the consternation of the Miskitos, who were near revolt.

By 1981, this five-hundred-man force had been loosely organized into what was called the 15th of September Legion, which refers to Nicaragua's Independence Day. It was led by a number of former noncommissioned officers of the National Guard with a sprinkling of former officers, the senior of whom was Col. Enrique Bermúdez. After a falling-out with Somoza, Bermúdez had been exiled to Washington, D.C., as the Nicaraguan military attaché during most of the period of Somoza's conflict with the Nicaraguan opposition. The Legion was conducting minor hit-and-run operations against the Sandinistas across the border.

There was also an organization of Nicaraguan exiles that was opposed to any association with former members of the National Guard. Called the Nicaraguan Democratic Union (UDN), it was led by Chicano Cardenal and the Chamorro brothers, Edmundo and Fernando, among others, all of whom had good anti-Somoza credentials. In the late summer of 1981, circumstances on the ground, not the myth of U.S. government pressure, forced a union between the Legion and the UDN. The new organization was called the Fuerza Democrática Nicaragüense (FDN). The Chamorros opted out; they couldn't stomach former members of the Guard in any form, or perhaps their reason was more personal. I suspect they felt their influence within the FDN would not be in keeping with their perceived stature based on their long opposition to Somoza.

Our intelligence told us that the Legion, now the FDN, was being trained, advised, and equipped by a small group of Argentines from the Argentine Military Intelligence Directorate. Their presence in Honduras was facilitated by Col. Gustavo Alvarez, commander of the Honduran uniformed police, FUSEP, who had graduated from the Argentine Army's Command and General Staff School. The effort had the support of the Honduran military and Honduran president Gen. Policarpo Paz, all of whom feared the aggressive behavior of the Sandinistas and thus sought a counterpoise.

Our inquiries in Tegucigalpa and Buenos Aires indicated that if the United States government were "serious" about doing something about the Sandinistas, our involvement with the FDN would be welcome, but if we were going to run when the politics became too hot and leave the guerrillas in the lurch, "forget it." Frankly, this position was all too correct; the sorry record of the United States in abandoning previously supported opposition forces, for whatever reason, was well-known.

I briefed the plan and the intelligence behind it to the RIG and went on to explain how we planned to implement our proposal. Assuming we reached agreement with the Hondurans and the Argentines, we would set up a tripartite arrangement. The CIA would provide logistics and training. We would train the Hondurans and Argentines in guerrilla tactics, weapons as necessary, and demolitions. The Hondurans in turn would train the Miskitos, because they could relate to them the best. The Argentines would train the Nicaraguans. We hoped that in this way the CIA could conceal its involvement to some extent. The tripartite group would decide on the operations and targets within Nicaragua and do the planning.

I told the RIG that we had to get rid of any members of the FDN with unsavory reputations from their days in the Guard, deserved or not, and prevent others from joining. Moreover, we insisted on respect for the civilian population in the operating areas and that the guerrillas pay for any food or other matériel needed. Furthermore, we intended to eschew economic targets, except for those supporting the infiltration of arms to El Salvador. To that end as well as others, the CIA was to keep all explosives under its control until issued for training or a specific operation.

The members of the RIG wanted to know how soon the CIA could get under way with operations inside Nicaragua. I indicated that assuming agreements were reached with the Argentines and the Hondurans, from the time President Reagan signed the Finding, we needed forty-five days to arrive in Honduras. Once there, we would begin establishing our base, bring in matériel and put together a logistics structure, and initiate training. I said that we would do this job with about ten to twelve permanent staff in country and of course TDY (temporary duty) personnel as needed. The first operation was planned for sixty days after that. We had already selected the targets, assuming our allies agreed. The looks on the faces of most of my fellow RIG members were of disbelief at the short timetable and limited manpower, except perhaps for Enders, who had seen the Clandestine Services move into Cambodia in the 1970s.

Another question was the weapons mix that we proposed to supply to the guerrillas. I replied that the basic shoulder weapon would be the Belgian FAL rifle; the U.S. Army M-60 machine gun (later the Soviet AK-47), ubiquitous now around the world; the Soviet RPG-7, a rocket-propelled grenade launcher; the LAW, a light anti-vehicle/tank weapon for use against trucks, bunkers, and the like; and a few 60-mm mortars. For the Miskitos, we planned to issue World War II–vintage semiautomatic M3 carbines. We were concerned that at least initially we would experience fire-control discipline problems, and a rifle with automatic capability could use a lot of ammunition quickly. The mix of the other weapons would be lighter and fewer, given the terrain and opposition the Miskitos faced.

I was asked why the Argentine military required training by us. I pointed out that they knew a lot about urban guerrilla warfare based on their successful operations against their own leftist urban terrorists between 1969 and 1979. But from what we could tell, they understood much less about guerrilla warfare in the countryside. The Argentine effort appeared very professional, at least from a distance. When the Argentines arrived in Honduras, they brought with them a psychologist/anthropologist to study the habits, mores, etc., of the Miskito Indians, who they correctly believed would eventually revolt against the Sandinistas' disruption and suppression of their way of life. By undertaking this study, the Argentines wanted to learn how to interact appropriately with the Miskitos to gain their confidence and support.

Why were the Argentines involved at all? I suspected that one factor was that the Sandinistas provided safe haven in Nicaragua to a number of Argentine terrorists, called Montoneros. It was a Montoneros terrorist team on contract to the Sandinistas that had killed exiled dictator Anastasio Somoza in Paraguay in 1980. Also, Colonel Alvarez's connection with the Argentines was a factor.

Someone brought up costs. I replied that assuming "go" by December 1, 1981, the cost of the program for the remainder of the fiscal year (ten months) would be about the flyaway price of a single F-16 aircraft, A or B version, Block 15. Silence descended. I pointed out that we had determined that to feed a guerrilla in the eastern sector—that is, the Miskitos —the cost was a dollar per day per man; in the western sector it was a dollar and a half. At about this point, my compatriots on the RIG broke into laughter, realizing that I had mistaken their silence for concern at the supposed high cost, when their reaction was exactly the opposite. The amount was trivial for such an undertaking, and they worried I was underestimating it.

Enders was under no illusions about the Sandinistas. When he went to Managua in August 1981 to talk to the Sandinista government, he was treated with unspeakable rudeness, topped by a litany of prior American offenses against the Nicaraguan people. This episode coincided with my covert action proposal. Enders had concluded that some military pressure on the Sandinistas was needed and might just get them to undertake some serious negotiations. Thus, he proposed a two-track policy of diplomacy and covert action. He proposed that we attempt to negotiate because that was what reasonable men should try to do. Even if it went nowhere, it provided the administration with cover with Congress. More importantly, it afforded Congress cover for the covert action with the Sandinista supporters in the United States. Thus, the covert action operation, which had been designed to modify the Sandinistas' behavior in the region and interdict arms, was always for Enders a prod to propel the Sandinistas into serious negotiations.

Unfortunately, Enders's two-track policy was suspect for many in the administration, particularly in the White House and perhaps even with Casey, although he was circumspect about it with me. I eventually concluded that it wasn't the policy that grated, for we continued for years to try to negotiate with the Sandinistas in one forum or the other; it was Enders himself. He was associated by many in the administration with Henry Kissinger, with whom he had worked closely in the past. Kissinger was regarded unfavorably as a Machiavellian conniver and sellout. This rubbed off on Enders, whose height (six feet eight inches) and low tolerance for the dim no doubt contributed. In the end, he simply was not trusted. Some in the administration believed that his two-track policy was a ruse. They feared that he would sell out the Nicaraguan guerrillas and the administration's policy of pushing the Soviets off the mainland of the Western Hemisphere in favor of some half-assed deal with the Sandinistas. After a clash (some said about the two-track policy) with Bill Clark, who had become the president's national security adviser, Tom Enders was reassigned as ambassador to Spain. It was a great loss, in my opinion.

I, too, had problems with the hierarchy. Within the Agency, Casey circumvented the usual chain of command for Latin American operations. Almost instinctively, we had a strong working relationship. When I took over the Latin America Division, Casey didn't say I should report directly to him, but he made it happen that way. He phoned me directly and met with me without my superiors, bypassing the deputy director, Bobby Inman; the DDO, John Stein; and the ADDO, Clair George.

Stein knew me and understood that this was simply Casey's style, and in any event I kept Stein informed about the content of my meetings with Casey. Stein didn't need any more face time with Casey than he already had and wasn't insecure. However, Inman and George and later John McMahon, when he became the deputy director, resented my special relationship with the DCI.

*   *   *

One late-October Saturday morning, I was in an official Agency vehicle along with two officers from the Directorate of Intelligence, headed for Andrews Air Force Base to board Air Force Two, the vice president's official aircraft, for a flight to Hartford, Connecticut. Vice President Bush's office had asked that the vice president be briefed on the current situation in Central America. An NSPG meeting was scheduled for the following Tuesday, and Bush wanted to be prepared. Because of the topics, both the DO and the DI would brief the VP, and Bush's staff thought this could be accomplished on the way to Hartford, where the vice president was making a speech.

We boarded Air Force Two, and shortly thereafter Bush's convoy arrived at plane side. After introductions all around, Bush immediately recognized me and called me by name. It had been four years since I had seen him, and he looked no different. Instead of briefing him about Central America, we sat on board and chatted about the past, particularly the Beirut evacuations and the Libyan struggle.

The briefing was put off until we reached the hotel, where a special room was arranged. The DI briefers led off with the situation status. Then it was my turn. Normally, because I was talking about operations, the DI briefers would have been asked to excuse themselves from the room on the basis of need to know. However, I had already sensed that when it came to Central America, the distinction between the DI and the DO was going to blur because unless the DI understood what the Clandestine Services was up to operationally in Central America, their intelligence analysis could be disastrously skewed. Therefore I made no move to exclude the officers from the Directorate of Intelligence; besides, no sources would be mentioned. This was the process that culminated in my concept for the Counterterrorist Center five years later.

Aside from the pleasure of seeing George Bush again, I had a specific reason for wanting to do the briefing. I wanted to get some sense of where Bush stood on the Central American issue, assuming that he represented the moderates within the Republican Party. I knew where the Reaganites were; however, I wondered whether there was possible disunity within the party over the issue. But Bush clearly signaled that he supported the administration in every respect on Central America and what the CIA was doing to contribute to the policy.

Flying back to Washington, I reflected on the irony of yet another chapter about to begin in the long, often bloody history of relations between the United States and Nicaragua. There are many fascinating ties between the United States and Nicaragua from the creation of the Nicaraguan National Guard to the establishment of baseball as a Nicaraguan sport. In the mid–nineteenth century, a Tennessee adventurer named William Walker led revolutionary forces and ended up proclaiming himself president of Nicaragua in 1856 for about a year. Shortly thereafter, the United Fruit Company began a crusade of political interference that lasted for nearly a century and inspired the term *banana republic*.

In 1911, the Americans sent the Marines into Nicaragua to separate warring factions, but the major intervention began in 1926 under Coolidge, when U.S. Marines were called in to defend the central government against a group of rebels led by Cesar Augusto Sandino. Although Sandino eluded capture, when the Marines were recalled under Franklin D. Roosevelt's Good Neighbor Policy in 1933, he and his band laid down their arms. Sandino was promptly murdered by the Nicaraguan National Guard.

Following Sandino's death, Gen. Anastasio Somoza García consolidated his power over the country, rigged an election, and established a family dynasty that lasted for forty-five years. The first Anastasio Somoza knew that the key to retaining power was to keep the United States happy, and it was only when his son broke that rule that the family's hold on the country was endangered. As anti-Somoza forces gathered strength in the late 1970s, they took the name of Nicaragua's martyr, Sandino.

Now the Sandinistas, in alliance with the Cubans and the Soviet Union, found themselves down in the lowlands running the central government, while the United States prepared to support opposing guerrilla forces occupying the mountains. This scenario was the exact opposite of what had happened in 1926–33.

The Nicaraguan covert-action planning proceeded apace, not just the paperwork to support the Presidential Finding, but also much more detailed preparations that would be needed to implement the Finding. The Central American Task Force, led by the able Jerry Svat; the International Activities Division, which provided the experts on political action, propaganda, and paramilitary operations; the Office of Technical Services, which was responsible for technical requirements including demolitions; and the Offices of Medical Services, Communications, and Logistics were all up on the step and fully behind the program. I was amazed to find that despite the 1978 reduction in force, resignations, and retirements, we still had a substantial cadre of experts in political action, paramilitary operations, and the logistics support for such. The CATF received a major augmentation in manpower to cope.

Headquarters was, of course, in constant touch with appropriate stations as it developed its plan. However, I knew that I needed to consult face-to-face with the station chiefs who would be on the front line of this event. Moreover, I wanted to gauge what lingering hesitancy might exist to an offensive covert-action program among them as a result of the Church/Pike investigations of the mid-1970s. Bringing the appropriate chiefs to Washington would be an opportunity to get their measure and thoughts en masse and in turn let them size me up.

They arrived for two days of discussions. Only those who would be involved—directly or indirectly—were present. After describing the program, I laid it on the line. I told them, "Okay, fellas, this is it. I want your ideas and trepidations."

Only two chiefs had any qualms. One had been around Latin America for years and had seen these kinds of operations come and go with varied results. In recent years, there had been few out-and-out successes, and I think he feared my plan wouldn't work. On the other hand, he might have been just too worn-out and bruised by what had previously happened.

Jack Devine was the other chief with concerns. He had been a young officer in Santiago, Chile, when the Allende episode had gone down. He'd worked hard on it, then seen his chief pilloried for his efforts. He was apprehensive about another potentially volatile operation and was frank in expressing his reservations. I appreciated his honesty. There were some, however, who were not so kind. They saw him as someone motivated largely by a desire to advance his career.

I had already decided that, given the unhappy recent history of the division and the high profile this operation would assume with the administration and Congress, I had to lead from the front. There was one crucial reason for this: if everything went wrong, if the operation blew up or if Congress came down hard on the Agency and the division once again, somebody had to be the scapegoat. I was not being altruistic or self-sacrificing; that is not really in my character. The simple fact of life was that I could afford to take the fall.

CHAPTER 12

Going to War

One could argue that it was rather sporty, perhaps even arrogant, to put together a covert action program without the agreement of our other key partners, Honduras and Argentina. However, my problem was rather like the chicken-or-egg paradigm. I wasn't absolutely sure the Hondurans and the Argentines would sign up, although our stations there thought so, but there was also no reason to get our allies in a lather until I was confident that we had a go from the president. That was effected on November 16, 1981.

Although we needed the official approval of Gen. Policarpo Paz, the head of the Honduran government, to operate within and from his country, we were already cooperating well with Honduran colonel Alvarez and his security forces, so the first step was to cement a relationship with the Argentines, whose interest in working with us was more problematic. Accompanied by my Central American Task Force chief, Jerry Svat, and Hank Booth and Mick Donahue, respectively Agency world-class specialists in guerrilla warfare and demolitions, I flew to Buenos Aires in mid-November 1981, shortly after the Finding was signed. I was to meet with Lt. Gen. Leopoldo Galtieri, the commander in chief of the Argentine armed forces. What was supposed to be a brief trip turned into a sort of state visit. On arrival at the Buenos Aires airport, we were met by an escort officer and a security detail from Argentine Military Intelligence; they remained with us throughout our stay. We were ensconced at the Hotel Plaza at the head of the famous shopping street Calle Florida. The security detail had set up a command post in a room opposite to the suite that Svat and I occupied. It was fitted with numerous radios and weapons. We were being accorded the type of security normally provided for a head of state. However, this was all for show, because the leftist urban terrorists had been decimated a year or more earlier. Svat and I rode in the lead vehicle, with a driver and bodyguard. Another car followed with our compatriots, and then finally a chase car with additional bodyguards. On one occasion, a taxi attempted to edge in front of us. The bodyguard nudged our driver, who blew his horn to attract the taxi driver's attention to the bodyguard's handgun aimed at him through the window of our vehicle. The cabdriver, startled, immediately drifted off toward the curb.

The initial meeting with General Galtieri was quite a scene. His rococo offices were furnished with mammoth, ornately carved dark furniture and heavy brocade drapes dripping with fringe. Our session began at 10:30 A.M. with several rounds of whiskey.

His primary concern was whether the United States would stick it out in the fight against the Sandinistas. Of course, I had no guarantee, but I firmly believed that President Reagan was committed, and I told him so. For the moment I skirted one potential complication. It was evident that the Argentines were ultimately aiming to bring down the Sandinista government. I thought this a rather grandiose goal when I considered the five hundred ragtag troopers along the Nicaraguan-Honduran border. Galtieri dismissed my negativism and looked vaguely amused when I restated our aims of interdicting arms and turning the Sandinistas inward. We let it go at that and departed for Military Intelligence Headquarters.

Unlike the Hondurans, the Argentines were a long way from home on the Nicaraguan-Honduran border and not threatened by the Sandinistas, either directly or indirectly. What were they doing in Honduras? The Argentines were philosophically anticommunist as a result of their own terrorist war and had a messianic vision of destroying communism wherever they could engage it. The Argentine military believed that the United States had abandoned the fight against Marxism during the Carter administration; they saw an opportunity to extend Argentina's influence in nontraditional areas by taking up the slack, much as Count Alexander de Marenches, the chief of French Military Intelligence, believed and did during the same period in the Middle Eastern arena. They were also in pursuit of a Cuban-backed Argentine terrorist group, the Montoneros, which had begun in Argentina in the 1970s. The Argentine military had been tracking them down at home since they took power in 1976. They had largely exterminated the Montoneros within Argentina; tragically they may also have killed associates of the Montoneros with less evil intentions. After the Sandinista victory in 1979, some of the surviving Montoneros had taken refuge with their ideological comrades in Managua. I could now answer definitively the question posed to me in the RIG as to why the Argentines were in Honduras.

Days passed. At Military Intelligence Headuarters, we were lectured on counterguerrilla tactics, largely urban in nature. Hank Booth, our paramilitary expert, concluded that the Argentines would indeed need some training in rural guerrilla tactics if they were to train the Nicaraguans. We were shown examples of the propaganda that was used on Argentine radio and TV to gather public support for the fight against the terrorists. It was truly imaginative and was successful. We witnessed a mock takedown of a terrorist safe house. Interspersed with all of this, we laid out our plan for the tripartite arrangement: who did what, the initial targets, and the timetable. We reached agreement, but clearly our goals differed. I thought I could contain the Argentine vision, or rather that reality would do that for me.

We had a final meeting with Galtieri, much the same as the first. A couple of rounds of whiskey were followed by a handshake that sealed our relationship. At no time during the meetings with Galtieri or the other Argentines were there any references to Argentina's dispute with the United Kingdom over the Falkland Islands, or the Malvinas Islands as the Argentines called them. Nor were there any hints that Argentina expected something in the way of recompense from the U.S. government for participating in the tripartite agreement. A week or so later General Galtieri became president of Argentina; I sent him a letter of congratulations.

I returned to Washington in time to hear Casey brief the Senate Select Committee on Intelligence (SSCI) about the new Reagan Finding we had drafted. Reagan had signed National Security Decision Directive 17 on November 16 providing policy guidance on Central America. He signed the Finding on Nicaragua soon thereafter. Casey had already briefed the House Permanent Select Committee on Intelligence (HPSCI) during my extended visit to Buenos Aires. The Senate briefing went well enough, but some opposition was already indicated. Daniel Patrick Moynihan, now a senator from New York, was concerned that the CIA was really out to overthrow the Sandinistas. In truth, no one in the Agency was going to shed any tears if Daniel Ortega, Tomás Borge, and the rest of the Sandinista ruling directorate found unemployment as a result of our efforts. However, with permission to work with a disorganized, small band of insurgents on the Honduras/Nicaragua border, no one knew better than I how far from that possibility we really were.

The next task was to go to Tegucigalpa and get the official seal of approval from the Hondurans. I flew to Miami, where Jerry Svat met me with a Learjet to take us to Central America. Why exactly he thought we needed the Learjet escapes me now, but it was a fortunate decision as events unfolded. The rainy season had begun, and we reached Tegucigalpa in the late afternoon. Colonel Alvarez headed up the small welcoming delegation, but everyone kept beating around the bush each time I tried to pin down when we would meet with the president, Gen. Policarpo Paz. Finally, Alvarez took me and our local CIA chief of station aside and admitted, "Look, you have to meet the president. He's got to chop this deal, but . . ."

"So what's the problem?" I asked.

"Well," Alvarez began reluctantly, "it's just that Paz has had too much to drink. We're drying him out over in the Tenth Battalion. He's been drinking for a few days, so I'm not sure when we will have him sober enough to participate in this."

We sat down with Alvarez and worked out the details of how the Hondurans and the Argentines would cooperate with the United States and flew back to Miami to await the completion of the general's involuntary detox program. In a day or two, we were told that we could return to Tegucigalpa.

The next morning after our return, we presented ourselves at Honduran military headquarters. Shortly, the door swung open and a short fellow in a white uniform, festooned with military decorations and with a wide blue presidential sash, entered almost bashfully into the room. I noticed a rather large spaghetti sauce–like stain had run a distance on the left breast of his otherwise white uniform. The poor president's face was ashen; he looked as if he were about to throw up. Most of the Honduran offficers seemed terribly embarrassed.

After a few short remarks on the purpose of the meeting, President Paz gave his blessing to the endeavor and left the room, barely acknowledging his fellow officers' salutes. No documents were signed, but the last leg of the tripod agreement, called La Tripartita, was now in place.

President Paz was a lame duck. In the fall of 1981, democratic national elections were held in Honduras. Roberto Suazo Cordova, a civilian, was elected president and took office at the turn of the year. Early in 1982, I called on Suazo, who reaffirmed Honduras's commitment to the tripartite agreement. Suazo chose Colonel Alvarez, now General Alvarez, as commander in chief of the Honduran armed forces. From our point of view, it was a great outcome, for it installed our friend in a position of greater power and responsibility. Over the years, I came to know Alvarez very well. He was a fine officer.

As I had promised the RIG, the CIA base for this operation was established in Honduras by January 15, 1982. It was in communications with Headquarters; supplies were brought in and training of both the Argentines and the Hondurans had commenced. At the same time, the division and its Central American stations were heavily engaged under the original Carter covert action Finding in political action and propaganda operations in Nicaragua and El Salvador; in training and supporting security forces in El Salvador, Honduras, and to a much lesser extent Guatemala in trying to interdict the arms flow from Nicaragua to various terrorist groups in these countries and combat the groups themselves; and in improving the collection of intelligence in the area and from Cuba.

With La Tripartita in place and preparations moving ahead rapidly to establish our presence in Honduras, we could now confront several other problems that needed attention. One was the political leadership of our nascent guerrilla group. Although there was nothing wrong with the anti-Somoza credentials of the current political leadership of the FDN, we needed to augment it with higher-profile individuals, capable of working together, and of less autocratic inclinations.

To this end, I met with Arturo Cruz Sr., who was at that time employed at the Inter-American Development Bank in Washington, D.C. Cruz, an intelligent, perceptive gentleman, had been the Sandinistas' first ambassador in Washington and had resigned when he could no longer defend or abide the totalitarian Sandinista policies or their coziness with the Communist Bloc.

Cruz met me at the entrance to his bank. It was a cold, gray, blustery Saturday afternoon in January 1982. We sought in vain for a place to have coffee and settled instead for a walk along the deserted streets. Cruz turned down my suggestion that he head the new political leadership, begging heavy family responsibilities that required his presence in Washington.

During the nearly one-hour stroll, Cruz did contribute to my education when he told me with great care and intensity, "You should always remember that Nicaraguans have a great weakness in that they are supreme individualists and find it nearly impossible to cooperate for long with one another."

While we sought out Nicaraguans, they also sought us. The Chamorro brothers, Edmundo and Fernando, aka El Negro, asked to meet with us. The CATF chief and I met them in a dimly lit lounge of a second-class hotel in northern Virginia. El Negro, apparently so-called because he was of darker skin than his brother, was an authentic hero of the fight against Somoza. On one occasion, he had fired two rockets from a room of the Intercontinental Hotel in Managua at Somoza's headquarters bunker. However, El Negro had few followers; he was a one-man adventurer in the Central American tradition who never really attracted a following, perhaps because of his lack of discipline and an inclination to tipple too much at the wrong times. The brothers, who had previously refused to join the FDN, now wanted us to put them in charge of it. We declined the offer but welcomed their participation. Eventually, El Negro did participate, first in the northern Nicaraguan sector and then in the southern one with Eden Pastora. Both were disastrous undertakings.

Another problem was the perception that our five-hundred-man guerrilla force on the Nicaraguan-Honduran border was led by former members of the Nicaraguan National Guard, whose purpose was to reestablish a Somoza-style regime. The Nicaraguan National Guard had been formed by the U.S. Marines during the American presence there in the 1930s as a means of shoring up the central government. The term *national guard* was used rather than *army*, but the Guard functioned like a combination army and police force.

When the Somoza family took over the government, it took over the National Guard as well, and the Guard became a major factor in keeping them in power. When Somoza fled (originally to Miami, and thence to Asunción, Paraguay), much of the top leadership of the National Guard went with him, and the Guard collapsed, enabling the Sandinistas to move into a power vacuum in Managua.

The generals and other high-ranking National Guard officers were rightly branded as Somocistas—they had surely supported Somoza's longevity and had participated in his human rights violations. Unfortunately, the entire National Guard was tarred with the same brush by the international media, and it stuck. The National Guard was perceived by the American public as sort of a Latin descendant of the Nazi SS. As in any military organization, however, the junior officers, noncoms, and run-of-the-mill troops had no political orientation. They had no special loyalty to Somoza; they followed orders. Nevertheless, we could never shake their tarnished reputation.

The other guerrilla force was composed of Miskitos, who are an indigenous people who inhabit the lush and remote coastal plain of Nicaragua along the Atlantic Ocean. Unlike many of the native peoples of Central America, their ancestry is not Mayan. The Miskitos are descended from Caribbean tribes who intermarried with black slaves who had been brought from Africa to work the sugar plantations. For many of them, Spanish is not their native tongue. Culturally and linguistically, the Miskitos have much more in common with their distant cousins on the islands of Jamaica, Hispaniola, and Cuba than they do with the inhabitants of the rest of Nicaragua. Indeed, the Costa de Miskitos, or Mosquito Coast, was for most of its history only nominally part of the country. Ungovernable and largely not worth governing, the Mosquito Coast had basically been left to its own devices over the years by the national administration in Managua.

That is, until the arrival of the Sandinistas. Determined to assimilate the Miskitos, they began a relentless program to force them to accept the Communist agenda they had foisted on the rest of the country. The Sandinistas grabbed private and tribal Miskito farms and businesses and announced the formation of state-run cooperatives. These co-ops were to dictate what crops would be cultivated and the prices at which they would be sold—to the government. Cuban teachers arrived to impart the lessons of Marxism to Miskito children.

The Miskitos weren't having any of it. They took to their unpaved streets in surprisingly well organized protest. The Sandinistas responded heavy-handedly. Tribal leaders were arrested; villages were burned to the ground and the occupants forcibly relocated. Horrified, many Miskitos simply pulled up stakes and fled across the Río Coco into Honduras. The Río Coco, though it formed the border between Nicaragua and Honduras, ran right down the middle of traditional Miskito lands and had both economic and spiritual significance for the tribe. Entire villages relocated en masse into Honduras. Indian anger at the Sandinistas prompted many of the exiles to take up arms and begin harassment raids against Sandinista outposts across the border.

Casey was astounded at how rapidly we moved and what we accomplished in such a short time and said so. I was persuaded that we had to move more rapidly to change the image of our guerrilla movement and find some counterbalance to the successful propaganda effort of the Sandinistas. From the beginning we had been sensitive to the fact that our Nicaraguan guerrilla movement needed a solid political element. There were DO officers who thought I emphasized preparing for guerrilla operations to the detriment of the political aspects of the movement as a whole, and maybe they were right. On the other hand, pressure was on me to provide a significant "bang" in Nicaragua soon in order to announce a change in the way the Sandinistas thought the game was played.

Because members of the FDN, like the 15th of September Legion before them, were working "against" the revolutionary Sandinistas, they inherited (with the assistance of the Sandinistas and the U.S. media) the appellation of *contrarevolutionarios,* which shortened to the *contras*—which is Spanish for "against." Contra conjured up a negative connotation that hurt the cause, above all in Washington. Despite the effort by President Reagan and others over the years to describe our Nicaraguan peasant guerrilla army as "freedom fighters," the term contra stuck.

Coupled with the contra label was that of Somocista. That no one associated with the FDN and its predecessor organization could be called a crony of Somoza—and thus a Somocista—mattered little to the media.

I needed someone in our Sandinista opposition mix who had at least the reputation of a shooter against Somoza's forces and who was regarded by the liberals and socialists in the United States and abroad as one of their own. I knew this someone could be the Nicaraguan Eden Pastora, aka Comandante Zero. I decided to seek his cooperation.

Pastora had long been an opponent of Somoza, and his "revolutionary" credentials were as good as any of the leading Sandinistas'—and in most cases much better. However, it was in 1978 when he burst onto the world stage. In that year, he slipped into Managua with a few dozen colleagues and seized the Nicaraguan National Palace. The palace housed not Somoza (who had taken up more secure lodgings) but the National Assembly and a wide assortment of Nicaraguan government offices. For three days his handful of men held fifteen hundred people hostage, including about fifty members of the Chamber of Deputies, demanding release of Somoza's political prisoners, including future Sandinista minister of the interior Tomás Borge. After tense negotiations brokered by Miguel Obando y Bravo, the archbishop of Managua, Pastora and his men left with the freed prisoners, half a million dollars in cash, and a gold Rolex watch lifted from the wrist of a hostage. This dramatic attack was the epitome of a flamboyant personal style that made him an almost instant folk hero.

When the Sandinistas finally ousted Somoza and divided up the spoils, however, Pastora was shoved to the side, despite—or perhaps because of—his popularity with Nicaraguans. Although the jubilant crowd in Managua chanted, "Zero, Zero," he was given positions of lesser importance—deputy interior minister, deputy defense minister—that did not jibe with his elevated opinion of where he belonged in the government hierarchy. He was deliberately excluded from the ruling directorate. Disaffected, he eventually took off from Nicaragua in a huff and traveled around Latin America looking for another place to be a revolutionary hero.

In hindsight, I think Pastora had come to a point where guerrilla warfare was a way of life for him. After the death of his *compadre* and supporter Omar Torrijos of Panama, in a plane crash in July of 1981, he seemed at loose ends. He tried his luck in Havana, where he took up support of a Central American noncommunist guerrilla group and decided to join their fight to overthrow their military opponents. During this period, he allegedly visited Muammar Qaddafi to raise funds for the group, and the $2 million he received was supposedly confiscated by Castro when it arrived in Havana. In despair he retreated to San José, Costa Rica, with a few followers and spent most of his time brooding and hunting sharks. San José was like a second home to him and was where his long-suffering wife, Yolanda, and three daughters lived.

The Agency had a good reading on his current foul mood, particularly for some of the Sandinista leadership, namely Interior Minister Tomás Borge and Defense Minister Humberto Ortega. Pastora had no real politics or ideology. However, he was certainly anti-Somoza; now he was anti-Sandinista to a degree, although he was still ambivalent about Castro. He was no democrat; he preferred a more "managed" form of government from the top. He was a cast-off hero of the revolution in Nicaragua, but still a golden boy of the left in Europe and a credible figure to U.S. politicians and the media. I assumed that he would be a great character, but I didn't know the half of it.

We arranged a meeting with Pastora in Acapulco, Mexico, in February of 1982. I had begun to travel under the pseudonym of Dewey Marone. Since my nickname of Dewey was well-known, it was obviously a poor choice. By the time I realized the screwup, the not-false-enough name had become set in concrete—or rather, set in a raft of alias documentation paperwork.

We met Pastora in a hotel suite rented specifically for the purpose. Neither we nor Pastora wanted anyone to know of his connection with the Central Intelligence Agency, for it would have ruined his reputation and usefulness. We picked a suite on the ground floor off a garden, so that we could reduce our comings and goings through the hotel lobby and thus limit our exposure. Although we knew that Pastora was traveling in alias, we had to assume the Mexican authorities might know of it from his previous visits to Mexico and have him watch-listed at the airport. Our countersurveillance picked up no indications of interest in him.

Pastora arrived with two other men. We weren't formally introduced, but I had reason to believe they were Leonel Poveda, aka Comanche, and Carlos Coronel. Poveda was a sidekick in the legendary seizure of the National Palace. Carlos Coronel had also been with Pastora since the fight against Somoza and was believed by many to be Pastora's political éminence grise.

Pastora in person was even more egotistical than advertised. Of medium height and build, he had an engaging face and personality to match. He could rarely sit for long, moving incessantly around the room, lecturing, hectoring, and gesticulating. He tended to refer to himself in the third person. Nevertheless, he struck me as a believable leader, someone who could ameliorate the Somocista/contra image of our guerrilla operation against the Sandinistas. I also thought that he could perhaps establish a modest force in southern Nicaragua, which could get at the many small airfields there being used by the Sandinistas to move arms by light aircraft into El Salvador.

I told him that we wanted two things: first, a public announcement of his break with the Sandinistas, and second, a tour of Europe to tell the leftists what the new Sandinista government was really doing. In return, we would support his organization for operations in southern Nicaragua. By the end of the first tiring and intense day, we were far from agreement. Pastora would not commit to a timetable for his public break with Managua, and we would not agree to his rather thinly disguised goal of being put in charge of the northern guerrilla front and ousting all the supposed Somocistas, which mainly meant Enrique Bermúdez.

Pastora always hedged when asked to quote chapter and verse on Bermúdez's offenses; as a military attaché exiled to Washington in the waning days of the Somoza regime, he'd had no opportunity to be tainted by any atrocities. Bermúdez had been given a clean bill of moral and ethical health even by the Carter administration, and he'd been part of the anti-Sandinista leadership since its earliest days as the 15th of September Legion. Although Bermúdez was certainly a decent human being, we didn't get along all that well because I think he sensed that I didn't have that much confidence in him. He had a great rapport with Alvarez, but I didn't feel he was the kind of dynamic military leader we needed for this particular kind of war. Moreover, he had been trained for conventional warfare and for the longest time had a problem accepting the need for guerrilla tactics. To his great credit, he eventually did and with good result. Furthermore, as the years passed, he grew in stature and competence as a military leader.

The second day opened with more of Pastora's ranting and raving and making speeches about the goddamned *comunistas* in Managua and the goddamned Somocistas we were supporting in Honduras. Although my ultimate game plan was for unity among the anti-Sandinista forces, the more I learned about Pastora, the more it seemed he would never make common cause with the FDN. Moreover, I knew full well that the Hondurans and the Argentines would never accept Pastora's overall leadership of the guerrilla movement because they questioned his military competence and believed that he was really a Communist. The southern front was one way of getting Pastora into the game without having to deal immediately with the hostility between Pastora and the anti-Sandinista leadership in Honduras.

Pastora's rambling diatribes on the Somocistas on the northern front, the perfidy of American policy and actions in Central America, and the CIA's unscrupulous ways and failure to support him in his fight against Somoza went on for hours on end. He continued to make all sorts of unrealistic demands for money and weapons, including artillery, and his requirement for total control of the contra operation became increasingly blatant. Toward the end of the day, perhaps because he was exhausted (I know I was), and because he also sensed we were not going to cave in to his more outrageous demands, Pastora suddenly seemed to want to come to closure. Poveda and Coronel played a useful role in this regard in their side conversations with him.

Pastora agreed to make a public break with the Sandinistas and Castro around the end of March 1982 and then leave shortly thereafter for Europe for discussions with socialist leaders. He would also begin to put together a political/military structure for a southern front that we would

216

support with funds and matériel. But then, Pastora dropped a turd in the proverbial punch bowl. He insisted that we make an airdrop of a few weapons and radios to a small group of noncommunist guerrillas that he was trying to support as an indication of his continuing Central American revolutionary credentials. Of course, it was also a test of our sincerity. No amount of argument would get him off his demand, and more and more it became a condition of his cooperation. I said that I would try to obtain approval, but no promises. With that, we departed more or less on friendly terms.

I flew directly to Washington and went straight from the airport to the Agency. It was February and was already dark outside when I asked to see Casey. I was ushered in immediately. Casey pointed to the wing chair beside his desk and I sat. I told him in detail about the meeting with Pastora with particular emphasis on the airdrop as an indicator of our bona fides. I told him that I believed we had to do it because without it, we didn't have a deal. No drop, no Pastora.

Casey was immensely pleased with the results. It took him about five seconds to grasp the issue of the airdrop and its implications. Just as he was about to nod his assent, Bobby Inman, the deputy director, walked in through the private door that connected his office to Casey's. By tradition, the deputy director had unimpeded access to the DCI, and as he strode in, he overheard my closing comments on the airdrop. Inman listened to me reiterate what I wanted to do, and the most amazing look came over his face. I think he regarded the airdrop as the most lunatic idea he had ever heard and thought that both of us were out of our minds to consider it. The concept that we would make an airdrop to guerrillas in a friendly country was beyond his comprehension. He was already angry that I was discussing Central America with Casey without his being present, and the possibility of the airdrop completely outraged him. I'm sure he also thought Pastora was a Communist. He glared at me, turned to Casey, and said, "That's the dumbest thing I've ever heard."

Casey replied, "Oh, come off it, Bobby." But Inman had turned on his heel and was already walking out of the room.

Bobby Ray Inman was not accustomed to being ignored or brushed aside. He had been director of the National Security Agency (NSA) for four years and before that was director of naval intelligence—both sterile, impersonal, and thus politically safe intelligence-collection organizations whose means rarely cause controversy with Congress or the media. Not known as a risk taker, he had an ego almost as big as Pastora's. He was also good at kissing up to the House and Senate intelligence committees, as his ample NSA budget had proven.

Inman was a great friend of Bob Woodward of the *Washington Post.*

They'd served together in the Navy. It was an open secret in Washington that Inman had been a source for Woodward. Casey later told me that he suspected Inman continued to be a source for Woodward after Inman came to the CIA.

In late February 1982 under a nearly full moon, the Twin Otter De Havilland aircraft banked, came around, and took up a new heading now on a south-to-north axis. The pilot was certain he had the correct longitude and latitude and time, but still no signal fire appeared on the ground. Then, suddenly, flames leapt skyward in the darkness ahead. The copilot saw the flames as well and opened the door on the side of the aircraft. The Otter began losing altitude, and when the pilot dropped his arm from its upraised position, the copilot pushed two bundles attached to parachutes through the door to the waiting jungle below. The pilot reported success to Headquarters by radio and readjusted his heading. I telephoned Casey and John Stein with the result. We had kept our bargain with Pastora with the RIG's approval; now it was his turn.

Our case officer in touch with Pastora reported that the latter was still dithering about when he would make his break with the Sandinistas, so I decided to play a trump card. Under a veil of intense secrecy, I brought Pastora to meet Casey in Washington, D.C. We brought him into CIA Headquarters through a special entrance underneath the building that only the director and a few other senior officers used, then up the director's elevator to the seventh floor. Few people ever knew Pastora was in the building.

The meeting was dramatic in the way only Pastora could make it. He spoke rather eloquently about freedom for the Nicaraguan people, condemned the Sandinistas for stealing the revolution, and berated us for supporting the Somocistas along the Nicaraguan-Honduran border. As a final touch, he took the brass, handmade dog tag from around his neck with *cero* (zero) imprinted on it (from whence came his nom de guerre) and gave it to Casey with a flourish.

Casey, for all his worldliness, appeared touched by this gesture. He clearly liked Pastora and also knew his political value in Europe, Latin America, and with the U.S. Congress. Comandante Zero promised Casey that he would make his public break with the Sandinistas "soon." I still feared we were caught up in the mañana syndrome.

In Nicaragua, our guerrillas were right on schedule. We had set March 15 as the date for our first operation: the targets were two bridges on the Pan American Highway. The highway was the main vehicular artery used by the Sandinistas to infiltrate arms to the Communist rebels in El Salvador via Honduras concealed in trucks and cars. The heavily used bridges would be dropped by Argentine-trained Nicaraguans. Because the two bridges would be felled simultaneously, the Sandinistas couldn't attribute their disappearance to a flood or other natural causes. This operation would be our calling card, a message that we were taking the war to Nicaragua. Having served notice to the Sandinistas, we would then lie low until the fall while training the Nicaraguans and Miskitos in the use of their weapons, communications, and guerrilla tactics, including respect for human rights in earnest.

On the night of March 14, the guerrillas penetrated into Nicaragua and blew the Somotillo and Ocotal bridges on the Pan American Highway. I requested aerial photo reconnaissance, which indicated that one was down completely; the other was severely damaged. Blowing these bridges was not a simple undertaking. In keeping with our policy, we had to train the Argentines how to reconnoiter the bridges. Once this was accomplished, the Argentines had to train the Nicaraguan recce teams and dispatch them to the bridges. That completed, we had to instruct the Argentines in how to demolish the bridges based on the reconnaissance data, and they in turn had to train the Nicaraguans. That all of this was accomplished within two months of going into operations along the Nicaraguan border with Honduras was of great credit to all participants.

The raid had the desired effect, and as we anticipated, the Sandinistas declared a state of emergency, suspended opposition political activity, and instituted direct censorship of the press. We knew from espionage operations within the Sandinista directorate that the Sandinistas had planned to institute these measures in the near future anyway; we simply advanced their timetable. But in truth their actions were exactly what we wanted. They exacerbated their problems with their own population and increased discontent, which we hoped would divert them from their aggressive designs on other countries in the area.

By this time, I knew that we had major problems with the Argentines and that our plan to remain in the background, providing logistics, training support, and operational advice, was unworkable. Not unreasonably, the Argentines resented our apparent taking over of their operation, although we tried to play only our behind-the-scenes role. One of the problems was that the Argentines had no appreciation for or understanding of rural guerrilla warfare; the same was true for the Hondurans and also for at least the initial group of guerrillas, who were former troopers in the Nicaraguan National Guard. As a result, their concept of operations tended to follow conventional warfare lines, which was useless, given the mountainous terrain of our operational area.

Furthermore, all our allies tended to ignore the logistics of guerrilla warfare and insist on developing a dangerously exposed and expensive airdrop capability. A second issue was the propensity of the Argentines and sometimes even Alvarez, probably out of frustration, to press for urban guerrilla warfare in Nicaragua. I opposed the concept. Urban guerrilla warfare can quickly become terrorism, or at least be perceived as such. The third problem was that although La Tripartita had called for the jettisoning of any former member of the Nicaraguan National Guard with even the least suspicion of previous criminal activity, we knew that the Argentines were fiddling around with some questionable individuals, including Ricardo "Chino" Lau, apparently for counterintelligence purposes.

For these reasons, I decided and advised the RIG that we had to assume the leadership role in La Tripartita, which meant that the CIA's profile would be raised. This was what we had sought to avoid, but I saw no alternative. Otherwise, we would never create an effective guerrilla force, and moreover, I was sure that eventually some dreadful incident would occur that would cause us endless problems in Washington.

We didn't announce the change; we just did it over time. The Argentines immediately sensed it, and the tensions in our relationship increased exponentially. Bermúdez didn't like it, for he had a cozy lash-up with the Argentines going back to the beginning and they had cultivated him assiduously. Alvarez, for all his close ties to the Argentines, seemed to be of two minds. Not unreasonably, he felt a strong loyalty to them for past and present support, but he was politically astute enough to realize what a disruptive force the Argentines had become.

On April 2, Brig. Gen. Mario Davico, director of Argentine Military Intelligence, came to see me in Washington to discuss various problems. I'd met him on my first trip to Buenos Aires and had conferred with him upon occasion since then. When he arrived in my office, he brought with him a beautiful cowhide-bound English translation of *Martin Fierro*, the classic Argentine novel about gaucho life. Because he knew that I had become interested in Argentina, it was a thoughtful and appreciated gift. I liked Davico; he wasn't a hard-liner; I thought we could work out our differences.

As we were discussing matters, my secretary came in and handed me a message. When I read it to Davico, his mouth dropped open. Claiming repatriation of Argentine lands, President General Galtieri had just landed thousands of troops in the Islas Malvinas. Most people, including the British to whom they belonged, knew them as the Falkland Islands.

Before Davico arrived, matters had already heated up in the area, but our intelligence estimates had dismissed the likelihood of major military action by the Argentines. Again, the wog factor was at work.

Davico's surprise seemed genuine. Even if he were a consummate actor, why would the chief of Argentine Military Intelligence be sitting in my office when the Argentine invasion went down? I concluded that he was undoubtedly aware of Argentine plans regarding the Falklands, but that the timetable had been accelerated and he found himself awkwardly in Washington with no instructions.

Given my firsthand experience with the inebriated haze through which Galtieri began his mornings on the few occasions I met with him, I could believe that the Argentine timing and plans might have gone askew while Davico was in transit to the United States. However, that he had received no instructions after his arrival was remarkable. It underlined to me that either the Argentines didn't consider La Tripartita card worth playing, or they assumed that with this alliance in place, the United States would out of loyalty not interfere in the Falklands. If the latter, they dangerously misread their history, particularly with reference to the Reagan administration.

From a policy standpoint, the Falklands invasion was a massive miscalculation on Galtieri's part. I believe they had counted on the distance between the United Kingdom and the Falklands to be the military determinative and thought that the British would negotiate. Like Hitler with Churchill, Galtieri totally misjudged the character of his opponent, Mrs. Thatcher. Reagan, with Caspar Weinberger leading the charge, rallied to the British side, and the Argentines eventually went down in defeat in June 1982. In Honduras, I expected increased problems with the Argentines, but they didn't happen. Tension remained as before between us over tactics and who was in charge, but to their credit they soldiered on until just before the Argentine democratic elections in the fall of 1983, then went home.

Meanwhile, weeks had passed since Pastora's promise to break with the Sandinistas, but still no statement was forthcoming. We became concerned that Pastora was perhaps trying to cut an eleventh-hour deal with the Sandinistas to rejoin the fold. We knew that Pastora's trusted aide Carlos Coronel was having ongoing discussions with some of the more moderate Sandinistas, including the minister of agriculture, Jaime Wheelock, in a move to bring Pastora back into the government in an enhanced position. The Sandinistas were clearly making every effort to block Pastora's announcement. I decided I had better go down to Central America and meet with Pastora. When I arrived, I was informed that Pastora had gone up-country or something, and our meeting had been delayed a day.

I had never been in this corner of Central America before. The delay afforded me the opportunity to witness our first delivery of supplies to Pastora's organization.

The grassy airstrip was out in the middle of nowhere. The reception parties, both ours and Pastora's, paced about in anticipation near dusk.

Security units reported no problems. Almost to the minute of its schedule, a dot appeared on the horizon to the north, losing altitude. Our radio operator established contact with the dot and gave it an all clear. The Twin Otter aircraft swept down over the airstrip to check for obstructions, such as cows and the like, made a series of banks, then settled in for its final approach. The plane landed, taxied to near where we were waiting, turned around to be ready to take off with its engines idling. Within minutes, it had been unloaded and the matériel placed in Pastora's trucks, which moved off into the night. With a wave from the cockpit window, the pilot pushed his throttles forward and the Otter was airborne in seconds. We went back to the hotel for a drink and to contemplate the next day with Pastora.

We cooped ourselves up in a seedy safe house with only straight-backed chairs. Even my gift of an M16 rifle with a 40-mm grenade launcher beneath its barrel failed to impress him. Several of his subordinates were present, in particular the questionable Carlos Coronel. I was determined to get a firm date for Pastora's announcement and an outline of its content. The air in the room became blue with a mix of his ranting about the Somocistas in the north and my cigar smoke. After nearly eleven hours of great pain and tension, we got agreement on a date and the general content of the declaration. On April 15, 1982, Eden Pastora called a press conference in San José and denounced the Sandinistas as "traitors and assassins." He called for the ouster of all Cubans from Nicaragua, branding them "instruments of intervention and death." He then cataloged the abuses of the Sandinistas, including restrictions on freedom of religion and the press, and persecution of the Miskitos. It wasn't everything I had wanted, but his announcement of a formal break with the Sandinistas caused a considerable stir in the media and in Nicaragua.

By now the Miskitos were in full and open revolt. To stem their flight into Honduras, the Sandinistas had started herding the Indians into what amounted to little more than concentration camps. Not only did they feel an ideological compulsion to bring the Miskitos under control, they also needed free access to the port of Bluefields, which was located in the heart of the Mosquito Coast. Though a rinky-dink harbor, it was the port of entry for Soviet, Bulgarian, and Cuban military hardware. Eastern Bloc weaponry came in at Bluefields and was then moved up the Río Escondido on roll-on/roll-off ships to a terminal, Arlen Siu, slightly above the town of Rama, then was off-loaded and trucked along the Rama Road into Managua. Without access to Bluefields, the Communists would have had to bring all these armaments through the Panama Canal.

We and the Hondurans began organizing and training the Miskitos, focusing on an emerging leader named Steadman Fagoth. Fagoth wasn't the only Miskito leader. Another faction was led by a fellow named Brooklyn Rivera, and they may have shared as much animosity for each other as for the Sandinistas. Part of the rivalry was personal. Fagoth had supposedly stolen Rivera's girlfriend and had eventually married her.

I met with Fagoth, who was relatively more stable than Rivera and had a larger following within the Miskito community. Moreover, he already had loose ties to the FDN, and the Hondurans accepted him. (Rivera later aligned with Pastora, but contributed almost nothing to the southern front.) With minimal training, once armed, the Miskitos insisted on going into action against the Sandinistas who were ravaging their homeland. The Miskitos were natural guerrillas totally at home in their swamps, savannas, and estuaries and were immediately successful against the Sandinista troops.

Pastora formed a political-military organization called the Democratic Revolutionary Alliance, or ARDE, and became its *comandante*. The political arm of ARDE was headed up by Alfonso Robelo. A tall, thoughtful, and articulate man with a large beard, he had a considerable following, both in Nicaragua and abroad. An educated gentleman, Robelo was a moderate with absolutely impeccable anti-Somoza credentials. Unlike Pastora, he was blessed with an even and reasonable temperament. He's one of the finest men I've ever known. A former member of the junta that had overthrown Somoza, Robelo broke with the Sandinistas when they would not tolerate dissent in Nicaragua. From our perspective, the linkage between Robelo and Pastora was positive, but eventually, however, I'm sure that Pastora's antics frustrated Robelo as much as they did us.

Pastora as a leader was a mixed bag of pluses and minuses. His military successes tended to be flash-in-the-pan outings like the takeover of the National Palace. These glamorous triumphs have their publicity value, but he had an ongoing penchant to play to the grandstands—to go for the extravagant gesture in lieu of solid progress.

All too often, Pastora's insistence on total control and his inability to compromise made him his own worst enemy. To be sure, he had compromised in other situations, most notably with the Sandinistas, and the results had turned out badly for him, but Pastora was an undisciplined leader with no concept of the need to delegate authority. He alienated and humiliated his subordinates, and they left him. Leonel Poveda's departure in total frustration was a monumental loss. I suspect that, like many Latino men, Pastora had a strong authoritarian streak in him; had he ever come to power in Nicaragua, he might well have tried to run the country as a benevolent despot, a caudillo, in the Latin American tradition.

Having said all that, the truth was that I liked Pastora. He was a colorful but ultimately very decent fellow whose ambitions and ego just consumed him. His unpredictability made him difficult to deal with. There were days when I could have dispatched him, and days when, I am sure, the feeling was mutual, but beneath all the posturing I sensed that he liked me a bit. Because of this relationship, generally speaking, when Pastora had to be handled, it was my job to handle him.

Following his dramatic press conference, Pastora agreed to leave almost immediately on a tour of European capitals. His mission was to talk with various people in the Socialist International and try to cut off the aid, moral or otherwise, to the Sandinistas that was still coming to them from Western Europe, particularly from France, Germany, Italy, and Spain. By early May, not accomplishing much because the European socialists were stiffing him at the Sandinistas' behest, Pastora had holed up in the Intercontinental Hotel in Madrid. The colleagues who had accompanied him had returned to Central America in disgust. Pastora showed no signs of returning to Central America. I needed him for a summit meeting in the Washington area of the leadership of the northern and southern fronts and La Tripartita. As it appeared to be the only way, a colleague and I left for Madrid to retrieve him. After subjecting us to yet another round of lectures and posturing, he agreed to return with us.

The three of us were ticketed on an Iberia Airlines flight from Madrid to New York. We'd outfitted Pastora with a disguise—wig and dentures—and false papers. Not only did we want to avoid media representatives chasing after him, but all of us were also concerned that the Sandinistas and Cubans might attempt to kill him—a not overly dramatic concern as later events proved. I thought Pastora looked a bit foppish in his wig, but he seemed to like it.

My colleague and I arrived early at the airport. I was relieved when the unreliable Pastora actually materialized at the ticket counter, in good time and incognito. I can't recall the reason, but we all were upgraded to first class. Entering the first-class section, my heart leapt when I noticed the publisher of Miami's largest Spanish-language newspaper, *Diario Las Americas*, Horacio Aguirre, and his wife settling themselves in their seats on the port side of the cabin.

I had met Aguirre several months before, when he had come to Headquarters to give Casey the benefit of his observations on Central America. I had spoken to him on the phone a couple of times after that. I tried to make myself small over by the window of my bulkhead, starboard seat, while my Agency companion sat in the aisle seat, shielding me as best he could. Aguirre, who was Nicaraguan, knew Pastora well, at least from pictures if not in person. I mused that the effectiveness of the Agency's disguise experts was about to be put to a real test. God knows what Pastora might have to say to Aguirre if unmasked during the seven-hour flight in front of us. I had my companion slip Pastora a note pointing out Aguirre's presence. In the end, Aguirre never realized I was on board or that Comandante Zero was sitting just a few seats behind him.

I felt it was imperative to get Pastora to the summit meeting that we hoped would bring some unity to the anti-Sandinista organizations. I wanted to bring about an agreement between ARDE (Pastora and the southern front) and the FDN (Bermúdez and the northern front) to form a joint organization, or at least to agree to cooperate and coordinate closely on political and military matters. We met at a hotel in Reston, Virginia, for two days. Attending were General Alvarez and two of his staff officers, Bermúdez, Pastora and two of his companions, and Clandestine Services officers from Central America and Headquarters. The Miskitos were absent because they were in action against the Sandinistas. We didn't have to contend with an Argentine presence because of the ongoing Falkland Islands War. But enough poison was in the air even without them. The conference went nowhere and degenerated into a series of side meetings of the various factions, with the Americans shuttling back and forth between them.

In addition to his now familiar diatribes about the Somocistas and the Argentines, Pastora had a new complaint: his organization was receiving second-class treatment in terms of funds and matériel compared with the FDN. This was not true, but it remained a constant refrain of his throughout my association with him.

The collapse of the summit underlined the need to build the political directorates of the FDN and ARDE and to bring the guerrilla components of these organizations under their control. I was under no illusion that this would be easy with Pastora and ARDE. I was fortunate in this regard because the new chief of the Central American Task Force, Jerry Gruner, was bright, politically astute, unflappable, and an able negotiator. He moved quickly to make this a reality.

Looking back, I sometimes wonder how I managed to keep so many balls in the air at the same time. I was frequently in Honduras, trying to keep all of the antagonistic factions from ripping the operation apart, and in El Salvador, determining what we could do better to improve the interdiction of the Sandinistas' arms supply to the insurgents there, to enhance the capabilities of the security forces, and to encourage the democratic political process under that grand gentleman President Duarte. Accompanying all of this in El Salvador were our efforts to penetrate the right- and left-wing political and insurgent groups sponsoring death squads, murdering not only their own countrymen but also American military assigned there.

Back at Headquarters, besides Central America, there were concerns in Mexico, the Caribbean, Cuba, and South America to deal with. In addition to the meetings within the executive branch, there were with increasing frequency briefings of the congressional oversight committees and their staffs, sometimes with Casey. The swelling of our Nicaraguan guerrilla ranks alarmed some in Congress. The political heat about Central America was rising in Washington, both in the media and on the Hill. Clearly, the Democrats had decided to confront the president over his Central American policy.

The days, including Saturdays, were long but fascinating. The first thing in the morning, when facing twelve inches or more of incoming and perhaps half as much of outgoing cable traffic to read, I was aided by strong coffee and a nice heavy-bodied, six-inch Honduran cigar. One of the perks of being in Latin America Division was access to a variety of fine cigars from Jamaica, the Dominican Republic, Honduras, Nicaragua, and once in a while, even Cuba. That I was able to do what I did was, of course, because I had a superb group of dedicated, loyal, and intelligent people from just about every major component of the Agency and beyond supporting our efforts, and not just in regard to Central America.

CHAPTER 13

The Two-Front War— Washington and Nicaragua

In the late spring of 1982, Bobby Ray Inman resigned as deputy director of central intelligence (DDCI) after an evening meeting with Bill Clark, the president's national security adviser. Inman's resignation seemed to surprise Casey, who was out of Washington at the time. When he returned, he didn't appear to have anyone in mind for the job and didn't move with alacrity to fill it, interviewing just one candidate, an admiral, before he lost control of events. Almost immediately after Inman left, the press and Congress began a drumbeat to have John McMahon, then the Agency's executive director, which many at the time regarded as a nonjob and holding position, named the DDCI. McMahon was certainly qualified. However, Congress's desire to have him in the job had less to do with his very real abilities and more with its view that he was sympathetic to its interests. McMahon was believed to be trustworthy, lukewarm on covert action, and thus a counterweight to Casey within the Agency. Casey, of course, knew this when he was more or less forced to appoint McMahon DDCI.

There is an interesting cultural difference between directorates within the Agency in how they view and interact with the executive branch and Congress. An understanding of this explains some things, such as the McMahon phenomenon.

The Directorate of Operations or the Clandestine Services has always "marched" for the president, no matter what his political party. On the other hand, the Directorate of Science and Technology, which is involved in large and expensive programs, usually of a technical nature, has a very different focus, and Congress controls its funding. The president is a beneficiary of its intelligence collection, but the implementation of its programs, the success thereof, and thus its officers' promotions depend on congressional financial largess. No wonder then that officers largely brought up in this directorate, such as John McMahon, develop an almost symbiotic relationship with Congress, in stark contrast with the Clandestine Services, which is beholden to Congress for little.

Lt. Gen. Paul Gorman, assistant to the chairman of the Joint Chiefs of Staff (JCS) and a member of the RIG, suggested that I occasionally brief the JCS on what I was up to in Central America. The chiefs seemed to find me amusing, probably because I came alone, carried my own briefing boards, and had a colorful pocket square hanging from my suit-coat pocket. I described what for them were some rinky-dink operations in Central America, which was an arena they or at least some of them wanted to avoid. One briefing occurred in June of 1982 shortly after McMahon was appointed DDCI.

These briefings took place in the "tank" in the Pentagon. The tank is a kind of military holy place, where the chiefs meet together to discuss and decide military issues. Within the room is a large U-shaped grouping of tables with various writing implements, paper, and munchies available at each seat. Because this was the Reagan administration, the munchies were a substantial jar of jelly beans at each position. At the top of the U was a stage for the briefers. The positions occupied by the chiefs and their deputies around this table are inviolable and permanent, probably through long tradition. Looking out from the stage, I saw starting from the left the chief of staff (COS) of the Army, in this instance Gen. Edward "Shy" Meyer; the chief of naval operations; at the bottom of the U the commandant of the Marine Corps; COS of the Air Force; the chairman of the JCS, in this case Air Force general David C. Jones; and finally the director of the JCS, a sort of chief clerk with the rank of major general who runs the bureaucracy of the JCS.

The guerrillas had already dropped the bridges in Nicaragua and were conducting limited operations within the country. The Miskitos were pressing the Sandinistas in the east. Perhaps the chiefs thought Clarridge was off on his own and might get them into a war in Central America, so they asked Tom Enders to brief as well on the political dimensions. He was supposed to go first; however, a call from his office indicated that he would be late, so I went ahead. Near the end of my presentation, the door of the tank opened and in came Casey and McMahon, who, after introductions, sat down behind General Meyer in chairs along the wall. Casey had brought McMahon to the Pentagon to introduce him officially to Secretary of Defense Weinberger, among others.

I finished my briefing, answered a few questions, and joined Casey and McMahon on the wall. Time passed. Enders still hadn't appeared, and no one said anything. Then, suddenly, General Meyer, looking at the chairman with his back to us, said, "I find it untenable that a military officer has not been appointed the DDCI." He went on and on in that vein. All were embarrassed with McMahon sitting there.

Finally, Casey, who was clearly searching for something to say to head off General Meyer, said, "Now, General, you've had a military man as head of CIA for the last four years," referring to Adm. Stansfield Turner. At this, General Meyer swiveled in his chair and faced us for the first time and said, "Mr. Casey, what you say is true, but that son of a bitch didn't do a goddamned thing for the military during all his time at CIA." I would have given much to know what Turner had failed to do, but at that moment Enders walked through the door and took the stage. Casey asked me to join him and McMahon in his car for the ride back to Headquarters. No one said much of anything during our drive back, but the next day Casey appointed Rear Adm. Edward "Al" Burkhalter as head of the Intelligence Community Staff, a booby prize if there ever was one and hardly what General Meyer had in mind.

Throughout my tenure as Latin America Division chief, there were periodic meetings of the National Security Planning Group (NSPG) concerning Central America. Sometimes these were simply for the purpose of bringing the president and the other members of the NSPG up to date on the situation there; others were for making specific decisions based on recommendations arrived at by the RIG. Often, these meetings were for "principals only."

Alan Wolfe's Second Dictum is that *principals only* are the two most dangerous words in the English language. This is because when cabinet officers attempt to make complicated decisions without subordinates who know the details, matters frequently go off track. This is not a negative reflection on the intelligence of the principals; their job is to see the broad scope of things, and the level of detail often needed for these decisions cannot be reduced to a briefing paper. Invariably, when an NSPG meeting was called for "principals only," Casey would call the president's national security adviser to have it changed to "principals plus one," which, if it involved Latin America, was me as the "plus one" for Casey.

The NSPG met in the Situation Room in the basement of the West Wing of the White House. You'd think that the U.S. national-security decision-making nerve center would be this big-deal kind of room, but it was actually quite tiny. It was pleasant enough, with a large maple table surrounded by chairs for the principals, but they had virtually no knee room. The president was on the end facing west and the national security adviser sat at the opposite end. Other members of the NSPG always sat in the same seats around the table. Another set of chairs was behind the principals for their subordinates. It was a squeeze.

Normally, Casey was asked to lead off with an intelligence analysis of the situation, which had been prepared by the Directorate of Intelligence. Usually he reworked it, often during the drive over from Headquarters. I would fill in the details, particularly on the operational aspects of the situation. Then, other members of the NSPG would express their views, and often the secretaries of state and defense and perhaps the chairman of the JCS would have specific briefings as well on the situation as they saw it.

Unless he needed a point clarified, the president would express his opinion only after everyone else had spoken. Reagan was impressive that way: he never tried to skew the meeting by speaking first and then letting everyone else fall into line. I certainly heard all of the stories about how he dozed off in other meetings, but I never saw him be anything except alert. When it came to foreign policy, especially Central America, he was right there and right on top of it. Over time, our guerrillas really became his boys. They were never the contras to him; they were always his freedom fighters. At the conclusion of the meeting, the national security adviser would sum up the results to ensure agreement and a written record was made.

Casey liked to go where the action was and had not yet been to Central America. He was always nattering at me about it: "Dewey, when can I go? When are you going to take me? Are we going soon?" Finally in June of '82 he and I and International Activities Division (IAD) chief Robert Magee flew to Honduras, aboard the vice president's airplane, Air Force Two.

When we landed, General Alvarez was on the tarmac to greet us. We met with him and with President Suazo as well. Our personnel gave Casey detailed briefings on the situation and their prognosis. Then we flew by helicopter to our training base, a former Honduran artillery facility called La Patarique, where the Argentines, despite the Falklands, were honoring their commitment and were fully engaged in training troops. These troops showed off their growing prowess firing mortars and machine guns, and Casey loved it. For him, I think it was a flashback to his OSS days during World War II.

Casey's visit gave the seal of approval from the Reagan administration and a boost in morale for everyone. He left no doubt with the Hondurans of the U.S. commitment. The trip was a huge success from Casey's point of view as well. When we got back, he could not stop talking about how much we had accomplished with such limited financial resources. I got the sense that the highest government circles were greatly amazed at how well this was coming together. I couldn't understand why he was so astonished by what we'd achieved; it was always my tendency to see the problems I still had to deal with, rather than how far we'd already come.

My biggest problem was that Congress was as hostile as Reagan was supportive. I had not anticipated the power of the anti-Sandinista movement within Nicaragua, which swelled the ranks of our volunteer camps on the Nicaraguan-Honduran border. Congress was startled by the dramatic increase in the number of troops and called me back repeatedly to testify, which I did, almost on a monthly basis. Senator Moynihan and others on both oversight committees hammered away that in the Finding briefed in November of '81, the Agency had said that the operation would involve only five hundred troops (slightly less than the size of the House and Senate combined). This was true, I explained, but I had not counted on the repressive tactics of the Sandinistas. Thousands of peasants had been pushed off their farms by collectivization, and thousands more had been enraged by the harsh measures taken against the Catholic Church in this most Catholic of countries. What was I supposed to do? Turn them away?

Guns and ammunition and food will always bring in a certain number of people, no matter what their political beliefs. However, the unsolicited rush of volunteers pouring over the Nicaraguan border demonstrated a genuine grassroots anger about the Sandinistas. From the summer of 1982 right through to the collapse of the government, the numbers kept increasing almost exponentially. At the end, we had close to twenty thousand guerrillas in the field, which is the largest guerrilla force ever seen in Latin America. The contras were a true anticommunist campesino army, a movement of peasants and small landowners—people with deep and abiding grievances against the Sandinistas.

Dealing with the mushrooming army took some adjustment. As the early volunteers progressed with their training, their growing numbers and enthusiasm made it difficult to keep them contained in the camps along the border. The idea of standing down and doing nothing but training after dropping the bridges wasn't going to work. They wanted to get at it and would engage in operations along the central mountain chain and its foothills that separate the western lowlands of Nicaragua from the eastern portion of the country. Occasionally, they would attempt—usually unsuccessfully—to take control of a town. Once they ran low on ammunition or whatever, they would retreat back to the border area for resupply. Overland logistics continued to bedevil us. Months later, we acquired a number of Honduran mules, hoping the guerrillas would use them to establish caches of supplies inside Nicaragua. Once inside the country, the guerrillas ate the mules! The guerrillas and their leadership wanted an easy solution, which they felt to be airdrops.

We also had disciplinary problems with some of the unit commanders, in particular one named Suicida. His depredations and murders inside Nicaragua could not be tolerated, and he was eventually tried and executed by the FDN.

Early in the summer of 1982, reconnaissance indicated a disturbing development under way with regard to the Miskitos. The Sandinistas with East German help were building a road from Matagalpa through the Miskito heartland northeast toward Puerto Cabezas on the Caribbean Sea. The Sandinista forces who were undertaking the subjugation of the Miskitos were dependent on air and ships traveling up the coast from Bluefields to keep their troops supplied. The road under construction would certainly facilitate their occupation and undoubtedly allow the Sandinistas to reinforce the area with troops to contain our Miskito guer-rillas. We noticed that the Sandinistas corralled all their trucks, tankers, bulldozers, and other heavy earth-moving machinery at a place called La Tronquera every Sunday. I asked that the FDN undertake a demolitions assault on this vehicle park to at least slow down construction.

This was not an easy operation because of the distances and terrain. An FDN recon team was first dispatched to the target, their trek taking one week each way over difficult terrain. After intensive training on where to place the explosives, the assault team left for La Tronquera. The team succeeded, doing major, irreparable damage to a large number of pieces of equipment. Unfortunately, one Sandinista died; he was asleep in one of the trucks when it went up, overlooked by the team.

Critics in Congress insisted that this activity and the burgeoning size of the army were proof that the CIA intended to overthrow the Nicaraguan government. (In fact, I knew some individuals within the administration who did advocate its overthrow, such as Haig, Constan-tine Menges, and perhaps Fred Iklé.) However, over and over I explained that even if we had wanted to, we did not have the capability to do that—barring direct U.S. military involvement, which Reagan had categorically rejected from the outset.

It was a ridiculous charge. Our guerrillas were never equipped or of the numbers needed to take on the Sandinista Army, with its thousands of troops. Moreover, its tanks and artillery and airpower were placed in the lowlands of Nicaragua, the only locale where a denouement of the San-dinistas could be affected. Sandino had failed in part in the 1920s and 1930s for the same reason. I believe that many of the most vocal critics in Congress knew that an overthrow was not possible but they used it as an excuse to pummel the administration and the CIA in particular.

The sad truth is that the Sandinistas and their leftist friends were far more effective in lobbying Congress and selling their story to the Ameri-can press than was the administration. It was slick and it was effective. They did just a super job of political action and propaganda, beginning with raising the specter of "another Vietnam" in Nicaragua. Most Ameri-cans were dead set against that kind of tar baby; they were also credulous enough to believe that Somoza had been so awful that anyone who gave him the heave-ho had to be better.

Countless Reagan speeches to the public seemed to have little effect in generating support for the contras. At first, the idea that the Sandinistas were as bad as, if not worse than, Somoza just didn't register. As time went on, Sandinista support in the United States was rising *despite* the awareness that their regime was growing more oppressive. The explanation foisted on the public by the Sandinistas and their supporters was that it was *our* fault. This was a masterstroke of public relations: the Sandinista spin doctors put forth the propaganda line that the CIA, through our Somoza retreads the contras, was going at them hammer and tongs, and that their tyrannical measures were needed to defend their country from us yanqui imperialist pigs.

The well-oiled Sandinista propaganda machine reached as far as my son Ian's prep school. He sent me a program from a weeklong workshop on Nicaragua and U.S. involvement. Although a State Department representative and someone from the Heritage Foundation were on the program, the deck was stacked against the official U.S. position. Other participants included two representatives of the Nicaraguan embassy, a pastor from a church in Cuba, a representative from the American Friends Service Committee, and a Maryknoll lay worker assigned to Nicaragua. I can only imagine what kinds of false accusations against his father and "the CIA war against the innocent people of Nicaragua" he had to listen to. In his small, precise handwriting, he provided his assessment of each speaker. He summed up the experience by saying, "As you can see, Dad, it is pretty one-sided, which really burns me up. A whole week of this stuff did confuse me. I need to talk to you about it to get my facts straight."

The churches in particular were influential in turning American opinion against the contras. The Maryknoll nuns were quite active in Nicaragua and were openly sympathetic to the Sandinistas. House Speaker Tip O'Neill had a maiden aunt named Annie Tolan, who took her vows as Sister Eunice of the Maryknoll order. After she died at the age of ninety-one, he was in correspondence with Peggy Healy, another Maryknoll nun in Nicaragua. The Catholic O'Neill absolutely believed whatever his aunt and Peggy Healy had to say. Based on their words, he took a moral stand against the contras that no amount of logic or information could alter. Because his close former roommate fellow Massachusetts Democrat Eddie Boland was the chairman of the House Intelligence Committee, O'Neill's moral objections probably took on even greater weight than they would otherwise have.

You cannot have 535 people up there on Capitol Hill all wanting to be secretary of state and setting foreign policy based on popularity polls, but late in 1982 that is exactly what happened. Between surveys showing that the American public was tilting away from supporting the contras, and Tip O'Neill blowing messages in his ear from his aunt Sister Eunice, Representative Boland decided to go after our operation. At first he wanted to try to cut funding entirely, but he compromised on a motion, the first of the Boland Amendments, that said, "None of the funds . . . may be used by the Central Intelligence Agency or the Department of Defense to furnish military equipment, military training or advice, or any other support for military activities, to any group or individual, not part of a country's armed forces, for the purpose of overthrowing the government of Nicaragua or provoking a military exchange between Nicaragua and Honduras." The House and Senate passed the amendment.

Our 1983 budget for the Nicaraguan Finding was about the flyaway price of a single F-15 aircraft, reasonably equipped. We used to joke that the U.S. Navy pushed trash of greater value off its carriers' afterdecks in a single morning than we had to spend for a year on our Nicaraguan operation.

Not that we didn't have other problems as well. The situation with the Argentines had deteriorated badly. In October 1982, Alvarez and I along with Task Force chief Jerry Gruner and the chief of station in Tegucigalpa, Don Winters, had to make a trip to Buenos Aires to attempt to straighten things out. The chief of the Argentine group in Honduras, Osvaldo Ribeiro, and his deputy were being obstreperous—and that was on their good days. On their bad days they were countermanding orders and second-guessing decisions that had repercussions not just in Central America but in the corridors of Congress as well. Having started out as a great asset, they'd become a liability. The trip results were not an unqualified success, but we reached a modus vivendi of sorts.

We were also continuing to have trouble getting units to go into Nicaragua and stay there, which is what was needed. Logistics was, of course, the problem. Without a more substantial presence and more dynamic operations inside Nicaragua, the driving force that would propel the Sandinistas into negotiations was missing. The Boland Amendment had been a shot across the bow. I was being exhorted to move things along faster. Casey's constant refrain rang in my ears: "Can't we get some more pressure on these people?" One of the first groups to make the move into Nicaragua was the Jorge Salazar Task Force, named after FDN directorate member Lucía Salazar's martyred husband. They were conducting operations in the Matagalpa area and we had begun supplying them by airdrop.

By November 1982, Gruner and Joseph Fernandez, who was in charge of political action for the Central American Task Force and a persuasive negotiator, had put in place a political directorate for the FDN filled with estimable individuals with impeccable anti-Somoza credentials and acceptable to the Hondurans and the Argentines. Bermúdez was initially leery of such a group because of the likely diminution of his power, but eventually he came around. The group selected Adolfo Calero as its leader, and a few months later, the political directorate assumed formal control of the military component of the FDN. In actuality, the control was brought about by an increasingly smooth relationship between Calero and Bermúdez. In the south, meanwhile, Alfonso Robelo put together a political directorate for ARDE, but not surprisingly, Pastora maintained iron control over military matters.

Calero was a man of immense integrity, calm, and quiet persuasion. Rather un-Latino in his emotional makeup, he had graduated from Notre Dame University, was a leader of the Nicaraguan Conservative Party, and a businessman. He had been imprisoned by Somoza twice. Other members of the directorate were Alfonso Callejas, a farmer and former vice president of Nicaragua who had resigned in a public break with Somoza; Marco Zeledon, a businessman active against Somoza; Indalecio Rodriguez, a veterinarian imprisoned by Somoza; the beautiful and intelligent Lucía Cardenal Salazar, whose husband, Jorge, had been brutally murdered by the Sandinistas; the brooding and unhappy former Jesuit Edgar Chamorro; and Bermúdez. Each had a portfolio of responsibilities to manage within the directorate. Under them were several other very accomplished individuals, such as Frank Arana, who handled such activities as the FDN's radio station. The station's power had been augmented and its strident anticommunism retuned to more appealing themes for the Nicaraguan population.

Nineteen eighty-three opened with the so-called Boland Amendment in place. In January, Gruner, Fernandez, and I were part of a group of Agency officers who traveled to Miami for a meeting with the FDN political directorate before its departure for Europe for discussions with European leaders. A rather large suite in a hotel had been rented by an officer who paid cash in advance. Agency personnel never used credit cards, for security reasons. He'd also paid cash for a quantity of soft drinks and snacks, but it was a long meeting and we ran out. Another officer called room service for some additional refreshments. Shortly thereafter, a hotel employee from reception called the room and politely said that the hotel could not accommodate our request for additional drinks because we were CIA.

The officer hung up the phone and repeated the hotel employee's statement to those assembled. All hell broke loose as we scrambled to close up files and fill briefcases for a hurried departure. We couldn't figure out how we had been compromised as CIA. And what did our being

CIA have to do with supplying the drinks anyway? Then, someone with some brains—I think it was Gruner—said, "In hotel parlance, *CIA* is the abbreviation for 'cash in advance.' Hadn't we done just that?" We had, and everyone calmed down and went back to work.

We were still having our troubles with contra rivalries, and above all with getting Pastora to go into military action along the southern front. Steadman Fagoth was still conducting independent operations with his Miskitos, but Pastora had hooked up with Fagoth's rival, Brooklyn Rivera. Rivera had some influence with the Miskitos and the Creoles along the coast south of Bluefields, but they weren't generating much activity. A third group of Miskito troops was under the command of Wycliffe Diego. Diego, a humble Moravian pastor with close ties to the traditional Miskito council of elders, was thrust into the leadership of the northern Miskito combatants when the increasingly bitter rivalries between Rivera and Fagoth threatened to bring down the resistance structure.

In an effort to get Pastora, Diego, and Rivera to pull their act together, I met with them in Panama. We met in a small no-stars hotel. The air-conditioning was out—and had been for some time. An interesting collection of gray and green mold was creeping up the walls. Overhead, the ceiling fan was twirling lazily. Pastora was as usual ranting and raving about not getting any supplies and about the goddamned Somocistas in Honduras. The discussion went nowhere. Brooklyn Rivera, who had been tippling heavily, began snoring on the settee. Diego left the room. An otherwise simple and dignified man, Diego sometimes unfortunately reacted to the stresses of revolutionary leadership by retreating to his room and locking himself in with a bottle. This was no way to run a war. The southern front was in danger of becoming a joke. I had finally given up on trying to integrate either politically or militarily Pastora's organization, ARDE, and the FDN.

Even if Pastora's troops in the area had been led by Sandino himself, we would still have had problems. The southern front backed up on Costa Rica. The Costa Ricans, with no military forces, were trying hard to stay neutral, even though the government was by now secretly quite fearful of the Sandinistas. By this time, most of Central America was eyeing the Sandinistas warily. However, the governments were reluctant to speak out publicly against them because they did not want to become targets of their subversive activities and also did not want to be openly associated with a policy supported by both the Argentines and the gringos. Because they were afraid of reprisals, there was no way the government in San José would permit us to have any sizable training facilities in Costa Rica from which to launch operations. I decided to pay a visit to Manuel Noriega to explore the possibility of setting up a training camp in Panama.

Whatever you may think about his ultimate fate, Noriega was an interesting character. He had a distinctive, heavily pockmarked face. He'd been almost a street boy in his youth, but someone had befriended him and sent him off to the Peruvian military academy.

When I first met Noriega in Washington early in 1981, he'd been a lieutenant colonel in charge of intelligence. In a meeting with Casey and me, he had indicated that Panama was in a delicate position vis-à-vis Nicaragua because the Panamanians had good connections to the Castro government, and Noriega was the primary go-between. He did not come out and say it, but he made it clear that the Panamanian leadership was beginning to question the Sandinistas' intentions.

Based on that conversation and subsequent developments, I knew that Noriega would not be entirely surprised by my request. He received me at his home, a rather modest dwelling not far from the Marriott Hotel. He was a great collector of frogs, made from a wide variety of materials, including some of semiprecious stones. In Spanish, *sapo* is a word for a toad or, perhaps in some cases, a frog and is also a colloquialism for "spy." Noriega didn't smoke, but he had a stock of fine Cuban Cohiba cigars available for those who did. Through his Cuban connections, he was able to get his supply banded with a personal label bearing his rank. Whenever we saw each other, he presented me with a box, and through his cigar bands I was able to chart his rise in seniority. I still have the last box he gave me, which say GENERAL NORIEGA.

Noriega was also fond of Old Parr Scotch. We drank a lot of Scotch together and always got along rather well. The allegations about his involvement in drug trafficking and money laundering were already in the press. Our DEA considered him more clean than not. He provided them with information that led to seizures of drugs and drug runners. Perhaps he was simply handing the DEA his rivals. DDCI McMahon didn't like the fact that we were talking with him. Sometimes in the spy business you don't have a choice with whom you deal; unfortunately, it is often the unsavory individuals who have the critical information.

When we got around to discussing a Panamanian training base for the southern front, Noriega was receptive. He was chief of staff of the Panamanian forces and offered us Snake Island, off the west coast of Panama, which had been sort of a penal colony at one time. The island was aptly named, for it was full of poisonous snakes. Almost immediately, we contracted through a Panamanian company connected with Noriega or the government to build a modest thatched-roof training center, primitive barracks, and the like for the southern command and brought in southern-front units, including Miskito Indians and Creoles under the command of Brooklyn Rivera. This lasted only a few weeks, and before we could deliver the beds for the barracks, Noriega sent us a message saying in effect that he had to renege on his offer. Elections were coming up in Panama, and he was nervous about Snake Island's becoming an election issue. At least, that's what he said. I suspect that it was pressure from Cuba that made him change his mind. Moreover, Noriega could no longer abide Pastora because of his erratic behavior. Noriega remitted to us the unused funds for the Snake Island venture.

Although Pastora continued to be a valuable political asset, we suspected that he was still trying to cut a deal with the Sandinistas. Pastora's deputy Carlos Coronel, through his connections with Agriculture Minister Jaime Wheelock, was the suspected back-channel conduit. Pastora's continued sniping at the other contra factions drained our energies. In addition, he became his own worst security risk. He could not resist a pretty face and a tight skirt. The Sandinistas knew this and sent women to visit him. Given both his colossal ego and his equally enormous libido, his Sandinista girlfriends easily got him to brag about his exploits, his grandiose battle plans, and the locations of his troops. It might have been comic if lives had not been at stake. Inexplicably, the press still loved him.

However bizarre matters were on the southern front, with the FDN, things were looking up. I gained renewed confidence as I saw how the political and propaganda efforts on the northern front had improved. The FDN had made some public relations inroads in Congress and had demonstrated that the new directorate was not just a bunch of Somoza outcasts. Moreover, even some doubters in Congress were beginning to concede that the contras were a legitimate peasant army.

The ranks of the contras continued to swell, aided by what seemed to be a never-ending procession of Sandinista stupidities. Their economic policies had not only alienated their trading partners, they put the Nicaraguan GNP into a tailspin. Consumer goods were in short supply and rationing was imposed. To bulk up the armed forces, they also instituted conscription, which they enforced by denying ration cards to families who couldn't prove that their children had enlisted. City youth were drafted into the militia and with little training or preparation thrown into the hills against the contras. With increasing frequency, these middle-class children of middle-class parents were being returned home dead. Although conscription was promoted as an effort to generate unity against "the common enemy," in general it worked against the Sandinistas rather than for them.

The most moronic of their efforts were launched against the Catholic Church, in particular against Miguel Obando y Bravo, the archbishop of Managua. With the possible but fading exception of Eden Pastora, Obando was the most highly regarded man in Nicaragua. His strength of character imbued him with a holy aura and an inviolable prestige not unlike that of Bishop Desmond Tutu of South Africa.

As if that were not enough, the Sandinistas also took on the pope. In March, Pope John Paul II visited Nicaragua, the first ever visit by the pontiff to the country. Nicaraguan Catholics (95 percent of the country) were ecstatic, but on the day of his homily in Managua, the Sandinistas planted a small group of demonstrators right below the dais. Shouting slogans and catcalls, they disrupted the speech by His Holiness. Sandinista audio technicians turned down the pope's microphone and amplified the demonstrators. It reminded John Paul all too much of his days struggling against the Communists in his native Poland, and his experience gave Archbishop Obando y Bravo about the best possible ally he could have hoped for.

During 1983, the need for a real FDN medical facility became acute, for we were taking casualties. Gradually, a medical component was put together, which would in time become a full-scale field hospital. Initially, it was staffed by Nicaraguan physicians and specialists who had fled or been forced out of Nicaragua by the Sandinistas and had largely relocated to the United States. At their own expense these individuals came on weekends to the Nicaraguan border area to perform operations and train medics and nurses. We owed them much.

However, we had big problems with insecure communications. We had provided the FDN guerrilla teams penetrating Nicaragua with radios and onetime code pads to encipher messages. Of course, it took time to encipher the messages, so they rarely did, often with disastrous consequences. Our guerrillas found themselves ambushed by waiting Sandinistas who had intercepted their message traffic in the clear. The Sandinistas, with East German help, became quite sophisticated in intercepting the guerrilla communications. Worse yet, they built fairly elaborate DF (direction finding) stations, which could actually pinpoint the locations where the transmissions originated.

Within Nicaragua, we stepped up our support to the anti-Sandinista underground. Because the resistance did not have access to printing equipment (which was carefully guarded by the government), we used balloons left over from operations in East Germany and Czechoslovakia in the sixties to drop propaganda leaflets in Spanish. We tried to fly these balloons over several of the larger cities; however, the winds were contrary. I never expected great things out of the balloons, which were only one measure among many.

We managed to smuggle a TV transmitter onto a hill in Managua where it could override the Sandinista TV station. The plan was to have the transmitter broadcast a prerecorded tape of Pastora speaking to the people of Nicaragua. This was a low-budget production directed by Linda Flohr, Task Force chief Jerry Gruner's most able executive assistant. It was so low budget that Linda produced the ARDE flag and the backdrops for the production on her sewing machine at home. She failed, however, to get Pastora to remove his gold ring and gold Rolex for the filming. The insertion team set up the TV transmitter and, in prime time, broadcast the tape of Comandante Zero preaching freedom to the people and blasting the Sandinistas. It had quite an impact locally. Since security in Managua was tight, the action couldn't be sustained, but it certainly reminded the people that the Sandinistas were not invincible, and that at least one of the anti-Somoza heroes was out there against them.

Moynihan, Boland, and the other long knives continued to circle us in the House and Senate. In May, HPSCI voted along party lines to zero out contra funding. A few days later, Casey testified before SSCI trying to salvage the situation. To restore the budget, he agreed to revise the Reagan Finding of November 1981 to broaden it beyond arms interdiction as the rationale for our involvement.

Meanwhile, pressure was building up within the administration against Thomas Enders, the assistant secretary of state for inter-American affairs, and his two-pronged approach to dealing with Nicaragua. The diplomatic track and the covert-operations track were always in his mind tandem approaches with the same objective, but no one made this crystal clear to Congress and the public. Richard Stone, a former senator from Florida, was brought in as a special negotiator to deal with the Sandinistas, but by this time, the paramilitary operations had submerged the diplomatic in the eyes of the media and Congress.

In May of 1983, in the first of a series of personnel changes, Enders resigned, and Langhorne "Tony" Motley replaced him. I had liked Enders and thought his two-track approach was absolutely valid. I also thought he got a bum rap as being "soft" on the Sandinistas. Motley, however, was and is a boon companion. Born in Brazil, Motley was a graduate of the Citadel who, after a career in the Air Force, had gone into real estate in Alaska. There he became involved in Republican politics and worked for Reagan's election. When the new administration came in, he was appointed ambassador to Brazil. He'd done an outstanding job there, and not just because he spoke Portuguese like a native. Tony is one of the brighter people I have encountered and is both articulate and well disciplined. Moreover, he nimbly navigates his way through political thickets and has an outrageous sense of humor that I find appealing.

I'd gotten to know him on a trip to Brasília in 1983. During the Falklands War, a British fighter had made an emergency landing there. Some of our air-to-air weapons were on board, and we wanted him to make sure that they didn't fall into the wrong hands. It was a ticklish assignment that he handled with great diplomatic skill. Tony took over leadership of the Restricted Interagency Group, or RIG, which Enders had initiated.

Other changes in the RIG cast occurred as well. Gen. Paul Gorman, our liaison with the Joint Chiefs, got his fourth star and was sent to Panama as commander of SOUTHCOM. He was replaced by Vice Adm. Art Moreau, who was totally supportive of our efforts in Central America and was eminently practical and intelligent. Nestor Sanchez was still part of the group, representing the Department of Defense. The two Agency representatives had been Latin America national intelligence officer (NIO) Constantine Menges and me. At about the same time that Motley took over, however, we also got a new NIO, John Horton.

Horton had been retired from the Agency for several years and was busy growing grapes in Maryland when he was recommended to Casey as a replacement for Constantine Menges, who had become a liability for Casey within the Agency. In the end, Menges had alienated too many people with his arrogance and extremist political views. Casey saw to it that Menges got a job with the NSC having to do with Latin America. Although Horton, a gentleman and certainly bright enough, had been deputy chief of Latin America Division and chief of the Soviet Division, somewhere along the way he seemed to have lost some of his nerve for covert action. Some say that he had taken to religion. Menges may have had his problems, but he was fully on board with the operation against the Sandinistas; Horton was never as committed to it. At first Menges continued to attend RIG meetings in his new capacity at the National Security Council. Increasingly, however, the NSC chair was occupied by a Marine lieutenant colonel named Oliver North. North was always supportive of what we were trying to do.

Mid-1983 was a low point in our Nicaraguan operations. For logistical reasons, we were still having problems sustaining guerrilla operations deep in Nicaragua. Volunteers were still coming in. I had taken to obtaining NSPG approval for the augmentation of our troop strength, to show Congress that it was the president, not just Clarridge and Casey, who had a hand in the decision. The Sandinistas were showing no willingness to negotiate seriously with Stone, Motley, or anyone else. Arms were still flowing from Nicaragua to El Salvador, including U.S. weapons that the Vietnamese had given to the Sandinistas. General Gorman was bringing U.S. military technical means to bear on the problem for the first time in any significant way. There was a lot of frustration in the administration.

Casey convened a meeting at Headquarters to discuss the overall problem and consider new ideas. Except for Jeane Kirkpatrick, U.S. ambassador to the United Nations, and Casey, the participants were at the subcabinet level and lower. Not much new came from the meeting. The most lively debate centered on forming a Nicaraguan government-in-exile in the northeast corner of the country. But this looked too hard, involving issues of recognition and the defense of the entity. Perhaps for Casey, the important result was that nobody had any better ideas than the CIA for coping with the problems.

In June, Casey wanted to go to Central America again, not just to go see the troops, but to get a firsthand assessment of the situation from his officers on the ground. This time he dragged DDCI John McMahon along with us—and *dragged* is the operative word. McMahon was not particularly in favor of paramilitary operations, an attribute that endeared him to Congress. Casey forced him to come along, not just to give McMahon a taste of what it was like on the ground, but to show Congress some solidarity. However, it was unheard of for both the DCI and the DDCI to be out of the country at the same time. John Horton, the new NIO for Latin America, was also a member of the party.

By this time our airfield at Aguacate had been improved and was in full operation. We were beginning to have quite a number of C-47s because we were now seriously increasing our airdrops of supplies to troops operating within Nicaragua. Casey was anxious to step up the program to what he thought would be the next level—guerrilla operations in urban areas. We were already making small forays into towns and cities for intelligence-gathering purposes, but he was talking about sabotaging targets and even engaging Sandinista forces. He believed that these activities would be the harder jolt we needed to prod the Sandinistas to the bargaining table.

In this rare instance, I disagreed with Casey. I knew him well enough not to take him on directly about it, but I was unequivocally opposed to what he wanted to do. For starters, the distinction between urban guerrilla action and terrorism was easily blurred. Even with military targets and careful execution, civilian casualties are almost unavoidable. Moreover, the Sandinistas were perfectly capable of detonating a school or a hospital and pinning it on us. Casey's approach risked throwing away all the goodwill we'd built up inside Nicaragua and generating howls of protest in Washington. Casey persisted, but I basically slow-rolled him on the issue. I saw to it that we never really took any action in that direction. I felt strongly that with all the other problems we had, it just wasn't possible to do it right, and even if we got it right, it would still come out wrong.

During this same trip, Casey went on to El Salvador, where, on behalf of the administration, he really laid down the law about the Salvadoran death squads. They would absolutely not be tolerated.

Reports of Sandinista atrocities were finally beginning to surface in the press. We wanted to be sure that the contras did everything possible to seize the ethical high ground in the conflict with the Sandinistas. Toward that end, we created a course in how the contras should deal with the civilian population. The course would set forth the basic rules of engagement, stating quite clearly what kinds of activities—rape, murder, plundering, and other crimes—were clearly off-limits, and on the positive side, listing measures that should be taken to gain the support of the local population. John Kirkpatrick, who had experience in Vietnam, was contracted to prepare the curriculum of the course and then go to the guerrilla camps and training facilities to teach it and train a group of Nicaraguan instructors to carry on his initial work. Later, Kirkpatrick was to prepare a manual incorporating his curriculum and other materials in English. After that, it was to be translated into Spanish and distributed to the guerrillas as part of their human-rights and other political indoctrination.

By this time we had fielded perhaps as many as three thousand Nicaraguan and Miskito guerrillas on both fronts. Our FDN training facilities were turning out one new company of one hundred men every two weeks, and volunteers were flooding in at an alarming rate, given our limited funds to support and train them. Senator Moynihan was apoplectic about the increasing numbers. Every time I went to the Hill to testify, he started hammering on me. In some ways, he reminded me of an Irish version of Eden Pastora, albeit far more pedantic. He'd just stand up and let fly with this incredible bombastic blast of polysyllabic rhetoric that went on forever.

The strange thing was that he could turn it on and off like a faucet. Once we'd stopped testifying, he could be quite cordial. One day after an appearance, he greeted me as he passed out of the hearing room. Not wanting to be unresponsive, I said, "How are you? And how are your silver Alexandrians?" Moynihan was taken aback. He had no immediate recollection of me in the context of his visit to Turkey in 1969, and from the quizzical look on his face he not surprisingly had no memory whatsoever of the cocktail party at my house—or his near tumble down my spiral staircase in the Izmir Palas.

Gradually, however, I could see it floating back to him as he began to put my name together with Istanbul. A broad smile crept across his face. "Oh, yes," he said with all the charm he was famous for. "I've still got those, and I want to tell you that is my retirement." Naturally, this interlude didn't stop him from lambasting me the next time I came to testify.

At both Motley's RIG meetings and gatherings of the National Security Planning Group (NSPG), members of the administration were becoming increasingly concerned about the possible introduction of MiG-21 aircraft into Nicaragua. Although the liberals in Congress didn't want to believe it, Sandinista pilots had been training on MiG-21s in Bulgaria since 1980. The Sandinistas would undoubtedly be able to put them in the air. Cuban and Nicaraguan laborers were lengthening an old Somoza runway to the west of Managua and protective revetments for the aircraft were being built—obviously in expectation of the MiGs. The introduction of these aircraft would dramatically alter the balance of power in Central America. The Hondurans had a good air force; in fact, it was the premier service in their military, but their elderly French fighters would be no match for the MiGs. At a meeting of the NSPG in the summer of 1983, every option possible short of introducing U.S. troops in the area was discussed. Present were all the "principals"—even Deaver, Baker, and Meese showed up.

We considered a scheme to take out the aircraft on the ground with an AC-130 gunship, the so-called Spectre gunship. The AC-130 was a beefed-up attack version of the C-130 cargo transport. Equipped with a 105-mm cannon and 40-mm and perhaps also 20-mm rapid-fire cannons, it could put down awesome firepower. Flying at night with infrared assistance, pilots could see the ground as if it were daylight and would be able to take out the MiG-21s in a single outing. The problem was how to cover it—the only people who could fly the AC-130 were U.S. Air Force pilots, and most of Reagan's advisers within the NSPG balked at direct involvement of U.S. military personnel. Training CIA personnel to man the gunship was considered. The aircraft would be "bailed" to the CIA by the U.S. Air Force. "Bailing" is a legal method by which the U.S. military can furnish the CIA with an asset it does not possess. However, once the mission was accomplished, it would be difficult to explain how it was done and keep the AC-130's involvement secret.

I thought I had the solution. I proposed that we take one of the FDN's C-47 cargo aircraft and equip it with one or more 20-mm Gatling-type rapid-fire cannons. Such a configuration had successfully been used in Vietnam (and later in El Salvador) and was called a Spooky. On the night of the operation the C-47, now an AC-47, would fly with the AC-130, but stay out of the latter's way. The next morning the FDN would take the credit. In the end, all came to naught over the problem of manning the AC-130; it was just too difficult to find a solution.

We also looked at the possibility of mining the Río Escondido. We figured the Soviets and the Sandinistas would off-load the MiG-21s at Bluefields, bring them upriver to Rama, then truck them to Managua. We would airdrop the mines into the river. The trouble with mines is that most of them are not selective—and the Río Escondido carried a lot of civilian water traffic. It was certainly possible that we'd end up sinking a boat full of orphans on their way to a picnic, generating a true PR disaster.

Command-detonated mines were possible, but complicated matters considerably. It would have to be done by parachuting special teams into the area and keeping them hidden while they waited for the ships carrying the MiGs to arrive. We had begun training an FDN paratroop unit for special operations deep in Nicaragua; in particular we wanted to take out a major high bridge west of Rama to cut the artery of supply of Soviet heavy military equipment.

The NSPG meeting ended without finding a solution, although everyone agreed that if we went for the Río Escondido option, only command-detonated mines were acceptable given the type of traffic on the river. As we were breaking up, President Reagan pulled me aside and asked, "Dewey, can't you get those vandals of yours to do this job?" He was suggesting that we infiltrate troops to the airfield and have them sabotage the MiGs on the ground.

The airfield was located in the plains of Nicaragua, where the heart of the twenty-five-thousand-man Sandinista Army was garrisoned. Although the contras were shaping up nicely, we weren't ready to infiltrate special teams into that environment with any chance of success. I had to answer, "I'm sorry, Mr. President, I don't think my vandals are quite up to the job."

Knowing Eden Pastora's tendency to play to the grandstands, part of our deal with him was that he was not to carry out any sort of spectacular operation without clearing it with us first. Because of the political ramifications, we'd also repeatedly told him to avoid civilian targets. Pastora wasn't doing much on the ground, but he was accumulating the beginning of an air force. He'd bought some commercial aircraft—a twin-engine Beechcraft, a couple of Cessnas, one or two helicopters, and even a hang glider. Pastora didn't drink, but he apparently took dumb pills, at least on occasion.

In the midst of our titanic struggle with Congress, Eden Pastora pulled off one of the great stupidities of all time. On September 8, Senators Gary Hart and William Cohen were due to land in Managua on a fact-finding mission. When they got there, the terminal was a shambles. Pastora had sent one of his Cessnas, laden with a brace of five-hundred-pound bombs, to attack the airport. The pilot mistakenly released his bombs at too low an altitude. The shock waves rising skyward from the explosion brought down the aircraft. The pilot died in the crash; unfortunately he was carrying some documentation that indicated a connection with the CIA.

Wonderful. Pastora had barely missed killing two members of the U.S. Senate, and at first blush it certainly looked as if we had put him up to it. It really made my day. It couldn't have been much worse—unless, of course, Cohen and Hart had been killed or injured.

The media went wild, and Congress was right behind them. Pastora couldn't figure out what all the fuss was about—it was his first experience with bad press. Meanwhile, I was trying to put the pieces of our credibility back together. At first, nobody was prepared to believe that the attack hadn't been ordered up from Langley. Naturally I was called on the carpet to give testimony on what the hell had happened. I spent a lot of time scraping congressmen off the ceiling, trying to convince them that this was entirely a wildcat operation. Fortunately I had the cable traffic to Pastora to back me up. We had clearly issued standing orders that he was not to do anything of this sort, and eventually I was able to convince our more reasonable lawmakers that whatever else we might be, we weren't *that* stupid.

Later in September, Casey briefed Congress on the revised Finding that Reagan had signed, broadening the scope of our involvement from the limited role of arms interdiction to that of bringing the Sandinistas to the bargaining table and pushing them toward democratization. The lawmakers were mollified, but I knew it was only temporary. We had to show results—not just in the growth in numbers of the contra fighting force, but real progress in getting the Sandinistas to sit down with us. Casey's continual chant stayed with me: "Can't we get some more pressure on these people?"

Just as I was developing a really effective response, I was forced to look to a problem looming in another part of my parish—Grenada. All I needed at this point was another crisis, but there was no getting away from it. Although the locale was different, some of the antagonists were the same. We were up against the Cubans and the Soviets once again.

CHAPTER 14

The Grenada Episode

Although I was devoting most of my time and effort to Central America and the war in Nicaragua, as chief of the Latin America Division, I was also responsible for the administration of stations in a vast area reaching from the Mexican border to Tierra del Fuego. I began to see disturbing reports from a small island in the Caribbean named Grenada.

For four years, that tiny nation (133 square miles; population roughly eighty thousand) had been ruled by an overtly Communist government, led by Maurice Bishop and his New Jewel Movement. Bishop had never tried to hide that he was Castro's protégé, but recently he had invited the Cubans into Grenada for a "public works" project, a new airport runway. The Cubans were not just there to pour concrete. They were paramilitary construction workers—Castro's version of our Seabees. The runway they were building was nine thousand feet long, far longer than any commercial airliner would ever need, but just right for Soviet and Cuban reconnaissance planes and other military aircraft.

On Wednesday, October 19, 1983, Bishop was murdered by other Communists within his political party. After more people were killed in ensuing incidents, we became concerned about the agitation and instability there. No one seemed to be clearly in control of the government; indeed, no one seemed willing to speak for "the government" at all. All the islanders knew that Bernard Coard and his wife, Phyllis, were the ringleaders behind Bishop's murder, but the Coards didn't publicly admit to being in charge of the government. The situation was of particular concern because a New York State–registered, offshore medical school called St. George's School of Medicine with about eight hundred students was located on the island.

The school administrators had developed a good working relationship with the Bishop government. The school brought in a lot of hard cash because the students bought all of their food from the locals. They also rented housing, had maids, and spent money in the bars and restaurants. Besides nutmeg, the school and its students were the island's only "cash crop."

The U.S. government did not have an embassy or a consulate in the country. The State Department covered Grenada through our embassy in nearby Barbados. With increasing concern, State Department officials consulted with the administrators of the medical school based in New York City. The med school authorities pooh-poohed the danger and assured us that their students were fine. Basically they were trying to convince us to butt out. Meanwhile, however, others began to believe things weren't so swell after all. From his new position at the National Security Council, Constantine Menges became alarmed at the prospect of yet another Soviet puppet regime in the Western Hemisphere with a brand-new military runway and a deep-water port. To Menges it seemed highly unlikely that all of that Cuban/Soviet activity was intended to boost the sales of Grenada's main export—nutmeg. It seemed far more likely that it was meant to boost Cuba's main export—revolution.

Others in the administration agreed with Menges, and they had the assessment of Tom Adams, the prime minister of Barbados, to back them up. I had come to know Adams on one of my trips. A British-trained barrister, he was a decent, thoughtful, intelligent man, a class act. Moreover, he'd done a remarkable job as prime minister of his country. Barbados had a stable, democratic model government that was admired throughout the Caribbean. If revolution was to be exported out of Grenada, it didn't take much imagination to figure out that Barbados and other islands would be likely targets.

In the early spring of 1983, increasing Soviet and Cuban activity in Grenada and the establishment of a military dictatorship in the former Dutch colony of Surinam on South America's northeast coast had alarmed Assistant Secretary of State Tom Enders. He proposed to Casey the formation of a military rapid deployment force in the Caribbean for possible intervention in these and future situations. The force would be composed of troops from Barbados and Jamaica, the only two Caribbean island nations with (minuscule) armies, and augmented by the Panamanian Defense Forces and a special Venezuelan commando unit. The United States would provide equipment, training, and transport. Casey liked the concept. I discussed it with Colonel Manuel Noriega in Panama, the Venezuelans, and Prime Minister Adams. Noriega and the Venezuelans were willing to consider the proposal. Adams was enthused, but we never got beyond the talking stage and eventually the Venezuelans had cold feet.

One of our biggest problems was that our intelligence about Grenada was lousy. Given what we knew the Cubans were up to, it should have been better. All we had was sporadic intelligence from agents who visited periodically, such as a leftist Caribbean journalist, who later turned out to have been doubled by the Cubans. Because we had no case officers on the island, we did not have a flow of current intelligence, and the British didn't have much either. We were operating virtually in the dark, without any means of monitoring the situation. I immediately moved to increase our intelligence-gathering capability, even before I knew what kind of action might be forthcoming.

Clearly, a lot of fighting was still going on within the ruling elite. Both Prime Minister Adams of Barbados and the U.S. ambassador to Barbados, Milan Bish, were pressing the United States for action. For Bish, who was a political appointee and a decent man, things didn't go fast enough. Not wise in the ways of bureaucracy, Bish would "back-channel" messages (use CIA rather than embassy communications) to me for the White House. This, of course, didn't endear him to Tony Motley. Bish meant well. Things were tense. Reagan advisers in the White House were reluctant to look as though the United States were acting unilaterally, but they were certainly taking both the vulnerability of the students and Menges's analysis seriously.

Meanwhile, back in Washington on Thursday the twentieth, National Security Adviser Bud McFarlane's deputy, Vice Adm. John Poindexter, convened a meeting of the Crisis Preplanning Group (CPPG) to discuss the problem. The group that met consisted primarily of the core members of the Latin American Restricted Interagency Group, or RIG—Tony Motley, Oliver North, Constantine Menges, Nestor Sanchez, Vice Adm. Art Moreau, and me. We met in Room 208 of the Old Executive Office Building, which North had just reconfigured with screens and monitors as a roomier, more high-tech version of the White House Situation Room. This was its maiden voyage. After assessing the situation on Grenada, gauging how it was likely to evolve over the next few days, and examining our options, we concurred on a course of action and prepared a recommendation to intervene for the National Security Planning Group (NSPG).

That same evening, Vice President Bush convened a little-used body known as the Special Situations Group, which he chaired. In addition to the above players, more senior officials were in attendance—including acting DCI John McMahon representing Casey (who was in Norway); Gen. Jack Vessey, chairman of the JCS; Bud McFarlane; Fred Iklé, the number three official of the Department of Defense; and Deputy Secretary of State Ken Dam. The meeting dealt principally with two issues. The first was the need to have the Organization of Eastern Caribbean States (OECS) request U.S. assistance in dealing with Grenada or, if you will, provide cover for the intervention. The second was McFarlane's idea to detach the Twenty-second MAU, the Marine Amphibious Unit aboard the USS *Guam*, for potential duty in Grenada. The Twenty-second MAU was a self-contained assault unit with about eighteen hundred Marines, plus helicopters, landing craft, and so on, part of the Sixth Fleet Carrier Battle Group. The Battle Group was steaming from Norfolk, Virginia, for the Mediterranean. McFarlane wanted to have the MAU circle Grenada to handle any contingency that might arise. Moreover, the MAU might intimidate the Grenadians into reasonableness regarding the evacuation of the medical students. The JCS were not enthusiastic about this idea and insisted on a presidential order to effect it. Reagan signed the order, and the MAU was visible offshore on the morning of October 22. With that, McFarlane left Washington with President Reagan and Secretary of State Shultz for a golf outing in Augusta, Georgia.

On October 21, the Organization of Eastern Caribbean States met in special session in Bridgetown, Barbados. The organization, led by the formidable yet personable figure of Eugenia Charles, prime minister of Dominica, officially requested U.S. intervention in Grenada to restore order and democracy.

Meanwhile, in New York the administrators of the medical school continued to be uncooperative, perhaps because they were misinformed by their staff on the scene who claimed there was no problem on the ground and the students didn't want to leave.

We were about to have a competent pair of eyes and ears on Grenada, however. On October 21, I told Linda Flohr, a case officer, to travel from Barbados to Grenada with State Department officer Ken Kurze and a British representative. Her purpose was to collect intelligence. The State Department handled routine consular matters on Grenada by sending three or four officers to the island from time to time from our embassy in Barbados. The embassy staff would charter a light plane, leave Barbados in the morning, spend the day on Grenada, and return at night. Their private plane was turned back by the Grenadians on the twenty-first of October but was allowed in on Saturday, the twenty-second. Instead of returning to Barbados, Flohr and Kurze stayed overnight on Grenada. Using as a cover story the need to visit the medical school and the off-campus students, Flohr was able to observe the Grenadian weaponry and its dispositions around the capital. She and Kurze were also able to meet for thirteen painful hours with what represented itself to be the new government in fruitless negotiations to allow the students to leave the island.

When I decided to send Flohr to Grenada, rapid communications was a major consideration. A case officer collecting intelligence needs to be able to relay it in a timely manner. The U.S. government didn't have an official installation on Grenada in which to place a satellite communications system (SATCOM), or any other system for that matter, and Flohr couldn't run around the island with a SATCOM or any other suitable system. The solution appeared to be simple: we'd ask the British to help us.

In the meantime, we would have to depend on her sending out her reports each afternoon when the State Department consular officers returned to Barbados after having completed their day's work on Grenada.

The British had an assistant high commissioner on Grenada. He reported to the British high commissioner (like an ambassador) on Barbados. The assistant high commissioner had a small office in St. George's, but he had a home on high land with a perfect view of the nine-thousand-foot airfield and half the island. I assumed the British would be more than willing to send the SATCOM into Grenada by diplomatic pouch, and Flohr, who had every reason to visit the assistant high commissioner's home, could operate it from there. Therefore I approached the British through my normal channels and the matter was referred to the British Foreign Office.

The Foreign Office left the decision to the high commissioner on Barbados. Unfortunately, the high commissioner was not on the island and his deputy was in charge. Deputies tend to be insecure in the absence of their boss. He refused to send in the SATCOM. Needless to say, most of the British who knew what was going on were chagrined, and the assistant high commissioner was beside himself. They, of course, were mindful of our support to them during the Falkland Islands War.

Without the SATCOM, and indeed without secure communications of any kind, Flohr's only choices were to continue to send out reports with her State colleagues returning to Barbados or to improvise—and that she did. The Grenada government supplied Flohr and her State colleagues with cars and young, heavily armed soldiers as drivers, who were to ensure that they did not roam around at will. But the soldiers really didn't know what to make of Flohr, referring to her as "girl" or "lady." Undoubtedly, because she was a woman, she got away with more than a male case officer would have. She had extraordinary freedom of movement, particularly around the sensitive airfield, and her intelligence reports reflected this.

On Saturday, October 22, with Reagan in Augusta with Shultz and McFarlane, Vice President Bush convened another meeting of his Special Situations Group (SSG) to consider Eugenia Charles's request. The participants were about the same as at the previous meeting. After considerable discussion, the SSG recommended intervention, and Vice President Bush got on the secure phone to Augusta. Even though President Reagan was on the golf course, the Secret Service and his vital communications link to Washington were right there with him. Bush put the president on the speakerphone and went through our recommendation and how it was reached. Reagan consulted briefly with Shultz and McFarlane, then said, "Let's do it."

The SSG also dealt with other issues before breaking up, including when President Reagan should telephone British prime minister Thatcher. After all, we were about to take down a member of the British Commonwealth of Nations. Decision: notify her at the last minute. There would be no briefings of the media and no media to accompany the troops (even the president's press secretary was to be kept in the dark). Lacking time to arrange for other Caribbean troops—what there were of them—to accompany our forces, it was decided that Marine major general George Crist would shuttle among the Caribbean nations lining up their military and police contingents for deployment as a security force after the completion of the military operation.

Finally, we needed to have Sir Paul Scoon, the governor general of Grenada, the representative of the British queen, sign a document requesting U.S. intervention. He apparently favored this action, but he was under house arrest. Although we had access to him, for security reasons we didn't want his signing in advance of hostilities. Therefore, a helicopter with officers bearing the document would go to his residence shortly after hostilities commenced. This legal nicety for the lawyers was almost a debacle in the execution.

On the surface, it looked like a go. After all, the president had given the order, but strangely it was an equivocal go as far as the U.S. military was concerned; they really wanted no part of it.

Meanwhile, as usual, the Clandestine Services marched to the president's orders. So did the State Department, for once—with Tony Motley's boot firmly up their ass. I returned to Headquarters and briefed key officers. We had already set up the Grenada Task Force to handle our activities connected with the intervention, with my deputy Herman Peklo [F] in charge. The chief of the responsible branch for the area, Norman Abood [F], a bright, aggressive, and resourceful officer, made ready to deploy to Barbados, pending going over to Grenada to take command of our operation there. We knew about eight hundred or so Cubans were on Grenada. Although most of them were military construction workers, we still wanted to debrief them and if possible recruit some of them. Therefore, fifty-two officers with good Spanish from various locations throughout Latin America were instructed to stand by for further orders.

Our job was to provide as much intelligence support to the military as we could. Aside from Flohr's report on the gun positions and the obstacles placed on the runway, some of which could be confirmed by aerial reconnaissance, we had precious little to add. Although most of the weaponry on the island was not very sophisticated, the Grenadians did have about one hundred Soviet-supplied twin-barrel, non–radar-controlled ZU-23-mm antiaircraft guns. They also had 12.7-mm heavy machine guns, often in quad mounts, which are good antiaircraft and antihelicopter weapons, as we found to our sorrow in Vietnam. We believed that these guns probably represented the most lethal weapons that our troops would encounter, aside from a few clunky Soviet armored personnel carriers with machine guns. Thanks to Flohr, we knew generally where some of these guns were being emplaced, but the junglelike growth on the island made pinpointing them with aerial reconnaissance unlikely in many instances. However, there was a solution.

Several years earlier, the Agency, in partnership with the Army, had developed small helicopters that made little noise as they flew and hovered. They were equipped with FLIRS, forward-looking infrared devices, which allow the operator to see at night almost as if in daylight. We believed that by deploying these helicopters, we could detect most of the heavy-machine-gun positions our troops would face. Thus, we leased two commercial versions of the C-130 Hercules aircraft and loaded two of the helicopters on each. With the permission of the Barbados government, they arrived there early Friday morning, the twenty-first. At one o'clock Friday morning, Prime Minister Tom Adams came out personally to the airfield to greet them. This was his first indication that the United States might be serious about doing something about the thugs on Grenada.

On the evening of October 22, as Admiral Moreau had previously requested, I showed up at the Pentagon for a meeting with Adm. Wesley McDonald, commander in chief of the Atlantic (CINCLANT), who had been put in overall command of the Grenada operation. The other participants were Moreau and McDonald's J-2 or intelligence officer, Capt. Tom Brooks, whom I knew by reputation from Turkey, where he had served in the mid-1960s.

I briefed McDonald on the Grenadian situation as we saw it and explained what Flohr could do and not do because of the lack of electronic communications. In great detail, I went over our deployment of the silent helicopters and told him we would begin flying to locate the gun positions when he so ordered. He acknowledged all of this but made no requests, except for his desire to have a Clandestine Services officer assigned to his command for the duration to handle any operational requirements. He already had an officer from the CIA's Directorate of Intelligence permanently assigned to his command.

The next event that affected Grenada came from out of the blue. On Sunday, October 23, Islamic terrorists on a suicide mission drove a truck loaded with explosives into the Marine barracks in Beirut. There were over 240 dead and 80 wounded. A somber and shaken President Reagan, together with McFarlane and Shultz, cut short his trip to Georgia and flew back to the capital.

Although they were reeling from the tragedy in Beirut, the Joint Chiefs saw Reagan's return to Washington as a chance to second-guess the operation in Grenada. They and Secretary of Defense Weinberger requested a meeting of the NSPG on the issue. When you carefully examine the logic of it, it was pretty damned cheeky. It was as if the Joint Chiefs were saying to the president, "Because Vice President Bush was sitting in your chair when this operation was green-lighted the first time, maybe you didn't really mean it. Wouldn't you like to think again?"

There was still some question in Washington as to whether the medical students on Grenada were frightened and really wanted to leave. It was a key issue on whether to intervene. I was in my office at Headquarters on Sunday in the late afternoon of October 23, waiting to go with acting DCI McMahon to the NSPG meeting, when I was handed an intelligence report from Flohr.

She had sent out this crucial information in a letter to her husband, who was on Barbados. She simply included her report within a letter to her husband and "mailed" it with one of her fellow consular officers. She reported that contrary to what the State Department had heard from college authorities in New York, the medical students were frightened and they all wanted out. Furthermore, some said they were being intimidated by their school administration. In fact, the school's authorities were pressuring the students by insisting that they would not refund the tuition of any student who chose to leave. Although the report had been automatically disseminated to all appropriate recipients, I brought it along to the meeting.

The worst nightmare of the administration had been that we would launch a full-scale assault of Grenada to rescue the students, only to find ourselves forcibly tearing them out of their quarters and off the beaches to "liberate" them and bring them home. Flohr's report made that scenario unlikely.

McMahon and I drove down to the White House Situation Room for the NSPG meeting. Casey was still in Norway. Everyone present was warily circling the question of whether Reagan's return put the decision to go back on the table. The major players were clearly holding their cards close to the vest. McMahon slid Flohr's report across the table to the president. He had not seen it before, nor had anyone else. The president read it aloud. Weinberger asked that the room be cleared, which meant getting rid of the "plus ones" and going to that dangerous configuration of "principals only."

After perhaps twenty minutes the meeting ended and McMahon gave me the thumbs-up. On the way back to Headquarters, McMahon told me that in the principals-only meeting Gen. Jack Vessey, speaking for the

Joint Chiefs of Staff, had referred to the president's upcoming reelection campaign and the wisdom of the Grenada intervention in that context. The president replied, "General Vessey, my reelection and national security issues are very divisible. We go."

With this reaffirmation to intervene and with the early-morning hours of Tuesday, October 25, selected as the assault date, pandemonium broke out within the military. Although the Marines (and by extension the Navy) were circling the island (thanks to McFarlane's foresight), none of the other services were willing to leave all the action to them. No one wanted to be left out of the first real military action since Vietnam, but this zeal had virtually nothing to do with Grenada, and everything to do with justifying military budgets on Capitol Hill.

The Army's regular units had to get a piece; the Air Force had to get in on the act; and then there were the Special Forces and the Rangers. I assume the military had a contingency plan for the assault on Grenada, but perhaps it wasn't dusted off until the evening of the twenty-third because nobody in the Pentagon had really believed they would have to go in. It looked that way from all the confusion surrounding the assault. Units seemed to be committed without coordination with others. All of the services seemed to have different radios or at least ciphers and had trouble communicating with one another.

In the midst of all this, a group of Navy SEALs were dropped in the water off Grenada to provide advance reconnaissance on the new runway and to set up homing devices near it for our aircraft. The weather conditions for this operation were marginal, and tragically four of the SEALs failed to make it to the Boston whaler boats waiting in the water. The remainder of the team had to abort when they spotted a Grenadian patrol boat. I had still not received instructions from Admiral McDonald to fly over the Grenadian gun positions. My officer at McDonald's command was brushed off by Captain Brooks when he asked about it.

Over the weekend, Castro dispatched a supposedly hotshot Cuban Army officer, Col. Pedro Comas Tortola, and others to Grenada to prepare its defense. They landed at Pearls Airport, a small airfield in the northeast corner of the island. The defense plan drawn up by the Cubans was later found in a government office. The Cubans had based it on what they had learned of U.S. military tactics from the Bay of Pigs incident. In hindsight, having the MAU prowling around was perhaps not the best idea, because it caused the Grenadians to refuse to negotiate the evacuation of the students. The Cubans told them they needed the students for hostages when the Marines came across the beach. This was the reason for all the Grenadian gun emplacements along the beach in front of the medical school campus—the Cubans apparently never anticipated a paratroop assault. Having cluttered up the nine-thousand-foot runway with bulldozers and other junk, they thought no aircraft could land and placed only one antiaircraft gun nearby. It seemed never to have occurred to the military "genius" Colonel Tortola that troops might parachute in, jump-start the heavy equipment on the runway, and drive it off, allowing our planes to land. Which is what happened. Once repatriated, Tortola was sent by Castro to Angola, where he was killed in the fighting.

Back at Headquarters after the NSPG meeting, I notified Flohr of the assault date and that she should be at the governor general's residence on the morning we went into Grenada, to be evacuated by the helicopter bringing in the team with the legal document for the governor general to sign. We also sent her a Motorola handheld radio of limited range, for passing intelligence to a CIA-controlled yacht that we were positioning off Grenada specifically to receive her transmissions. However, the U.S. Navy shooed all the private yachts out of the area, and we were unable to coordinate quickly enough with the Navy to allow our yacht to remain in place.

Flohr received this message the morning of the twenty-fourth. That afternoon she went up to the governor general's residence to visit Sir Paul. He was still under house arrest and the area was ringed with armored personnel carriers and antiaircraft guns because Maurice Bishop's killer, Bernard Coard, lived in a mansion next door. Noting no proper landing site for our helicopter within two miles of the governor general's residence, except perhaps for its tennis court, she said good-bye to Sir Paul, adding that she was sure the United States would do everything to free his country, and went back to her hotel. There, failing to make contact with her radio, she telephoned our facility on Barbados. She reported on the military dispositions around the governor general's residence, the lack of a landing site, and the gun positions she had observed on the beaches in front of the medical school on her way to her hotel. This was against security procedures enacted for her safety, but the situation clearly called for it. She then wisely departed for the safety of the British assistant high commissioner's home, where she continued to try to establish radio contact.

At first light on Tuesday, October 25, the main part of the operation began, with the various American forces approaching the island from all directions. Ranger units dropped on the not-yet-completed Cuban runway. Marines landed on the east coast, near the Pearls Airport. Resistance was relatively light, although the Rangers were taking casualties. They cleared the runway and planes with additional troops poured in.

The CIA and the State Department had been asked to perform a small but crucial mission: to deliver the letter requesting U.S. intervention to

Governor General Scoon for his signature and to evacuate him and Lady Scoon from their residence.

At least as important as the mission we were asked to accomplish was the one that went unasked for. The Pentagon never took us up on our offer to fly reconnaissance of the antiaircraft machine-gun emplacements. Our silent helicopters never left the field, but we soon had reason to wish they had. To deliver the letter, the military provided a Black Hawk helicopter from Barbados at first light on October 25 after the commencement of hostilities, carrying my Caribbean Branch chief, Norman Abood, a State Department officer, a few members of Navy SEAL Team Six to secure the area, and a CIA radio operator. As the helicopter made its approach to the governor general's residence, it was hit by antiaircraft fire and nearly blasted out of the air. The machine-gun positions were there, just as we had expected they would be and as Flohr had reported. Given what we knew or suspected, why did we go in? There was little choice. Sir Paul's signature and above all his safety were paramount political considerations.

The SEALs bravely slid to the ground on their slick ropes. However, the helicopter had been so badly hit that it could hardly fly. It departed for the USS *Guam* offshore, with everyone else (and the letter) still on board. The letter to Governor General Scoon was not delivered until much later. When the helicopter landed on deck, the pilot couldn't shut down its engines. The ship's crew had to douse it with fire hoses and basically drown the engines until they stalled out. Injuries to Abood and others on board were mercifully minor. It could have been much worse, but I was appalled that it had happened at all. The military had not taken out the gun emplacements because they didn't have enough precise information about them—the very information that we had offered to obtain for them.

As the assault continued, resistance stiffened, and our troops were not prepared to deal with it. A SEAL unit that had been assigned to hit the radio station ran into such heavy fire that it had to pull back; some Marines from the east side of the island were brought in to solve the problem. Gen. Paul Gorman's SOUTHCOM Army forces in Panama actually had to recall some of their AC-130s, which were being used without their guns for intelligence collection over El Salvador, reinstall their weapons, and send them in to reinforce the effort on Grenada. The accurate, concentrated fire from these Spectre gunships allowed the SEALs to protect the governor general, and his wife and servants, and withstand the siege of the residence until relieved by other American troops. Finally the Eighty-second Airborne was committed.

President Reagan's conversation with British prime minister Thatcher was not much better. She didn't much like the idea that the U.S. government was taking down one of her Commonwealth countries. On the evening of October 26, I was at home when I received a call from Don Gregg at the White House. Gregg, a wonderfully bright gentleman and former CIA officer, was now Vice President Bush's foreign policy adviser. Gregg confirmed that the fighting on Grenada was still rather intense and that, although an American victory was assured, Castro had ordered his troops to fight to the last man. To avoid further unnecessary casualties on both sides, Vice President Bush wondered if I could get a message to Castro on behalf of the U.S. government, asking him to have his troops cease hostilities. I told Gregg I would try.

I knew immediately that the only available, quick channel to Castro was Manuel Noriega. I telephoned Casey, who had returned to the United States, explained the vice president's request, and my solution. Casey said to go ahead. In the interest of speed, I asked the Operations Center at Headquarters to patch me through on a normal telephone circuit to chief of station Panama. We double-talked what I wanted; he understood immediately and left to meet with Noriega, who did not connect with Castro but with one of his senior officials. Castro, of course, chose not to issue any order to cease hostilities.

Once the intervention was in the mop-up stages, I decided I ought to go to Grenada and see my fifty-two or so troops, who were busy chatting with the captured Cubans. As I was making plans to go, the military was still all over Grenada, but no ranking officer from the Joint Chiefs of Staff had yet set foot on the island. I didn't want to embarrass the military. I called up Adm. Art Moreau to tell him I was leaving. I didn't have to draw a road map for Art. He realized that if I got down there first, the Washington wags would be tut-tutting that the CIA had managed to get its responsible chief down there but the military had not. Moreau bundled JCS chairman Jack Vessey onto a plane and got him there a few days before I arrived.

Our personnel had commandeered a large bungalow on a bluff over the airport that also looked out over the ocean. There was one workable toilet, no water for bathing, and military MREs to eat. Everyone slept on the floor because there weren't enough beds. The Cubans had been rounded up into a barbed-wire compound for debriefing. Although the interrogations were not proving especially revealing, the warehouses where all the Soviet and Cuban munitions had been stashed told the real story. For an island with minimal security problems, there was quite an arsenal. The weapons were not particularly advanced, but they certainly were plentiful—too plentiful, indeed, to presume they were all going to remain on Grenada. The inescapable conclusion is that these weapons had been stockpiled to mount Communist insurrections on other islands in the southern Caribbean. Constantine Menges had been right about that.

There was a disturbing aspect to my visit. When I arrived, I noticed a rather large number of Army Special Operations Forces (here I am not speaking of the Green Berets but a special unit) were billeted with my officers. I was introduced to many of them, and there was a real sadness about them. Abood explained that the "straight-leg" or regular Army had ostracized these men and he had rightly taken them in. These Special Operations Forces had been given some of the toughest and best-defended positions to take, such as the prison and the fort, among other sites. These special, small units are trained and equipped to fight particularly at night. Their small numbers and the targets assigned mandated a night operation on Grenada. Unfortunately, their helicopters were delayed leaving Barbados and arrived at their targets in broad daylight. As they went in, the units took a pounding and initially failed to take most of their objectives. Fortunately, they sustained few casualties. The regular Army, which has always regarded these special troops with disdain, rubbed in their "failure." A sorry, ugly business.

As the years passed, I had much more to do with this fine special unit, and although nothing was ever said, I suspect one of the main reasons why it and the Clandestine Services got along was because of our help during Grenada. For me personally, I have been proud to know and have been associated with such excellent officers as, now generals, Bill Garrison and Pete Schoomaker, among many others.

I was astonished that the Army would turn its back on its own, but I was even more astonished when General Vessey had the temerity to write Casey to complain that the CIA had not provided adequate tactical intelligence to the military during this operation. Tactical intelligence is, of course, the jealous purview of the military, until they find themselves without it. After Casey showed me the letter listing five deficiencies and I got over my pique, I felt sorry for Vessey, who had really been sand-bagged by his staff with this one.

Responding to Vessey was child's play, beginning with the failure of the military to use the silent helicopters, failure ever to provide any tactical intelligence requirements or anything else to the officer I had assigned to Admiral McDonald's command at Norfolk, and going on from there. Then, there was the complaint that the military had had to use tourist maps when they went into Grenada. The Defense Mapping Agency, not the CIA, is supposed to produce maps of foreign countries for the U.S. military. We heard nothing further from General Vessey.

I nominated Flohr and others for CIA medals and signed seemingly hundreds of "well done" letters for other CIA personnel who had contributed to our effort in Grenada. For some reason, it took many months for the medals to be awarded. Meanwhile, the State Department had acted with alacrity (probably Tony Motley at work), and Flohr received the Department's Superior Honor Medal for her State Department accomplishments during Grenada and was handed her laurels by Secretary of State Shultz himself.

CHAPTER 15

Hardball in Nicaragua

"Can't we get some more pressure on these people?" Casey's sense of urgency with respect to the Sandinistas continued to grow and paralleled my own. It was time to turn up the heat, to bring the war to the Sandinistas in a way that would give them a compelling reason to come to the negotiating table.

Ringed by El Salvador, Honduras, and Nicaragua, the Gulf of Fonseca is a horseshoe-shaped bay that is one of the few inlets in the otherwise even Pacific coastline of Central America. The mouth of the gulf is narrowed by the Cosigüina Peninsula of Nicaragua, which juts into the opening from the south, making the run from the Nicaraguan side to the Salvadoran side a scant twelve miles.

The Sandinistas were quick to take advantage of this geographic proximity. A substantial portion of the arms smuggled into El Salvador were gathered at various points on the Cosigüina shore and transported by water across the Gulf of Fonseca. In addition, the East Germans and the Cubans had helped the Sandinistas construct an intercept site on the peninsula. Located near the caldera of a dormant volcano, this electronic listening post (disguised as an agricultural station) intercepted communications throughout El Salvador and from our contra camps on the Honduran-Nicaraguan border. By this time, the U.S. military was becoming heavily involved in trying to interdict the Sandinistas' arms supply to the Salvadoran insurgents, largely by technical means, so American security was at stake as well.

The same geography that made it a good intercept site also made it susceptible to attack. The Salvadoran Air Force, which had a tactical interest in this endeavor, gave us permission to use their airfield at Ilopango, so the FDN brought down all five of their Cessna push-pulls with seven-round 2.75-rocket pods on each wing from Aguacate. The unfortunate truth is that 2.75 rockets aren't very accurate, unless they're in the hands of an absolute expert who has had a lot of practice. The Cessna push-pull is a small passenger plane of commercial manufacture with one engine fore and another aft of the cabin. These aircraft had originally belonged to the Nicaraguan National Guard in Somoza's time and had been flown out by Col. Juan Gomez and others to Honduras when Somoza fled. Colonel Gomez, who now commanded the FDN air force, was a remarkable man and skilled pilot of great courage and determination, which could also be said of most of his fellow pilots.

At Ilopango the Nicaraguan pilots and ground crew gassed up the planes and loaded the ordnance in the pods, then staged to a smaller field closer to the Gulf to top up their fuel. The scene resembled something out of World War II. The planes stayed low and skimmed the Pacific to avoid radar detection, then began slowly climbing to attack altitude. This took twenty minutes or more for the heavily laden and unwieldy aircraft. They were vulnerable to almost any form of gunfire from the ground. The pilots attacked at four o'clock in the afternoon, coming out of the sun to limit the effect of any ground fire. The "William J. Casey Memorial Operation" was under way. The pilots did a reasonably good job of hitting the intercept station, considering the instability of the rocket platform, undoubted stress, and limited practice with the rockets. Eventually the Sandinistas restored the site to operation, but the idea that we could hit them there was a shock. It was a start.

We decided to go after the gunrunning that was originating from the Cosigüina Peninsula and from small inlets along the Nicaraguan Pacific coast. It was time for an operation that would answer some of the yelping in Congress about what the contras had to do with arms interdiction into El Salvador. Sandinista fishing vessels left tiny ports along the Gulf of Fonseca and the Pacific coast laden with guns and equipment and dropped them on the beaches on the Salvadoran side before returning to Cosigüina with their hauls of fish and Pacific lobster. We infiltrated by land a group of FDN commandos into a Sandinista staging area, where they destroyed some of the boats and weapons storage areas. To be really successful at intercepting these arms, I knew we had to come at them from the water, and to do that we needed to contend with the Sandinista patrol boats.

I had always been fascinated by the Q-boats that the British used in World War I. These were specially equipped merchant ships with sides that dropped down to reveal large cannons mounted inside. When German submarines surfaced to blast away with their deck guns at what they thought was an unarmed freighter, the British would drop the sides and blow the submarine out of the water. I wanted to use the same concept against the Sandinista patrol boats that were protecting the gun smuggling to El Salvador.

My plan was to mount some concealed 106-mm recoilless rifles on what looked to be a fishing boat. With our budget stretched thin, I figured I could afford this. My troops humored me and led me to believe they were hard at work on building one of my Q-boats. They skillfully hid the fact that my idea wouldn't work—until they came up with something much better. About all it had in common with my original concept was the name—the Q-boat.

The ever-resourceful officers in the Clandestine Services' Maritime Branch got Customs to give us two fast Cigarette-type boats that had been confiscated from drug runners. We were fortunate to have a Navy SEAL named Bill Shepherd assigned to the Clandestine Services. An Annapolis graduate and naval architect, Shepherd, who eventually became an astronaut, supervised the adaptation of the Cigarette boats, cleverly revamping each one into a mini man-of-war. After beefing up each boat structurally, he mounted a 25-mm chain gun forward of the helmsman's position, more or less amidships. Originally developed for the Bradley fighting vehicle, an armored personnel carrier, the chain-gun could penetrate the armor on Soviet T-55 tanks. Shepherd then retrofitted the stern to be able to hold other heavy items and installed a 40-mm automatic grenade launcher. These launchers didn't have much range, but if you had to make a run for it, they would make life unpleasant for someone pursuing you.

To increase the reach of the Q-boats, we leased a ship whose original function was to support offshore oil-drilling. We called it the Mother Ship. With a small bridge forward toward the bow, there was a long, flat deck for cargo. It was cozy, but the deck could handle three Hughes 500 helicopters, which we equipped with 7.62-mm miniguns and the ubiquitous 2.75-rocket pods. Under the flat upper deck, we installed two hydraulic ramps so that we could winch the two Q-boats out of sight belowdecks and launch them rapidly. We ended up with a great Trojan horse that could deliver the two well-armed and fast-moving Q-boats wherever we wanted them, supported by a trio of small helicopter gunships. To preserve the ship's cover during the day, the helicopters came aboard only at night for operations.

The Q-boats were to work against arms smuggling up the coast from Nicaragua to El Salvador, to deal with the Sandinista patrol boats, and to begin an offensive against economic targets along the Pacific coast. At the beginning of the Nicaraguan endeavor, we had decided to eschew attacking any economic targets. The conventional wisdom of guerrilla warfare supports this decision, but it is wrong as an all-encompassing principle and needs to be examined on a case-by-case basis. The argument goes that by destroying economic targets, the guerrilla alienates the very population he needs for support. Not necessarily. Each particular circumstance requires specific analysis, not blind acceptance of the conventional wisdom. I am not talking about general economic warfare of total destruction, but rather thoughtful, selective acts to conclude conflicts of the type more likely in our future and certainly applicable to the Nicaragua of the 1980s.

The selective destruction of economic targets and in some cases even an economic blockade, if seriously implemented, hurts the well-off minority of the country, which usually includes its leadership proportionally more than the majority of the population, who do, or in extremis can, live on much less and who will eventually seize on the minority rather than the "enemy" as the source of their grief. Countries like Nicaragua, which are dependent on bulk exports and at least a minimum of imports to keep things going, and which have only a single main port—in the case of Nicaragua, Corinto—are particularly vulnerable.

(Unfortunately, I came to all this wisdom about one year too late, and by the time we changed our strategy and began to hit selected economic targets, Congress had decided to cut off funds for the Nicaraguan program.)

So, I told the RIG that I thought we should change our strategy and begin attacking selected economic targets. All agreed, and at this stage, given the limited activity anticipated, no one thought the decision needed ratification at an NSPG meeting; of course, principals were to be informed. The FDN guerrillas began blowing up the odd power station and transformer clusters and hitting storage depots of the much-despised agricultural collectives. Because the Sandinistas were still coercing the farmers to sell their products at confiscatory prices, destroying cotton, coffee, sugarcane, and other crops in these storehouses didn't bring us any ill will. As far as the campesinos of Nicaragua were concerned, the contras were blowing up stuff the Sandinistas had already stolen from them.

In keeping with our new policy, we attempted a major operation in terms of the difficulty of the target—the Corinto Bridge, linking a causeway from the mainland with Corinto. If the bridge went down, Nicaragua's ability to move its export commodities to Corinto for shipment would be inhibited.

We began training the FDN SEAL team and reconnoitered the bridge to determine where to place the explosives and assess the Sandinistas' security.

Days later, the Q-boats launched the divers, and over the next twenty-four hours or so, the diving team made two attempts on the bridge, both unsuccessful. On the last, some equipment and demolitions were abandoned by the divers and found by a Sandinista patrol. Subsequently, the Sandinistas increased their security around the bridge, which made further attempts to destroy it with divers highly imprudent. Fortunately, the

FDN divers suffered no casualties. One who failed to make it back to the Q-boats took refuge in a beach cabin. His distress signal was picked up by one of our helicopters looking for him, and it landed on the beach and retrieved him. Landing in Nicaragua was forbidden by standing order, but on this occasion we were grateful for the pilot's willingness to risk the charge of insubordination.

The Q-boats could hit targets that were out of reach by land, including one area where the Sandinistas were particularly vulnerable—their oil supply. Since about 1980, the Mexicans had been furnishing oil to the Sandinistas on credit. As the Nicaraguan debt mounted and payment looked increasingly uncertain, the Mexicans were getting leery of continued shipments. Meanwhile, Mexico began having its own economic problems, and Pemex, the state-owned Mexican petroleum company, began making noises about turning off the spigot.

The Nicaraguans had an oil refinery near Managua run by Exxon. No port served the refinery directly; crude was off-loaded at a mooring facility, named Puerto Sandino, in the Pacific Ocean south of Corinto. Mooring the ungainly tankers at the offshore terminal was a difficult operation. Pilots had to maneuver the tankers inside the buoys and tie up at a five-point anchoring rig. Once the ship was more or less steady, it would connect its off-loading hose to a large-diameter pipe that ran underwater to holding tanks onshore. Another pipeline ran overland from the storage tanks to the Exxon refinery.

Under Chief Robert Magee, the International Activities Division (IAD) had begun to develop a cadre of Latin American and European officers with particular specialities who were contract employees of the Agency. The Agency had always had people who served in this capacity; however, their numbers were much reduced after Vietnam and during the Carter years. Our Latino officers came from all over Central and South America, and it was interesting to see how the press treated them. At the same time that the Agency was being berated in the media for using "mercenaries," we were also being crucified for using "real" CIA employees in operations against the Sandinistas.

This was not the issue. In a legal sense, there is little difference between CIA staff and contract employees, and no legal impediment to using either of them in operations. However, an internal CIA decision was made that no staff employees would engage in operations, only the support thereof, in order to assuage Congress. The Hispanic contract employees were dubbed UCLAs, or unilaterally controlled Latino assets, and among the crews that Magee developed and trained were helicopter pilots and several teams of divers.

In October of '83, we used the Q-boats to drop UCLA divers offshore at Puerto Sandino to set charges on the underwater pipeline between the tankers and the holding tanks onshore. We knew a tanker was due to off-load soon, and we were amazed when it docked and pumped its load without difficulty. We repeated the operation twice before we discovered the problem. Our divers had blown up sections of the pipeline, but on both occasions, the Sandinistas had cleverly sent their own frogmen in after ours and put some kind of flexible hose onto the ends of the still-intact sections of pipe to make up the difference. On the last attempt, our assault came under fire from Sandinista ZU-23-mm shore batteries, which fortunately were not radar controlled. Our Q-boats returned fire with their 25-mm chain guns while extracting our divers. Even though these operations were not successful, they loved them over at the White House.

In October, we went after the port of Corinto, Nicaragua's only significant commercial harbor on the Pacific coast. The target was the port's single, large Dutch-built crane, which was essential for loading and unloading cargo.

In the evening, the two Q-boats moved up the dredged channel that led into the port from the ocean. One of the Q-boats got stuck on a sandbar, and people on the main pier—unaware that this was one of our vessels—waved and gave encouragement until the boat was able to move. Once free in the channel, the Q-boats came parallel with the pier, and the crews opened fire with their 25-mm chain guns on the loading crane's control house. Then the boats went behind the pier into another channel to turn around to head back to sea. The crews took advantage of targets of opportunity not specified in their orders.

On their left were a series of oil and gas storage tanks. The chain guns fired on the tanks, and one after another, they blew up. The crane was badly damaged and out of order for some time before replacement parts were acquired from the Netherlands. Hitting the tanks wasn't part of the original plan, but it was one helluva colorful improvisation. Over three million gallons of fuel burned. The entire town of Corinto, about twenty-five thousand people, was evacuated. The "War of the Pacific" was on.

By anyone's definition, this was "more pressure," and although Casey and the White House were pleased, Congress was not. These activities brought further charges that we were trying to overthrow the Nicaraguan government, charges fed by the continuing efforts of the clever and efficient Sandinista and Cuban propaganda campaign. The Sandinistas were increasing the size of their armed forces, stifling dissent, and clamping down ever more harshly on their own population, all the while maintaining that our activities made them do it. If only the CIA would stop its aggression, they said, they'd turn back into a peaceful republic.

With repression on the increase and the economy in a nosedive, contra recruits kept arriving in the FDN camps. Trying to make my budget stretch to cover an ever-larger contra army was a constant problem. That fall, we had eked out the equivalent of a not-too-well-equipped F-15 from Congress. To get that, we had to swallow a second Boland Amendment, stipulating that $24 million was the most that could be spent till October of 1984 "by the CIA, the Department of Defense, and any other agency or entity of the United States involved in intelligence activities" to support military operations in Nicaragua. As the guerrilla force continued to grow and the administration continued to call for more pressure, it soon became apparent that we were going through the $24 million very quickly. I knew it would never last till October.

Times were lean, but we received a windfall. Under something known as Operation Elephant Herd, we acquired surplus weapons (some called it junk) from the Pentagon. When the Israelis withdrew from Lebanon earlier in '83, they left with all of the weapons and ammunition that they had captured. Maj. Gen. Richard Secord at the Pentagon had talked the Israelis into giving the United States some of this hardware. The Pentagon gave it to the CIA for its inventory, and we moved it to our warehouses on the Nicaraguan-Honduran border. The Israelis did not earmark these weapons for the contras, as is claimed. They simply gave them to the U.S. government.

We ended up with a veritable United Nations of munitions. There were only a few Russian AK-47s, a number of Swedish "K" 9-mm submachine guns, and other assorted shoulder weapons such as the Soviet SKSs. Curiously, there were about ten thousand German Mauser bolt-action rifles, mostly of Czech manufacture (of World War II vintage). These were from the Israelis' own stocks and had been rechambered from the original German 8-mm to the NATO 7.62-mm standard. Finally, there was a plethora of Soviet heavy weapons, including recoilless rifles and 82-mm and even 120-mm mortars, all with ammunition. Exactly what a guerrilla force would do with 120-mm mortars escaped us at the time, but later they proved their worth in defense of the guerrilla camps against Sandinista incursions.

Congress interpreted this acquisition as defiance. I had unarmed men sitting in tents on the Nicaraguan-Honduran border, but our legislators felt that procuring weapons without using up my budget allocation was a deliberate circumvention of their will. Clearly, not only did Congress hold the purse strings on the war against the Sandinistas, it intended to use them as a rein—and if need be, as a noose. The U.S. military, which had been about to give or bail to us some transport aircraft and other items from National Guard units (which was headed for the scrap yards), decided that they couldn't risk incurring the budgetary ire of Congress and rescinded their offer of further hand-me-downs. These C-7s would have been invaluable to the Nicaraguan guerrillas for airdrops and would have saved lives.

I increasingly had the feeling that we were racing against time. Casey's pleas to step up the pressure took on added gravity. He wanted more ideas out of all of us in the RIG. Unless we could get the Sandinistas to negotiate, eventually, I feared, Congress would cut us off.

Absorbed by the war, I was in Central America constantly. At home, I was a shadow man. I had no personal life. For months at a time I barely saw my family, the other division chiefs, or anyone else in Washington, except those connected with my work. There were other problems besides Central America, such as the drug issues in Jamaica, Mexico, Peru, and Bolivia; improving counterintelligence operations against the Soviets along the Mexican-U.S. border; acquisition of advanced Soviet military hardware; and Cuban intelligence operations (my great "failure").

I really had only two times in the day when I could think and strategize—to take the long-range view. One of those times was in my Jeep. I owned a CJ7 Jeep, the rear of which was fitted with two bumperettes for protection. When I went to Grenada after the intervention, an officer of the Eighty-second Airborne Division gave me a divisional bumper sticker that stated WE KICKED ASS IN GRENADA! I placed it on the left rear bumperette of my Jeep. A short time later, I was given another bumper sticker by the United Students of America, which read, NICARAGUA NEXT! This went on the other bumperette. My friend IAD chief Bob Magee thought I was being too provocative. Frequently, motorists would come alongside me, honk, and give a thumbs-up. Only once (in Baltimore) did a driver honk and shake his fist at me, and later someone punctured two of my tires with a sharp instrument in the CIA parking lot! The Jeep is long gone, but I still have the bumperettes.

The other chance for reflection was in the evening at home. Actually, it was seldom evening when I arrived at the house—more often it was night. All too frequently my son Tarik was asleep when I got home and still asleep when I left early the next morning. Whatever remorse I felt that my son was growing up without me was counterbalanced by my belief that what I was doing was important.

Toward the middle of January 1984, an NSPG meeting on Nicaragua decided to increase the size of the guerrilla force once again, as a means of putting more pressure on the Sandinistas. The administration was highly frustrated. I knew that augmenting the guerrilla force would not bring the solution it wanted. Besides, I could not afford to arm more guerrillas.

The guerrilla task forces were doing better. Monty Duncan [F], who I had pressed to take over our operational base in Honduras in early 1983, had done wonders against formidable odds, not all of the Sandinistas' making. By dint of his perseverance, the guerrillas were penetrating farther into Nicaragua, sometimes almost to the Rama Road. They were also staying inside longer thanks to airdrop resupply—we had caved to some extent on this issue.

I still needed a better idea to bring the Sandinistas to the negotiating table. Toward the end of January, having just received from Casey's office the official minutes of the NSPG meeting on increasing the guerrilla force, I arrived home from the Agency early enough for once to do something other than fall into bed. I remember sitting with a glass of gin on the rocks, smoking a cigar (of course), and pondering my dilemma, when it hit me. Sea mines were the solution. We should mine the harbors of Nicaragua, Corinto and the oil facility at Puerto Sandino in particular. The export season in Nicaragua was coming up, and if we could block their shipping for even a short period, it would be enough of an economic hardship to bring them around. As Tony Motley was fond of saying, "People don't move to the negotiating table simply because it's a nice piece of furniture." To this day I wonder why I didn't think of it sooner.

People seem to get all bent out of shape about sea mines. Sea mines damage property primarily, but somehow they have been pegged as dastardly, inhumane weapons. Like chemical and biological warfare, sea mines have become ordnance pariahs that "civilized" nations somehow should be above using.

I have always found it peculiar that people (including congressmen and the media) who seem to have few qualms about equipping military forces with mind-numbing lethality find sea mines distasteful. The irrational assumption behind this aversion is that it is somehow better to kill people with some weapons than with others; or worse, that it is better to kill people than to cause damage to inanimate but valuable objects, such as ships.

In fact, fewer people have been killed by sea mines than by any of the other means of destruction we have invented over the centuries. Mining is one of the least cruel and most economical means of warfare, especially if you warn your enemy and interested third parties that an area is mined.

Mines aren't glamorous, but they are cheap and effective. To me, they were the answer. I knew, of course, that the Agency had built a stockpile of precisely the sort of mine I needed. We had considered their use in the Río Escondido earlier. These were built out of sewer pipe and weighed about three hundred pounds, so they could be handled without special machinery. Each Q-boat could carry two, one on each side toward the stern.

The Mark-36 fuse system used on them was sensitive to hull pressure and the acoustics from a vessel and magnetics, as well as any attempt by divers to deactivate them on the bottom of the sea. Our imaginative technicians made major innovations to the Mark-36 system. They installed a self-destruct mechanism on each mine, which could be set for detonation at any time; we usually set them for thirty days. Moreover, they devised a self-neutralizing device that would cause the batteries of the fusing mechanism to run down and thus deactivate the mine without an explosion, if we wished. Everything was done to limit the risk to human life, including that of the enemy. No one wanted to blow up any ships; we wanted to stop the ships from coming into the harbor.

We called them firecracker mines because they made a lot of noise but would not do much damage. It occurred to me that we should plan to have the FDN notify Lloyd's of London after each insertion of mines into the Nicaraguan ports. I fully expected that port traffic would be radically reduced and eventually halted as a result.

I was aware of the potential political fallout from the use of sea mines. I knew that as a result of sea-mine warfare during the Russo-Japanese War, an international conference had been held at The Hague in 1907, resulting in a treaty on sea-mine warfare. The next morning, I sent an officer to the library to do some research. He discovered that the 1907 Hague Convention covered free-floating mines, not tethered mines or mines that rested on the bottom. As far as I could determine, no international convention made what I was considering an illegal act of war.

Having checked out international law, I told Motley what I was thinking and requested a special meeting of the RIG. When I explained how the mines worked, Motley, tongue in cheek, referred to them as a "loud fart." He and the rest of the RIG were completely enthusiastic about the idea. The RIG drew up a recommendation for a special meeting of the NSPG. George Shultz was out of town. His deputy, Ken Dam, was a cautious individual; however, Motley got him to support the mining. Casey was also away, which meant I had to deal with McMahon. I was a little worried about how he would react, but he liked it right away. At the NSPG meeting, after considerable discussion of the pros and cons of the mining, in the end, without any disagreement from any of the principals, the president gave the go-ahead.

The 1984 campaign of the War of the Pacific opened on January 4. The Q-boats, supported by the Hughes 500 helicopter gunships and our "mini-AWACS," a multisensor-equipped Merlin aircraft, hit the Sandinista naval base and weapons depot at Potosí on the Cosigüina Peninsula. Potosí was a staging area for gunrunning into El Salvador, and also the home port for several patrol boats. A shot from the chain gun hit the main terminal, which went up in flames, but during a heavy firefight one of the Q-boats had engine problems and was dead in the water. Its possible capture or destruction appeared very real. The second Q-boat was maneuvering to tow it, but the intensity of the enemy fire made its success problematic.

The Mother Ship, crewed by CIA staff and contract personnel, stayed in international waters. It was equipped with satellite enciphered communications (SATCOM), as were some of the helicopters. The specifics of immediate command and control always remained with the Mother Ship, but the SATCOM allowed us to give instructions, if necessary, and to monitor events from the Operations Center in Headquarters in Langley.

For actions of this magnitude, I normally returned to Headquarters after dinner at home to follow events via SATCOM in the Operations Center. Thus I was at Headquarters when the boats got into trouble. I heard Rudy Enders, chief of the Clandestine Services' paramilitary operations, describing the situation. Enders (no relation to Thomas Enders, Motley's predecessor at the State Department) had traveled to Central America to check on his officers, and I knew that he had gone on board the Mother Ship for the same purpose.

I quickly realized from the noise that he was up in one of the helicopters, which was about ready to begin a rocket and machine-gun attack on one of the Sandinistas' gun positions and a patrol boat. The helicopter pilots flew with night-vision goggles, which gave them an advantage in this situation. I broke in on the SATCOM link and, in the most modulated voice I could muster, said, "Rudy, why the fuck are you up in that helicopter when you know it is against our rules to be directly involved in hostilities?" I don't recall his reply, but he argued that the situation with our boats mandated his helicopter joining the attack along with another one.

I gave the okay. The helicopters, with Enders on board one, went in. With the choppers distracting the Sandinista patrol boat with rocket and machine-gun fire, the Q-boats' 25-mm chain guns continued to engage the shore facilities. The crew of the disabled Q-boat restarted its engine, and everyone made a safe withdrawal. I don't think my blood pressure went back to normal until I heard that Enders was safely out of that helicopter and back on the deck of the Mother Ship.

On February 7, we mined the oil facility at Puerto Sandino. This was the opening shot of the mining campaign. Two Q-boats went in, released four mines, and shot up the Sandinista oil storage tanks on the cliff. They got heavy return fire from the ZU-23-mm guns and one of the Q-boats lost power. The other Q-boat moved in to tow it, and our helicopters stood by to provide covering fire. The Q-boats and helicopters returned safely to the Mother Ship. Immediately the FDN made a public announcement of the mining and notified Lloyd's of London and the international shipping community. What mystified me was that the shipping didn't stop—either the insurers and the international shipping lines didn't know or they didn't care.

In late February we sent the Mother Ship with the Q-boats south, through the Panama Canal and up the Mosquito Coast. To take some of the pressure off the Miskito Indians, who were being harassed by Sandinista patrol boats, we put down some mines at tiny Puerto Cabezas, near the Nicaragua-Honduras border. At the somewhat larger port of Bluefields, Soviet and Bulgarian ships continued to bring in all of the military equipment used by the Sandinistas. I didn't think our mining operation would bring that to a halt, but I thought we could give Pastora a hand on the southern front by dealing with some of the patrol boats that operated out of there. At El Bluff, which sits at the mouth of the Bluefields harbor, the Q-boats put down four mines. When these went off, they sank or heavily damaged four Sandinista patrol boats. The Q-boats also shot up the oil storage tanks in the ports along the Atlantic. If the remaining patrol boats didn't have any fuel to run on, they wouldn't be giving Pastora or the Miskitos too many problems. Earlier, a Miskito underwater demolition team had gone in at Puerto Cabezas with limpet mines against the hated Sandinista patrol boats, and this had caused the Sandinista announcement that they were being mined.

Having done what we could for the effort along the Atlantic Coast, we sent the Mother Ship back through the Panama Canal to resume the War of the Pacific. By the fourth of March, both Corinto and Puerto Sandino were mined, the latter for the second time. Despite warnings to Lloyd's of London, the ships still kept coming to Corinto. Not surprisingly, they started to get hit. A Dutch dredger and a Panamanian-registered ship were damaged in Corinto, as was a Sandinista patrol boat. *Los Caribes,* an old Cuban rust bucket flying a Panamanian flag that continually plied the route between Corinto and Havana, hit one of the mines and was so badly damaged that they towed it to Cartagena, Colombia, and sold it for scrap.

Both the Mexicans and the Dutch closed up shop in Nicaragua— which was exactly what we'd been hoping would happen. The Dutch suspended all dredging operations at Corinto. Dredging there was essential to keep the harbor open; without it, the littoral drift of silt and sand would soon render Corinto too shallow for seagoing vessels. For the Mexicans, who still hadn't been paid, the mines were the last straw. Citing the danger and a stack of overdue invoices, they refused to send any more petroleum to Nicaragua. However, the Soviets stepped in and began shipping oil to the Sandinistas. This of course made for one of the world's longest supply lines, and I figured that if we could cut it, the Sandinistas would be at the bargaining table in no time.

On the seventh of March, the Q-boats went after the Sandinistas' oil storage facility at San Juan del Sur, just north of the Costa Rican border. Once there, however, they came under intense crossfire from the Sandinistas and were pinned down in the bay. Again, one of the Q-boats had lost power. Our helicopter gunships moved in and provided suppressing fire on the Sandinista gun positions until the Q-boats could safely withdraw. The petroleum tanks on shore exploded in fiery eruptions, and secondary detonations suggested that ammunition dumps had gone up as well.

On March 20, despite all the warnings, a Soviet oil tanker, the SS *Lugansk*, put in at Puerto Sandino. It was carrying 250,000 barrels of crude oil. Because maneuvering a loaded tanker into the five-point offshore mooring rig was a job for an experienced helmsman, the Soviets had taken on an American pilot working for the Panamanian Canal Commission when they came through the Canal. As he began maneuvering to tie up the ship, the *Lugansk* hit one of our firecracker mines. The mine's effect was magnified because it hit the starboard forward compartment, which was empty. The pilot (who was debriefed later back in Panama) said it knocked him right off his feet. The Soviets unloaded their oil nevertheless.

About a week later we set more mines at both Corinto and Puerto Sandino. An outbound Japanese vessel loaded with cotton took a hit, and several more Sandinista patrol boats were damaged. Then one morning I got a news report that a British P&O (Pacific & Orient) freighter, the SS *Iver Chaser,* had hit one of our mines and taken a large jolt in its bow. Although the ship was not severely damaged, it was bad timing, since Motley and I were each scheduled that day to see Sir William "Bill" Harding, the senior British Foreign and Commonwealth Office official responsible for Latin America, who was visiting Washington. Motley and Harding had been ambassadors to Brazil at the same time in the early 1980s; they were also rather good friends. I immediately called Tony, who was at that moment meeting with Harding. Pulling him out of the meeting, I said, "Look, Tony, a British freighter took a hit at Corinto from one of our loud farts. No one was injured; do you want to tell Harding? If not, I'll tell him when I see him later today."

"No problem, Dewey," Tony told me. "I'd be delighted to tell him." Motley was like that. He didn't shrink from the difficult, and besides, he probably enjoyed informing Harding, with the implication that the British should discourage their shipping from servicing the Sandinistas. I later met with Harding for lunch at Headquarters. A marvelously intelligent and worldly gentleman, Harding took the incident in stride.

Other nations were certainly having second thoughts. After the Dutch and the Mexicans opted out, hull insurance rates for ships calling at Puerto Sandino or Corinto went up. No less than eight foreign merchant ships refused to put in at Nicaragua's Pacific ports that spring. We later learned from an intelligence report that the Sandinistas had agreed among themselves that they would have to come to the negotiating table if we had kept up the mining for one more month. All we had to do was stay the course.

It was not to be. We had made no effort to keep the mining a secret. We'd briefed HPSCI and SSCI as we were supposed to, and the FDN had publicly informed Lloyd's of London about the mines. In Congress, Eddie Boland's House Intelligence Committee jumped down Tony Motley's throat about the mining, and one member started making reckless allegations that we were "killing innocent sailors from other countries." Motley brought him up short on that accusation, real fast. "Let me put this thing in context," he replied coolly. "Fewer people were killed by these mines than died at Chappaquiddick."

At least HPSCI had the decency to own up to the fact that they had been briefed, which is more than I can say for the Senate. The Senate Select Committee on Intelligence was briefed about the mining on multiple occasions. Maybe Casey didn't make a big deal of the mining, but he didn't make a big deal of a lot of things. That was his way of presenting a briefing, and he was already notorious for it.

The mining was just another operation consistent with a Presidential Finding—the idea that he and I should have gone to SSCI and rubbed their noses in it and made a big presentation about it is absurd. There is no legal requirement for the Agency to brief members of Congress on each individual covert operation we undertake. That the mining wasn't highlighted in yellow, spelled out in capital letters, and stuck on the front page of their agenda doesn't mean we were trying to obscure what we were doing. Even if the senators themselves didn't get it when Casey said it, they had hot- and cold-running staff members who were paid to cull this kind of information from the briefing materials we prepared.

We briefed the Senate Intelligence Committee on the eighth and the thirteenth of March—by which time several ships had already struck the mines. The Sandinistas had publicly complained that we'd mined their harbors. For goodness' sake—if the Sandinistas were whining and the contras were informing Lloyd's of London, how the hell can anyone believe we were trying to keep it a secret from Congress? Furthermore, making an issue of the fact that CIA foreign contract personnel were doing the mining and not the FDN, which was taking credit, was totally specious. The CIA was not legally limited in this regard. We were proud of the mining—we knew it was working. There were few casualties. Coffee, cotton, and sugar continued to pile up on the docks in Corinto, waiting for increasingly reluctant ships to come and haul it away.

SSCI members had numerous opportunities to find out, both direct and indirect. Two senators who missed the SSCI group session, Patrick Leahy of Vermont and Claiborne Pell of Rhode Island, were given private briefings. Casey had invited some of the members to Langley for a breakfast meeting. I was called to meet informally with the Senate Armed Services appropriations subcommittee on another matter having to do with Central America in mid-March. This meeting was chaired by Warren Rudman of New Hampshire. We had both grown up in Nashua—he'd lived not far from me and we'd been in the Boy Scouts together as preadolescents. This was the first time I had met him in Washington.

The appropriations subcommittee shared at least two members in common with SSCI, the "crossovers" Walter Huddleston from Kentucky and Fritz Hollings from South Carolina. During my appearance before the appropriations subcommittee, I spoke directly about the mining in some detail. Huddleston and Hollings were sitting right there—you'd think if it were such an unknown they would have rushed to report back to their colleagues at SSCI. Moreover, no one else on the committee reacted to my briefing on the mining, which suggests that it was general knowledge in the Senate by that time.

The news of the mining hit the press in the worst possible way. On the evening of April 5, Barry Goldwater was speaking before the Senate on behalf of our added appropriation of $21 million. Without it, the $24 million we'd won in October would soon be exhausted. Goldwater was recovering from hip surgery, and on this evening he was in Bob Woodward's words, "well medicated." When Sen. William Cohen (who, together with Gary Hart, had narrowly missed Pastora's dim-witted attack on the airport in Managua) showed him an SSCI staff memo indicating that CIA contract employees, not Nicaraguan contras, were involved in the mining, Goldwater overreacted. Instead of checking it out and getting more information from us, he read the classified memo into the *Congressional Record*.

Up until this point, Goldwater had always been a staunch supporter of the Agency. I have to wonder whether if he had been unmedicated, he would have gone public with sensitive intelligence information in such a bull-in-a-china-shop manner. SSCI staff got the speech expunged from the *Congressional Record* as a breach of security (which was no small task), but the damage had already been done. A reporter from the *Wall Street Journal* had witnessed Goldwater's address; the next morning we were front-page news.

The mining became a Big Deal. Congress and the press have this mutually reinforcing relationship—they incite each other to greater heights of hysteria. The name-calling began, and those who could tried to run for cover. Ken Dam, Shultz's deputy at State, said to Motley with a stammer, referring to the mining. "How do these things happen?" "Not so fast, Ken," said Motley, who had almost as little patience for cowardice as he did for stupidity. Tony reminded him that when he represented Shultz at the NSPG meeting, he fully supported the decision to mine the Nicaraguan ports. In a way, the manner in which so many in both the executive and the legislative branches of government feigned ignorance about the mining was a precursor to the collective amnesia that fell over Washington when the Iran-contra affair broke.

When the hounds of the press started baying that the CIA had committed an "act of war" without notifying Congress, no one took the time to look back through the testimony to see what had actually transpired, at least not on the Senate side. We'd made no less than eleven separate briefings to various House and Senate gatherings. Goldwater, who continued to labor under the delusion that the SSCI had never been told about the mining, fired off his famous "Dear Bill, I am pissed off!" letter to Casey.

In the midst of all this nonsensical furor, Vice President Bush and Don Gregg, his national security adviser, did me a signal honor. Don asked me to come to the vice president's office in the White House to discuss with Mr. Bush the mining operation and my prognosis for Nicaragua. We discussed these matters for about twenty minutes, then a photographer appeared to take a photo of Vice President Bush and me; in other words, I was being afforded a "photo opportunity" to show the vice president's solidarity with the Agency in its beleaguered circumstance. As always, George Bush was a class act.

On April 9, the last engagement of the War of the Pacific was fought. Our helicopter gunships were launched and went in at San Juan del Norte to support a column of ARDE guerrillas dispatched by Pastora against that target. Earlier, an ARDE commando unit had failed in an attempt against the overland pipeline from Puerto Sandino to the Exxon refinery near Managua.

Casey was summoned to Capitol Hill to testify on April 10. As we began readying the testimony documenting the history of our mining program and how Congress had been notified along the line, no one had to tell me that the senators would be loaded for bear. Casey was always a last-minute man when it came to getting ready to speak before Congress. It didn't matter who had prepared the briefing. He always redid it at the last minute, adding and subtracting and tinkering with the language. I don't know whether he ever really knew what it took for his two marvelous secretaries, Betty Murphy and Debby Geer, to whip his material into shape on such a tight deadline, but it absolutely amazed me that they always got him out the door.

Casey and I rushed to the SSCI meeting. His testimony was still warm from the typewriter as we jumped into the director's elevator and headed down to the underground garage beneath Headquarters. We climbed into the back of his Oldsmobile, with his artful driver Ennis Brown and a security officer beside him. A chase car followed us. As we drove out of the parking structure, Casey was already blue-penciling his draft, making further changes. On this day we were later than usual, and traffic was snarled; the security officer turned to the director and said, "Do you want to use the equipment?"

Casey's eyes lit up. "Using the equipment" meant throwing the red light on top of the car and turning on the siren. Casey loved this stuff, and it did help us move through the traffic faster, and more often than not he cut his timing so close that using the equipment was essential.

We arrived at the SSCI hearing as the senators were filing in. I was already seated next to Casey at the witness table when Moynihan stormed in—late. His face was so gray it was almost black. Consistent with my lifelong habit, my legs were crossed at the knee as I sat. Moynihan plopped down in the vice chairman's seat and glowered across the room at me. Then he yelled into the open mike, "Uncross your legs!"

It was not an auspicious beginning. Naturally, I didn't comply and the entire hearing just went downhill from there. The philistine committee members ranted and raved. It didn't matter how much evidence we presented to prove that we'd told them about the mining, they chose to ignore or trivialize it, and Moynihan led the pack. Gone was any of the good-natured bonhomie that the silver Alexandrians had engendered.

Meanwhile, Teddy Kennedy rammed through a condemnation of the mining. Although it was nonbinding, it declared that "no money could be spent for the planning, directing, or support of the mining of the ports or territorial water of Nicaragua." It passed the Senate by a vote of 84 to 12. Perhaps realizing by now what he'd set in motion, Goldwater was one of the dozen who voted no.

Chagrined as he was, for the sake of the contras Casey ate crow on Capitol Hill. He went to see many of the SSCI members privately. He sent Goldwater a written letter of regret. He even went to see Moynihan again, hat in hand, and asked him to reconsider his resignation from the SSCI. On April 26, he made a mea culpa, *mea maxima culpa,* to the Senate Select Committee on Intelligence and got pounced on for his pains.

At least one honorable legislator could not stomach the hypocrisy of it. After one of Casey's appearances and after all the witnesses had departed, Sen. Jake Garn of Utah spoke the truth. Rising to leave the committee room, he turned momentarily to his fellow members and shouted, "You're all a bunch of assholes! You know that we got briefed!" Vice Chairman Moynihan demanded that Garn smile when he called him an asshole, so Garn looked Moynihan in the eye, gave him a big shit-eating grin, and stomped out the door. By this time, however, the damage was done: Congress and the media had whipped themselves into a froth. The facts no longer mattered.

We sent the Mother Ship bearing the Q-boats back down the Pacific coast, through the Panama Canal, and toward home. We had placed only seventy or so mines in the entire endeavor. Getting the Sandinistas to negotiate in good faith, which would have been accomplished with another month or so of hardball, took another five years of agony, blood-shed, and dying. Warfare is stupid and destructive, but some forms of it are better than others. That which is of enough significance to advance the resolution of the conflict with minimal casualties on both sides is superior and in a way productive. The mining was just that.

CHAPTER 16

Phasing Down

Everything we'd accomplished with the contras was now at risk. After the mining contretemps in Congress, the extra $21-million appropriation appeared doomed. Moreover, the House and Senate might even zero out the contra budget entirely for FY 1985, beginning in October 1984.

When the second Boland Amendment had been attached to the last appropriation in December, Casey found himself in a precarious situation. Like President Reagan, he deeply believed in the cause of the contras. However, he also knew that as director of the CIA, he had to protect the integrity of the Agency against repeated attacks by some members of Congress. The Agency could not go through another Church/Pike *mano a mano* with Congress and survive with its vital functions intact.

Casey found an ally in National Security Adviser Bud McFarlane, who was directly responsive to Reagan's concerns about not abandoning the contras. Boland II allocated a maximum expenditure of $24 million by "the CIA, Department of Defense, and any other agency or entity of the United States involved in intelligence activities." McFarlane's National Security Council (NSC) gave advice on defense and security matters to the president; it was not one of the agencies included within "the intelligence community," and it had not been an "entity . . . involved in intelligence activities"—at least up to that time. Therefore with respect to the Boland Amendment, the NSC was in legal limbo. (As others including former NSC adviser Mike Ledeen pointed out, if Congress had intended that *no* entity of the government—intelligence or otherwise—spend money on the contras, there existed unambiguous and time-honored language for saying exactly that, and Eddie Boland most assuredly knew what it was.)

As far as Casey was concerned, this was a loophole big enough to solve both his problems. Because the NSC could take the point on matters that the CIA was enjoined from pursuing, the contras could be sustained, and the Agency would stay out of hot water on Capitol Hill.

That may have been the grand strategy, but knowledge of it was strictly confined to the highest levels of the administration. Unbeknownst to me, National Security Adviser Bud McFarlane and DCI Casey had already begun contingency planning and had started to look for alternative sources of revenue to support Reagan's anti-Sandinista freedom fighters in case Congress cut us off at the knees. During the Iran-contra hearings, the investigating committee's lawyers tossed a memo at me and asked me to explain it. Written by Casey on March 27, 1984, it was an Eyes Only note to McFarlane that dealt with obtaining funding for the contras from other countries. I'd never seen the memo before, and I told them so, but they kept insisting that somehow I should have known about it. In hindsight, it's clear that Casey never showed it to me as a way of protecting me, and by extension the Directorate of Operations, from involvement in something that was obviously pushing the envelope of the Boland Amendment.

One of the sources of supply that Casey and McFarlane had considered was South Africa. During 1982–83, I had been asked to give briefings on our Nicaraguan operations to General Van der Westhuizen, chief of South African Military Intelligence, during his visits to Langley. He invited me to come to South Africa to see how his organization provided logistics support to Jonas Savimbi and his UNITA freedom fighters against the Marxist government in Angola and its Cuban supporters. Savimbi and the South Africans had had a great deal of success against the Cuban and Angolan troops and had captured a lot of equipment from them.

My South Africa trip was for information and had the approval of the highest levels of the State Department, thanks to Tony Motley. Savimbi's forces were facing some of the same Eastern Bloc weapons that the contras had been confronting in Central America, and I wanted to know how they were dealing with them. The South Africans had also solved the logistics problem of supplying Savimbi's guerrillas, the enigma that still nagged us in Nicaragua. The South Africans had made some interesting innovations in airdrop techniques, particularly in setting up arrangements on the ground to avoid having their resupply aircraft flying over areas with antiaircraft-gun concentrations.

We had information to share with them as well. Savimbi's UNITA troops were facing some of the Cuban paramilitary personnel whom we had captured on Grenada the previous October and later repatriated to Cuba. Our intelligence indicated that as punishment for their defeat they had been shipped off to support the Marxists fighting in Angola and Namibia. The names of these Cubans might be useful to the South Africans and Savimbi in inducing defections from among them. Moreover, we agreed to broadcast the names of Cuban troops killed or captured in Angola into Cuba as a means of inducing dissatisfaction in Cuba with its involvement there. Castro suppressed information on casualties; families went for months before learning of the deaths of their sons.

I left for South Africa in early April, but before my trip Casey and I agreed that I would not discuss South African support for the contras. Casey coveted the cache of arms that the South Africans had captured from the Cubans in Angola and would have loved the poetic justice of putting them in the hands of the contras. Nevertheless, political realities dictated that the Agency not ask for South Africa's help in Central America nor accept it if offered. In Congress, mixing the near-leper status of South Africa, whose government was still steadfastly clinging to its domestic policy of apartheid, together with the high profile of the anti-Sandinistas would be political dynamite. CIA procurement of "tainted" South African aid for Central America would have been the last straw on Capitol Hill.

To show what a hall of mirrors the congressional political climate had become, however, Casey did ask that I explore potential South African support for anticommunist Afghan rebels. The CIA Afghan program enjoyed great popularity on the Hill—whether this was because the Communists in power in Afghanistan were less mediagenic than the Sandinistas or because they were geographically more distant from the floor of the Senate or because no one's maiden aunt was connected to a religious order there is a matter of conjecture.

I dutifully asked General Van der Westhuizen if he could spare any supplies for Afghanistan, but he told me that all of the captured Cuban matériel was recycled to Savimbi; if I'd been running that operation, I'd have done the same thing.

During the Iran-contra hearings, both Congress and independent counsel Lawrence Walsh made an issue of this South African trip. In his final report, Walsh claims he "decided not to pursue false statement and perjury charges" against me in connection with the trip, and that his reasons are set forth in a "classified appendix." The only people with me at the meeting were General Van der Westhuizen and the local CIA chief of station, who told me that his recollection of what happened matched my own.

I returned from South Africa just as all hell was breaking loose in the House and Senate over the mining of the harbors. By coincidence, all hell was also breaking out on the southern front. On April 12, Pastora and his ARDE forces had actually launched an attack and captured San Juan del Norte, a small Atlantic town with a tiny port just on the Sandinista side of the Nicaragua–Costa Rica border. (Place names, like many other things in Nicaragua, can be vexing—San Juan del Norte, on the Atlantic [east] coast, is actually farther south than San Juan del Sur, on the Pacific [west] coast.)

On the one hand, I should have been pleased that Comandante Zero had done anything at all. On the other, he'd taken an objective of no military importance—a hamlet with a population of one hundred people defended by a Sandinista garrison of just seventy soldiers. Worse, he'd chosen a target he couldn't possibly hold, even though he had reinforced it with Soviet recoilless rifles and mortars that we had supplied from the Israeli largess. The "glorious victory" in San Juan del Norte was yet another in his long string of grandstand plays. From the moment of Pastora's great triumph, it was obvious to me that the Sandinistas were going to have to retake the town, for their image if nothing else. Pastora invited all the media to the town to fawn over him before the roof fell in. Less than a week later, the Sandinistas got tired of Pastora's strutting and gloating and swatted him back into the mangrove swamps that ringed the town.

Pastora's men left behind CIA-supplied secure-communications equipment, potentially compromising future operations. Worse, Comandante Zero had squandered all of his heavy ordnance in his conquest of San Juan del Norte. His timing was terrible. I couldn't replenish the stuff he'd wasted. Our supplies were low, with no guarantee that they would improve. The $24 million was almost exhausted.

After heading back to the banks of the Río San Juan, Pastora was bitching about his plight and bad-mouthing the Agency to everyone. McFarlane at the NSC was trying to pull off what I'd attempted earlier—to bring about some semblance of unity between the ARDE forces on the southern front and FDN contra factions based in Honduras. Alfonso Robelo, who headed ARDE's political wing, was willing to consider it, but Pastora was still insisting on being made the caudillo—over Bermúdez, over Calero, over Robelo, over numerous Chamorros, over everybody.

Over my dead body. We'd given him all this matériel and he'd burned it in a pointless operation at San Juan del Norte, leaving behind our communications equipment. For this he expected to be put in charge of all the contra forces? As far as Langley was concerned, whenever Pastora was a pain in the ass—which was quite often—he was *my* pain in the ass to deal with. It was time to pay him a visit. I had no illusions. It was going to be a very heavy meeting.

We met in a safe house. He arrived with his entourage and immediately launched into his customary litany of complaints: that I gave everything to those Somocista thugs in the north; that, like all of the goddamned gringos, I had failed to fulfill my promises; that he needed more weapons and ammunition. I told him, "Comandante, I am out. I am out. There is almost nothing left."

He responded, "How come you take such good care of your friends the Somocistas in the north? Look at their operations. According to radio reports, they are practically down to Matagalpa."

"Look, Comandante," I said, "how many troops do you have now?"

"Seven thousand," he said, looking me in the eye and lying to me with a straight face.

I didn't take it personally. I knew that in the macho mind-set of the Latin culture, truth was often quite elastic, especially when a man's honor was at stake. In this case, Comandante Zero was stretching it to the breaking point. My officers working with Pastora told me that he had no more than a thousand troops, perhaps only half that, and most of his best officers and men of any real ability, such as Leonel Poveda, had already drifted away from him.

"Okay, Comandante. I have some Mauser rifles. That's all I've got." Sadly, that was the grim truth.

Pastora was furious. He wanted automatic weapons, not vintage bolt-action rifles. Suddenly, he jumped up and yelled at me, "You can't do anything right! Look at this!" With that, he focused all of his frustrations on a single subject and vented over a most unlikely grievance—his underwear.

He dropped his pants. "Look at this goddamned underwear you air-dropped to us last night! This underwear is made for a six-foot-two gringo and I'm a five-foot-four Latino!" To demonstrate, Comandante Zero grabbed the waistband and pulled it right up to his neck. I had to admit that the fit was not good—this was one of the rare screwups by our logistics people.

"Can't you people do anything right!" he screamed. Eyes bulging, nostrils flaring, Pastora was in a rage. If this was typical, small wonder that his best troops had left him.

This was not a private tantrum—the entire scene was taking place in front of his people and mine. It crossed my mind that Pastora's guru and aide-de-camp, Carlos Coronel, whom we still suspected of double-dealing, might carry word of this bizarre behavior back to Managua. Meanwhile Comandante Zero stood there fuming with his pants around his ankles and his Fruit of the Looms around his neck. If only I'd had a camera. For Daniel Ortega, Jaime Wheelock, Tomás Borge, and the other Sandinistas, it would have been the ultimate Kodak moment. Pastora refused the Mausers. Not surprisingly, we did not part on warm terms.

There wasn't much good news that spring. Shortly after my unpleasant encounter with Pastora, I had to fly to Tegucigalpa to see Honduran president Suazo and his new military chief, Air Force general Walter López. In an unexpected move, on March 31, Suazo had removed our friend and ally Gustavo Alvarez from command, and indeed from the country. In collusion with López and other military officers (who claimed Alvarez was abusive to subordinates and colleagues), Suazo had Alvarez taken prisoner at San Pedro Sula Air Force Base. They put him on a plane and gave him a one-way ticket to Miami.

All of us at the Agency, including our Tegucigalpa chief, Don Winters, and the U.S. ambassador to Honduras, John Negroponte, were completely blindsided by the coup. Naturally, Suazo knew that Alvarez was close to us. He was afraid that if we had gotten word of a plot to oust Alvarez, we would have warned him—which undoubtedly we would have done.

From what I could understand, Suazo had become fearful that Alvarez was planning an overthrow of his government and probably figured the CIA would help him. This, of course, was false. We never had any indication that Alvarez had any such intentions. However, other members of the Honduran military possibly fomented and fed Suazo's fears for their own ends.

Much as I lamented Alvarez's departure, I still had to play out the hand in Tegucigalpa. The Hondurans were crucial to the contra effort, no matter who was in command. I had to reforge a positive working relationship with General López and President Suazo. Ollie North and I went down to Tegucigalpa to meet with López and the new military command. The U.S. participants represented the Washington Restricted Interagency Group. Gen. Paul Gorman came up from SOUTHCOM headquarters in Panama; ambassador John Negroponte was there as well.

The Hondurans were more worried about Nicaragua than ever, and they were putting a lot of heat on us to give them F-5 aircraft to counter the anticipated arrival of the MiG-21s for the Sandinistas. They wanted more military and economic support from the United States. They never actually said that we owed them this assistance in return for their support of the contras, but that is what it really came down to. We reached agreement with the Hondurans without any real commitment from our side, although the U.S. military had already taken measures to improve the capabilities of the Honduran Army.

The Alvarez affair had curious repercussions when I was in Panama for a meeting with Manuel Noriega a few weeks later. As usual, the meeting was held at Noriega's home, and he got out the Old Parr and the Cohiba cigars. Something was clearly bothering him. He was pacing around the patio, skittish and irritable, and liquor did nothing to calm his nerves. Finally he wheeled around, glowered at me through eyes narrowed to angry slits, and spat out one word: "Alvarez!"

I suspected where this was leading, but asked, "What about him?"

"Why did you do it?" he asked, poking me in the chest with his finger. "Why did you get rid of Alvarez?"

Alvarez and Noriega had a love-hate relationship. Though they didn't like each other, there was a grudging admiration between them. "We didn't get rid of Alvarez. We had no idea that it was going to happen. It was an intelligence failure," I confessed.

Noriega's eyes took on a cold, hostile cast. "I don't believe you. Why did you get rid of him?"

I tried repeating the message. "We didn't. Alvarez was our key man in the Honduran government. Getting rid of him would be the last thing we'd do."

I could see that I was getting nowhere trying to convince him. I could also see the machinery in gear behind his eyes, turning events over and over, wrestling with several things that just didn't make sense to him. First, he couldn't imagine why we would have dumped our friend Alvarez. Second, he didn't understand why Clarridge—who'd always been pretty much straight up with him before—was lying to him about not knowing. He rejected out of hand the idea that we weren't behind Alvarez's ouster. Noriega firmly believed that the CIA knew everything before it happened and was usually the one that made it happen.

Behind it all was Noriega's clear recognition of the parallel between his situation in Panama and Alvarez's (former) situation in Honduras. Both were powerful military leaders with strong ties to the United States in countries with relatively weak democratic institutions. Now one was gone, and as far as Noriega was concerned, we would be coming for him next. No amount of denial from me had any effect on him.

"Do you know what's important to me?" he shrilled, again jabbing his index finger in my chest. "Do you know what I care about? I care about me! And my wife and children."

"And, of course, Panama," I added, trying for once in my life to be a good diplomat.

"Panama?" He looked at me and spit out incredulously, *"Panama?* What the hell are you talking about?"

His paranoia was five years too early, but from the coup against Alvarez onward, Noriega was always looking over his shoulder, straining to hear the footsteps of Uncle Sam. As everyone knows, Noriega is now in prison in the United States, after having been forcibly extracted from Panama by the U.S. military and tried and convicted on drug charges. Even at that, he has fared better than General Alvarez. In January 1989, Gustavo Alvarez, who had been allowed to return to Honduras, was gunned down near his home in Tegucigalpa. Members of a leftist guerrilla group called the Cinchoneros claimed responsibility for his murder.

Since 1983, there had been blips, not hard intelligence, that the Sandinista government was, for a price, allowing drug-running aircraft en route from Colombia to the United States to make refueling stops in Nicaragua, as Castro was doing in Cuba. In addition, there were persistent rumors of a cocaine-processing facility under Sandinista protection in the dense Nicaraguan jungle north of the Río San Juan, not far inland from the Caribbean Sea.

In the early spring of 1984, U.S. Drug Enforcement Administration (DEA) officials asked the CIA for technical support for one of their enforcement operations. The DEA had gained the cooperation of an American pilot, Barry Seals, who owned a Korean War–vintage cargo aircraft with which he conveyed drugs from Colombia to the southern United States. The aircraft, a C-119, had a rear cargo door that opened like a clamshell. The DEA wanted us to conceal two cameras in the cargo area shooting backward through the clamshell doors. The cameras would be activated electrically and surreptitiously by Seals in the pilot's cabin.

According to the DEA, within a few days Seals was to take delivery of a cargo of cocaine at the Sandinistas' major military airfield west of Managua and fly it to Florida. Because there would be no compromise of the CIA's methodology if the DEA went into court with the photographic evidence, and because it was our duty to support the DEA technically when we could, I agreed.

About a week or so later, I was shown some startling photographs. U-2 aerial reconnaissance photographs showed Seals's plane on the Sandinista runway, but the pictures from the cameras in the plane's cargo bay were mind-boggling. There was Pablo Escobar, one of the major Colombian drug thugs, along with others, loading sacks of cocaine aboard the C-119. Among the others was Sandinista minister of interior Tomás Borge's executive assistant Federico Vaughan. To cap it all, one of the photos showed a clearly marked Sandinista military fuel trailer alongside the clamshell door, standing by to refuel the aircraft.

A few weeks later, I was at the Old Executive Office Building to see Casey in his office there and afterward dropped in on Ollie North. He asked me to stick around to join a meeting he was having with two DEA officials, then produced the photographs of the cocaine loading at the Sandinista military airfield. The DEA officers arrived and explained that Seals had delivered the cocaine to Florida. After it was off-loaded and was being moved by a van, the DEA had arranged an accident for the van, so that the cocaine was "found" and seized. They hoped this drew suspicion away from Seals. Apparently, he was to make another run from Nicaragua, and the DEA officials were rightly nervous about his safety.

North said that with the DEA's approval, the White House wanted to give the photographs to Florida senator Paula Hawkins, chairwoman of the Senate Caucus on Drug Abuse, so that she could use them at a special press conference to expose Sandinista collusion in drug running to the United States. What North didn't say was that Senator Hawkins had a tough reelection campaign coming up in November and the White House must have hoped the press conference would help her. North and the White House also hoped that the exposure of the Sandinistas would help swing votes in Congress in support of funding for the Nicaraguan guerrillas in 1985. The DEA officers didn't much like the idea and left to seek approval, which was given. Hawkins acquired the photos from the U.S. attorney in Miami who used them in the arraignment of eleven people on drug-related charges. The senator's press conference was a media nonevent and she lost reelection in November. Not only did the press ignore the incriminating evidence, but as far as I could detect, so did most of Congress, especially the Democrats. Apparently teaching Ronald Reagan a lesson by withholding the 1985 funding for the contras was more important to them than fighting the drug problem poisoning America.

Years later, a B film called *Doublecrossed* was made with DEA's obvious connivance, claiming that the CIA had wanted the cameras mounted on the C-119 and was ultimately responsible for the murder of Barry Seals in Louisiana by a Colombian drug cartel. Such is the dishonesty and insecurity of our DEA colleagues.

By late May 1984, I had to meet with the FDN political leadership. They read the U.S. press and knew that the funding for 1985 was in jeopardy. Calero, Robelo, and others had been making their case to Congress, with little success. I didn't look forward to the meeting, but they had to hear it from me that the 1984 money was about to run out. Certainly it would be gone by August, and the mood in Congress was clearly to punish President Reagan, and by extension the contras, for the CIA "sin" of having mined the harbors of Nicaragua. Once again, the United States government was about to betray another guerrilla group of its own devising.

My meeting was at FDN headquarters, a house in Tegucigalpa containing both offices and living quarters. Not all members of the political directorate were present. Oliver North happened to be in Honduras on some other business and I took him along. By this time, North was the sole representative of the National Security Council at Motley's RIG meetings.

I told the FDN leaders candidly about the funding situation with Congress, but I also assured them, "President Reagan will never let you down." I didn't know this for a fact, but I did know that Reagan identified with the contras. They truly were his freedom fighters. He was committed and I knew he wouldn't let them hang out to dry, if he could possibly avoid it. How he might help them, I had not a clue.

In the burgeoning mythology of the Nicaraguan war, this gathering became the "turnover meeting" at which I supposedly anointed Ollie North as the new American coordinator for contra funding and weapons supply. That is simply not true and would be entirely contradictory to the practices and policies of the CIA. The idea of my turning over a CIA operation to anyone other than my CIA-appointed successor would have been unimaginable. Now, was North introduced at this meeting? Yes, he was—in the same way that you would introduce anyone who accompanied you. North already knew many members of the FDN directorate because on occasion they came to Washington and would meet with the NSC on tactics and other matters. North was introduced to those he did not know, but I did not pass the baton, as it were.

From Augusto Sandino to Anastasio Somoza to Pedro Chamorro, political murder is a tradition long practiced in Central America. On May 31, an attempt to assassinate Pastora nearly succeeded. Comandante Zero had called a press conference in his base camp at La Penca, just inside the Nicaraguan border. (For fear of Sandinista reprisals, the Costa Ricans would not permit him to pontificate on their soil.) Twenty-four members of the international press corps who covered Central America had been taken by jeep into the rain forest and had boarded canoes with Pastora's men for the last leg of the journey to La Penca.

Just as Pastora was beginning to address the group, there was a large explosion. A man posing as a Danish photojournalist named Per Anker Hansen had concealed a bomb in a camera case and detonated it by remote control from outside the farmhouse where Pastora was speaking. Three reporters and five soldiers were killed by the blast, and Pastora was seriously injured.

By now, the list of suspects who might have wanted to kill him was legion. The only credible suspects were the Sandinistas, the CIA, and alienated current or former contras.

Naturally, Comandante Zero accused the Agency of setting him up and complained mightily from Venezuela, where he was recovering. We may not have been delighted with his behavior, but Reagan's executive order barring assassination was unambiguous, and in any event there are many ways to deal with these problems short of killing.

"Per Anker Hansen" was never caught, but it's apparent that the only people with a real solid motive to kill Pastora were the Sandinistas. They had attracted terrorist assassins from all over the world, including Montoneros from Argentina and ETA (Basque Independence Organization) veterans from Spain. Several months after the attempt at La Penca, an ETA operative was apprehended in San José as he was sketching the layout of Pastora's home.

The Sandinistas had also tried to kill Pastora once before. In late June 1983, a Nicaraguan vice minister of commerce named Rodrigo Cuadra had arrived in Costa Rica. Cuadra claimed to have renounced Marxism and volunteered to work with Pastora for the overthrow of his former Sandinista comrades. His pronouncements were sufficiently convincing that Pastora accepted him into the ARDE hierarchy without further investigation.

On July 3, 1983, Cuadra and a companion died in an inadvertent car-bomb explosion while en route to Pastora's headquarters in San José. The bomb they were carrying—in Cuadra's briefcase—was set off by the high-frequency radio transmitters at the main San José police station, not far from the offices of the southern front.

Per Anker Hansen's bomb at La Penca had also been triggered by radio, and another suspicious coincidence at La Penca points to Sandinista involvement. Comandante Zero's favorite girlfriend was a Nicaraguan woman who called herself Nancy. Virtually since he announced his opposition to the Sandinistas on April 15, 1982, everyone around Pastora had warned him that she was a Sandinista spy. On May 28, three days before the assassination attempt, Nancy hightailed it back to Managua. The timing of her departure strongly suggests she had advance knowledge of the assassination plot, and shortly thereafter, Managua's newspapers published every word of the detailed intelligence she brought back with her.

Pastora came to Washington in July and we had a more pleasant meeting, which turned out to be our farewell. He was pretty much recovered from the bombing, but I found him less flamboyant and considerably chastened by his brush with death. By now the Agency was completely out of both weapons and money; we'd cut off military support to the southern front. Alfonso Robelo had left ARDE and had begun a rapprochement of sorts with Adolfo Calero and the other contra leaders of the FDN. Eventually, along with Arturo Cruz Sr., they formed a new united contra effort called UNO.

In many ways, aside from the dead on both sides, Pastora was the tragic figure in this unnecessarily long war in Nicaragua. Had he played his cards reasonably, he could have had most of what he wanted short of being the caudillo.

I had fully expected to disengage from my role as chief of Latin America Division in the summer of 1984. I had told Casey that three years in the job was enough. Also, I was a liability when it came to dealing with Congress, where sniping at Clarridge had become a popular sport on Capitol Hill, especially in the Senate. If Moynihan and the others couldn't get at the DCI, they'd take potshots at me. I didn't especially mind it personally, but I didn't want congressional animosity toward me to affect the Directorate of Operations any more than it already had. For the good of the DO, it was better for me to take a job with a lower profile, where I would spend less time dealing with Congress. Above all, I needed something that would give me more time at home.

John Stein, who had joined the Agency with me, had left his position as the DDO and been reassigned as inspector general, the Agency's internal watchdog. Clair George, the former associate deputy director (ADDO) under Stein and then chief of legislative liaison, figured he was next in line to be DDO.

The only potential obstacle in Clair's way was me. I think he was anxious that Casey was going to bypass him and tap me to be head of the Directorate of Operations. To some extent, George's concern was legitimate. My relationship with Casey was close enough that if I had requested the DDO slot, he would probably have let me have it. However, I didn't want the job for several reasons. First, the position should handle budgets, personnel, and Congress. Former DCI Stansfield Turner had that one right. After being the target of opportunity in the congressional shooting gallery since August of 1981, I sure as hell had had enough of Congress, and I think the feeling was quite mutual. Second, I don't think DDCI John McMahon, Casey's number two man, would have felt comfortable with me. I believe he wanted somebody he could more easily control, so in July of '84, Clair George was appointed.

I was slated to become chief of the European Division. In late July, toward the end of my time as Latin America Division chief, Casey, Clair George, and I went to Panama for several days of meetings. We met with the Central American station chiefs, with General Gorman, and naturally, with Noriega. The discussion with the latter centered almost exclusively on seeking his help in monitoring terrorist suspects transiting Panama from Europe to Nicaragua. He agreed to help.

The rest of the discussions were strictly informative and uneventful. Casey got a good feeling for what we would be going up against, and the station chiefs got a dose of cold water on what they could expect in the way of support from Washington. Once again, by chance, Oliver North was there, and so Casey included him in some meetings. Much false speculation—all of it in hindsight and filtered through the gauze of the Iran-contra media circus—has been made concerning those meetings. This is the trip where Casey allegedly set up North to take over the CIA's functions with respect to the contras. But it simply isn't true. We didn't take him with us down there, and he didn't go to Panama to participate in our consultations.

Just as I was transitioning to my new post, there was one final blowup in Congress. During our Central American visit in the summer of '83, Casey had suggested that more attention be paid to the political and psychological aspects of the war and to avoid the criminal type of activities undertaken earlier by Suicida.

An ex–Army officer who had served in Vietnam named John Kirkpatrick was contracted to prepare the training syllabus and then train a cadre of guerrilla instructors in Honduras. Once this was accomplished, the training course was converted into a manual in Spanish for the guerrillas. Kirkpatrick adapted instructional materials that the Army had used in Southeast Asia, tailoring them to fit situations that contra guerrillas were likely to encounter in the Nicaraguan countryside. Most of the manual is pretty standard, warmed-over Vietnam-era winning-hearts-and-minds-of-the-people advice, telling the contras how to interact with the local populace. To give the pamphlet added legitimacy, Kirkpatrick attributed authorship to Tayacán, a legendary Central American Indian warrior.

Kirkpatrick did not prepare the manual in a vacuum; he worked in cooperation with FDN director Edgar Chamorro, and with Noel and Laura Ortiz, who together ran Radio 15 de Septiembre, the contra radio station. The booklet was produced under the supervision of a Spanish-speaking woman assigned to the political-action section of the Central American Task Force. This officer's job was to review its contents line for line and arrange its production in Spanish.

Several thousand copies were printed in late 1983. Before distribution, Adolfo Calero, head of the FDN directorate, quite justifiably objected to several passages. One section that was removed discussed "leading demonstrators into a confrontation with authorities, so as to provoke riots or shootings which may cause the death of one or more persons who would become martyrs" (page 71). Another section discussed how contras could "neutralize carefully selected and planned-for targets, such as court judges, cattle judges, police or state security officers, CDS chiefs, etc." (page 33).

At Calero's instruction, eight pages were surgically removed by contras wielding razor blades on the already-bound manuals. Chamorro, whose assignment within the directorate was PR and media relations, had four pages revised, reprinted, and inserted loose where the objectionable pages had been. Chamorro did not revise the page containing the word *neutralize*, despite Calero's objections.

The manual was not exactly a best-seller in Tegucigalpa. For about a year, piles of them languished in the FDN offices, readily available to the press and indeed anyone who walked through the door. In the meantime, Chamorro's relationship with the other FDN directors became increasingly testy, and General López and the new Honduran military command found him insufferable. In September, the Hondurans told the FDN that

Chamorro was PNG—persona non grata—and after a trip to the United States, he was refused entry back into the country.

In mid-October 1984, a copy of the original, unrevised manual was leaked to the Associated Press in Washington. We suspected Edgar Chamorro was responsible for the leak (he denied it), perhaps in a fit of childish pique over his banishment. Chamorro's nose had been out of joint ever since Adolfo Calero was chosen as president of the contra directorate. Naturally, he felt that the post should have gone to him. What had been of no great concern to the press corps in Honduras when it was published a year earlier suddenly aroused a feeding frenzy in the American media, just a couple of weeks before the presidential election. There was outrage, particularly regarding the passage dealing with "neutralizing" Sandinista officials—the same one that Calero had asked to be removed. The press interpreted the passage to suggest that the CIA condoned and actually sanctioned assassination by the contras; the booklet was quickly dubbed "The Murder Manual" in the media. Congress went into a tizzy as everyone jockeyed for position, trying to use the issue for political advantage.

As with the mining of the harbors, the facts got so buried in the ballyhoo that they no longer mattered. The most important one is that the word *neutralize* in Spanish has the same range of definitions as in English, including its primary meaning—to offset, counterbalance, or nullify. Only through our violence-saturated movies and television has it become a euphemism for killing. Many other do-it-yourself guides to grassroots rebellion and civil disobedience use the same terminology. Kirkpatrick, indeed, had not even used the word *neutralize* in his original text; instead, he wrote of "removing" Sandinista officials—terminology that doesn't carry nearly so much implied lethal baggage. Only when the manual was translated into Spanish was the word *neutralize* inserted; with a bit more diligence by our Task Force officer and teamwork on the part of Edgar Chamorro, it would have been removed and the entire commotion would have been avoided.

With the presidential election fast approaching, Casey was under political pressure to appease Congress. In the internal investigation that followed, the Task Force officer responsible for the manual denied her responsibility to the CIA inspector general, even though the insertion of the word *neutralize* had happened under her supervision. Casey decided to issue reprimands to five officers in the chain of command involved with the manual, among them former Honduras station chief Don Winters, Joe Fernandez, who had been head of the Political Action Unit, and Vince Cannistraro, Central American Task Force chief.

When the reprimands were announced, many of the Latin America

Division officers, not just those being reprimanded, were appalled at the blatant politics of it all.

At this point, Casey and I had two different objectives. He was going for damage control, trying to limit the effect of the "Murder Manual" on Reagan's reelection bid. I was concerned about morale in the Latin America Division. It occurred to me that both Casey's objectives and my own could be met by one single solution. Clair George and I went in to see him about congressional testimony on the subject. During the discussion, I said, "Look, this thing is plain and simple politics. Congress really wants my head. Why don't you give it to them? If you give me the reprimand, Congress will back off." It didn't occur to me that I was offering to do anything particularly extraordinary. From the minute we started gearing up in Central America, I had decided to lead from the front, not from the rear, and thus be in a position to take the fall in a circumstance such as this one. When I made the offer to Casey, Clair's head jerked around toward me in disbelief.

I pressed Casey to give me the reprimand, but he was unconvinced. "Look," he said, "the buck has to stop somewhere. If you get the reprimand, maybe I should get a reprimand. Maybe the president should get a reprimand." He dismissed it out of hand. I tried to persuade him twice more in subsequent conversations, and he refused.

Some of the reprimanded officers, including Task Force chief Vince Cannistraro, refused to sign their reprimands, which has no official consequences, but it caused an internal uproar anyway. Clair George was furious—primarily, I suspect, because he had assured Casey that he could deliver signed reprimands and it would all go away quietly, but it didn't. George never forgave Cannistraro in particular for refusing to sign his reprimand, which had interesting ramifications.

One day as my tenure was winding down, Tony Motley asked me to come over to see him at the State Department. When I arrived, several of his colleagues were there. Shortly thereafter, Casey showed up, and together they presented me with the State Department's Superior Honor Medal.

Within the CIA I was notoriously "antimedal"—that is, I was particularly opposed to the handing out of awards simply because an officer had held a certain position. At that time, almost every departing division chief in the Clandestine Services received the Distinguished Intelligence Medal, the highest decoration for intelligence activities. I strongly feel that no one should get an award just for showing up and warming the chair for years on end. Medals should have meaning in part through their being rare. Giving prizes by rote demeans the value of awards for valor and meritorious service that have been hard-won, often at great personal cost. Having said that, my Superior Honor Medal is genuinely special. It had never been given to anyone outside of the State Department before for activities not directly connected with the Department's mission. Tony Motley was almost as pleased as I was, for he had had to jam the issuance of the medal through a reluctant State Department bureaucracy to the secretary himself.

No one should be proud of the cowardly way in which the U.S. Congress pulled the rug out from under the contras in October of 1984. There was yet another Boland Amendment—this one the most restrictive of all—which barred all funding for the contras by agencies or entities of the United States involved in intelligence activities. Then to salve their consciences and in anticipation of the tidal-wave reelection of Reagan in November of 1984, Congress passed a bill providing humanitarian assistance to the guerrillas. Interpreting this law became a cesspool of legal hairsplitting and eventually caused many problems for those caught up in the unhappiness of the so-called Iran-contra affair two years later.

In 1982, someone pasted on the wall of the Central American Task Force the "Six Phases of a U.S. Government Sponsored Covert Action: Enthusiasm—Disillusionment—Panic—Search for the Guilty—Punishment of the Innocent—Praise and Honor for the Nonparticipants." For many in the CIA during the last decade, this is truth.

In 1990, Violeta Chamorro won the presidency away from Daniel Ortega in free elections. The largest guerrilla army ever assembled in the Western Hemisphere had won, perhaps not as they wanted and not with a victory parade through the streets of Managua. But they had won. Those who seek to diminish their contribution to the establishment of democracy assert that it was the collapse of the Soviet empire that really forced the Sandinistas into elections. If that were the case, why is Castro still dictator of Cuba?

There had been too much tragedy on both sides of the conflict in the interim, including the cold-blooded murder of Gustavo Alvarez, to be elated about an outcome that could have happened six years earlier. I was in San Diego when I learned of Mrs. Chamorro's victory, and I tried unsuccessfully to contact Calero, Robelo, and others. I did connect with Enrique Bermúdez. After my congratulations, I asked him for the phone number of Osvaldo Ribeiro, the Argentine military officer who had been the first adviser to the contras. Though Ribeiro and I had had our run-ins, I thought I owed him a call, thanking him for getting the ball rolling and sticking it out despite the Falkland Islands War. I suppose Ribeiro was momentarily flabbergasted that I had called. However, he recovered and rather emotionally thanked me.

Bermúdez is perhaps the most tragic casualty of the entire endeavor.

He was there at the beginning; he was there at the end. After Violeta Chamorro's election victory, he returned to Nicaragua, which was probably a mistake. In February of 1991, just a couple of months after the election, he was murdered in a parking lot. He was done in Sandinista style—two shots behind the ear with a special KGB handgun. The weapon was double-barreled, somewhat like a derringer, did not utilize rifling, and used air pressure to simultaneously propel two AK-47 bullets at a low velocity on exactly parallel tracks into Bermúdez's brain, killing him instantly. I was told that the special ammunition for this weapon was issued only on the personal, specific order of Humberto Ortega, the Sandinista minister of defense, who continued on in the same capacity under the democratically elected President Chamorro. When a U.S. newspaper published an article linking Ortega to the murder, he denied the charges.

PART IV

FIGHTING NEW ENEMIES

CHAPTER 17

Chief of European Division, 1984–86

It was time for me to disengage from the war against the Sandinistas on any number of grounds. I had put on weight and took off twenty-five pounds on a pasta diet over about a month. I had sacrificed any semblance of a normal family life during my tenure as Latin America Division chief. Although Cassi and Ian were now adults, my youngest son, Tarik, was just eleven. He was a bright child who could fix all kinds of mechanical things, but he found school a bore. This needed to be remedied, and I was ready for a change of pace.

Clair George wanted me out of the way, and Congress had seen enough of me, but Tony Motley at the State Department argued that I was still needed in the Latin America Division. Given the cutoff of funds and the likely turmoil within the Nicaraguan resistance, he felt that I had to give continuity to U.S. efforts. Admiral Moreau at the JCS and Oliver North at the NSC echoed this sentiment to Casey. As a result, the DCI delayed my transfer from June to October.

Casey called me into his office one afternoon during the early summer. He came right to the point, as usual: the person appointed by Clair George to replace me as head of the Latin America Division was a really decent gentleman but not particularly assertive. Casey also realized that the head of the Central American Task Force (CATF), Vince Cannistraro, would be leaving his post in early 1985. Casey was concerned about the leadership vacuum and the continuity of knowledge about the Nicaraguan operations. His solution was to select Cannistraro's replacement now and to have him understudy Vince until his departure. Such a situation is never workable in reality, but I didn't argue. Of more importance was who would be Cannistraro's replacement.

The obvious selection was Alan Fiers. I knew Casey had become acquainted with him during his visits to Saudi Arabia, where Fiers had most recently been posted, and that the DCI had developed great respect for his capabilities. Fiers was slated to take over the large and important Afghan operation, but I believed Fiers was needed to head the Central American Task Force. The Afghan operation managed a large logistical supply line with hardly any direct involvement in the Afghan War, either militarily or politically. Central America and the Nicaraguan resistance were much the opposite. Casey agreed and said that he would discuss it with Clair George. Fiers's nomination as Central American Task Force chief was announced shortly thereafter.

George had always been upset by Casey's go-to-the-source management style. In the CIA, the people who had the smoothest working relationships with Casey were those who accepted his ad-lib administrative technique as part of the job, such as John Stein, and even John McMahon (although he didn't like it). Those who tried to fight it, such as Bobby Ray Inman and Clair George, succeeded only in making themselves unhappy.

To get the traditional chain of command back in place, George's game plan appeared to be to replace me with a less aggressive personality and to substitute a more pliable person for Cannistraro. George had wanted to get rid of him ever since he had refused to sign his reprimand over the psych-ops handbook. Fiers's appointment upset his plans, and Casey continued to circumvent the org chart. Instead of dealing with the division chief, he went one entire organizational layer lower and dealt directly with Fiers as head of the Central American Task Force.

Predictably, the understudy plan didn't work. Cannistraro had to leave his post early. Clair George probably would have buried Cannistraro because of his extreme pique over the reprimand refusal. I asked Casey to help find him a job in the NSC with Ken de Graffenreid, who headed up the intelligence section. Cannistraro continued to be a thorn in Clair George's ass from this position, as there was no love lost between the NSC intelligence group and George, particularly on counterintelligence and Afghanistan.

After helping to put Fiers in place and to evacuate Cannistraro, I took over as chief of the European Division in October 1984. I am a firm believer that when you change posts, you should quite literally close one book and open another. This procedure was not always followed in the Clandestine Services, which has security implications that show up in instances such as the Ames case. If a "no legacy" policy had been enforced, there would have been no reason for Ames, when assigned to the Agency's Counter Drug Center, to spend a lot of time in his old division, the Soviet Division, discussing operations and reading and filching paper on behalf of the Soviets.

I turned all of my attention to Europe. I involved myself in the ongoing Central American activities only when I ran interference between Oliver

North and Central American Task Force chief Alan Fiers. North and Fiers were both griping to me, calling each other sons of bitches. I spoke to them twice on the telephone individually and told them they had to work together. The problem was that Fiers's job and North's responsibilities overlapped, so they were often poaching on each other's turf.

I could understand Fiers's position. This was a CIA operation. However, Oliver North's responsibilities were rapidly expanding because the CIA had been sidelined by the congressional cutoff of assistance to the contras. By the middle of 1985, every warm body inside the Beltway was aware that Oliver North was out there drumming up money for the freedom fighters in Nicaragua on behalf of the White House. The topic was hard to avoid. It was the worst-kept secret in Washington.

Everyone was also aware that North was running a huge arms-supply operation with the money he raised. Everybody knew that he was doing this—and that he was not doing it on his own authority. Of course, when Walsh's Iran-contra investigation descended, most administration officials conveniently forgot about North's involvement in running the arms resupply.

For me, Europe was a downshift in activity compared with Latin America—almost anything would be. The emphasis in Europe was on espionage rather than covert action. One primary concern was to stop Soviet theft of technology, often referred to as tech transfer. Through the efforts of the KGB and the GRU, and through collusion with European, Japanese—and American!—businessmen, the Soviets had cleverly managed to get hold of high-tech equipment and know-how that was embargoed under COCOM, the Coordinating Committee for Multilateral Export Controls, an organization set up by NATO in 1949 to regulate the flow into the Communist Bloc of Western technology that could be used for military purposes.

In 1981, French president Mitterrand had authorized a French intelligence service to reveal to us the FAREWELL operation, which had been run by the French against the KGB. A Soviet agent had revealed the details of the Soviets' massive acquisition of COCOM-embargoed technology, particularly computer technology, largely with the connivance of unscrupulous businessmen.

It was a shocking revelation. Before my arrival in the European Division, a number of successful, high-profile, and subsequently public operations had been run to counter this Soviet activity, and a few businessmen, both in the United States and abroad, had gone to prison. A primary focus of the Soviet acquisition activity was computer technology, particularly the Digital Equipment Corporation's VAX series—a state-of-the-art computer for weapons development.

Compared to where we are now with computers, this was the Stone Age, but already the importance of computers in weaponry and defense was clear. That the technology was progressing rapidly and that computers would be crucial in the future was even clearer. Soviet computers in the mid-1980s were extremely primitive and not evolving at a rate that could keep pace with the West. Soviet weapons labs were already in dire need of more computer power, and the Russians knew that tech theft is a lot faster and more efficient than R&D.

I saw two factors inhibiting our efforts. One was a need for greater coordination in Washington among agencies, and I established closer working relationships with them. Secondly, the Soviet tech-theft operation was frequently not confined to a single geographic area. Thus it was not under the purview of a single Clandestine Services operating division. For example, embargoed technology might have been loaded on a ship in Genoa bound for Bombay. The operation had begun on the European Division's turf and was heading into the Near East Division's jurisdiction. Near East Division's equities in India might be such that it would not want to undertake an operation to confiscate the equipment in Bombay. Adjudicating this dispute at the level of deputy director of operations often took so much time that opportunities for interdiction were lost. A more centralized approach was needed within the U.S. government and the Agency, but the best I could do was to create a unit within the European Division to centralize our own divisional efforts.

There was some success in simply confiscating shipments, but this was a defensive approach; we needed an offense as well. However, some handwringers within the Agency opposed aggressive solutions. They feared that some malfunctioning device stolen by the Soviets would end up, for example, in a Soviet airport air-control system, rather than a weapons lab, and its failure would result in the crash of an aircraft full of innocent civilian travelers arriving in Moscow from Novosibirsk.

I had to make a number of trips to Europe to maintain effective relationships with foreign intelligence services. I also played host to wave after wave of European guests who came to Langley for discussions on such issues as tech theft and terrorism.

In addition to my own guests, I sometimes had to deal with Casey's visitors, who were legion. He would see almost anybody; he loved to talk to people. Some were men he'd known from the OSS; others were business contacts. He thought that other people out there, particularly in industry and banking, had a large amount of information. Still others were absolutely off the wall.

If the visitor said something that had to do with Europe, I got a phone call from Betty Murphy, his intrepid secretary, to come up and see Casey and an odd sod who purported to have "important information." Sometimes he did; more often he didn't. If the latter was the case, gentle disposal became my task.

The European Division was and is the largest division in the Directorate of Operations in terms of manpower, but during my tenure as division chief I would happily have sacrificed quantity for quality. I didn't have enough manpower with the skills and education that we needed to do the job. I was saddled with an overabundance of yuppie spies who cared more about their retirement plan and health insurance benefits than about protecting democracy. For them, the CIA was just a job.

It was not just a question of ambition; it was also a question of ability. My staff both in headquarters and overseas was proof positive that the CIA was no longer attracting America's brightest. Many junior officers lacked writing skills. I had no more than a handful of officers whose educational credentials put them on an equal footing with their European counterparts. This is not just Ivy League snobbery. Graduates of American universities whose biggest claims to fame are a lively social life and a successful football team often just don't have the intellectual horsepower to go head-to-head with graduates of major European universities.

By the late 1960s, top American students were much more interested in entering private industry than government service, including the CIA. Although Ivy League schools such as Brown, Yale, Dartmouth, and Columbia had traditionally been great recruitment centers for the Agency, that conduit had already started to break. Agency recruiters began to recruit from universities where the level of education was frankly less demanding.

This situation deteriorated further in the wake of the Vietnam War, particularly after the Pike/Church investigations. Few quality students showed interest in coming to the CIA. The on-campus network of professors who had identified potential candidates for us also eroded. By the mid-1980s, except for certain bastions in the South and Southwest, that top-drawer university infrastructure was all gone.

This recruitment difficulty was exacerbated by a drive to eradicate the taint of "elitism" from the Directorate of Operations. The DO had formerly been called the Clandestine Services, a name that had evoked a cloak-and-dagger image in the general public, and that had reinforced our "elite" reputation. For the CIA, the "elite" status of the Directorate of Operations was a big PR problem. We'd been hit with many zingers about it, both in Congress and in the press, and many people now thought we needed to be taken down a peg.

In a democracy such as the United States, egalitarian sentiment runs strong and deep, and elitism in almost any form is suspect. For those who grew up believing that anyone could be president, it's not a big leap of logic to conclude that anyone should be able to become a case officer in the CIA. And anyone is whom we started to get. Part of the problem lay in the dual definition of the term *elite*. In the Directorate of Operations, we unquestionably did think of ourselves as *elite*—a collection of the brightest and most dedicated men and women our country could produce, committed to the defense of America and one another. The U.S. Marine Corps regards itself in much the same way, that is, as an elite body of personnel devoted to the defense of our country. It is just that, and it has a positive image; no one belittles or takes potshots at it. When we were accused of being an elite in the press, however, the word was the same but the image became perverted. Journalists reveled in portraying us as a bunch of blue-blooded fops sitting around that bastion of privilege, the headquarters at Langley, clipping coupons, giving one another secret handshakes, and spying as a lark until the rest of dear old Mumsy's trust fund kicked in.

Relations in the DO or Clandestine Services were like kinship, analogous in many ways to the hoplites of the famous ancient Greek infantry phalanxes of the classical period. Although a few officers and secretaries had serious family money, the majority of us were middle class, albeit with quality educations. We were not ethnically homogeneous. Our kinship was based on shared values and experiences, and an unspoken ethic of loyalty up and loyalty down. This wrought a consensus on strategic objectives—above all, the containment of the Soviet empire—and a shared belief that the kinfolk's service to the country was not just a job, but a mission and a duty.

You don't have to be Albert Einstein to be a good case officer. (I would argue that officers with Ph.D.'s were not usually successful in the Directorate of Operations because they rarely can see black or white, only complex, murky grays. Thus, they never seize the moment to make a successful recruitment. Their ability to overanalyze prevents them from acting.) However, you do have to be able to make yourself interesting to your targets. In that regard, we found ourselves really outclassed in Western Europe, where our unlettered junior case officers had difficulty maintaining relationships with their more sophisticated, better-educated opposite numbers.

In many ways, being a case officer in Western Europe is a great deal more difficult than being a case officer in the third world. Stations are larger there than elsewhere because you need more personnel to get the job done. When you are trying to recruit someone in sub-Saharan Africa, for example, you can count on the attractions that are hard to come by there—particularly gourmet food, fine liquor, and the latest videos (especially pornographic videos). If you are trying to get a diplomat or local citizen to your home as part of a recruitment effort, inviting him over for some good Scotch, locally unavailable, and a private screening of *Debbie Does Dallas* is a good technique.

In Europe, they don't need you. They've got good Scotch; they've got pornographic videos; they are well paid. Moreover, younger Europeans don't believe they owe anything to the United States for World War II and its aftermath. The young German feels no guilt, and the young French no debt. The CIA case officer has to find another means to lure his target deeper into the relationship to effect the recruitment. He needs personal and intellectual qualities to sustain a continuing relationship with a target individual, to keep him coming back so that development can proceed.

Suppose you believe that an enterprising Frenchman is getting ready to ship a load of COCOM-embargoed computers to 'Aqaba, Jordan, and on to Basra, Iraq. Because you know that the French government will not cooperate to block the shipment, your objective is to seek the clandestine assistance of an officer in the export licensing department of the appropriate French economic ministry, who happens to be a graduate of the elite Ecole Nationale d'Administration, to help you to thwart this endeavor. Over a glass of Kroenenberg beer, the fellow warms up to you and in a friendly manner starts talking about some of his favorite literature, including the works of Albert Camus and Jean-Paul Sartre, or perhaps some obscure regulations of the European Economic Community.

So far, so good—in fact, very good. This is the beginning of an opportunity. You need to see him additional times to continue his development and build up his confidence in you. On his part, why should he do so? You'd better be able to say something intelligent about Camus and Sartre, if not the esoteric regulations—just to appear worthy of further contact. Too often, our case officers had no idea who Sartre was and knew nothing in detail about the European Economic Community. Every time they opened their mouths, their ignorance showed. Not surprisingly, the Europeans found little reason to maintain contact with them, and many of our recruitment efforts failed.

I should probably have been happy that my case officer was out having drinks with this fellow at all. At least he was trying. Case officer developmental activity was way down all over Europe when I took over the division, and one of my primary tasks was to kick-start some of these moribund stations into increasing their activity. Strangely enough, one of the reasons things were slow was the strength of the dollar.

Although a plummeting dollar is bad for the standard of living of Americans stationed overseas, it's made to order for the spy business. When case officers can't afford to go to lunch or dinner on their own because it's too expensive, they know they can still go out for a nice meal on Uncle Sam, since part of the business of developing somebody is taking him out for dinner. When I was chief in Rome five years earlier, the dollar was low against most European currencies, which made the developmental activity of my case officers shoot way up. Throughout the early to mid-1980s, the dollar continued to rise against the pound, the franc, the lire, and the deutsche mark. My case officers could now afford to take themselves to lunch or dinner without needing to write it off as an operational expense. Development activity in Europe dropped off markedly.

Productivity fell even further when word processors were introduced into our offices. Historically in the Clandestine Services, almost every chief of station has had a devil of a time getting his case officers to write contact reports. The result of an agent meeting has two principal parts to it. The first is the intelligence obtained from the agent. The second is the contact report, dealing with operational aspects, including security issues, your target's motivation, current personal problems, etc. Officers reported whatever intelligence their agent had, but getting them to write up the contact report in some detail, including psychological insights, was often like pulling teeth. This data is essential as a foundation for the next officer who takes over the agent, or if the agent goes bad and you have to figure out what happened.

By 1985, practically every case officer was issued a word processor. Now, rather than skimpy or absent contact reports, I began having the opposite problem. The goddamned contact reports ballooned. In fact, the case officers spent more time writing up contact reports than they did out on the street doing what they were supposed to do.

A third problem was the proliferation of videos and satellite TV, which provided new sources of previously unavailable home entertainment. This caused case officers to stay at home rather than seek entertainment outside for the purpose of meeting and developing potential targets of intelligence.

Our troubles with case officers and word processors soon started to look less significant than the burgeoning problem of terrorism. Just as I was coming into EUR in late 1984, a bomb exploded in the hotel in Brighton, England, where Prime Minister Thatcher was staying. Two weeks later, Indian Prime Minister Indira Gandhi was assassinated in New Delhi. Five weeks after that, yet another American was kidnapped in Lebanon, and a Kuwaiti airliner was hijacked to Teheran. The pace picked up in 1985. There were more Americans abducted from the streets of Beirut, and a rash of airline hijackings and explosions. In particular, the hijacking of TWA Flight 847 and the long negotiations with the terrorists traumatized the U.S. government and led eventually to the decision to form Vice President Bush's Task Force on Combating Terrorism to improve the efforts of the U.S. government as a whole in confronting the problem.

Many of these events had a European connection, even if they happened elsewhere. Europe was awash in terrorists. Not only were there homegrown groups such as the Irish Republican Army, the Red Army Faction, and the Red Brigades, there were also Middle Eastern terrorist groups operating in Europe, such as the Abu Nidal Organization, various Lebanese Shiite groups, and Al Fatah, some with state sponsorship by countries such as Libya and Syria.

As serious as it already was, the situation worsened further when, on October 7, 1985, a group of Palestinian terrorists under the direction of Mohammed Abul Abbas, aka Abu Abbas, hijacked the *Achille Lauro*, an Italian cruise ship, off the Egyptian coast and headed it toward Syria. Abu Abbas was the leader of a breakaway faction of Al Fatah, still closely associated with the latter and under the umbrella of the PLO. The White House sent elements of the Joint Special Operations Command (JSOC) team under the command of Gen. Carl Stiner to the Mediterranean, with the objective of boarding the ship and capturing the terrorists. As yet there was no game plan, but it was important to move the JSOC into position, since the trip from the United States to the Mediterranean would take half a day.

When Abbas's men asked the Syrians for political asylum, the State Department began pressing hard on Syrian president Assad to stand firm against demands. With world attention focused on the hijacking, the Syrians blinked. They refused the *Achille Lauro* permission to dock at the port of Tartus. The terrorists murdered Leon Klinghoffer, a wheelchair-bound, elderly American Jewish passenger, and threw his body overboard.

Abu Abbas was not on the ship, but was directing the effort long distance. Using the code name Abu Khaled, he radioed his henchmen to stop the killing and turn the *Achille Lauro* back to Port Said, Egypt. Meanwhile, the JSOC had devised an attack. SEAL Team Six was positioned on a Navy ship just over the horizon. They planned to board the ship silently from the stern, which was not visible from the bridge. When darkness fell, they would storm the ship and free the hostages.

Before they could carry out the plan, however, the *Achille Lauro* was permitted to dock in Egypt. The four hijackers left the ship and surrendered to the Egyptians, who had promised them safe passage out of the country. President Hosni Mubarak said that he had agreed to the devil's bargain because the *Achille Lauro*'s Italian captain had assured his government that no passengers had been harmed.

It was a lie. Mubarak could not, and as it turned out would not, surrender an Arab brother. The Egyptians were telling the world that the terrorists had already left when we learned that Abbas and the others were still there. They were to leave Egypt on an Egyptair jetliner bound for Tunisia.

A friendly country had been monitoring the situation and passed to the U.S. government details about the Egyptian flight. At the NSC, the problem fell within the purview of Oliver North, who by this time had a number of portfolios. North and other staff members came up with an intercept plan modeled on a strategy used in World War II, when Admiral Yamamoto's aircraft was identified, followed, and shot down. North and other staffers at the NSC proposed intercepting the Egyptair flight over international waters and forcing it to land, thereby enabling us to apprehend Abbas and make him stand trial.

I was at the Pentagon on other business and dropped in on my friend Adm. Art Moreau. I heard him provide the rules of engagement via EUCOM to the intercepting aircraft of the Sixth Fleet. F-14s from the USS *Saratoga* forced the Egyptair jet to head for the NATO base at Sigonella, Sicily. The jetliner, the first of a parade of planes bound for that destination, was followed by five aircraft from the *Saratoga* and two C-141 transport planes carrying General Stiner and members of the JSOC.

The Egyptair flight landed, and the C-141s followed in directly. Stiner's men then surrounded the aircraft and were in turn surrounded by several units of Italian carabinieri. An acrimonious exchange began between the Americans and the Italians. Although we hoped that we would be able to get custody of the terrorists, the Italians insisted that they had jurisdiction. They had a point—the NATO base was on Italian soil; the *Achille Lauro* was an Italian ship. Things were tense, and the JSOC refused to back down. For a while it was unclear whether Stiner's men would have to fight the terrorists or the carabinieri.

Eventually it was decided that a firefight with the Italians was not in our best interests. In the end it didn't matter. Despite an impassioned telephone call from President Reagan to Prime Minister Craxi, the Italians wimped out and let Abu Abbas and his fellow terrorists go to Yugoslavia and then on to Baghdad. Prime Minister Craxi was more worried about pissing off the PLO than President Reagan. It was yet another sign to the administration that terrorism was out of control.

CHAPTER 18

The Iranian Episode

On November 22, 1985, I got an early-morning call at home from Oliver North. He said, "Look, I got a problem. And it involves Portugal. I need to see you in the office as soon as possible. I'm going to need some help with the Portuguese government." He said it was urgent. I called the responsible branch chief and told him to send a message to Lisbon to stand by to receive message traffic from Washington. It was about 4 A.M. when I arrived at Headquarters. I entered the northeast entrance of the largely empty building without any premonition of what nonsense would afflict me for years because of the events to follow.

I settled in behind my desk. The branch chief informed me that Lisbon was standing by. North arrived shortly thereafter. I was not certain what kind of help he needed, but my guess was that it involved a delivery of arms to the contras. Two days earlier, he, Vince Cannistraro, and I had met for a drink at Charley's Place on Route 123 in McLean. I initiated the gathering, as I had not seen either of them in some time and Charley's Place was a mutually convenient location. Much was later made of this meeting by Lawrence Walsh and the Iran-contra prosecution squad, but there was nothing conspiratorial about our get-together, nor the conversation.

Ollie had been the last to arrive, and as was his custom, he was hyperventilating. He always had more things to do than time to do them. He talked about a problem he was having shipping arms for the Nicaraguan freedom fighters from Eastern Europe via Portugal to Honduras and Guatemala; the pipeline was clogged in Lisbon. The rest of the conversation largely dealt with politics between the NSC and the Directorate of Operations, specifically the problems Cannistraro was having with Clair George over Cannistraro's analysis of the Afghan operation on behalf of the NSC. Iran did not come up. After drinks, we parted ways.

When he arrived at Langley, North quickly explained that his difficulty did not involve Central America. Nevertheless, it was no small matter. Ollie thought arrangements had been locked up to secure landing privileges in Lisbon for an Israeli El Al 747 cargo aircraft, but the deal had fallen through—after the 747 was already airborne. Unless we could intercede quickly with the Portuguese government, the plane would have to turn back.

North told me the aircraft contained oil drilling equipment bound for Iran. He told me that this shipment was a crucial step in a two-pronged effort with the Iranians—as an opening to the "moderates" and as a step toward getting the American hostages out of Lebanon. The Iranians had a strong connection to the Hezbollah extremists who were holding the hostages. The aircraft was going to Portugal to sterilize the Israeli connection for the Iranians. Once in Lisbon, the cargo would be reloaded onto non-Israeli aircraft and shipped on to Iran.

The world now knows that this was a shipment of HAWK missiles, a surface-to-air weapons system, and several people have suggested that I should be angry with Ollie about his deception. That's nonsense. Intelligence organizations survive by compartmenting data and restricting access to knowledge. To assist Ollie North by providing communications for his effort to procure landing rights, I had no need to know the real contents of that aircraft. The need-to-know principle is fundamental to the intelligence business, and I've always been comfortable with it. Even with the highest security clearances, you will not receive certain information unless it's necessary for you to have it to do your job. I didn't question whether North was telling me the truth or even the whole story. It's inbred into anybody who's in the spy business not to ask a lot of questions until you know you're entitled to the answers.

The idea that it was drilling equipment was not as far-fetched as the media and prosecutor Lawrence Walsh made it sound. The Iranian economy was based on oil, and from the days of the Shah their equipment was all U.S. made. Moreover, I had seen intelligence reports that the Iranians were scouring Europe for spare parts (and I would have produced them at my trial). I was also aware that the Israelis had been pressing Bud McFarlane, the president's national security adviser, for an opening to Iranian moderates. The Israelis hoped that if the moderates gained power, Iranian support of Islamic extremists in Lebanon would be reduced. A shipment of oil drilling spare parts to Iran to keep their economy going, in exchange for more clout for the moderates, the release of some hostages, and the possibility of pulling the plug on Islamic Jihad in Lebanon, didn't sound at all implausible to me.

But it was not my job to read between the lines. From my perspective it didn't matter whether it was oil drilling equipment, HAWK missiles, or high-tech life-support apparatus for premature infants. The problem for me was that sending *anything* to the Iranians was a violation of the U.S. embargo on Iran and a contravention of U.S. policy of not negotiating with terrorists. I knew that the president had the authority to change and/or lift the embargo on his own, but I also knew that I'd seen no evidence that Reagan had altered his position. I had also seen no evidence that Reagan had changed his mind about negotiating with terrorists.

When Ollie first told me what he needed, I reflected to him that this was against U.S. policy regarding terrorists, and that I didn't like the idea. He told me that the president had approved both lifting the embargo and negotiating for the hostages. I had said my piece, and that was the end of it. The Directorate of Operations marches for the executive, of which the National Security Council (NSC) is a part, and you don't try to sabotage something when the decision has been made by the president to go forward. After hearing North on the phone with McFarlane in Switzerland and his deputy, John Poindexter, at the White House, I knew the White House clearly wanted this shipment to go through. Equally obvious was that none of these men was acting on his own authority—orders had come from higher up.

At the time, a CIA regulation said, "Support requested by or extended to the White House office, excluding the production and dissemination of foreign intelligence, must have the prior support of the Director." Apparently that regulation had been put through sometime in the wake of Watergate. Frankly, I wasn't aware of it, and I don't think that very many others in the Directorate of Operations knew about it either. Had I known of it, I'm not sure what I would have done. Although I still had no "need to know" exactly what North was doing, I knew—as did everyone in the DO and in the entire building—that Casey would want the NSC supported. The prospect of telling him that we had not cooperated with a direct request for assistance from Oliver North and the NSC was something few would want to contemplate. I assume that North's activities would have had de facto "prior support of the Director"—that is, a blanket okay from Casey—since the White House was clearly providing the authority for the action.

The relationship between Casey and North has been much discussed in the media. Although it may overstate it to call it a father/son relationship, William Casey had a lot of respect for Ollie. He could get things done, and that mattered to Casey a great deal. North frequently sought Casey's advice. Many if not most of their consultations were informal. Casey maintained two offices, one at the CIA, and one on the third floor, Suite 345, of the Old Executive Office Building, which he used quite often. The NSC also had offices there; North's was in Room 302. If he wanted to see Casey at the CIA, Ollie had to check in, go through security, and put on a badge. At the OEOB, all he had to do was walk down the hall.

North set himself up in my outer office. He needed access to our secure communications with Lisbon to work on the landing rights problem. I sent the cables via my "privacy" or "back" channel to Lisbon. A privacy channel is the way a division chief communicates with his chiefs on matters that are particularly sensitive—usually personnel matters. Cables in this channel are supposed to be destroyed on both ends after ninety days. Knowing this, I asked my secretary to set up a special file for these cables, separate from the regular files, to have a record of events. I did this because I still clearly recalled Ted Shackley's admonition to me. In 1977, Shackley was the associate deputy director for operations (ADDO). He gave me advice, saying, "When you support another agency, keep a detailed record, because when it all goes south, guess who's holding the sack."

This was a Friday morning, and Casey, McMahon, and Clair George were all away from Washington. Ed Juchniewicz, the ADDO, was running the Directorate of Operations. A copy of all incoming and outgoing divisional back-channel cable traffic is sent to the office of the deputy director of operations; thus Juchniewicz and his staff had full access to our communications between Washington and Lisbon. The DDO and ADDO read the divisional back-channel traffic first every day, unless some other crisis took precedence. What was going on was so unusual it must have been brought to Juchniewicz's attention immediately.

At North's behest I contacted our chief in Lisbon, telling him to pull out all the stops to secure landing rights for the El Al aircraft. My efforts were not isolated—the flight was nearing the turnaround point and North was trying anything he thought would work. Bud McFarlane was yanked from a meeting with Presidents Reagan and Gorbachev in Switzerland to place a call to the Portuguese foreign minister to see if he could get the needed clearance.

It was all in vain; the El Al plane had to turn around. Once the aircraft returned to Israel, North had to figure out an alternative means to get his shipment to Iran. Even if landing rights had eventually been secured in Lisbon, the El Al 747 was no longer available to fly the cargo there. The shipment was stuck in Tel Aviv.

The problem rattled on through Friday, the twenty-second. North wanted Lisbon to contact his confederate Richard Secord, who was going by the alias Richard Copp, to see about arranging other transportation. For me this episode was the first time Secord's name had surfaced—I'd never heard of him before. When it became clear to North that Secord could not solve the problem from the Lisbon end, Ollie asked me, "Can you recommend an aircraft charter company that can provide a couple of 707s to get this stuff out of Israel?"

This was no time for the yellow pages. I contacted the CIA Air Branch and said, "Look, this is what I need. Who do you suggest?"

"Give us some time to think about it," they responded. A couple of hours later, they got back to me. Air Branch proposed that North use St. Lucia Airlines, which was the CIA's proprietary airline. St. Lucia provided air support for Agency covert action, but also operated as a commercial freight hauler.

Well, I'm not stupid. At this point, I understood that we as an agency might be on the brink of getting into this endeavor. We'd no longer be simply providing communications; we could be perceived as participating in NSC activities. When I realized that this might bring the CIA into North's operation, I called Ed Juchniewicz for approval.

I didn't think I had to fill him in on the situation—it was evident from the cable traffic exactly what was going on. I told him about my discussions with Air Branch and said, "This is what North is asking for. The recommendation from Air Branch is for the use of our proprietary."

I didn't have to draw Juchniewicz a picture of what that meant. He had just one question: "Is this a straight commercial deal?" I told him that it was. North's operation would lease the planes and pay St. Lucia, which in this transaction was not much different from United Parcel Service or Federal Express.

It was important to the Agency that North pay for the use of the aircraft and pilots. If the arrangement had not been a commercial one and no money changed hands, then it would have become a CIA covert operation in support of the National Security Council. The distinction was crucial. Juchniewicz and I both knew that this would require a Presidential Finding and put us into a whole different ball game. With the understanding that it was nothing more than a commercial arrangement, Juchniewicz gave his okay.

St. Lucia Airlines dispatched a 707 with German contract pilots to Tel Aviv to load the shipment. Their last charter had been to haul chickens around Europe—they had to clean the feathers out before they could reload. They also had to reconfigure the 747-style packing to suit the smaller aircraft. Our next hurdle was to arrange flight clearance for the 707. At first the plan was that the St. Lucia aircraft would substitute for the 747, pick up the North shipment in Tel Aviv, and haul it to Portugal. However, we still were having landing-rights problems in Lisbon.

Then we got more bad news. Late on Friday the twenty-second, Secord lost his hold on the chartered Nigerian DC-8s that had been waiting in Lisbon to take the shipment on the last leg of the journey. That meant that the 707 in Tel Aviv would have to make the trip to Iran. One way or another, I knew we had to get clearance to overfly Turkey. Turkey was all but unavoidable—unless we wanted to fly down the Red Sea, around the Saudi Arabian peninsula, and into Iran at Bandar Abbas. This route had apparently been used for the August shipment of TOW missiles to Iran, but was ruled out this time for reasons unknown to me.

The Turks were leaning toward granting permission to transit their airspace, but wanted to know what was on board. I cabled Ankara that the flights contained oil drilling equipment. Meanwhile, we needed to find an alternative to Lisbon to obscure the fact that the flight had originated in Israel. Finally we settled on routing the aircraft through Cyprus. There the pilots would file a new flight plan, which would not mention that they had originally come from Tel Aviv.

The situation was becoming tense, because apparently the Iranians were putting pressure on North through the Iranian intermediary for the entire affair, Manucher Ghorbanifar, to put up or shut up regarding the shipment.

On November 24, the St. Lucia aircraft left Tel Aviv for Iran, with a stop in Cyprus. While the 707 was airborne over Turkey, I got another cable from Ankara, reporting that someone from the Turkish Foreign Ministry had spoken with the Turkish air traffic controllers. According to the cable, the controllers had asked the pilots about the contents of the aircraft and were told it was a shipment of weapons. The controllers had reportedly relayed this information to the Foreign Ministry, which asked our chief if this was the case.

In drafting a response, I queried North directly about what was on the plane. North confirmed that the shipment was oil drilling equipment, and I sent a message to that effect to the Turks through the station.

During my testimony before the Senate Select Committee on Intelligence, I really got hammered on this issue, but the great leap of faith here is not whether I believed North when he told me that the shipment was oil drilling parts. The real question is whether you believe that Turkish air traffic controllers actually demanded that the pilots tell them what was on board the aircraft. When I was testifying, Sen. Lloyd Bentsen was the only person present who knew enough about how the worldwide air traffic control system is structured to see my point. He said, "It's inconceivable that an air controller would ask the pilot what he is carrying. It's not their business."

He was dead right, of course. I believe that the pilots did not tell the air traffic controllers that they were carrying weapons—I believe that they were never even asked. I think that someone in the Turkish Foreign Ministry decided to go on a fishing expedition and just threw out the question to our Ankara chief to see what the response would be. I suppose it is possible that the Turkish Ministry of Foreign Affairs could have asked the controllers to pose the question; however, based on my knowledge of Turkey, this would have required more rapid coordination than is usually the case in that country—or most countries. The flight eventually arrived in Iran, but the entire process had been harrowing.

North told me there would be further shipments. That made sense, since the St. Lucia 707 would never be able to carry the cargo from a 747 in a single load. I immediately started looking for a cleaner way to camouflage the Israeli origins of the flight. Because the aircraft had left Tel Aviv without a cargo manifest, things had been dicey in Cyprus, and the pilots had had to really dance and talk fast to get into and off the island.

The Cyprus landing had sanitized the Israeli connection to the satisfaction of the Iranians, but it had given us one hell of a problem with the Turks. Because of the Turkish confrontation with the Cypriot ethnic-Greek government, the Turks were insisting that flights over their airspace not originate in Greek Cyprus. I began communicating with other stations, looking for a substitute location where the aircraft could land and refuel prior to heading for Iran. Throughout Sunday the twenty-fourth, I continued to send and receive messages looking for this alternative and was still working on the problem when McMahon came back into the office on Monday morning, November 25.

He was briefed by Juchniewicz about the activities of the weekend and reportedly went through the overhead. Apparently, at a meeting on the seventh floor, McMahon asked the Agency's chief legal counsel to prepare a finding to cover the Agency's involvement in the shipment, even though it had been paid for as a commercial transaction. Late that same afternoon, he called me. Although McMahon had a reputation as a screamer, he knew better than to scream at me. As calmly as he could manage, McMahon told me that whether or not I thought there had been a straight commercial arrangement between St. Lucia and North, we needed a Presidential Finding to do what we were doing. He told me we needed the Finding because the items in the shipment were embargoed, but this, of course, was incorrect. The president can lift an embargo at will and had obviously done so. Interestingly, during this conversation McMahon never mentioned missiles, either because he assumed that I knew there were really missiles on board—or because he thought that I still had no need to know. McMahon certainly had to have known they were weapons, because within the Agency, only he and Casey had been briefed on the Israeli initiative involving arms to Iran that had begun over the summer, and less than two weeks earlier, they had been told by McFarlane about the Israeli plan to move arms to Iran.

McMahon subsequently maintained that he also told me that Monday afternoon to stop supporting the NSC. Yet, if he had instructed me to shut down the operation entirely, it would have ended immediately. The Agency is hierarchical—people follow orders. It's not like I'm running my own private CIA and can do what I want. If McMahon had really issued that directive, the first time I sent a message that contravened his orders, the deputy director of operations, Clair George, would have seen it right away. The hammer would have come down from Clair: "For chrissakes, Clarridge, shut it down!" It never happened, and I continued working on a solution to the Cyprus problem until the sixth of December when North, of all people, phoned me to say that I could cease my efforts. With hindsight, I think that the decision to desist for the time being was due to the fact that the Iranians were irate over the model of the HAWK missile that they had been sent. It was not the one they wanted. Thus, both sides were regrouping as to what to do next.

After that, I had nothing to do with the Iranian operation, since it was not in my bailiwick. If the Directorate of Operations was going to really get involved in supporting the NSC, this was a task for the Near East Division, within whose jurisdiction Iran and Israel fell—not my European Division.

Who knew what and when? Casey had known about the missile shipments and their purpose from the beginning. McFarlane had briefed key national security officials in August about the first shipment of TOW missiles from Israel, which Reagan had approved. Shultz and Weinberger were opposed. Furthermore, a week before Ollie North asked for my help, Casey and McMahon had met with McFarlane and Poindexter. McMahon's notes indicate that McFarlane had briefed them on further plans to move Israeli arms to the Iranians.

It's clear that Reagan was frequently briefed on the situation, and the idea that anything had gone very far without his knowledge is just unrealistic. Reagan may never have been a nuts-and-bolts kind of president (except for matters that particularly interested him, such as the hostages and the contras), but in this case even if he didn't have a commanding grasp of all the details, he certainly understood what the deal was. He knew about the overall tactic of trying to find the opening to the Iranian moderates. He certainly knew that this had to include the hostage issue, and that arms were being supplied. He was under intense pressure from the families of the hostages to do something.

On at least one occasion, Casey made it clear to me that the president was aware. In the late spring of 1986, John Poindexter, who had replaced McFarlane, began to have some real queasy feelings—understandably enough—that this operation wasn't going well. Casey's antenna (North?) detected this and he called Poindexter, who was unavailable. When Poindexter later returned the call, I was in Casey's office. Although I was privy to only one end of their conversation, the subject was clear. Casey gave Poindexter a lot of encouragement to stay the course. Afterward, Casey remarked to me that the president was really feeling the pressure from the hostage families personally and was pressing his staff to find some solution with the Iranians. I suspect that it was this increasing pressure to find almost any way out of the impasse that drove McFarlane, North, et al., to travel to Teheran in May of 1986.

Vice Adm. John Poindexter is one of the finest human beings I've ever met. He is first and foremost a naval officer, and naval officers don't go off and do things without the approval of the chief. Although Poindexter tried to shield the president in his testimony, Oliver North was right: the president surely knew what was going on. It is inconceivable, knowing McFarlane and Poindexter and their military backgrounds, that they would have been off on their own on this issue at any time. Naval and Marine officers are well-known for their respect for the chain of command.

When did I become aware that the true contents of the aircraft was missiles and not drilling equipment? On Saturday the twenty-third, North apparently authorized Charlie Allen, the national intelligence officer (NIO) for counterterrorism, to show me a sheaf of cables. (From the inception of the opening to Iran and the hostages-for-arms deal, Charlie Allen had been assigned by Casey to provide intelligence support to North and the NSC on these matters.) The cables were a bunch of telephone intercepts between Iran and someplace in Europe, where Manucher Ghorbanifar, the go-between, was working out the details of the deal with Iran. Allen would later testify that among other information in those cables was that the shipment included weapons for Iran.

That Saturday morning I remember Charlie Allen running around with a big stack of papers. He left them with me for a time, and I remember taking a look at the first page in the pile. These transmissions were difficult to read and understand—they were full of code words and elliptical references. I didn't do much more than glance at them. I could see it would take an age to wade through all that stuff, and I didn't have the time. This operation really had nothing to do with my division. I was simply passing messages and facilitating overflight clearances.

In the ensuing years during the brouhaha with Congress and Walsh over the so-called Iran-contra affair, they tried to make an issue over the fact that I was in the office on a Saturday morning. Somehow that "proved" that I was deeply involved in North's operation and thus knew that the cargo was missiles. What these worthies didn't understand was that I was at Headquarters almost *every* Saturday morning, frequently to work on the annual fitness reports, or PARs, of my officers. Performance appraisal reports are a time-consuming burden, but I've always tried to take them seriously. PARs are important to people's careers. Saturdays were when things such as PARs got done, because usually not a lot was going on.

It's hard to pinpoint exactly when I knew for sure that the shipment was missiles and not oil drilling equipment. At some point, I learned it informally, probably from either Allen or North, for I was not a participant in the discussions on the seventh floor where the future of this operation was being discussed and the Presidential Finding was being concocted on November 29. In any event, I certainly knew by December 6, when Clair George and I discussed North's telephone call about closing down further efforts to find routes into Iran and George briefed me on the Finding.

My mistake during the Iran investigation was in telling the truth when I said that I did not recall exactly when I learned that it was missiles rather than oil drilling equipment. I should not have been honest. I should simply have picked a date and stuck to it, and that would have been the end of it. There was nothing illegal, the Finding issue aside, about what was done. When the CIA knew it was missiles rather than oil drilling equipment was never an issue, except in the context of accusations of perjury during the ensuing endless investigation. Bizarrely enough, my honesty led to the charges of perjury against me, and for me it was a costly mistake—with a $200,000 legal fee attached.

After all was said and done, we had nothing to show for our efforts. No hostages were released, and the administration continued to be under pressure from the families and the press to solve the problem. The TWA Flight 847 hijacking, and our inability to nab Abu Abbas in Sicily, continued to rankle. Terrorism pushed everyone's hot button.

Then just before New Year's, the Abu Nidal Organization shot up the Rome and Vienna airports, killing nineteen people, including five Americans. The TV coverage was gruesome and the president was stunned. Casey told me that Reagan took the losses personally. The attacks strengthened resolve in Washington to take action to neutralize the terrorist threat. I didn't know it yet, but I was about to get another assignment.

CHAPTER 19

The Revolution Within

Blood and bodies were everywhere. Amid the shattered glass and twisted metal at the El Al ticket counters in Fiumicino in Rome and Schwechat in Vienna were the vestiges of Christmas packages, souvenirs, and other reminders of people on holiday. The Abu Nidal airport attacks shocked the nation. Innocent Americans were dying in terrorist acts abroad, and their government couldn't protect them. Like the hijacking of TWA Flight 847 in June and the *Achille Lauro* incident in October, this was terrorism in its purest form. And it had the desired effect—it heightened the fear of anyone traveling anywhere. Many Americans changed their destinations or just stayed home.

Prior to these atrocities, the idea of getting machine-gunned at an airline ticket counter was beyond anyone's worst nightmare. There were no threats, no demands, just senseless murder and a scene of violent mayhem at the airport. Returning the terrorists' fire, Italian carabinieri—stationed as airport security—were shooting wildly, almost indiscriminately, with their Beretta submachine guns. In contrast, an El Al security officer fired one shot from his nine-millimeter gun at a distance of sixty feet and hit a terrorist right between the eyes. In Rome, an eleven-year-old American girl named Natasha Simpson, already wounded, was killed by Abu Nidal's terrorists with an extra fusillade to the head. Her father held her as she died.

The murderers were hailed as "heroes" by Libya's Muammar Qaddafi. The products of Palestinian refugee camps, the assassins were boys and young men who had been doped with amphetamines and told to fire into the airport crowds. Many of the attackers were just a few years older than Natasha Simpson.

For me these airport hits were the last straw. I could see what terrorism was doing to the American people, to our government, and—without exaggeration—to the civilized world. The loss of innocent lives and the ensuing media maelstrom damned near engulfed official Washington. Certainly the upper echelons of the executive branch had become preoccupied with terrorism; it cast a shadow over the Reagan presidency that just wouldn't go away.

Shortly after the attacks I went up to see Bill Casey in his office on the seventh floor. I sat in that familiar colonial wing chair beside his desk. Casey looked tired. I told him, "We've really got to do something better to fight terrorism. I think we can be smarter about confronting the problem." I knew we had to take a more vigorous approach to Abu Nidal and his kind. I knew what would happen if we failed to act. The incidents would become bolder, bloodier, and more numerous. My words echoed Casey's feelings. As he looked out the window toward the Potomac, he confessed that he was under intense pressure to show more initiative in counterterrorist matters. Reagan was holding Casey's feet to the fire to take action—soon.

In a sudden burst of animation, Casey told me to take two or three months to study the terrorist problem and come up with a position paper and a game plan to fight terrorism more effectively. After the New Year, I turned over the European Division to my able deputy and began my new work immediately.

Clair George gave me an office down the hall from Casey's on the seventh floor, between his and the office of DDCI John McMahon. I knew it was unlikely that I would return to my post as chief of the European Division. Although nothing was said outright at our meeting, both Casey and I knew that I would head up whatever new activity came out of my research and analysis.

In terms of CIA experience, I was suited to remake our approach to terrorism. From 1968 in Turkey, to the Arab world in the mid-1970s, through Rome, to Latin America, and finally Europe, probably no one in the CIA had had more experience with it than I did.

I made the rounds within the CIA, went to the Pentagon, the State Department, the National Security Council, and the Joint Chiefs of Staff, and talked to everybody to get their input. Vice President Bush's Task Force on Combating Terrorism was just about to issue its recommendations, and I spoke with Adm. J. L. Holloway, who was heading up the Task Force. (Although he did not reveal the information to me at that time, the Task Force also had a secret recommendation that the CIA should take a more offensive posture against terrorism.)

I talked to virtually everybody in town who had any thoughts on the matter. Although Holloway was up to speed on Task Force recommendations, my discussions with others in the administration were not very enlightening. In all fairness, colleagues from other agencies could not provide much insight on how the CIA could confront terrorism more effectively. But I knew it was good politics to give everyone a hearing.

Even within the CIA, few people had any useful suggestions, with the exception of some officers from the Office of Technical Services, the group that supports the Clandestine Services. One of these officers, Mick Donahue, was in the forefront of analyzing and often modifying terrorist weapons and technical devices. He had thought a lot about terrorist issues, and he had examined their tactics more thoroughly than anyone else with whom I spoke.

In three weeks, I did my interviews and wrote a paper that contained an analysis of the problem and my recommendations. It was completed by the end of January. It was probably the most brilliant paper (or at least the most cogent) that I had ever put together or ever will—because my thoughts on the subject were really clear. I knew exactly what had to be done, and I was able to get it down in a minimum of pages and in simple language.

The CIA had four problems in dealing with terrorism—our major obstacles that kept us on the defensive. The first was psychological—our defensive mentality; the second was bureaucratic or organizational; the third was analytical; and the fourth was technological. Of these, the bureaucratic and the psychological problems were by far the most serious—solve those, and the rest would be much easier to deal with.

I knew what the psychological problem was. Terrorism is effective if you just try to contain it, if you stay in a defensive mode. If, however, you go on the offensive, you defuse much of the potential threat. I proposed a new orientation, taking the CIA from a defensive to an offensive posture. Up until this point, terrorists had operated knowing there was little chance of retribution or of their being brought to justice. I wanted to change that forever.

The bureaucratic problem was that we at the CIA, like other agencies of the executive, are organized along regional geographic lines. But terrorism never fits one particular piece of real estate. It is effective precisely because it spreads all over the map. An Arab terrorist group may be based in Libya or Syria, but its operations are likely to take place in Rome or London or Athens. Within the Clandestine Services, which division has jurisdiction—the Near East or Europe? Geographic divisions of responsibility create jurisdictional and coordination squabbles that play right into terrorists' hands.

For some time, the Agency had been dimly aware that we needed to centralize the effort against terrorism, but before I prepared my analysis, our results had not been successful. We had established a small terrorism staff, but it had no power. It could only *advise* the geographic operating divisions (Europe, Near East, etc.) on what to do. Without adequate personnel, money of their own, and a mandate to confront the problem, their advisory status meant that no one had to take them seriously. This problem was not unique to the CIA. The same organizational conflicts that existed among its regional geographic entities and between them and the powerless staff established to combat terorrism existed within the State Department and elsewhere.

It sounds absurd, but our efforts against terrorism were failing because terrorism wasn't anyone's number one priority. Internal politics within the CIA, and among the CIA, State Department, Pentagon, NSC, and FBI, were crippling efforts to deal with one of the most important issues facing the administration. Small wonder that we were always scrambling to respond after each new terrorist incident. Small wonder that the public viewed us as powerless—in a way, we were.

The third problem I identified was inadequate analysis of data to support counterterrorist operations—and a corollary failure to centralize the available data. I suspected that we were not making use of a lot of information about terrorists in various briefs and files around the CIA. Mounting operations against terrorist groups takes a lot of analytical work—if you hope to have any success. It's a business of minutiae—collating bits and pieces of data on people, events, places. It's often compared to a jigsaw puzzle, and the analogy is fitting. However, the Agency had failed in this area.

No operating division of the Clandestine Service—and I knew this from firsthand experience as chief of Arab Operations in the Near East Division in the 1970s—has the manpower in either quality or quantity to do the required analytical work. Most intelligence assistants and analysts in the Operations Directorate had come up through the ranks. Many of them were surely bright enough; some were not. Bright or not, often they lacked advanced education and training. In any event, there weren't enough of them to do the job required. Frequently, they were diverted by their bosses from one crisis to another, never able to complete any one project. They had plenty of other things to do besides work on terrorism. There was never a dedicated focus—even in the Palestinian Branch within the Near East Division—on terrorism, day in and day out.

On the other hand, the Directorate of Intelligence had a unit specializing in terrorist groups. They did have the analysts—both in terms of quantity and quality—to do the job. Therefore, we clearly had to take this analytical group out of the Directorate of Intelligence and bring it together with operational elements from the Directorate of Operations' geographic divisions. By doing that, we would get centralized data and analysis, and this critical mass could develop plans and support operations to go after terrorists.

Fourth, counterterrorist operations were going to need direct technological support, and in a different manner from how the Agency had been accustomed to providing it. This was a job for the Directorate of Science & Technology, but fighting terrorism didn't give us the luxury of the normal five-year development cycle for high-tech gadgets. We needed simple, cheap, low-tech stuff that worked even in parts of the world where electricity and flush toilets were luxuries. I called it the Radio Shack approach to research and development—taking pieces of existing things off the shelf and putting them together to deal with a particular situation in no more than a year. I am amused that nearly ten years later, the U.S. government and the Defense Department in particular have gone to COTS (commercial off the shelf) technology as the wave of the future.

My analysis of the problems argued for a centralized effort within the CIA with participants from all four directorates. Thus, I proposed the establishment of a new Counterterrorist Center (CTC), merging personnel from the Directorate of Operations, Directorate of Intelligence, and the Directorate of Science & Technology, but located within the Directorate of Operations because the emphasis of the Center would, of course, be on operations. The Directorate of Administration was also brought into the mix because it could provide administrative people and because of its Office of Medical Services. Among its other resources, Medical Services had psychologists on its staff who dealt with the psychology of negotiating with terrorists.

What I was actually proposing was nothing less than a revolution within the CIA. The CTC was absolutely without precedent—the Agency had never organized across directorate lines for anything before. Each directorate had always been a sacred fiefdom unto itself. Each had always been headed up by a deputy director, a monarch of his own domain who guarded his territory jealously, and subordinates with geographic regional responsibilities did likewise. The CTC was roughly analogous to a new and autonomous branch of the armed forces, with a mandate to commandeer staff from the Army, Navy, Marine Corps, and Air Force.

All change is threatening. I anticipated opposition, and I got it. Most of it came from within the Directorate of Operations, with staunch opposition both from the European and the Near East Divisions. Because I got immediate strong support from Casey, McMahon, Robert Gates, and to a lesser extent Clair George, the antagonism was subtle at first—no one would take on this group directly. Gates was a particularly strong proponent of the Center concept. It appealed to others who, like him, espoused the one-Agency theory. As time went on, however, the European and the Near East Divisions really dug in their heels. Within the Near East they looked on the CTC as an insinuation that they hadn't done their job against terrorists, and to some extent that was the case. I was brought up in the Near East Division and had run Arab Operations. I knew that the terrorism problem was beyond *any* one geographical division. Despite Near East Division's misgivings, my paper went forward to Casey and was, without change of a comma, approved for implementation. Finally, we were on the offensive. And so was the rest of the executive branch, thanks to the recommendations of Vice President Bush's Task Force on Combating Terrorism.

Although I was not aware of its work at the time I wrote my paper for the Center, the Task Force was looking at the same problem from the viewpoint of the entire government and coming up with many of the same recommendations. One of the primary outcomes of the unclassified portion of the Task Force report was the formation of an interagency committee under the direction of an officer of the National Security Council. At this time that was Oliver North. North was ably assisted by his deputy Robert Earl—a much-admired fellow Marine officer and Rhodes scholar. The committee included Jerry Bremer from the State Department, Charlie Allen from the National Intelligence Office, Richard Armitage representing the office of the secretary of defense, Oliver "Buck" Revell from the FBI, Lt. Gen. John Moellering representing the Joint Chiefs of Staff, and myself from the CIA. The purpose of this committee was to avoid interagency fighting by allowing the White House to adjudicate all disputes in this area. It worked. This group coordinated well together and there were a minimal number of conflicts.

The establishment of the Counterterrorist Center and the subsequent Presidential Finding allowing the CIA to undertake covert action to counteract terrorism—with or without the help of foreign governments—provided the wherewithal finally to get on with the task. For a long time we had had reciprocity agreements with other countries on criminal matters. However, as the Abu Abbas incident in Sicily proved, many governments didn't treat terrorists—even those known to have murdered defenseless people in cold blood—as criminals and would not turn them over to us. Nor, in many cases, would those governments prosecute these criminals themselves. However, now the CIA's authority to search out terrorists and to assist in bringing them to justice was coupled with another new weapon, the Omnibus Crime Act of 1986. This law established the United States' legal right to capture abroad terrorists who had committed acts against American citizens and to return them to the United States for prosecution.

Casey grinned broadly when he told me that he was looking forward to his next trip up to the Hill. Congress did not get to approve or disapprove the Presidential Finding; they just had to be informed. After all the trouble we'd had dealing with the House and Senate over Nicaragua, it was refreshing that when Casey and I came to talk about the CTC, they thought we were on the side of the angels. Even the Agency's worst foes in Congress had no choice but to support the CTC.

That doesn't mean there wasn't a bit of congressional whining about the prospect of kidnapping terrorists to return them to the United States for trial. What did these worthies think the terrorists were going to do— step right up and volunteer for a free ticket to the USA to be prosecuted? Even within the Agency there were whimpers of concern, especially from some in the Clandestine Services—of all places!

As anticipated, I became head of the Counterterrorist Center, and the offensive began. Despite a Presidential Finding that authorized the formation of the counterterrorist action teams and the parallel recommendation supporting these from the Vice President's Task Force on Combating Terrorism, the idea made some congressmen edgy, perhaps because of the term *action team*. But that was a lot more soothing than calling them strike teams. No amount of explanation could convince some of our lawmakers that we weren't putting cadres of hitmen on the CIA payroll. The job of the counterterrorist action teams was to track terrorists, carry out surveillance, and assist in capturing and returning them for trial in the United States. We had two action team contingents, one composed of U.S. nationals and another of foreign citizens. Members of both groups were chosen for a wide variety of special skills, including use of weaponry, knowledge of aviation or navigation, and foreign language fluency.

The foreign national–staffed action team came primarily from the Middle East. Members were recruited using a principal agent who developed and ran his own network of subagents. This action team was to be used for surveillance and countersurveillance in support of case officers working against a specific target. Whenever a case officer was to meet with a terrorist, particularly one volunteering his services or in a cold approach in a bar or other semipublic place, I wanted to surround him with heavy countersurveillance—preferably with sawed-off shotguns under their raincoats—to protect him.

I thought the foreign action team was important because I knew that the CTC might eventually be operating in backwater parts of the Middle East—places where Americans, even those of Middle Eastern heritage, could never look inconspicuous. However, many in Congress opposed the use of foreigners, even under the direct guidance of CIA case officers. Within the DO, some people were worried because Congress was worried. Others were concerned that the foreigners might slip their collars, go off on their own independent operation, and point the finger at us when it was done. Eventually, the pressure was just too heavy and the foreign action team was disbanded.

Howard Freeman, the most highly decorated CIA officer (holding medals both for his intelligence successes and for valor), was in charge of the teams. He was ably assisted by Tim Geraghty. Geraghty was the superb Marine Corps colonel who had taken the fall for the suicide bombing of the Marine Corps barracks in Beirut, despite his many urgent messages to his commanders to allow him adequate means to secure his compound. His troops were placed in an impossible position because they were no longer considered neutral in the Lebanese civil war. They were called upon to support the Christian forces. Then this great tragedy occurred and he took the responsibility. As a result, he left the Marine Corps, a loss to that service of one of its finest officers. We were delighted to be able to use him in our counterterrorism efforts.

For some time, Casey had been forming the opinion that some CIA activities required a different sort of individual than the normal Clandestine Services case officer. Because of their specialized training, he had concluded that policemen would have a useful role to play, so early on in the formation of CTC, we decided to recruit some. They would be used not only for the action teams, but would be trained for case officer roles. This program was anathema to many in the Clandestine Services leadership. The program was derisively known within some circles as the "Casey's cops" program.

Despite this opposition, we did contact a number of urban police chiefs to talk about recruiting officers for counterterrorism action teams. We got a lot of support—and many chiefs referred officers to us who they thought would be able to do the job. The sheriff of San Diego, John Duffy, became a particularly strong supporter of this program. Of course, I didn't get cooperation from everyone—Darryl Gates, the chief of the LAPD, told us to pound sand right away.

Within the Directorate of Operations, many case officers were adverse to participating in counterterrorist operations. They viewed it as "police work" and felt they had not joined the CIA to be cops. If they had wanted to pursue that career, they would have joined the FBI, the DEA, or police forces.

I ended up with several action teams staffed with U.S. personnel, both men and women. Some were military; some were policemen or policewomen; some were neither—and they were among the finest and most dedicated human beings I've worked with. The screening of these recruits was some of the most vigorous I have seen, including psychological testing. Frankly, many, particularly from the police forces, failed to meet our criteria. Several of these recruits had particular qualifications, including language skills, that were most important to us. Some of the women had military service backgrounds, including experience with lethal weapons. One member of the team had been a mercenary in Africa. Another, who was to play a crucial role in a later operation, had been a U.S. Navy SEAL.

We were in business on February 1, 1986, but there was considerable discussion about what my title should be. I think Clair was worried that I was going to aim for something like associate deputy director—to a bureaucrat in a bureaucracy, these things matter. I think we settled on a hybrid, deputy chief of operations for counterterrorism.

I didn't care what they called me—regardless of how the organization chart was laid out, functionally I was running my own show, and it was going to work the way it had worked in Latin America. In other words, no matter who was in between, a direct pipeline would go from Casey to me and back again. That was Casey's choice, not mine.

Staffing was one of our first undertakings in the struggle. To carry out my mandate, the CTC had to function as an operational unit; it would not be advisory. To be effective, we had to stay small. I ran it as a hands-on operation. I told Casey that I wanted twenty-five people from the Directorate of Operations, and I wanted them by name. He agreed. I got the people I wanted, despite pressure by DO division chiefs to discourage volunteers. We also frankly "stole" some of our best personnel from other divisions and offices. I took my able deputy from a position in the European Division. He was one of the few senior officers in the DO who had any firsthand experience fighting terrorists.

With the establishment of the CTC, I knew we were going to write a lot of papers, policies, and Presidential Findings, so I wanted a first-class executive assistant. I managed to steal Linda Flohr, the woman case officer who had done such a superb job in Grenada. She became invaluable and was responsible for riding herd on the mountain of paper we generated. I was also fortunate to obtain a magnificently competent secretary, Sarah Clinger [F]. Cheerful and unflappable with all hell breaking loose, Sarah was a steady, positive influence on our surroundings—a real rock. Numerous others, whose names I am not permitted to reveal, volunteered to join the CTC; all highly skilled, energetic, and creative individuals.

Because Gates was solidly behind the idea of the CTC, I obtained the entire unit from the Directorate of Intelligence that was concerned with terrorism. The leader of this group was Betsy Graves, a marvelously intelligent woman who did not suffer fools gladly. She quickly made herself indispensable and became the third-highest-ranking officer in the CTC, in charge of the combined operational/analytical structure of the organization.

On the technical side, however, I didn't know whom I wanted from the DS&T since I didn't know its personnel well. I asked for seven or eight people, but I didn't ask for anyone by name. I'm sure that the techies that the DS&T thought it was fobbing off on me were misfits and troublemakers, but to me they were jewels. I found that they were original thinkers being given a chance to try out their extraordinary ideas.

Freed from DS&T bureaucracy, my techies exceeded all my hopes and then some. Their relocation to the CTC gave them a place to stretch their imaginations. Taking my Radio Shack mentality to heart, they became my tech wizards. For example, to send a wayward oil producer a message, they devised a way to make his pipeline flow backward from the seaside oil terminal to his oil wells in the outback.

One immediate problem I faced was simply finding offices for our Center. The original small terrorism staff unit in the Directorate of Operations had recently been set up with secure communications, television monitors, and facilities for twenty-four-hour-a-day crisis management. Initially, I moved into this tiny area with my staff. As a virtually nonstop cigar smoker, I nearly asphyxiated my colleagues with blue smoke. I am told that in the morning, my troops knew I was already at my desk from the smell of cigar smoke in the elevator on the first floor. (I must add a belated note of apology to Betsy Graves for how much she must have suffered throughout the months while we were waiting for more spacious quarters.)

This diverse group of DO, DI, DA, and DS&T people began working well almost immediately. They pretty much jettisoned old geographic and directorate loyalties and quickly jelled as a unit. The synergy we got from putting these people together produced some remarkable results within a short time. Despite a high degree of camaraderie within the CTC, however, hostility from "outsiders" began almost at once and was never entirely resolved. Despite Gates's support, we had problems with the Directorate of Intelligence, where some senior officers thought that the CTC was set up to undermine them and to circumvent their "unbiased" analysis.

Difficulties with the traditional geographic divisions of the Directorate of Operations were even more acute. It all came down to turf, and it turned ugly. Obstructionism was rampant. We were dependent on the DO's geographic divisions for communications, among other things. Those divisions have command over the stations in their territory abroad. Often, the stations were cooperative, but the division headquarters was not. The CTC, with no personnel in stations abroad, had to operate through the established field stations. That meant we needed the divisions to clear our cable traffic to their stations.

It may sound like a small matter, but it wasn't. To send a CTC cable to Beirut, it would have to be released by the chief of the Near East Division. A cable to Rome had to be released by the chief of the European Division. Both the European and Near East chiefs by their attitudes let it be known to their troops that they really were not behind the CTC. This situation was a real "embuggerance" and witless. The CTC had some of these divisions' best personnel, and they should have trusted them.

That CIA colleagues were making our job harder—and sometimes a lot harder—greatly hurt CTC morale. To me it was just unconscionable. I knew I could ask Casey to intervene in really serious matters, and often enough nothing less than a fireball from the director was needed to get people moving. But I could get fireballs from Casey only so often. The rest of the foot-dragging we just had to either endure or circumvent. In most cases we prevailed in the end, but it was debilitating to my troops and took up a lot of time.

Before leaving the Agency, I proposed that centers like the CTC be established to contend with the narcotics problem, tech theft (now called proliferation of weapons of mass destruction), counterintelligence, and economics because of their nonspecific geographical nature and for reasons of mass. Since my departure, all but the latter have been put in place.

CHAPTER 20

On the Offensive

The first order of business for the CTC was to improve our intelligence-collection operations against terrorist groups. The CTC simply didn't have enough manpower to vigorously pursue all of the terrorist groups simultaneously. In February 1986, two groups were of obvious high priority: the Abu Nidal Organization (ANO) and Hezbollah, both active and dangerous. State-sponsored, these groups had the resources of entire nation-states behind them. Their activities were more than likely to be carried out internationally, and Americans were among their favorite targets. Though we did not ignore other Palestinian and Lebanese terrorist groups or some of the European terrorists, they were given lesser priority.

The ANO went out of its way to target innocents, even children. The only ANO terrorist who survived the massacre at Fiumicino Airport in Rome carried a note vowing, "As you have violated our land and our honor, we will violate everything, even your children." The CTC estimated that more than three hundred people had died and almost six hundred had been wounded in ANO action by 1986.

Next to Peru's Sendero Luminoso and the IRA, the Abu Nidal Organization was probably the most professional terrorist organization in the world at the time. A breakaway unit within Al Fatah, ANO's sworn enemies were Israel and its supporters (including the United States), as well as moderate Arab governments (such as Jordan, Kuwait, and Egypt). From Abu Nidal's point of view, even Yasir Arafat of Al Fatah was a moderate.

The official name of the ANO was the Fatah Revolutionary Council, but the group seemed to take a particular delight in inventing mysterious and melodramatic cover names when "claiming responsibility" for various terrorist actions.

ANO leadership demanded unswerving allegiance and unquestioning obedience to orders. Explanations were seldom given. The ANO employed highly sophisticated tradecraft, including rigorous compartmentation and secure electronic communications. Terrorist operations were planned at a high level without the participation of the lower-echelon personnel executing the plan. Cadres would be given training and sent abroad not knowing their objective. They'd enter a country "clean" and be met by a support team, providing instructions, weapons, and explosives. The number of people who knew the whole picture was very, very small. If something went wrong, individual terrorists knew nothing, and they could compromise or betray virtually no one else in the organization, even if they wanted to.

Recruitment into the ANO was based largely on intimidation and family ties. Brother would recruit brother and then become responsible for ensuring he didn't screw up. Punishment for a lapse in loyalty was severe: if a brother strayed from the reservation, his sponsor and other members of his family were killed.

I recognized that the family-retribution aspect made penetration of the ANO particularly difficult. The ANO, like other professional terrorist organizations, vets a new recruit by making him commit an outrageous act—bank robbery; assault on members of a rival group; murder—to prove his allegiance to the organization. This not only tests the loyalty of the newcomer, it also gives the ANO something that might be useful later to keep an individual in check. Thus, right away we had a problem infiltrating the organization, because the CIA cannot allow anyone under its direction to commit such acts.

Secondly, terrorist groups ask for and expect immediate compliance with orders. If a CIA-recruited apprentice terrorist is asked to commit a felony, maybe he has time to tell you, and maybe he doesn't. If he does tell you and it's a murder, what do you do? This was a long-standing problem that I first dealt with in the 1970s when I was deputy chief of the Near East Division for Arab Operations. We had made an important recruitment, a crucial penetration of a terrorist group. Our agent had been asked to commit what would have been a major felony in the States. There was no way I could let him do it, and no way to fake it, but I urgently wanted him to keep his connection with the group. Our doctors came up with a possibility: some pills he could take to make him vomit blood—just not his blood. By taking these pills at the last minute, he'd get out of participating in the crime, but wouldn't lose credibility—or perhaps his life. I thought it was a great solution, but Stansfield Turner, who was DCI at the time, vetoed it outright. To this day I can't imagine what the hell was going through his head. We had to abort the operation completely and lost the agent. (Interestingly, in recent years Turner has proclaimed himself a counterterrorism expert.)

In 1986, however, Turner was history and the necessity to deal with terrorism was paramount. Therefore, innovative means of maintaining a recruit within a terrorist organization—short of shooting somebody—

were permissible. On a number of occasions, we staged operations that pretty much followed the ANO's instructions to our agent, but were totally scripted and controlled by us. No one got hurt.

In our efforts to maintain our agents in terrorist organizations, a number of other government agencies assisted us. In one case, the assistance of Marine commandant P. X. Kelly was invaluable. Frankly, without the cooperation of Kelly and others, we could never have maintained these agents in place.

We had two initial breaks in our efforts against Abu Nidal. First, we made a significant recruitment within the ANO. Though he was slow to reveal information, some excellent handling by the case officer brought him around. Second, the analysts from the Directorate of Intelligence took all of our accumulated data on the ANO from both the DO and the DI and analyzed it piece by piece, generating a full picture of the organization for the first time. Frankly, we knew more than we thought we did when we put all the pieces together. We were euphoric that the CTC was able to move so quickly against a terrorist group that had been considered invincible by other counterterrorist organizations.

From our ANO agent penetration, we began to accumulate a lot of knowledge about Abu Nidal's "diplomacy" and his financial dealings and uncovered for the FBI his network of "sleeper" terrorists in the *United States,* Mexico, and northern South America. This coupled with our newly centralized CIA data revealed an ANO funding channel through the London branch of the Bank of Credit & Commerce International, which led us to ANO activists and backers in France, England, and Germany. Abu Nidal had an extensive commercial network in Eastern Europe, Greece, Cyprus, Yugoslavia, and to a lesser extent, Western Europe. These businesses had three purposes—their profits financed the organization; their structure provided cover and support apparatus for terrorist operations; and they gave cover to Eastern European intelligence services in some instances. Under the umbrella of these "legitimate" businesses, the ANO could move and hide funds, acquire and transport weapons, and arrange meetings and liaisons. We were able to document any number of deals involving East Germany and/or Poland that put weapons in the hands of the ANO and other Arab terrorist organizations, as well as patron states such as Libya, Iraq, and Syria.

The head of the ANO commercial empire was Samir Hasan Najm al-Din, a businessman who lived in Warsaw and specialized in the gray arms market. Najm al-Din not only supplied the ANO with ordinary weapons such as pistols, rifles, and submachine guns, he was also able to procure sexier and more deadly paraphernalia such as surface-to-air missiles and portable antitank missiles.

After reviewing this astonishing network of terrorist support, I arrived at the conclusion that the best way to attack Abu Nidal was to publicly expose his financial empire and his network of collaborators. However, the Clandestine Services was concerned about these methods and their effect on our sources. This was a new tactic that ran absolutely contrary to our operational mode and the espionage business.

As time went on, however, it looked more and more as if revealing this information was going to be more effective than simply continuing to gather intelligence about Abu Nidal. Going for extraction of wanted ANO members was impossible, given their location, largely in southern Lebanon and Libya. Finally, we decided to go for the public exposé, revealing the support of some countries for the ANO in an effort to embarrass or pressure them into desisting.

Initially, we attempted to deal through traditional diplomatic channels—having assumed that the State Department was genuine in its pledge to work with other U.S. government agencies. My opposite number at State was a dynamic, intelligent, no-nonsense fellow named Jerry Bremer. As bad as I had it with obstructionism within the CIA, he had it far worse. The geographic bureaus within the State Department frequently blocked him. Each time he needed a major decision, he had to go upstairs to either Secretary of State Shultz or to the undersecretary for political affairs.

The CTC provided Bremer with the data to prepare démarches on Abu Nidal to be presented to the various governments who were harboring his activities. A démarche is the diplomatic equivalent of a demand, and the concern within the CIA over surfacing our ANO intelligence was nothing compared to the nervous sphincters at State over the wording of the démarches. Bremer and I met with representatives from the geographic bureaus at State and went through the evidence with them, line by line. We provided extensive proof of ANO terrorist activity within their jurisdictions. Nevertheless, both the bureau representatives in Washington and the officers in embassies abroad resisted them.

Finally, watered-down démarches were forwarded to the embassies for delivery. We later learned that these démarches were further diluted by the embassy officials who delivered them. The démarches rubbed these countries' noses in our undeniable evidence and demanded that they close the ANO down within their borders. However, because the démarches were so vacuous, the countries concerned took no action.

Frustrated by the lack of results from the démarches, I came up with another idea. "Forget the politely worded pleas for diplomatic courtesy," I said to Bremer. "Let's publish the infamous facts for the whole world to see, and let the chips fall where they may." I proposed that the Department of State issue an explosive little tome called *The Abu Nidal Handbook*. And to my delight (and amazement) they did, after an enormous amount of pain.

Bremer fought huge battles simply to get the regional bureaus to agree that we at the CTC really did have evidence against the ANO, and that our data was valid enough for public presentation. A sizable nucleus of people in the State Department believe that U.S. foreign policy should be the art of not antagonizing other nations. They are more interested in being neighborly than in executing the foreign policy interests of our government.

Yet, Hitler did not become less aggressive when Neville Chamberlain began pandering to him. Instead, he got more ambitious because he knew he could get away with it. I knew the escalation of activities by Abu Nidal, abetted by his knowledge that such countries as Poland, East Germany, Yugoslavia, Greece, and Cyprus would not take action, was no different. Our effort became bogged down in a long and tiring fight with the State Department bureaucrats. Essentially, they didn't like the idea that we had hard, cold evidence that even some U.S. allies were allowing terrorists to operate within their borders because they were intimidated by the consequences of throwing them out. Despite Jerry Bremer's strong support, the regional bureaus at State now tried to water down *The Abu Nidal Handbook*.

The Abu Nidal Handbook laid out chapter and verse on the ANO, its members and accomplices, and its crimes. It even had an organizational chart. Starting with Sabri al-Banna (Abu Nidal's given name), it set forth in great detail much (but by no means all) of what we knew about the organization, including the address of Najm al-Din's headquarters in Warsaw, his home address, the addresses of companies he did business with, and the litany of bombings, hijackings, grenade attacks, and assassinations for which they were responsible. Many ANO addresses were within countries friendly to the United States.

The publication of our handbook had the desired effect. Governments in Europe squirmed, but they terminated their dealings with Abu Nidal. Even the Poles and the East Germans divorced themselves from him. I had the CTC continue to monitor carefully to make sure that Najm al-Din and the others didn't just reestablish their gray-market arms dealings under better cover. As far as we could tell, we really did shut them down.

By mid-1986, we had developed enough data on potential ANO targets abroad that we decided to make some recruitment pitches to Abu Nidal Organization personnel in various countries. Most of the approaches did not result in agent penetrations of the ANO, and I was disappointed by our lack of success. But our pursuit of Abu Nidal's organization and personnel eventually paid off in a very different way.

Seeing his financial empire under attack and listening to reports of CIA efforts to recruit his cadres, Abu Nidal was aware for the first time of a concerted offensive against him—we were coming after him and his people. He, like many in his line of work, was paranoid. The CTC fueled his hysteria over plots against him—feeding fear to a paranoid is something we know how to do. Not surprisingly, Abu Nidal panicked. Those who reported having been approached by us were not rewarded for their loyalty, because Abu Nidal never quite believed that anyone in his group had turned us down. Their loyalty was suspect thereafter, and the punishment for disloyalty was torture and death.

By 1987, a fearful Abu Nidal had turned his terror campaign inward. The ANO was starting to drown in the blood of its disciples. A simple allegation was sufficient; usually there was no investigation. Accused followers were tortured to confess, then executed on the basis of that confession. After the effective ANO apparatus in southern Lebanon fell under suspicion, over three hundred hard-core operatives were murdered on Abu Nidal's order. On a single night in November of 1987, approximately 170 were tied up and blindfolded, machine-gunned, and pushed into a trench prepared for the occasion. Another 160 or so were killed in Libya shortly thereafter. Distrust reached high into the politburo ruling the ANO. Even his closest surviving lieutenants began to believe that Abu Nidal was insane. Abu Nidal's paranoia, fed by our crusade against him, caused him to destroy his organization.

Years later in London, I was reminiscing over pink gins in our club, the Oriental, with a foreign-intelligence colleague, a great bear of a man and dear friend. We agreed that we had succeeded in beating Abu Nidal in a way we had never anticipated, that the techniques of publicity and other actions to stimulate paranoia had succeeded beyond our wildest hopes.

I realized that something similar had happened in Nicaragua. By maintaining support for the contras we signaled our resolve to the Sandinistas. Although our guerrilla efforts failed to bring the Sandinistas to the bargaining table as we had intended, their pressure helped to force democratic elections and the Sandinistas were defeated. We won in a way we had not foreseen. That is how we also won the Cold War! Resolve will eventually always win out over temerity, if the cause is fundamentally right.

The demise of the ANO was a clear-cut victory for the CTC and the CIA. Abu Nidal went to ground and hasn't been much heard from since. As a terrorist threat to be reckoned with, he appears to be finished. There are several morals to this story. First and foremost, it validates my theory about the need to adopt an offensive posture against terrorists. Secondly, there are lessons here for the war on drugs. We can use the information we gather about drug lords to embarrass those who support or tolerate them. The same sort of paranoia exhibited by Abu Nidal is rampant among drug barons. Drug cartels have their internal feuds and their senseless purges. By applying what we at the CTC learned, their paranoia can be used to our advantage. Let them eat themselves. It is an issue only of applying imagination to the problem.

In the mid- to late 1980s, Libyan head of state Muammar Qaddafi was Abu Nidal's primary benefactor. Anti-American and anti-Israeli activities were Qaddafi's primary focus, but he was also vehemently anti-French and anti-British—an obsession that even extended to supplying weapons to the Irish Republican Army.

On April 5, 1986, a bomb exploded inside the rest room of La Belle discotheque in West Berlin, a nightclub notoriously popular with U.S. servicemen. An American sergeant and a Turkish woman died. Over two hundred people were injured. We in the CTC knew that Qaddafi's fingerprints were all over this operation. We were aware even before the bombing that some atrocity was in the works. In late March an intercepted message from Tripoli to various "people's bureaus" said, "Prepare to execute the plan."

The night of the bombing, two more messages were acquired, both sent from the East Berlin people's bureau back to Tripoli. The first said, "We have something planned that will make you happy." The second announced that an event "had occurred" and that it would not be traceable to Libyans in East Germany.

These intercepted messages were the "smoking gun" that cried out for a response. The question was, what kind of action to take? I sat in on a number of meetings in the White House Situation Room as we looked at our options for punishing Qaddafi. From a CIA operational perspective, we could undertake nothing that delivered a sufficiently effective message. A diplomatic protest seemed insufficient, which pretty much left a military response.

Once we decided to retaliate against Qaddafi with a military air strike, selecting the targets became the primary focus. The objectives selected were a compromise between what we wanted to hit and what we thought we could hit with minimal danger to both American pilots and civilians on the ground. One of the targets the CIA and other agencies very much wanted to strike was Al Arafiq, the Libyan Intelligence Bureau, which had instigated the "execute the plan" message resulting in the disco bombing.

Al Arafiq was housed in a Y-shaped building in downtown Tripoli. A strike by a cruise missile fired from a submarine was the first alternative considered. The problem was that the cruise missile was originally designed to carry nuclear warheads. With nuclear munitions, it doesn't much matter if you are precisely on target—the missile could land fifteen miles from the bull's-eye and still attain its objective. Obviously we were not going to use nuclear warheads against Qaddafi. However, the guidance systems for the cruise missile were not precise enough then to ensure that we would hit only the Intelligence Bureau and not adjacent structures with a conventional warhead. The French embassy was across the street. President Reagan was not willing to countenance the chance of collateral damage to the French embassy, so the Y-shaped building was dropped from the list of targets. The remaining targets were the military airfield and Qaddafi's standby command post in Benghazi; the frogman school; the military side of the international airport in Tripoli; and Qaddafi's personal compound and command center, Al Azziziyah, or Splendid Gate.

In the late afternoon of April 14, the president, together with Casey, Poindexter, Shultz, and Weinberger, briefed the congressional leadership on the attack. Shortly thereafter, Robert Gates invited Casey, Clair George, me, and others for a drink in his office to listen to the incoming reports.

The raid sent a hell of a message to Qaddafi, but it was not an unqualified success. The military had a great deal of trouble hitting its targets accurately. In all fairness, it wasn't their fault. The French refused permission for the F-111Bs staging from England to overfly France. Therefore, American pilots had to fly out to sea around France and be refueled several times en route. Their strike was to run from south to north, to provide more surprise. At the same time, the Navy came in from the north with A-6 attack aircraft from our carriers. Considering that the F-111B pilots and weapons officers had been subjected to a long, unnecessary flight by the French and were under considerable pressure during the strike, it is not surprising that their attack was less than perfect. One F-111B dropped one of its two-thousand-pound bombs late and we hit the French embassy anyway. In fact, we hit the portion of the embassy housing the French intelligence unit. Luckily no one was hurt. The local station chief of the French Intelligence Service had just left the building. I saw Gen. Rene Imbot, the head of French Military Intelligence, shortly after the incident. As a good friend both professionally and personally, he understood that it had been a mistake and laughed about it, particularly when he learned that we had gone out of our way to avoid such an incident.

We also took a beating in the media because of what happened to Al Azziziyah. Although the two-hundred-acre compound was the nerve center for Qaddafi's terrorist offensive, it was also his home. His residence remained standing, but all the doors and windows had been blown in. There were casualties within Qaddafi's family. Two of his sons, ages three and four, were wounded, and a little girl who was described as his adopted daughter was killed. Qaddafi himself was not harmed.

Were we trying to kill him? You be the judge. Nine F-111Bs, each carrying four two-thousand-pound bombs, were tasked with attacking Al Azziziyah. At six hundred miles per hour, a pilot could not be certain of hitting Qaddafi's command bunkers and avoiding his residence. Given the magnitude of the raid, the inescapable conclusion is that it would have been acceptable within the administration if Qaddafi had died in the bombing.

A day or two after the Libyan raid, I chatted with Casey. "We have to find a better way to send a message to outlaw nations that we don't like their behavior—short of sending in squadrons of F-111Bs," I told him. I also told him that I found our government's position against eliminating totally unprincipled rulers who threaten or carry out indiscriminate acts of terrorism hypocritical. We in the CIA had our hands tied. We can't put out a contract to eliminate a Saddam Hussein or a Qaddafi, nor are we allowed to pursue an operation to simply shoot them down and spare their families.

Yet, the president authorizes the military to carry out air attacks that may or may not hit and kill the real target. Why is an expensive military raid with heavy collateral damage to our allies and to innocent children okay—more morally acceptable than a bullet to the head?

Casey shrugged. He agreed, and he knew that I had not come to discuss hypotheticals with him. He wanted to hear about my better way. I told him about an idea that the CTC was working on. One of the technical geniuses in the Center thought he could develop a system that would send a clear message, with poignant effect, but with minimal loss of life for the recipients, and none for our delivery personnel.

Casey was fascinated and approved the development. We brought our Radio Shack approach to R&D to bear on the problem. In just over a year we had tested out the device. Shortly thereafter we had five of them operational at a total cost of less than $8 million. Part of the money was furnished by Charlie Hawkins, then a deputy assistant secretary of defense, who saw the device's applicability to military problems. About two years later, the Army gave up on developing a similar but "gold-plated" device, but only after they had spent $900 million on it. In 1995, a joint U.S. military service effort for a similar device was canceled because of technical difficulties after $600 million was spent.

Meanwhile, the hostage dilemma in Lebanon continued, and one element of the CTC worked this problem exclusively in an attempt to penetrate the Hezbollah organization. This intractable tragedy overshadowed many other activities of the U.S. government. It certainly had a profound influence on the White House. Moral and humanitarian concerns dominated President Reagan's thinking, and he was constantly urging his staff to find ways to resolve this matter. Meanwhile, the hostage families were frequently interviewed in the press, keeping pressure on the CIA and all of the other agencies to focus on this problem. We were aware that North, with the support of the Near East Division, was still attempting to secure the release of the hostages through some sort of deal with Iran.

Although the CTC had nothing to do with it, Charlie Allen, the national intelligence officer (NIO) for counterterrorism, was still providing intelligence support on the hostage dilemma. Allen was "co-located" with the CTC. Some of the Center's group working on the Hezbollah problem had originally been under his aegis, and after we amalgamated, Allen remained the point man for intelligence on the hostage problem for the government at large. He was a bit of a maverick: bright, absolutely dedicated, on occasion short on diplomacy, and a workaholic.

The CTC focused on two aspects of the hostage situation. First, we were trying to penetrate the Hezbollah apparatus in Beirut for general intelligence on their activities. Second, we were gathering information in support of a possible military operation. Our thrust was to try to infiltrate people into West Beirut to determine where the hostages were being held.

We knew that Hezbollah held the hostages, or at least most of them. Although the kidnappers had used a variety of names in their abductions, they were not necessarily different groups. Hezbollah was a small, closely knit group of people, and West Beirut was a no-man's-land run by fundamentalist gangs and some gangs with no affiliations—a totally hostile area in which we found it nearly impossible to operate.

To draw a parallel, imagine that Manhattan, Staten Island, and the rest of the boroughs of New York City have all been taken over by gangs. A little gang of twenty people is sitting in Brooklyn—they're your target. Imagine Jersey City, New Jersey, as our Beirut station. You're trying to work against that little Brooklyn gang from Jersey City across the entirety of New York City, which is all enemy territory. Then imagine Langley, Virginia, as Yokohama, Japan, from which CIA Headquarters is trying to manage the problem and give instructions to Jersey City.

To limit the exposure of our personnel, we had little presence in East Beirut. However, we were still vulnerable. Meanwhile, back in "Yokohama," we looked for openings that could level the playing field, especially those that could be undertaken in friendlier territory. One of the operations we attempted before the CTC was officially established was to apprehend Imad Mugniyah, the Shiite leader of Islamic Jihad. Islamic Jihad was the extremist cell of Hezbollah that had kidnapped our Beirut station chief, William Buckley, early in 1984. Mugniyah was also tied to the Iranian Revolutionary Guards in Lebanon's Bekaa Valley, and from there straight through to Iran itself.

In the fall of 1985, Mugniyah had been sighted in Paris. Since I was head of the European Division, this put him on my turf. We may not have been able to get at him in Beirut, but in Paris we had a much better chance of apprehending him. I went to Paris to evaluate alternatives with the French. We considered kidnapping him ourselves, but instead we organized through the French. The French appeared interested for their own reasons. In the end, Mugniyah escaped, probably with some unofficial French connivance. As an irritating footnote to this episode, a friendly French official even passed along a photograph taken of Mugniyah in the airport, on his way to board a flight for Beirut.

Frankly, our penetration efforts in Beirut had little fruition. To put agents into Beirut, we began recruiting in the Detroit area, which has one of the largest concentrations of Shiite Muslims in the United States. However, we found that Hezbollah and their allies became increasingly suspicious of people returning from the United States—even their own relatives.

The CIA did build up an infrastructure to support possible attempts by the military in the event that the hostages were found, but we knew we would not be part of the rescue effort. I also knew that the chances of pulling off a hostage rescue from West Beirut were slim. The U.S. military insisted on having "American eyes on the hostages" before risking any American lives in a rescue attempt. As an officer, if you are going to commit U.S. forces, you owe it to them to make sure they're not walking into a trap, and that the dangers are worth the risk. The military was willing to depend on CIA Lebanese agents for getting them to and from the target, but they weren't willing to depend on them for saying the target was there.

I understood why the military wanted that confirmation, but it was a real limitation. Discovering where the hostages were located was difficult enough, but infiltrating a member of the American armed forces into West Beirut or the Bekaa Valley—even one of Lebanese descent—to make a visual sighting of the hostages was a tough and risky proposition.

At the same time and very much connected with the hostage rescue efforts in Beirut was the attempt to use arms shipments to Iran to bargain for their release. Although it was never really clear how much control the Iranians had over Hezbollah, that campaign was very much alive. Even if Hezbollah was taking direction from Teheran and a release was negotiated with the Iranians, we assumed that Hezbollah would keep a hostage or two as protection against retaliation by the Americans.

However, except for Charlie Allen's intelligence coordination activities, the CTC had nothing to do with the Iranian connection. We were working on the other end of the problem—trying to find out where the hostages were, pointing toward a military operation to get them out. Charlie would brief me from time to time, but I really didn't follow it on a regular basis. In the absence of the Near East Division chief, I did sit in on one meeting at CIA Headquarters with Ollie North and Richard Secord. It was the first time I'd ever met Secord. I stayed for about ten minutes as they were discussing the prices charged to the Iranians for weapons. Using the profits for the contras was not North's idea. It came from an Israeli named Amiram Nir, often described as the "Ollie North of Israel."

Neither Caspar Weinberger nor George Shultz supported the arms-for-hostages deal or, for that matter, any opening to Iran. To be sure, they never really took Reagan on about it, either—and they should have. They had better access to Reagan than anyone else and should have been more forceful in voicing their objections. That would certainly have been better than going around whimpering after the fact, saying they were opposed all along.

Casey supported President Reagan's need to move on the hostage issue—and, more importantly, the opening to Iran. I don't know how Casey felt about the moral issues of the arms/hostage exchange, but he knew the administration could have no opening to Iran without dealing with the hostage situation. In Casey's support of providing intelligence to Iraq in its war with Iran, he was aligned with Shultz and Weinberger. The U.S. intention was to assure no clear-cut winner in this conflict. Disagreement on the hostage issue was but one of the reasons why Casey and Shultz were on the outs with each other. Casey didn't much care for George Shultz.

Meanwhile, Bremer and I went to South America to talk to the Colombians, Peruvians, Ecuadorians, and Panamanians about terrorism. The latest buzz was about "narcoterrorists"—thugs involved both in drugs and terror. We were discussing this topic with León Febres Cordero, the president of Ecuador, when the subject of Manuel Noriega came up. The *presidente* told us that Noriega was his most reliable source of information on narcotics trafficking. He said, "I get lots of support for antidrug activity, but it's Noriega who calls me up in the middle of the night and gives me actionable intelligence. I move on the information he gives me, and he's always dead right."

It occurred to me that perhaps Noriega was just feeding Febres information on Noriega's competitors in the drug trade. Letting the Ecuadorians do his dirty work would surely have been safer than doing it himself. On the other hand, Febres's account meshed with the position of the Drug Enforcement Administration. The DEA had told us that they were getting great support in Panama, and from Noriega in particular, in interdicting drugs.

It's certainly possible that both the DEA and Febres Cordero had been hoodwinked. The relationship between Noriega and the U.S. government had already started to deteriorate over charges of drug trafficking and money laundering. The last stop on the trip Bremer and I were making was Panama, so I called on Noriega.

We talked about terrorism and what he could do to track people coming through Panama. In particular we discussed augmenting the capabilities of a special unit of the Panamanian Defense Force as a counterterrorist team. Noriega had always maintained a close relationship with the Israelis. He had an Israeli "security" adviser, Mike Harari, and a house in the exclusive Tel Aviv suburb of Herzliyya. The unit I was interested in had actually been developed by the Israelis during the Carter administration at the time of the Panama Canal crisis. In the event that the negotiations with the United States failed, the unit would sabotage the Canal. Noriega was positive about cooperating, and we agreed to discuss details at some future date.

That was the last time I saw Manuel Noriega. Our counterterrorism efforts in Panama were overtaken by the swirl of political unrest surrounding him and his desperate attempts to stay in power. I am quite prepared to believe that he was involved in the drug business to some degree, but I never saw any evidence that he was a user himself, and I find it a little bizarre that the DEA, unless they're suppressing what they knew, didn't get some real smell of his activities when they were nosing around down there. I'm not saying that he was a humanitarian, and I have no truck with his manipulation of the democratic process in Panama and possibly violent crimes. But I have some real problems with how the United States got rid of him. Above all, I believe that our invasion of Panama and all the chaos that followed need not have happened.

Our real objective was to get him to leave the presidency, and we didn't do a good job in that regard. The Bush administration was aware of at least three people who knew Noriega well and had some credibility with him. There was, above all, Nestor Sanchez, who was my predecessor as head of Latin America Division; there was a former CIA chief in Panama; and there was me. When the time came to negotiate Noriega's departure from power, they didn't send any of us. Instead they sent people he didn't know, who delivered heavy-handed messages that offered no solutions for him or his family. There is nothing wrong with heavy messages, but in his culture, by whom and how they are delivered is key.

If the right person had been talking to him, the invasion, the bloodshed, and the expenditure of millions of dollars could have been averted. The "right person" could have been any one of us, but Nestor Sanchez knew Noriega best. I think Nestor was never sent because the administration felt that he was biased in favor of Noriega. They should have known that Nestor is enough of a soldier to follow his instructions—and I think that he would have been able to edge Noriega peacefully out of the presidency and into a nice cozy exile somewhere.

It's hard to imagine that any of the three of us could have done much worse than what happened—unless you assume that our government didn't seriously want to cut a deal with Noriega, that we backed him into a corner to give some facade of legitimacy to the invasion and drug trial that followed.

Part of Noriega's problem was his appearance. With his scarred face, he looked like someone that central casting would send in to play the part of the corrupt narcotics dealer. If Noriega had been five feet ten and handsome (say, like Omar Torrijos before him), he probably wouldn't be where he is today. The reverse is also true. I know individuals in the CIA who are a little short on brainpower but long on looks and social graces who got a lot further than their IQ should have taken them. As Alan Wolfe used to say (I believe it was his Ninth Dictum), "If so and so [a good-looking fellow, now a GS-18, but short on brains] were five feet seven and had a wart on his nose, he would still be a GS-14 [lieutenant colonel grade]."

In the aftermath of Noreiga's conviction on drug charges, DEA clearly felt tainted and vulnerable for having given him a clean bill of health over the years to the State Department, CIA, White House, and other government agencies. Apparently, to offset this embarrassment, several former DEA senior officers somehow recently persuaded a writer to provide a book of thinly disguised fiction that excuses DEA's "blindness" regarding Noreiga and lays it on the CIA's withholding information about his drug activities, the CIA's insistence on his preservation because of his "overwhelming importance" in supporting the Nicaraguan contras, and so on.

This is DEA insidious nonsense. To take only one example: Noreiga never was at any time a real factor for the CIA in the contra operation; however, the DEA needed to explain why the CIA had "insisted on protecting him," which excused the DEA's culpability.

The DEA has always been a curious formulation in terms of personnel and operating procedures, probably because of the nature of the work. Many in the government regard it as an organization largely staffed at all levels with marginal humans devoid of talent except for breaking down doors. This is wrong. The DEA's overriding problem is that it has a serious inferiority complex vis-à-vis the FBI, CIA, State Department, and a number of other government agencies. It needs to grow up, confront its failures, stop blaming others, and get on with its business. Some real leadership might help; it has never had any.

The CTC did not ignore Europe. We often ran joint operations with the Europeans against non-European terrorist groups, but we believed that the Europeans were far more capable than we in penetrating their homegrown groups. We saw our role largely as one of providing intelligence, by-products of our operations elsewhere, and technical assistance to support their efforts.

Early in 1987, an innovative and energetic technical officer in the CTC came to me with a proposal that we ask American industry about their new technological developments that might be applicable for countering terrorism. Twenty-five companies were identified, and letters were sent to the chief executive officers, inviting them to CIA Headquarters, with their principal research and development specialists, for a full day, which included a morning of top secret briefings on the terrorist threat and our problems in dealing with it, lunch with the director, and an afternoon of technical discussions. Five companies were invited in every two weeks. We were hoping that a few of these companies might have "skunkworks" that had technology that could be rapidly deployed to help us with our problems.

At the end of one of the afternoon sessions, an officer who had accompanied his CEO mentioned that his division had developed a technology that detected weapons caches, which are difficult to find by normally available techniques. I could think of no immediate application, but I filed it away in my memory.

A couple of months later, I was in Paris and Chuck Cogan and I met with French minister of interior Charles Pasqua. Chirac was then prime minister, and Paris was in panic over a number of bombs that had exploded, killing several and wounding many, in shops and arcades along the Champs-Elysées. The newspapers were speculating that if the government couldn't handle this problem quickly, Chirac might fall. Pasqua discussed this problem at length and mentioned that a large cache of explosives in the Fontainebleau Forest was the source of material for these terrorist bombs. However, an army of police and military with probes and other devices had failed to locate it. I remembered my conversation with the industrialist visiting the CIA. I cabled Headquarters and asked them to contact the company concerned, evaluate the likely effectiveness of the technology, and if positive, make arrangements with the company to support the French.

Company technicians, together with French and American security personnel, eventually found the cache of explosives, which contained, along with many kilos of the Czech explosive Semtex, a rather large quantity of heroin. This was a Shiite fundamentalist operation. Although we had asked Pasqua not to give the U.S. government or the company concerned any credit for their assistance, he did exactly the opposite in a press conference (but managed to leave the company's name out). This is the same Minister of Interior Pasqua who, in another incarnation early in 1995, in a political act condemned even by many in his own government and press, accused America of industrial espionage against the French. So much for gratitude! Merci, Monsieur Pasqua.

CHAPTER 21

Bring 'Em Back Alive— or Not

The Libyan raid by the United States on April 14, 1986, was followed by a flurry of violent terrorist acts, and more were to come. In Lebanon, two Britons and one American were murdered on April 17. On the same day, security staff at El Al Airlines at Heathrow Airport in London found a suitcase bomb in the carry-on baggage of a pregnant Irish woman. The bomb had been given to her by her Jordanian boyfriend, Nizar Hindawi. She would have been killed with the other passengers if it had been placed on board the flight. The Justice Department had secured sealed indictments against terrorists who had carried out airline hijackings or other crimes in which American citizens or property had been attacked. In addition to Abu Nidal and Abu Abbas, we were authorized to apprehend and return to the United States for trial a number of others.

One of them was a Jordanian explosives expert named Mohammed Rashid. Rashid was part of a Baghdad-based terrorist organization calling itself the 15 May Group (after the birthdate of the state of Israel), headed by his mentor, a master bomb maker named Abu Ibrahim, who had a talent for making hard-to-detect bombs. Rashid, his apprentice, had learned his deadly trade well; the CIA had been tracking him for years.

On August 11, 1982, a bomb went off on Pan Am Flight 830, which was airborne from Hong Kong to Honolulu via Tokyo. A sixteen-year-old Japanese boy named Toru Ozawa was killed and fifteen other passengers were injured. The bomb had been planted beneath Ozawa's seat. Airline records revealed that three members of a Moroccan family named Harouk had been sitting in that row on the Hong Kong–Tokyo leg of the trip, but had left the flight in Tokyo. A fingerprint left on the stub of Mr. Harouk's boarding pass revealed that Harouk was in fact Mohammed Rashid. His Austrian-born wife, Christine Pinter, aka Fatima, whom he had met during his terrorist internship with the Baader-Meinhof gang, and his son were his traveling companions.

The incident was not gory enough to receive much media attention, but for the CIA it was troublesome. The bomb was made of plastic explosive. It had passed through airline security devices, which were metal-sensitive and intended for weapons detection. The device was barometric, set off by a change in cabin pressure, yet small enough to be hidden underneath an airline seat. It could be armed by a terrorist who would be able to disembark before it killed unsuspecting passengers.

Two weeks later, on August 25, Pan Am maintenance workers in Rio de Janeiro discovered an unexploded bomb attached to the bottom of a seat cushion in a plane that had just come in from Miami. It was not just the Miami–Rio passengers who had been reprieved. The bomb had actually been placed on the aircraft by one of Rashid's coconspirators for a flight from London to New York. It had been programmed to detonate at about the same time as the Hawaiian bomb. Wrapped in burgundy plastic and not much bigger than a paperback book, the bomb was a Frequent Flier. It had flown around the world for fourteen days and forty thousand miles without going off because the terrorist had broken off a portion of the safety pin, leaving the nib stuck in the bomb. Rashid was undoubtedly responsible. The device contained a length of gold-plated nickel wire identical to a fragment that had been removed from the body of the dead Japanese boy.

On August 30, just five days later, a distraught Palestinian businessman named Adnan Awad visited officials in the U.S. embassy in Bern. Guilty over the potential loss of innocent lives, he confessed that he had left a suitcase bomb in his room at the Noga Hilton in Geneva. The U.S. diplomat who debriefed Awad notified the Swiss federal police, who located the luggage but not the bomb. Awad had to draw a diagram of the suitcase interior before the Swiss could find it.

To prove to the Swiss that he had been sent by the 15 May Group, Awad called Abu Ibrahim in Baghdad and said he was out of money. A courier named Abu Saif arrived shortly thereafter, bringing $1,500 in cash. When the Swiss searched Saif's shoulder bag, they found that a portion of the lining had been removed. The lining was made of burgundy vinyl and matched the wrapping of the bomb found in Rio.

Rashid was later implicated in the 1983 killing of Palestinian moderate Isam Sartawi in Portugal (an Abu Nidal hit). In a retrial, he was found not guilty of murder after he confessed to serving as a decoy to draw attention away from the real murderer who was never caught. Rashid was, however, sentenced to three years in prison for using a forged passport. The Portuguese released him nearly two years later, and he disappeared.

Since 1983, not much had been heard of Rashid. Early in my tenure at the CTC, we received an agent report that Rashid and his family were living in a North African city. To the casual observer, the ever-resourceful

Rashid appeared to have taken up a new line of work, ceramics, manufacturing dinner plates. Actually, the plates were made of plastic explosive.

The CTC, with the help of local CIA personnel, zeroed in on his life and his habits. We observed his patterns of movement and his associates. We knew where his house was and had surveillance on the office where he made his explosive plates. We even had video of his activities. Casey and I discussed the possibility of seizing Rashid and returning him to the United States for trial, but the CTC action teams were still in training and Rashid might change location quickly.

I suggested to Casey that perhaps the leader of another North African country might be willing to help deliver Rashid to us. Casey and this leader were friends, and this country had been a victim of some of Rashid's terrorist activities. Casey sent this leader a message asking him to receive me. Although his nationals would conduct the operation, the CTC had a plan to camouflage the leader's involvement. In and out quickly. Minimum of personnel, supported by excellent intelligence on the continuing whereabouts of Rashid. It appeared to be operationally feasible.

I flew to meet the leader. He received me warmly and graciously, which I took as a sign of the rapport that he and Casey shared. I launched into my pitch—most people have no idea how much salesmanship is involved in the spy business. As soon as I presented my plan, however, political realities intervened. He turned me down cold. The potential political fallout from the mission, he told me, was just too great. Everything depended on absolute secrecy, which no one could guarantee. If his role in handing over Rashid to the Americans became known, the damage to his regime, both internally and internationally, would be far too severe.

As much as I wanted his help, frankly I could see his point. We were looking at the upside of our proposed operation; the leader had long ago learned that the key to surviving as a head of state in the Arab world was a healthy respect for the downside. That left us fresh out of possibilities for apprehending Rashid. We were left with monitoring his activities, and waiting for another opportunity.

Another terrorist under sealed indictment was a Lebanese Shiite named Fawaz Yunis, who on June 11, 1985, had hijacked a Royal Jordanian Airlines plane from Beirut. He and his comrades subdued the eight guards on board the aircraft, disarmed them, tied them up, and beat them. In an ordeal that lasted more than two full days, Yunis ordered the pilot to fly to Tunisia, where an Arab League summit was convened. Yunis had hopes of delivering a diatribe before that august body, but he was refused permission to land at Tunis and returned to Beirut.

As he postured in front of the aircraft reading his prepared statement for the benefit of the TV cameras, his compatriots evacuated the passengers and crew and placed explosives on board. Just as he finished his harangue, they shot up the plane, setting off the explosives. The jetliner blew up on the tarmac, becoming a huge fireball and giving the media its lead story on the six-o'clock news.

Fawaz Yunis hadn't killed anyone; the airliner was Jordanian; and the crime was committed on Lebanese soil. However, three Americans were on board. Although they were released unharmed, the Omnibus Crime Act allowed the FBI to take jurisdiction in the case. In all honesty, from one to ten on the scale of terrorism, Fawaz Yunis was at best a three. (Abu Abbas was an eight; Mohammed Rashid was a nine.) But unlike Rashid, he was accessible. We were pretty sure we could get at him, and I knew that by capturing him for trial we would make our intentions clear throughout the terrorist community.

Two days after he blew up the Jordanian aircraft, Yunis surfaced again in connection with the hijacking of TWA Flight 847, which was commandeered en route to Athens and flown first to Beirut and then to Algiers. After it returned to Beirut, an American hostage named Robert Stethem was shot in the head and thrown out the front door of the aircraft onto the runway. Yunis was among the reinforcements who had boarded the plane shortly after Stethem's murder. With him was the Imad Mugniyah, head of Islamic Jihad, the group responsible for blowing up the Marine barracks in Beirut in 1983 and holding the hostages in Beirut. Amal militia chief Nabih Berri ultimately brokered the release of the hostages through dealings with the White House and with Syria's Hafiz Assad and Hashemi Rafsanjani of Iran.

Yunis was never one to keep a low profile. Through our sources we had learned of his whereabouts and had developed a substantial dossier on him. We knew he was living in Beirut, but that he did travel. At one point during Oliver North's efforts to free the hostages in Beirut, he had several DEA officers assigned to him. They were looking into contacts in the drug world in Cyprus, which spilled over into Lebanon, who could be useful on the hostage problem. These DEA officers had acquired a source, Jamal Hamdan, who was quite reliable in providing information about drug traffickers. Hamdan had been friendly with Fawaz Yunis since 1981 and had even served as a sort of mentor to him in the shadowy world of Middle Eastern black-market commerce.

Before he took up air piracy, Yunis had been in another line of work—he was a used-car salesman in Beirut. Generally speaking, there is a lot of "glory" but not much money in terrorism, and Yunis had a wife and two young sons to support. Now he was unemployed and strapped for funds, so he was trying to get into the drug business.

I was delighted. Drug running would give the CTC a good cover to lure

Yunis out of Beirut to a place where he could be shanghaied and taken to the States. In spring of 1987, a series of high-level sessions began among officials of the CIA, Pentagon, State Department, NSC, FBI, and Justice Department about bringing Yunis to the United States for trial. We called it "extraction," as in the removal of a bad tooth. In terms of coordination among branches of the federal government, we were really breaking new ground. That process, as effective as it can be, is seldom efficient—the bureaucratic rigmarole in setting up the apprehension of Fawaz Yunis was more complicated than the operation itself. I listened to a great deal of posturing; I found it necessary to massage any number of overblown egos.

Everyone wanted in on the action. Each agency had a need to shine (or a need to justify its budget). On the other hand, because no one wanted to look bad if the deal went sour, there was a great deal of jockeying for safe positions.

The final result of the interminable meetings was what the FBI called Operation Goldenrod and an agreement on the "rules of engagement" for seizing Yunis. The Justice Department, which would prosecute the case once Yunis arrived in the States, set most of the ground rules. They needed to establish a clean and unbroken line of jurisdiction, from the time of his apprehension to his delivery onto U.S. soil. This meant that Yunis had to be apprehended by the FBI in international waters or airspace, remain in constant custody of the feds, and remain clear of the turf of any other sovereign nation—for the entire duration of his four-thousand-mile journey to the United States.

The CIA would run the extraction operation—up to a point. We would dangle the bait, set the trap, and be sure that the target was delivered into the FBI's hands in international waters. The CIA can't arrest anybody, so that job fell to the FBI. To keep the case "clean," we couldn't even be present when he was arrested. We were required, however, at the point he departed for his rendezvous with the FBI, to have "U.S. eyes on the target"—to make sure that he was in fact the same Fawaz Yunis who stood on the tarmac in Beirut in 1985.

The key to the operation was Jamal Hamdan. Hamdan had already proven that he could entice Yunis out of Beirut and into neutral territory, but Jamal himself was a problem. He wasn't exactly Snow White—in fact, he was a murderer in the context of the Lebanese civil war, which bothered some folks in the administration. One of his requirements for cooperating with us was that he and his entire family be given asylum in the United States—a reasonable request under the circumstances.

Hamdan had left Beirut to live in Cyprus because he had made a lot of enemies in Lebanon. His family was still there and elsewhere in the Middle East, however. He was concerned about retaliation against his relatives after his role in delivering Fawaz Yunis became public. He saw this operation as his and his family's ticket to safety, for under normal circumstances his unsavory reputation would have precluded the offer of asylum. Only after a great deal of discussion in Washington about this issue was permission granted.

Hamdan lived in Larnaca, a Cypriot coastal town. With our encouragement, he intensified his relationship with Yunis by telephone, and an initial operation was undertaken to obtain, in effect, a confession from Yunis regarding his part in the Jordanian Airliner hijacking. The Justice Department really wanted this evidence badly. Hamdan was set up in an apartment in Cyprus. Yunis was invited to visit him there, and after a few drinks he bragged about the Jordanian hijacking and about his involvement in TWA Flight 847. Knowing that Yunis needed money, we also provided Jamal with a lot of it to throw around. Hamdan assured Yunis that he, too, would be rolling in cash if he would be willing to work for a drug dealer named "Joseph."

Yunis was extremely interested and returned to Beirut to await a signal from Hamdan to return for a meeting with Joseph. We began to consider how we were going to extract Hamdan's immediate relatives, including a number of children. This was no small matter, especially when we had to do it at the last minute without arousing suspicion. These were not experienced global travelers by any means. We had to get them tickets; we had to get them money; and most important, we had to arrange U.S. visas for them, something not easily obtained for Lebanese in the Middle East, for fear that they would never leave the United States.

In the warlike atmosphere of Lebanon and other Middle Eastern countries, these were major logistical problems—and the timing had to be exquisite. We couldn't extract them ahead of time or we would tip our hand. We worked out plans to move them on the morning that the operation was activated. We also had to quietly prepare them for the journey and make sure they understood the need for absolute secrecy, without telling them why. All it would take was the sudden purchase of an expensive new pair of shoes by a sister and the offhand comment that she was going on a long trip to compromise the entire operation.

Because Yunis's terrorist act had been perpetrated against the Jordanians, we asked them if they would like to participate with us in apprehending Yunis and have him stand trial in Jordan. The Jordanians were not interested.

By the end of summer, everything was in place. At yet another interagency meeting, which Clair George attended with me, Yunis's extraction was set for September 13. On the way back to Headquarters, Clair turned to me and said, "I think you better go out and run this one."

I was not particularly surprised that he made this suggestion, but it was not the way the Clandestine Services normally handled such matters. To my knowledge, the Directorate of Operations had never sent a senior officer from Washington into the field to run an operation. I had a lot of confidence in our fine and able chief on Cyprus, whom I knew well.

On the other hand, I could see Clair's point. The extraction was going to involve some heavy hitters from the Pentagon and the FBI, and he wanted someone of comparable stature to represent the Agency in the field, in case anybody tried to pull rank and override our command of the operation. I think Clair had another reason—if the whole thing went south, I'd be the convenient scapegoat to take the blame.

The plan was relatively simple. Hamdan would arrange for Yunis to meet with Joseph, the drug kingpin, on his yacht out in the Mediterranean, where the FBI would be waiting to take him into custody. Pulling it off, however, was another matter. Twelve miles is a long way offshore—beyond the sight of land—and even an Onassis-class yacht looks rather small out there on the open water, if you can find it. Jamal had no boating experience whatsoever, but he did have a brother named Ahmad [F], whom Yunis knew and trusted. Because Jamal didn't feel it was safe for him in Lebanon, we had been using Ahmad as a middleman in dealings with Fawaz Yunis in Beirut. We brought Ahmad to Cyprus. A bright young man with no experience operating a motorboat, he would become the helmsman of the motorboat that would take Yunis and Hamdan to the FBI.

Although we could relatively quickly teach Ahmad how to handle the boat, teaching him how to navigate out of sight of land was impossible, given our time constraints. A group of us were sitting around my office, worrying this issue, when it occurred to me that we could station small, easily maneuvered picketboats at intervals from the shore to near the yacht, off which Ahmad could key as he roared out to the rendezvous with Yunis aboard. This concept was accepted and then modified. We settled on one picketboat stationed out near the yacht, and another boat with a touristy-looking couple joyriding about in the ocean who would lead the way—hopefully in an unobtrusive manner. The couple was carefully chosen from our U.S. action team. He was an ex-SEAL, and she was a former Army officer.

Meanwhile, we leased an eighty-one-foot yacht, the *Skunk Kilo*, for Joseph, a name that seemed to suit a drug baron. A joint team of CIA and FBI personnel would board the *Skunk Kilo* and sail to a rendezvous with the USS *Butte*, a munitions ship of the Sixth Fleet, which was to support the operation. At that point, the FBI would take over control of the yacht; they believed that they had personnel capable of navigating to and holding the precise longitude and latitude off Cyprus for the offshore rendezvous with the motorboat bearing Yunis.

The FBI staffed the *Skunk Kilo* with their counterterrorist Hostage Rescue Team (HRT) for the takedown. This was fine by me, since they hadn't seen any action as yet, and this was just the kind of mission they'd been established to handle. The trouble was that the HRT team was all male. I thought that a yacht belonging to a drug kingpin would have some ladies on board. I suggested that the FBI put a couple of bikini-clad women agents on the boat as window dressing, but they were mightily opposed. This was to be an HRT takedown and an HRT collar. Period.

After all we'd gone through, I didn't want Yunis having cold feet at the last minute, so I took the matter up with my friend and counterpart, FBI executive assistant director Buck Revell. Revell twisted an arm or two, overcame a mountain of male-chauvinist resistance, and forced the Hostage Rescue guys to grudgingly accept the presence of three women FBI agents.

The operation got under way when a Clandestine Services maritime officer was dispatched to Cyprus to train Ahmad to drive the boat. CIA and FBI officers boarded the CIA-chartered *Skunk Kilo* and began steaming for the rendezvous with the USS *Butte*. Other CTC officers supporting the operation left the United States by various routes and entered Cyprus. I disembarked into the hot and dusty atmosphere of Cyprus, passing through customs and immigration without incident and noting no particular interest taken by the authorities in the arriving passengers.

Stepping out of the entrance of the Larnaca airport, I made eye contact with the local CIA chief. I followed him at a discreet distance, and after a few twists and turns we drove off in his car. Frankly, he looked rather glum. We had planned to drive some distance out of town to rendezvous with some other personnel who had already arrived in Larnaca for the operation.

The chief informed me that the good news was that Yunis was already in Cyprus. However, the serious bad news was that the local Cypriot authorities had Yunis on a watch list and were apparently searching for him in hotels and other locations. My chief concern now was whether we should risk going forward with the operation. Yunis's being picked up by the authorities would be bad luck. Worse than that was the possibility that we could all be compromised in the process.

After joining up with some of our colleagues, we sat in an outdoor restaurant and discussed the dilemma. The maritime officer who had arrived a week earlier to train Ahmad in boat handling reported that Ahmad was proficient enough to follow the lead boat manned by the couple to the picketboat within sight of the yacht. Ahmad was a quick study. Howard Freeman, who, among other things, was to positively identify Yunis, was also there, as was a female CTC case officer who was handling liaison with the special team members.

The mood of the group at the restaurant was somber and tense. Much effort had gone into this operation. Ships were at sea, everything and everyone was in position. We felt enormous pressure to go ahead. It seemed to us that the only solution was to move Yunis—and of course Hamdan with him—from Hamdan's apartment where they were staying to another location. Why not the hotel from which we expected to initiate the operation? Weighing the various risks, I gave instructions to move Yunis there.

On Friday, September 11, Yunis and Hamdan moved into the Sheraton Limassol hotel, just a floor below our command post, so that we could keep an eye on them. Hopefully, the transfer would cause the local constabulary to lose track of Yunis for a couple of days—long enough to complete the operation. It was risky to have him check into the hotel—where his passport would be recorded—but it was an even bigger risk to leave him at Jamal's house in Larnaca, when the police knew of the connection between them. In making the move I was counting on the weekend to give us some breathing room—no one was apt to check passports in a high-priced tourist hotel until Monday. By that time, Fawaz Yunis would be on the way to Washington.

The chief and I met with Hamdan and Ahmad to explain why we had to make the move to the hotel and generally to boost their morale. We arranged to divert Yunis at the apartment and met the brothers at a safe house. This was the first time I had met with them face-to-face, but I was impressed by their cooperative spirit and eagerness to proceed. Jamal may have been a killer, but he certainly didn't look the part. Ahmad was certainly bright and seemed to have good judgment.

Our command post was in the honeymoon suite on the top floor of the newly constructed hotel. The radio operator and I were registered in the suite. Howard Freeman, the female case officer, and our local chief had each taken separate rooms. My being present during the operation did not seem to upset the chief, and I went out of my way to ensure that he was running the operation. This seems to have worked.

Fortunately, the suite was large—we filled it with people and equipment. Many U.S. government agencies were involved, and they all wanted to be up-to-date on the operation as it unfolded. As a result, we had an extensive communications network, including satellite communications, or SATCOM, whose antenna was directed—unobtrusively, we hoped—toward the living-room window. We had enciphered SATCOM links to CIA Headquarters in Washington, which, in turn, had a relay to the White House, to the FBI, and to the State Department. The U.S. military command in Stuttgart, Germany, insisted on monitoring our communications because of its responsibility for the USS *Butte,* and, of course, we had communications with the USS *Butte* and the *Skunk Kilo.*

We also had less powerful handheld radios for communications among the suite, the picketboat, and the lead boat. These pieces of communications gear turned out to be a problem. Maybe we asked too much of them, although God knows how many times we had checked and tested them.

Getting all of our gear into the hotel without being conspicuous was quite a feat. Your typical tourist arrives with sunscreen, a suitcase, and a Nikon, not with rather large aluminum boxes of telecommunications equipment—these were the days before laptops and cellular telephones. However, the fact that the hotel had just opened worked in our favor. There were few guests, and the management was still bringing in furnishings and other bulky objects of their own. Actually, we blended in well, and we billed our aluminum boxes as containing photographic equipment.

That the hotel was brand-new didn't serve us well in one regard, however. The manager was so goddamned delighted that a big spender from the States had rented one of his suites that he kept sending emissaries to the room with fruit, flowers, candy, and booze. We met a veritable parade of bellhops and waiters at the door, accepted their gifts, and prevented them from entering. Finally, the female CTC officer solved the problem. She donned one of the suite's bathrobes as if that were all she was wearing, put a towel over her hair as if it had just been washed, and answered the door. After two such encounters, the management finally got the message that this was a private party and stopped sending us gifts.

On Saturday, September 12, Ahmad reserved a rental speedboat for the following morning, while we checked and double-checked our arrangements. The FBI on board the *Skunk Kilo* were ready to go—in fact, they were loaded for bear. Additional FBI personnel boarded the yacht from the Navy munitions ship the USS *Butte,* armed not only with their own weapons but with the additional firepower they had borrowed from the Navy. My friend Buck Revell was on board the *Butte* running the FBI end of the operation. The CIA personnel had left the yacht for the *Butte,* so that no CIA personnel would be present when Yunis was arrested.

That evening Hamdan gave Yunis a nice send-off—the two of them spent the night with a brace of Colombian hookers who happened to be plying their trade in the hotel cocktail lounge. The following morning, Ahmad brought the speedboat around at about eight. We watched with apprehension, waiting for Jamal and Yunis to appear in front of the hotel and move toward the pier. There was some delay, perhaps caused by hangovers from the night before. Finally, they showed up, dressed in bathing trunks and T-shirts. Clearly, no one was carrying a weapon. Howard Freeman was on the dock looking properly touristy. As they boarded, he made the positive "U.S. eyes on the target" ID of Fawaz Yunis. He signaled to us in the suite, and that message was forwarded to all participants in our SATCOM network. We also asked Headquarters to activate the complex plan for moving Hamdan's extended family out of the Middle East to the United States. Their tickets, funds, and necessary visas had all been pre-positioned for this moment. Ahmad slipped the bowline from the dock's cleat and slowly edged out of the marina for the open sea, with Yunis and Jamal aboard.

Hours earlier, the picketboat had departed for its position near the yacht. The couple in the lead boat were making waves all over the sea in front of the marina on this hazy morning. Right away things started going awry. We had major problems with both navigation and communications. The picketboat reported that it had been unable to find the *Skunk Kilo,* which had drifted off its designated longitude and latitude. Finally, sporadic communication was established between the yacht and the picketboat, and eventually the picketboat established a visual with the yacht.

Meanwhile, the speedboat with Yunis was roaring out to sea, following the lead boat with the couple aboard. Because the *Skunk Kilo* was out of position, the picketboat was out of position. Thus, the longitude and latitude that the lead boat was headed for to make the rendezvous was incorrect. Moreover, the picketboat, the lead boat, and the suite were experiencing intermittent communications blackouts with the handheld radios. The lead boat could not maintain communications with the picketboat long enough to get a fix on what its new course had to be to reach the yacht. Coupled with the extremely hazy conditions, which made visual navigation difficult, we had the makings of a major disaster.

However, we in the command post in the suite were unaware of the problem, though we had sensed from the picketboat's comments on his difficulty in finding the *Skunk Kilo* that something was askew with its location. We assumed that the lack of communications between the picketboat and the lead boat was simply a matter of security.

I did know, however, approximately how long it was supposed to take Jamal, Ahmad, and Yunis to get to the yacht, and I knew that they were running overtime, then way overtime, in making the rendezvous. I began pacing. At about this time, the suite reestablished contact with the picketboat near the yacht, who reported that a large Soviet roll-on/roll-off ship had just crossed his bow headed for Limassol port. However, he reported no sighting of the lead boat, and of course, no sighting of the boat containing Yunis. The maritime officer aboard the picketboat knew that he and the yacht were out of position, and the lead boat and the motorboat bearing Yunis somehow had to be vectored to the yacht.

The former Navy SEAL, the helmsman who was handling the lead boat, also knew something was wrong—he was too far out at sea and had obviously overshot both *Skunk Kilo* and the picketboat. Being resourceful, he took the initiative to turn back, with Ahmad following at a considerable distance. Yunis was beginning to be nervous about being out of sight of land. After making his turn toward shore, the helmsman of the lead boat finally reestablished contact with the picketboat. The picketboat asked him when and if he had seen the Soviet ship. The lead boat had seen the ship. By calibrating its course and the time when it was sighted by both the picketboat and the lead boat, the helmsman of the lead boat was able to vector himself toward the yacht. Ahmad duly followed him on the new course to the *Skunk Kilo*.

Yunis and Jamal boarded the *Skunk Kilo* and admired the pretty women in their bikinis who were sunning themselves on deck. As Jamal had forewarned Yunis, they were both immediately frisked. Here we had a terrorist in a bathing suit—what the FBI thought he might be hiding, I have no idea. After the FBI made their own positive ID of Yunis, they slammed both him and Jamal to the floor—none too gently, either—and cuffed them. (We had requested the FBI to treat Jamal as hostile to maintain the fiction that he was not part of the operation.) Yunis suffered hairline fractures of both wrists. The *Skunk Kilo* then rendezvoused with the *Butte*, and Yunis and Hamdan were transferred onto the munitions ship. At about this same time, one of Hamdan's sisters, her husband, and their children transited Larnaca Airport on their way to asylum in the United States. Other members of the Hamdan extended family were proceeding to the same destination via other routes.

The *Butte* steamed through the Mediterranean for four days to meet up with an aircraft carrier, the USS *Saratoga*. Yunis and his FBI keepers were airlifted onto the *Saratoga*, then almost immediately put on board an S-3 Viking for the long flight to Andrews AFB in Maryland. Our CIA group dismantled the operations center in the suite and checked out of the Sheraton Limassol, once again spreading out to various nearby hotels. For security reasons, we could have only the briefest celebration, a handshake with the participants who had been operating outside of the hotel suite. Over the next two days, we took differing routes back to Washington, D.C.

When the operation was still in the planning stages, where Yunis should be tried had been discussed. Vicki Toensing, a former assistant to Sen. Barry Goldwater who was now in the Justice Department specializing in terrorist problems, wanted very much for him to stand trial in Washington, D.C. Her husband, Joe DiGenova, was the U.S. attorney for the District of Columbia, and out of her presence we mused about how the prosecution of Yunis, following on the heels of his pursuit of crack-smoking mayor Marion Barry, would be good for Joe's career. In any event, no one had a compelling reason to try him anywhere else, so the capital was fine by us.

Yunis—dressed in a straitjacket, lying on a stretcher, and drugged—was flying with such an entourage that the S-3 had no room for a copilot. Fortunately, one of the FBI agents was an aviator and had some hours in the S-3. He was able to spell the Navy pilot from time to time, as the flight to Andrews lasted 13 hours and turned out to be the longest S-3 flight in history—it made the *Guinness Book of Records*. Because Yunis couldn't touch foreign soil (we'd have had to turn him over if he did), there were two in-flight refuelings by KC-10 tankers. Finally, Yunis landed at Andrews and was put on trial. DiGenova got his conviction. As far as I know, Yunis is still working on thirty years in Leavenworth.

(Not long after our return to the capital, Vice President George Bush—always the thoughtful gentleman—invited some of us from the various agencies who had participated in the operation to his home at the Naval Observatory for a round of thanks. The only photograph that exists of the event shows just the backs of the heads of the participants, for security reasons.)

I recall sitting at my round table that served as my desk in early 1988, undoubtedly smoking a good cigar, when my deputy practically fell through the door waving a cable reporting that Rashid and his wife had been spotted in an African country. The opportunity we had missed in the North African city two years before had surfaced again. We began to examine the possibilities of extracting him. This operation was extremely complicated and would entail landing in the desert, in-flight refueling, and other problems that clearly required considerable U.S. military assistance. We further surveilled Rashid and developed good sources both in and out of the local government to help us. We made arrangements with the Air Force to have a Pathfinder team dropped into the anticipated landing area to test the soil for its suitability to handle a C-130. Discussions of the plan were held with administration officials just below cabinet level.

As the planning went forward, many—both within the CIA and elsewhere—felt that it was too complicated and risky. I did not minimize the problems, but I felt it was worth doing. As usual, the difficulties of international politics played a large role: we had to arrange complex aircraft movements up to the country of Rashid's refuge without drawing attention to our activity. We had worked out the operation with our military to a gnat's eye and believed that the operation was entirely feasible.

Unfortunately, it was clear from the beginning that new CIA director William Webster didn't have the stomach for bold moves of any sort, much less a fairly daring extraction of a dangerous terrorist. Webster talked about possible violation of international law every time this operation was discussed. Prior to a National Security Planning Group (NSPG) meeting to make a go/no-go decision on this operation, a subcabinet committee meeting on terrorist issues, including this operation, asked for a military evaluation of our plan, which had been drawn up in conjunction with the U.S. military. The job was given to then Lieutenant Colonel, now Major General, Schoomaker.

On the morning that Schoomaker's recommendations were presented at the NSPG by the vice chairman of the JCS, neither of us was in attendance. After the meeting, I got word from Webster's office that the JCS had recommended on the basis of Schoomaker's report that the NSPG terminate the Rashid extraction. I was told that General Schoomaker's report had been very negative. Yet, while the NSPG meeting was going on, General Schoomaker had been sitting in my office and he told me that he had written a report endorsing the Rashid extraction and had recommended NSPG approval.

This officer is not a liar. He is as straightforward and honorable an officer as they come, and we had known each other for some time. It was also his job to go get terrorists. He may have suggested modifications to the plan, but he recommended that it go forward. I suspect that the JCS had plenty of wet palms about the tricky air aspects in this operation and concerns about how it would look if they failed. Remember that the chairman of the JCS at this time was the "go and hide" submariner, Admiral Crowe. Unlike the naval aviation crowd, the submarine service has never been noted for its daring. That, probably combined with Webster's cold feet, was enough to kill the extraction in the NSPG. I guess the group simply claimed they were following General Schoomaker's recommendation so that no one else had to take any responsibility. Or, perhaps General Schoomaker thought the risks worthwhile, but the group couldn't stomach them.

In the end, Rashid and his wife were forced out of the African country and went to Greece. Under considerable pressure from the U.S. government, the Greek authorities arrested him and held him pending trial. Although the Greeks were on the verge of letting Rashid slip away yet again, we arranged, among other pressures, to have Adnan Awad testify at the trial, and the terrorist was sentenced to a mere eighteen years in prison.

Many more sealed terrorist indictments are still sitting in the U.S. attorney's office in Alexandria, Virginia. Some of those named are still active in Palestinian organizations, and a lot of us have not forgotten what they did. As "normalization" with Yasir Arafat and the Palestinians goes forward, I have to wonder whether our government will pursue the likes of Abu Abbas or not. If these terrorists are never prosecuted, they will have fared better under our system of justice than I did.

PART V

ATTACKED FROM WITHIN

CHAPTER 22

Iran-contra Investigation

"It's really gonna hit the fan this time! Aren't you glad you're not in Latin America Division anymore?" one of the CTC wags teased me. On October 5, 1986, the Sandinistas shot down a C-123 transport plane over Nicaragua that had been engaged in contra resupply. They captured the only survivor, a man named Eugene Hasenfus. Hasenfus was a "kicker"—someone who literally booted supplies out of the open hatch of the aircraft when it was over the drop site. Dazed, scared, alone, and clearly no genius, Hasenfus was paraded in front of the TV cameras by the Sandinistas. He told his captors that he was under the impression that he worked for the CIA. Papers on board the downed aircraft linked it to Southern Air Transport (SAT), which had formerly been a CIA proprietary.

The press was having a field day at the expense of the Agency, and yes, I was relieved that dealing with this problem was not going to be my responsibility. However, it didn't raise many eyebrows among Washington insiders. Hasenfus's capture was new news, but the contra resupply effort itself was old news—North's operation had been discussed on the cocktail circuit for well over a year. Nevertheless, some faces in the administration were red because an American had been caught, and the timing couldn't have been worse. With congressional elections less than a month away, the Democrats in Congress asked Ed Meese for an independent counsel to investigate whether there had been ongoing U.S. support for the contras at a time when it was prohibited by the Boland Amendment. The FBI and the U.S. Customs Service also launched investigations into SAT involvement.

A month later, a new load of manure came at the administration, this time from a different direction. A small Lebanese magazine named *Al Shiraa* reported that the United States had been selling arms to Iran. Iran's Speaker of the Parliament, Hashemi Rafsanjani, one of the "moderates," confirmed the report the following day.

The news of the weapons sale caused genuine astonishment inside the Beltway. In the press and in Congress, many were angry over what was perceived as hypocrisy and double-dealing by the Reagan White House. The government had been pressing hard on our allies and indeed on the rest of the world not to sell arms to the Iranians, and here we were doing it ourselves.

Right about here is probably where the administration lost the battle for public opinion. George Shultz openly broke ranks and appeared on *Face the Nation* saying, in effect, that he had nothing to do with it and didn't approve of the arms sales policy. In a series of briefings and public addresses, Reagan denied that the administration had sold arms in exchange for release of the hostages. It was one of the few occasions when his skills as the Great Communicator failed him. If the cabinet had presented a united front, if Reagan had come forward and stated his sincere desire to bring the hostages home, and if he had explained the actions of the government in that light, there would have been controversy, but nothing like what followed.

Both the Iran and the contra stories took on lives of their own in the press. Every day there were new headlines, and Reagan's changing explanations didn't satisfy anyone. Allusions to Nixon and Watergate abounded. The president was in a reactive rather than a proactive posture.

Both the House and Senate Intelligence Committees demanded that Casey come down to testify. Up until this point all this had almost nothing to do with me, or with the CTC, but it didn't matter. The entire Agency mobilized to assemble the pieces and prepare Casey to go to the Hill. He was due to testify before Congress on November 21.

Former DDI Bob Gates, who earlier in the year had become deputy director of the Agency after McMahon retired, was put in charge of pulling all the information together. A lot of us were called in on a Saturday to work on the testimony. I suspected that the issue of the November 1985 shipment of HAWKs might come up, so I called the woman who had been my secretary when I was chief of the European Division. She was still in that position. I asked her whether she still had my back-channel cable file on the shipment. When she told me she did, I was pleased because I knew the file would document what had happened.

Documenting what everyone else had done was another matter. It didn't help that Casey was out of the country, visiting the contras with Latin America Task Force chief Alan Fiers. The Boland Amendment had just been lifted on October 1, and Casey was anxious to see how the freedom fighters had held up during the official funding drought. The FBI was swarming all over CIA Headquarters taking depositions.

Gates's task was made much more difficult by the fact that no one person in the CIA had the complete picture. Maybe the only person who knew how the jigsaw fit was Oliver North, but North had more than enough troubles of his own. On the NSC side, North's number one, National Security Adviser John Poindexter, was scheduled to testify before HPSCI and SSCI on the same day as Casey, and everyone knew that any discrepancies between their statements would be relentlessly dissected.

Casey returned from Central America late on the nineteenth of November, two days before his testimony. The following day he conferred with Poindexter, then returned to Langley for a final meeting up in the director's conference room. The place was full of people who had gathered to complete the draft of his statement. As was customary, Casey waited till the last minute to put it into final form. This time, however, he may have waited too long. There was a lot we in the Agency didn't know, and even what we did know wasn't in one neat pile. Just one day before he was slated to speak on the Hill, his statement was still very much a work in progress.

The meeting was a round-robin session, with papers being passed around the conference table and people scurrying in and out bringing cables and file documents. Casey's statement was continually revised as pieces of information fell into place and as he continued to suggest changes.

Because the text of his statement remained so fluid, considerable erroneous speculation has arisen about a conspiracy to doctor Agency documents for Casey's appearance. No official CIA paperwork was modified. What was going on was much more like a group of students working together on a big term paper the night before it's due. Pieces of the assignment had to be divvied up and then reassembled as one coherent document. The style and content of each segment had to be made consistent from one section to an other. Like any term paper, the material for the footnotes had to be in order; we had to have everything listed in the bibliography. And it had to be ready by morning. I imagine that by the time it was done, parts of it did indeed look as if it had been written by committee, which is not necessarily a good thing. It may not have been an A paper, but it was not felonious.

Casey went before HPSCI (pronounced "hipsy"), the House Permanent Select Committee on Intelligence, early on the morning of the twenty-first. He testified before SSCI (pronounced "sissy"), the Senate Select Committee on Intelligence, just before lunch, then returned to the House for round three in the afternoon. By all accounts, Casey was by no means forthcoming with the legislators. This was consistent with his prior appearances before the House and Senate. Because he suspected the committees of leaking information to the media, he did not volunteer information and answered questions within the narrowest context possible. His suspicions were not unfounded. Shortly after his appearance, details of his testimony found their way into the press.

In some accounts of Casey's testimony, he is accused of trying to claim that we in the Agency still thought we were shipping oil drilling parts, and not missiles. I don't know whether Casey misspoke or became confused or whether someone misconstrued his notorious mumbling. Casey would never have claimed that the November 1985 shipment to Iran was oil drilling equipment because he had been briefed by McFarlane in August on the plan to exchange missiles for hostages. It was always clear to him that St. Lucia Airlines had ferried HAWKs from Israel to Iran in November of 1985; he would never have denied this. What he was probably trying to say was that when the Agency's St. Lucia Airlines ferried the HAWK missiles, those of us involved thought it was carrying oil drilling spare parts.

Other Agency personnel also testified before the committees, including me. I had a date with SSCI on December 2, and with HPSCI on December 11. As usual, I went down beforehand to talk with the staffers so they could play their game and ask the right questions. During this warm-up session, Tom Latimer, the senior staffer on HPSCI—and no friend of the administration—pulled me aside. "In all honesty," he confided, "if North really funded some of the freedom-fighter supply effort out of Iranian funds, this was one of the greatest covert operations of all time." I suspect that this was an underlying feeling on the part of many members of the committee, once you got past the politics. On the House side, some admired the reason for these actions and the boldness of the venture.

In the Senate it was a different kettle of fish. The Senate Select Committee on Intelligence had a new room where the interrogation was held. The senators all sat up on a raised platform so they could look down on their witnesses—all that was missing were their togas. It was a metaphor for their attitude. By and large, the questioning was hostile.

According to their rules, you could have a personal lawyer present, but not an Agency lawyer representing the Agency and you in your official capacity. (None of us, of course, had personal lawyers.) I found this more than ironic, since the senators asking the questions are almost all lawyers themselves. Moreover, sworn testimony before the Senate can be used against you in a court of law. The terrorist accused of blowing up the Federal Building in Oklahoma City had more protection of his legal rights—and more access to counsel while being interrogated—than I did.

I did not realize it, but Casey was already ill. He had never resembled the picture of health, and when he returned from Central America, I thought he looked a bit under the weather, but I wasn't surprised. Heat, humidity, rounds of meetings, and a helicopter trip into the jungle were not the best prescription for a man in his seventies, especially on the eve of a command performance before an audience of eager piranhas. Other than what I took to be a touch of jet lag, however, I hadn't noticed anything unusual—and I was seeing him a good bit on terrorism matters.

The day after Casey's testimony, staff members from the attorney general's office combed through the NSC offices. They found an undated Ollie North memo to the president clearly indicating that profits from Iranian arms sales were earmarked for supplies for the contras. At a press conference on Tuesday, November 25, Reagan announced the resignation of John Poindexter and the firing of Ollie North. Atty. Gen. Ed Meese then publicly revealed the diversion of funds from Iran arms sales to the contras.

The press howled, and Iran-contra investigations became the biggest growth industry in Washington. Meese agreed to seek appointment of an independent prosecutor. The White House decided it had to have its own inquiry into the NSC. There were more rounds of testimony on the Hill for Casey, and more rounds of preparation within the Agency. On December 8 it was House Defense Appropriations; on the tenth it was House Foreign Relations. On the eleventh it was back to HPSCI.

On the sixteenth, Casey was due once again before SSCI. He never got there. On December 15, Bill Casey suffered a seizure in his office and was taken to Georgetown University Hospital. Nobody realized how serious his problems were.

Casey's seizure was the result of a brain tumor, a fast-growing lymphoma that had spread its malignant web through much of the left side of his brain. Neurosurgeons removed it, or as much of it as they could, on December 18. Radiation treatments were planned to kill off whatever was left.

While they were boring a hole in Casey's skull, I was testifying again, this time before the President's Special Review Board, aka the Tower Commission. This White House commission was to determine if significant structural problems existed within the NSC and the way national security issues were handled within the executive branch. The commission consisted of three men with time on their hands—former senator John Tower; former national security adviser Brent Scowcroft; and former senator, former secretary of state, and former unsuccessful vice-presidential candidate Edmund Muskie.

Billed as the "three wise men," they had much more in common with the Three Stooges. The commission had no subpoena power, and both North and Poindexter, through their attorneys, turned down invitations to appear before them. Hence the commission was investigating a matter in the complete absence of firsthand information from the two men who probably knew the most about it. Undaunted, they proceeded.

When I testified, Tower sat directly across from me, with Muskie and Scowcroft beside him, to his right, in that order. It was about two o'clock in the afternoon, and Tower, not to put too fine a point on it, seemed drunk. He could keep his head up only by staring at a picture right over my head. Muskie seemed to be there in body but not in spirit or intellect. Scowcroft looked like he was dozing half the time and appeared to have to lean on his hands to focus his attention on the proceedings. They asked few questions—the director of the commission, Rhett Dawson, did almost all the talking.

Assistant Secretary of Defense Rich Armitage followed me in the witness chair. After his testimony, he asked the chief staffer how he did. "Well," Armitage was told in reply, "you certainly did a lot better than Clarridge. We couldn't get anything out of him."

They were trying to extract knowledge that I did not have. Without Poindexter, without North, and now without Casey, the staff of the Tower Commission were pushing the theory that a diabolical genius was somewhere, and somehow I was it. They were trying to make me into the éminence grise behind the Iran-contra linkage. I didn't tell them what they wanted to hear, but I told them everything I knew.

The following day, at the request of Atty. Gen. Ed Meese, Lawrence Walsh was appointed special prosecutor by the U.S. Circuit Court of Appeals for the District of Columbia. This put Iran-contra in an entirely different light, taking it out of the political arena of presidential commissions and congressional committees, and placing it into the realm of the courts. Even though the investigation was just beginning, the press hinted at possible hefty fines and prison time.

My cardinal regret of this entire business is that I didn't get a personal lawyer sooner—a lot sooner. The Agency's lawyer can represent you only in your official capacity and may be reluctant to, or under pressure not to, furnish you with sound advice—like keeping your mouth shut. To really protect yourself, you have to get your own attorney at your own expense, if you think you need one, or even if you don't, as in my case. Oliver North did that, and Brendan Sullivan did an admirable job of keeping his client from being railroaded.

And it would have happened. Between Thanksgiving and Christmas of 1986, a dense gray fog of amnesia had settled over Washington. All those people who had been delighted to share cocktail confidences about what North was up to promptly forgot all about it. The whole city was in denial. As soon as *contra* got hyphenated with *Iran,* no one wanted to be associated with any memory of it.

Nevertheless, I did not get legal counsel. Naively, I felt that since I hadn't done anything wrong and since my files were there and intact, I had nothing to worry about. My deputy at the CTC advised me to get counsel anyway. North and Brendan Sullivan said the same thing. It was good advice and I should have listened, but I was worried about the cost.

Generally speaking, the problem is not that you've done anything criminal. (If you have, that's another story.) The difficulty is that in your initial deposition or testimony you forget, misremember, or misspeak. As soon as that happens, you've set yourself up for a charge of perjury—and this occurs in the very earliest stages of the investigation. I want to establish a foundation so that if Agency people ever get into that position again, they won't have to think twice about retaining good legal help. The purpose of the foundation would be to give someone legal advice and protection at the outset, when they are most vulnerable.

Also, some in the Agency exerted none-too-subtle efforts to discourage me and others from getting legal counsel. Word came down from the seventh floor that getting a lawyer suggested that you believed you were guilty of something. Clair George was firmly opposed for that reason. Alan Fiers, to his credit, was in favor, probably because he had a much better understanding of what was at stake. He had sort of a firefight with George over the issue, but he didn't get a lawyer either—at least, not at that time.

Without an attorney of my own, I gave a deposition before the Walsh gang. An Agency lawyer from the CIA Office of General Counsel (OGC) accompanied me, but was not allowed to sit in. John W. Keker, the fellow who deposed me, eventually became one of the prosecutors against Ollie North. He didn't ask me many questions, but instead occupied himself spinning conspiracy theories at me and asking what I thought of them.

Mostly he was conjecturing what the quid pro quo was with the Hondurans for letting us use their country as a base of operations against the Sandinistas. He figured that we had somehow secured the help of the Hondurans during the Boland Amendment cutoff by promising them military and economic aid. Maybe, he suggested, that assistance had even been part of the deal while I was still division chief in Latin America.

Did the Hondurans expect some help? Yes. Did they they ask the ambassador for some? Yes. Was a deal cut during my tenure in Latin America? No. This would surely have come up in our Restricted Interagency Group meetings at the State Department, but it never did. Keker kept throwing out variations on this theme, with different mixes of "conspirators" who might have colluded to keep this promise of assistance to the Hondurans under wraps, but there never was a conspiracy by anybody—and I told him so.

Remarkably enough, I never met Walsh himself. My so-called deposition with the conspiracy-minded Keker was the only contact I had with Walsh's office for about three years (and after that only through my lawyer), until I met one of his subcronies at my arraignment.

The first reports after Christmas had been very optimistic for Casey's recovery, but in the meantime, Bob Gates became acting director of the CIA. Sadly, so much turmoil was going on within Langley over Iran-contra that we barely had time to weigh the gravity of Casey's condition. By mid-January of 1987, however, the flow of positive news from the hospital had slowed. William Casey resigned from his hospital bed at the end of the month.

The Tower Commission issued its report in late February. As a result of his performance, John Tower was a leading contender to replace Casey. (Acting Director Bob Gates, who would have been the obvious first choice, had been eliminated as a candidate because he was "too close" to Iran-contra.) The idea of Tower as DCI would have been ludicrous if it hadn't come so close to happening.

Instead we got William Webster from the FBI. In early March, Reagan asked Webster to move over to the CIA from the Bureau. Before heading up the FBI, he had been a lawyer, then a Missouri district and federal appellate court judge. Since we at the CTC had been working so closely with the FBI on terrorism, we had already heard a lot about Webster, none of it good.

From street level up to the top echelons, people at the FBI briefed us in detail about how much they detested Webster. Some despised him because they thought he was an egotistical lightweight, a social climber, and a phony. An Amherst graduate but still something of a hayseed, he seemed to have decided that he belonged in the Eastern Establishment and was going to gain entrée to it, one way or another. Playing tennis was important; so was being seen at the right soirees. Interestingly, soon after his arrival, Webster traveled in a fancy Learjet to make speeches. Casey had made do with a humdrum prop-driven Gulfstream, but apparently that wasn't good enough for "Judge" Webster, as he preferred to be called.

Personality shortcomings aside, Webster was in my view ill suited to lead an agency whose perspective was international in scope: he lacked experience in foreign affairs. Early in his tenure as DCI, Clair George invited him to a Directorate of Operations staff meeting to familiarize him with what was going on. Each division chief gave a bit of information about what his area was working on. We started off with Europe. The minute we left Europe and started on the Near East, Webster took out his ever-so-elegant burgundy, calfskin, monogrammed Filofax, and flipped to the maps in the back. I sat there wondering whether the man who had taken over as head of the CIA was looking for Morocco on the map.

We could probably have overcome Webster's ego, his lack of experience with foreign affairs, his small-town-America world perspective, and even his yuppier-than-thou arrogance. What we couldn't overcome was that he was a lawyer. President Zia of Pakistan asked him what in the name of Allah a lawyer was doing heading up a spy agency, and Webster could never really answer the question.

All of his training as a lawyer and as a judge was that you didn't do illegal things. He never could accept that this is *exactly* what the CIA does when it operates abroad. We break the laws of other countries. It's how we collect information. It's why we're in business. Webster had an insurmountable problem with the raison d'être of the organization he was brought in to run.

That Webster was so out of sync with the purpose and principles of the Agency made Casey's absence all the more noticeable. After his resignation at the end of January, there was still talk about his eventual recovery, perhaps even a post as special adviser to the president. In late March, however, it became clear that Casey was never going to get well. Sophia took him back to Mayknoll, his home on Long Island. William Casey continued to decline and died there on May 6.

Ollie North called me to ask whether I wanted to go with him to the funeral service. By this time Ollie was hotter than a $2 pistol; the press was tailing him everywhere. I've never been ashamed of my association with Ollie, but since the investigators were hell-bent to uncover a high-level intrigue between the CIA and the NSC (even where none existed), being seen with him would just have added fuel to the fire. The conspiracy fanatics would have "proof positive" of collusion between North and me. I told him that attending the funeral with his flying phalanx of journalists was probably not the most considerate thing to do, since it would detract from the solemnity of the occasion.

I suggested that it would be better for us "coconspirators" to attend the wake rather than the funeral. Ollie called Sophia to ask whether this was acceptable to her, and she graciously told us to come ahead. We employed a bit of tradecraft to shake off the media as we separately went into the Hill Building on Seventeenth Street, where Williams & Connolly, Brendan Sullivan's law firm, had its offices. We chatted for a bit, then Ollie, his bodyguard, and I went down the back stairs. North had a security detail from the Naval Investigative Service, since he'd received threats from Abu Nidal and company. Williams & Connolly had a car waiting for us in the garage next door. We sped off to National Airport and caught a plane to La Guardia. In New York we were met by other security personnel, who took us out to Long Island.

We arrived at Mayknoll well in advance of the formal beginning of the wake. We were welcomed effusively by Mrs. Casey, her daughter, Bernadette, and her son-in-law, Owen Smith. Then we were ushered into the kitchen, where we met Casey's relatives. Ollie and I spent the next four hours drinking with the family. (He had a good reason to linger—he had been held in contempt for challenging the independent counsel's statute and he was due to report to jail as soon as he returned to Washington.) There was a great deal of warmth and remembering and coming and going. Everyone was telling stories about Bill—it was an Irish wake in the best sense of the word.

In Ollie North's book, he tells an anecdote from the wake about a relative who said that Casey had looked up from his hospital bed and said, "He'll never get away with it," ostensibly referring to Reagan's denial of involvement in Iran-contra. Some have questioned whether that statement was ever uttered. I can attest that the relative made the statement that North quotes.

After sharing our reminiscences in the kitchen, North and I went into the living room, paid our final respects to Bill, and exchanged more stories about Casey with past and present members of the administration who were also attending the wake. We stayed long enough for Ollie's attorneys to be sure he wouldn't go to jail, returned to La Guardia, and then to Washington.

Casey's passing coincided almost exactly with the beginning of televised public testimony before the Senate and House committees investigating the Iran-contra affair. Richard Secord was the first witness on the fifth of May. The hearings rolled on through the spring and into the summer, but everyone was waiting for the Main Event—the testimony of Oliver North. In the press, there was an almost palpable sense of giddy expectation about North's appearance. The long knives were sharpened in anticipation that Ollie would finally be "called to account" and "get what was coming to him."

North began his testimony on July 7. The chief counsel for the Senate, Arthur Liman, resembled the stereotypical slick, sneaky lawyer, a man for whom every day is a bad hair day. John Nields, the chief counsel on the House side, looked like the hippie leftover that he is. As Liman and Nields began their interrogation of North, the House and Senate committee members fell to sniping at one another. Liman had been criticized for being too aggressive in his questioning of Richard Secord. Some members now thought that Liman was too soft on North; others felt that Nields was too tough. Some thought the reverse.

Still others crabbed because they thought Nields and Liman were hogging the limelight and not giving the real stars, the members of the House and Senate, enough face time before the TV cameras. Moreover, the new made-for-TV setup in the Senate Caucus Room, which was supposed to reinforce the majesty of the senators and congressmen and intimidate the witnesses, worked to their disadvantage.

With all due respect to Senator Inouye for his wartime service, he was the wrong man for the job. Television is first and foremost a visual medium, one that encourages people to think (rightly or wrongly) in stereotypes, and to see confrontations as good guys versus bad guys. Studies have shown that most viewers get their primary impression from what they see, not what they hear—and what they saw in these hearings was a Japanese-American senator scowling angrily down on a stoic U.S. Marine. With Inouye up there on the dais and Marine lieutenant colonel Oliver North down in the trenches below, in full dress uniform, laden with medals, many viewers interpreted the scene, subliminally if not overtly, as a metaphor for the taking of Iwo Jima from the Japanese in 1945. I was not the least bit surprised that the hearings turned Oliver North into John Wayne in a matter of days.

I believe that one of the key reasons for his success was that North knew that his ultimate judge and jury were outside, not inside, the hearing room. He'd always had a way with words, but in front of the cameras North was able to turn what might have been a star-chamber inquiry into his own platform in defense of truth, justice, and the American way. In two terms in office, Reagan was never able to bring public opinion around to support the contras. North defended his actions in part by steadfastly maintaining that it was morally bankrupt of Congress to abandon our commitment to the Nicaraguan freedom fighters and leave them defenseless against the Sandinistas. In doing so he struck a chord in the American conscience and generated a groundswell of support for the contras that was many times more powerful than anything the president could have hoped for.

Through it all Brendan Sullivan was there, whispering in North's ear as the questions were being asked, parrying with Liman, Nields, and the committee members like a fencing master. Anything but a "potted plant," Sullivan had obtained a grant of limited immunity for his client before he would let him appear before the committees. Whatever North said to the legislators couldn't be used against him in court. The more North talked, the less Special Prosecutor Lawrence Walsh had to work with.

I knew my turn in the barrel was coming up soon. In the midst of trying to run the Counterterrorist Center, I was busy giving depositions to various lawyers who had been brought in by this joint congressional committee. I decided maybe I ought to get my own lawyer. Brendan Sullivan hooked me up with an attorney whom I met once, but for some reason we never spoke again.

Once again, I had no personal legal representation. Even if I hadn't done so before, this is where I should have retained personal counsel, and not to have done so was a mistake.

Meanwhile there was a big to-do about testimony from those of us in the Agency—Clair George, Alan Fiers, and me. Congress wanted us to appear on television like everybody else so they could get their publicity mileage out of the hearings. These fellows just didn't get it. After North's testimony, the only people getting good PR from their appearance at the hearings were answering questions, not asking them. Worse, viewers were starting to get upset because the proceedings were dragging on, disrupting regularly scheduled programming, particularly soap operas. The CIA maintained that because we in the Agency were undercover, we couldn't appear on national TV. The committee claimed that we were so senior in the Agency, and so well known in Washington, that we had no cover—everyone knew who we were. The merits of the argument soon became secondary as the issue became an arm-wrestling contest, a power struggle. Discussions went back and forth, but nothing was resolved.

At last Congress decided to forgo our appearance. This looked like the final decision, so I left for a vacation at my home in the Bahamas. I'd been there only two or three days when the committee changed its mind and decided to let us appear in closed-door private sessions. I had no telephone in the Bahamas, and it took some doing to get hold of me.

After I was yanked back, I had just enough time to unpack, and no time to prepare for my testimony, which was scheduled for August 4. Prior to my appearance, I had some perfunctory consultation with Agency attorneys from the Office of General Counsel, but their client was the CIA itself, not individuals within it. The Agency attorney assigned to the Directorate of Operations was John Rizzo. In retrospect I think that Rizzo believed his primary job was to protect the head of "his" Directorate, DDO Clair George. Years later, we discussed the past with no rancor; I always liked John Rizzo, perhaps because he is smart, smokes cigars, has a fine sense of humor, and dresses well.

I was to be the debut Agency witness, which struck me as odd since I would have expected the higher ups, in this case DDO George, to lead off for the Agency. But committee staffers told me the Agency wanted *me* to testify first, and I can only assume that George and Rizzo hoped that once the senators and congressmen had vented their collective spleen on me, Fiers and especially George would have a much easier time of it.

The morning of my testimony, I was accompanied by a lawyer from the

Agency's Office of General Counsel named Kathleen McGinn. A bright and attractive redhead, with six-shooter eyes and tongue, she knew that what was going on was sheer political posturing, not issues of legality and illegality. To her great credit, when Congressman Dante Fascell, head of the House Foreign Affairs Committee, told her to leave, she didn't budge. Fascell maintained that because she was appearing as a representative of the Agency, she couldn't represent me personally, which she wasn't; she was my attorney in my official governmental capacity. She just took him on and continued to sit there. Finally he just shut up.

Once we got past the opening maneuvers, I heard mostly the same questions that I'd been hearing since Thanksgiving. One of the few members of Congress who actually seemed interested in shedding light on what had happened was Bob McCollum, a congressman from Florida. He, together with Tina Westby and Diane Dornan of his staff, were asking questions that clarified the issues involved.

Many of the rest were just trying to make waves and make the Agency look bad. One of the investigators the committee had hired was a former CIA case officer named Tom Polgar. Polgar had been our last station chief in Vietnam, but had retired with a chip on his shoulder. After he'd left, he had come to me when I was chief of European Division asking for a contract job to do some work in Germany, but I had turned him down because what he had to offer was already extant in the German station. Maybe he had it in for me personally, and I think he held considerable animosity toward the Agency.

What was a former case officer doing in the employ of a Senate committee? How did he get there? I suspect it was good old-fashioned nepotism. Among the committee members was Sen. Warren Rudman from my home state, New Hampshire. He and I had grown up only a few blocks apart in Nashua and had been Boy Scouts together. One of his chief staff members was Polgar's son. I can only assume that Polgar junior had sold his boss on the idea that a former Agency officer like his dad would know his way around the CIA to where the bodies were buried. Polgar senior had virtually turned the Agency upside down in a fruitless search for the phantom "missing cable."

The "missing cable" became the linchpin of the case against me, such as it was. The cable supposedly "proved" conclusively that I knew that the November 1985 shipment was missiles, not drilling equipment. The chief in Lisbon, who had been appointed to his position by my predecessor, maintained to investigators that he had sent me a cable, when we were still trying to obtain landing clearances from the Portuguese, stating that Richard Secord, North's confederate, had told him that the flights from Tel Aviv would contain missiles being sent to Iran in exchange for hostages. I'd been at loggerheads with this individual over his requests for more staff. More personnel wouldn't have helped him—what he needed was more vigor in getting results from the staff he had.

The phantom cable that he claims to have sent containing this information was never received in Washington. Interestingly, when first asked about the matter, the Lisbon communicator did not recall a cable. But when later requested to go to Washington for further questions, his memory "improved." Judging how important the contents were, you'd have thought he would have remembered it right away.

I'd kept records of all my cable traffic and didn't have a copy, nor did the DDO's office. There were allegations that Clair George and I had destroyed the incoming copies, but in addition to us, four or five other people at Headquarters would have seen it—had it really existed. They didn't, and no such cable has ever been found by anyone.

The questioning had become routine by now, but a little comic, if sick, relief occurred during break time. Warren Rudman came down from Mt. Olympus to make small talk. He actually had the gall to ask me, "Do you still have a lot of relatives in New Hampshire?" Real subtle.

I always enjoyed testifying before Congress. Although it did nothing to bolster my confidence in our elected officials, I found it amusing. Most people don't like testifying because often our legislators rant and rave and posture and try to degrade you.

I certainly wasn't at all intimidated by the array of august personages before me. After all, I'd been giving briefings in Washington to high-ranking officials in all branches of government since I returned to Washington from Rome in 1981. I have a good memory and can retain considerable detailed information when I feel it is significant; otherwise I discard it. Because I had the facts at my disposal, I didn't have to fumble for a response and was not at all hesitant about answering their questions. I was not about to be bullied, although they certainly tried to do that. This exchange was typical:

MR. FASCELL: You got a phone call from Colonel North and you jumped to. Why is that? In November of 1985, North called you on the phone, said you got to do something. Why did you do anything?

MR. CLARRIDGE: Because he said it was an urgent matter. He may have said it was life-and-death.

MR. FASCELL: Suppose I'd have called you up. What would you have done?

MR. CLARRIDGE: Probably done the same thing.

MR. FASCELL: Now you really got me. I'll try that with the CIA first chance I get.

MR. CLARRIDGE: Got to call the right person.

MR. FASCELL: Oh, I see. So you were tasked by the director to do something?

MR. CLARRIDGE: No, I was not tasked by the director.

MR. FASCELL: You voluntarily did it on your own?

MR. CLARRIDGE: Ollie North calls up and says that he needs some urgent assistance—

MR. FASCELL: Yes. I know that.

MR. CLARRIDGE: And it becomes clear that he is the National—

MR. FASCELL: Is he your boss?

MR. CLARRIDGE: No, he's speaking for the National Security Council.

MR. FASCELL: Are they your boss?

MR. CLARRIDGE: No, they are not my boss.

MR. FASCELL: Did you check with Casey?

MR. CLARRIDGE: No. He was not in town.

MR. FASCELL: Did you check with his number two?

MR. CLARRIDGE: No.

MR. FASCELL: You didn't check?

MR. CLARRIDGE: All I was asked to do was to provide some communications assistance.

MR. FASCELL: And you did it?

MR. CLARRIDGE: And I provided the communications assistance on my own.

MR. FASCELL: Well, let me ask you this then. Did you do anything else for North?

MR. CLARRIDGE: Well, let me think. You mean—

MR. FASCELL: Starting November 22, 1985, up until the time he quit? You see what I'm getting at?

MR. CLARRIDGE: No, I don't think I did anything.

MR. FASCELL: Is he running you or are you running him?

Fascell's final question suggested what I had begun to suspect. Some members of Congress, the Walsh crowd, and some in the administration itself thought I was the éminence grise behind Oliver North. He couldn't have done what he did without professional advice from someone in the intelligence business.

Committee members were not accustomed to dealing with a witness who had all the data in his head; more often, those who appear before the committee make promises to check their notes and "get back to you with the information." In this instance, they were grilling me with facts that had come from me initially—much of it was cables from my own files. I was accused of being glib, which they also assumed was arrogance. I knew that what the committee members really wanted, always want, was someone to kiss their asses.

The last thing Clair George had said to me before I left for the Hill to testify was, "The minute you get back to Headquarters, come see me." After testifying I returned to the office. When I got into Clair's office, he was there waiting for me with Fiers and Rizzo, the Directorate of Operations lawyer from the OGC. I'm sure they expected me to come back all bloody and battered.

I felt terrific. When I told them it was a nonevent, Clair's face fell. My last words as I slipped out the door were, "See you, fellows. I'm off to the Bahamas."

CHAPTER 23

The Long Good-bye

Director Webster may not have had experience or special interest in foreign affairs, but he knew how to genuflect to congressmen. When Webster's confirmation had dangled before SSCI in the spring, he pledged to keep the committee "fully informed" about covert activities. That was exactly what they wanted to hear.

Webster apparently got the message and was crowned by SSCI in April and by the full Senate in May. I'm sure Webster understood the political imperatives, but even he knew you couldn't say "Off with their heads!" without first having a trial. That must have been a problem for Webster, since no one in the Agency had been found guilty of anything in a court of law, and the Walsh investigation wasn't moving fast enough to suit his purposes.

Nevertheless, Webster knew that he had to do something to satisfy Congress. There had been rumblings to that effect even before I testified at the joint committees in August. According to a July front-page story in the *Los Angeles Times,* a dashed line was already tattooed across my neck. Those ever-popular anonymous sources had told the paper that Webster planned to remove both Clair George and me.

In September, Webster mobilized yet another investigation of me, Clair, Alan Fiers, Charlie Allen, Joseph Fernandez, et al., concerning CIA activities in Iran-contra. This one was to be "internal" to the CIA. It was also to be "independent" and "unbiased." Sure. Some of us had already been cleared by a previous internal CIA investigation by our own inspector general, Carroll Hauver.

For his internal investigation, Webster chose a lawyer named Russell Bruemmer. Bruemmer was a member of the Washington law firm of Wilmer, Cutler, & Pickering, but he was not by any stretch of the imagination independent, unbiased, or impartial. Bruemmer was Webster's boy all the way. He'd been Webster's law clerk at the federal appeals court. When Webster first came in to head the FBI in 1978, Bruemmer had followed along like a spaniel and become Webster's first special assistant. When the word came down that he had started rooting through the files, I expected an invitation to chat with him. I didn't get one.

In November 1987, Clair George and I were at a dinner party at the home of one of our Western European counterparts posted to Washington. I had still heard nothing from Bruemmer, but suddenly Clair turned to me out of the blue and said, "I'm retiring. Why don't we retire together?"

For a moment I was taken aback. I said, "What the hell would I retire for?"

When Clair said that he was going to leave before Bruemmer's report came out, it occurred to me that perhaps he knew something I didn't know. Nevertheless, I wasn't about to run or be forced out. I told Clair, "This is battle-stations time. This is not get-out time."

Just before Christmas, I got my first and only phone call from Russell Bruemmer. He said, "Do you have anything to say?"

I didn't know it yet, but it was the equivalent of the hangman asking the prisoner if he had any last words before the hood and noose were slipped over his head. "What do you mean?" I asked.

What he meant was, did I have anything to add to what I'd already said—to the FBI, the House, the Senate, the House and Senate together, to the Agency's inspector general, and to the Tower Commission? That was all he wanted to know, and that was the extent of our conversation. He didn't ask me any other questions. His investigative technique with Charlie Allen, Alan Fiers, and the others was exactly the same. He never really talked to any of us so-called "suspects."

Late December is traditionally peppered with Christmas parties all over the building. Clair George had all the division and staff chiefs up to his office for noontime drinks. It was going to be a somewhat somber event, since after our conversation Clair had gone ahead and announced his retirement. We knew that this would be his last Christmas gathering, and Clair was on edge, some said. It mystified me, because as far as I could see, none of the Iran-contra controversy was rubbing off on him or Central American Task Force chief Alan Fiers or Latin America Division chief Jerry Gruner. Except for Fernandez and Jim Adkins, who had just been forced into retirement, the others seemed immune. This gives you some idea of how little I understood of the contra side of the affair—as subsequent events proved.

I was looking forward to Christmas this year because Helga, Tarik, and I were going to Germany to spend the holidays with her mother and brothers. We needed time together as a family. Neither Helga nor Tarik had said much, but I knew that the last year had been difficult for them. My name kept showing up in newspaper headlines. Tarik faced awkward questions and sidelong glances at school.

While we were all in Clair's office sipping grog, I got a call that Webster wanted to see me. I went to his office, and before I even sat down, he said, "I think you ought to retire."

Webster waved Bruemmer's "report" in my face. Bruemmer had never spoken to me, except for that one phone call a couple of weeks earlier. All he'd done to create his document was to regurgitate everything from the depositions and testimony to the FBI, the Tower Commission, the joint House and Senate committee, and all the rest and wrap it all up in one tidy package for hizzoner, the judge and jury.

It smacked of Stalinism—with Webster playing Vishinsky—but even then Webster couldn't get it right. He told me I didn't obtain appropriate authorization when I told North to use St. Lucia Airlines for his November 1985 shipment. How could he even suggest that I had acted outside the chain of command in involving the air proprietary? I asked him if he had ever heard of Ed Juchniewicz. Webster replied, "I don't want to discuss it!"

Of course he didn't. The full report of the congressional committees investigating Iran-contra had been published a month earlier. Surely Bruemmer and Webster had received copies. It was not a unanimous document by any means, but the minority report had completely exonerated me, and even the Democrats had cleared me on that particular allegation. The committee's conclusion on this point was clearly stated on page 181: "Clarridge's actions resulting in the involvement of the air proprietary were at North's request and with the authority of CIA Associate Deputy Director of Operations, Edward Juchniewicz."

Webster handed me a letter and told me of its contents. I was reprimanded, demoted one grade, and could not get any medals, stipends, or special bonuses for two years. And, I was to be reassigned from the Counterterrorist Center.

Demotion was meaningless because everyone at the top grade levels was paid approximately the same anyway. And I had no use for medals except for valor or a significant intelligence coup. The only part of Webster's "punishment" that concerned me was leaving the CTC, because I didn't feel that I had quite finished my job there yet.

Everyone was waiting in Clair's office for me to return from my session with Webster. When I filled them in, all semblance of Christmas cheer evaporated. It was proof, as if anyone needed it, that Webster was just what some at the FBI had always maintained he was: a lightweight and an Eastern Establishment wanna-be with no semblance of moral or political fiber.

What was at stake here was a fundamental issue. This was the beginning of the end of the unwritten code that all of us in the Agency had lived by—Loyalty Up and Loyalty Down. In the CIA that I knew, this tradition was strong. Now, it was broken, and by the DCI himself. His trashing of that code is one of the most significant casualties of this tumultuous period—with far-reaching implications for the future.

My associates in the Directorate of Operations took it harder than I did. I already had my own private game plan for the future. Although I had no intention of doing so on Webster's terms, I was actually quite willing to retire from the Agency.

I had been thinking about retirement since early in the fall of 1986, well before the Iran-contra scandal broke. At the time, the CTC was getting its act together and starting to move on some of its targets, and I had the rare luxury of looking a little bit down the road. Once I got the CTC fully up and rolling, I knew that it was time to leave the Agency because there was nothing else I wanted to do there. I had been in charge of three divisions, counting the CTC, which was unusual in the DO. Also, I had had a large station abroad, and I had no interest in going overseas again to repeat that experience. I wanted something altogether new.

I thought back to an evening discussion I'd had with Casey. I was having trouble recruiting police for the CTC because of the cultural resistance in the DO, and I was a bit frustrated at all the roadblocks I was coming up against within the CIA on a variety of issues. I had looked at Casey—knowing that he could solve this problem by fiat—and said, "You've got the best job in the Agency."

He didn't miss a beat. "You're dead wrong," he replied. "I've given you the two best jobs in this organization during my tenure—chief of Latin America Division and chief of the Counterterrorist Center." He was right. When I thought about the prospect of leaving the CTC, there really wasn't another position I coveted.

Before I left for Germany, however, I did what I should have done from day one of the outbreak of the Iran-contra affair—I got a lawyer. Bill McDaniel was a heavyweight—he'd clerked for Supreme Court justice Harry A. Blackmun, worked for Williams & Connolly, had his own practice, and had a reputation around Washington as a tough son of a bitch. Right now that seemed to be exactly what I needed.

That I had secured legal representation made the Agency nervous, and stewing about it while I was gone on vacation made them even more nervous. When I got back from Germany, my deputy told me that in my absence, an attorney from the Office of General Counsel (OGC) had been nosing around the CTC. "He was extremely antsy," my deputy told me. "He was down here asking questions, trying to find out why you've got a lawyer." His sly smile assured me that the attorney hadn't gotten very far.

Not surprisingly, right after I got back, I got a visit from an OGC lawyer. The fellow was amazingly fidgety—you'd have thought that *I* was investigating *him*. He told me, "You know, it's pretty useless for you to get a lawyer to go to court over this."

I said, "Over what?"

"Over the reprimands and internal problems."

I let the jumpy OGC officer prattle on. The less I said, the faster he talked. It was a bit of tradecraft—he was revealing more of Webster's hand by babbling than I could ever have hoped to discover on my own. The lawyer mentioned that a case that would test the DCI's authority on hiring and firing would soon be heard by the Supreme Court. The light came on, but I said nothing. Finally, he went away.

Now, I knew that I had them by the balls. I was now in a position of strength to deal with my departure from the Agency on my terms.

From what the OGC officer had said, the OGC apparently believed that I had retained McDaniel to fight my reprimand through the legal system, but I hadn't. I had retained McDaniel to write a rebuttal to the nonsense that Bruemmer had put into the record, but the real reason I'd hired him was to defend me against Walsh. If the Agency thought I was guilty of something, that was a powerful argument for Walsh to pursue me. Lawrence Walsh was still spending the taxpayers' money in the ongoing criminal investigation of the Iran-contra affair, and I had already been notified that I was a "subject" of investigation.

I suspected the reason the OGC and Webster were concerned about my taking the DCI to court over the reprimands was directly connected to the upcoming case before the Supreme Court, which challenged the DCI's authority under the National Security Act of 1947 on firing and the CIA Act of 1949 on hiring.

The director of the CIA is one of the few people in the federal government who by law has unconditional authority to hire and fire, without giving any reason, to protect the security of the Agency. For some time now a legal challenge to the DCI's hiring and firing power had been making its way through the courts. Based on homosexuality, this lawsuit was one of the Agency's most sensitive personnel matters, and it went to the heart of the powers of the DCI. Both a lower and an appellate court had already ruled in favor of the plaintiff in this case.

The case was due to be heard by the Supreme Court within a matter of weeks. Perhaps Webster and the OGC were worried that McDaniel was going to file a complaint challenging my reprimand, and by extension the legal basis for the director's authority to hire and fire at will. The public taste for news about Iran-contra had not abated. They knew there would be a lot of publicity if I filed suit. The actions of the DCI against me could appear to be capricious and arbitrary. Someone in the press would surely be clever enough to juxtapose the two stories, mine and the case of the homosexual. It would be another black eye for the Agency and would make the court case under review appear to have more merit and perhaps influence its outcome. After having put all of this together, I knew that I had Webster where I wanted him.

Since our little chat before Christmas, I'd been getting a lot of support in the form of condolence notes and phone calls from highly placed people in the administration and the Republican National Committee. I got a very nice note from George Bush on December 19:

Dear Dewey,
   Sometimes life doesn't seem all that fair. In my line of work you learn that friendships count. I just want you to know you have my friendship—and you also have my respect and high esteem. That won't ever change. Have a wonderful Christmas and an even better New Year.
George Bush

Then upon my return from Germany, Gen. Colin Powell, the national security adviser to President Reagan, wrote me on January 10, 1988:

Dear Dewey:
   I just wanted to thank you for your support and education of me over the past year. I wish you all the best wherever the future takes you.
Colin Powell

Someone in the White House told me to call Jeane Kirkpatrick, who had left her position as ambassador to the United Nations and had returned to teaching. She was also writing a newspaper column and supposedly wanted to do a column on what had happened. When I got her on the phone before I left for Germany, she said, "Well, I guess you must be delighted with your country and what it is doing to you, after what you have done for it!" She gave me every indication that she was going to write me up in one of her columns, but she never did. I've often wondered why. Perhaps she thought better of it, or perhaps someone advised her not to do it. I suppose I should have contacted her again, but I was afraid I would embarrass her.

Interestingly enough, the system never actually got around to demoting me—out of sheer bureaucratic sloth. Meanwhile, they brought Dick Stolz out of retirement and back to the Agency to become the new DDO after Clair George retired. He had been a classmate of Webster's at Amherst and had been head of European Division in the late 1970s, and I had worked for him briefly before I went to Rome. I'd always thought he was a decent man, but not very dynamic, and certainly not bold. Oddly enough, he'd twice been passed over to become DDO, once by Stansfield Turner and once by Casey, who chose the execrable Max Hugel instead. Hugel had lasted no more than a couple of months, but by that time Stolz had retired in disgust. If he'd hung in there, he would probably have been DDO a lot sooner.

After he'd been DDO a couple of weeks, Stolz called me into his office and said, "What are we going to do, Dewey?" This was code for, "When are you going to retire?" Knowing what I knew about the nervous folk in the OGC and the DCI's office, I told him that I didn't have any intention of leaving and—to stick it in a bit farther—told him that McDaniel had about finished dismantling Bruemmer's report.

Stolz said that even if I didn't retire, he thought it was probably time that I left the CTC. I knew what he meant. Within the CTC a full-scale insurrection was in progress. I had gone to the mat for my staff when I had to. Now they wanted to do the same for me. People were openly resentful. My staff sprouted Dewey Clarridge T-shirts, Dewey Clarridge buttons. They even sent one over to Vice President Bush, who sent back one of his election buttons. Webster may have demolished Loyalty Up and Loyalty Down within the Agency as a whole, but inside the CTC it was still alive and well, and it had accomplished much. For the Center to survive, I had to get everyone back to doing its real work.

I told Stolz, "Let's talk about *your* problem." What I said, between the lines, was that I was willing to cut a deal. My goal was to blackmail the Agency into my leaving on my terms—they still didn't know I had already decided to go over a year previously. And, the possibility of taking them to court was still out there.

I wanted to continue as head of the CTC long enough to calm everyone down and get them back to work. I also wanted the CIA to make a "good faith" effort to find me another job. This was a totally tongue-in-cheek request. (I knew full well that they wouldn't really do a goddamn thing, but it was amusing to query Stolz periodically on his progress—or the lack thereof.) In return, I would retire and agree not to press a lawsuit—which, of course, I had no intention of doing anyway.

Stolz said he would relay my requests to Webster and became the go-between for the DCI and me. Webster thought the deal was okay in principle, but wanted me to give him a date when I was going to retire. I couldn't resist tweaking him. I said to Stolz, "I think that after the Republican National Convention might be a good time."

Stolz's eyes bulged at the prospect of selling this idea to Webster. There was still snow on the ground, and the Republican convention was slated for August 1988. Webster knew I had connections to George Bush.

As far as I was concerned, however, it was just another piece of blackmail. I had no intention of staying that long.

Finally I told Stolz I would retire on June 1. Webster agreed and started counting the days. Seeing the T-shirts and the accolades, Webster must have realized that I had more support in the Agency than he had surmised. There came a series of going-away parties, mementos, and plaques, all of them heartfelt, some touching, others humorous. Among other things, the Office of Technical Services gave me a model of the mine we had used in the harbors of Nicaragua. The fellows in demolitions used small explosive charges to blow an inscribed bronze plaque for me and gave me a dummy round from the 25-mm chain gun we had used on the Q-boats. I got another plaque from the Secret Service, and one from the Justice Department men and women who had worked with me on the Fawaz Yunis case. There was a letter from Al Gray, the commandant of the Marine Corps. And the FBI had me over to a big lunch with all the people I worked with. Buck Revell organized it. I suspect that, in a way, they were sticking it to Webster, who was anathema at the FBI.

There were also a number of mementos from the CTC. The group as a whole gave me a very apropos original 1863 Thomas Nast engraving entitled "The Life of a Spy." Many from outside the Agency were also most kind in words or deeds, such as former Naval intelligence officer Tom Duval and Carl Haas and his wife, Bernie, owners of a world-class Indy Car racing team. Needless to say, I was greatly touched by all of this thoughtfulness, and these mementos are among my most treasured possessions.

I invited Mike O'Neill, who had been Edward Boland's counsel at HPSCI during my seemingly countless appearances before that committee, to one of my going-away parties. We had a nice chat. He made an interesting remark, perhaps only because I was leaving: "You never told us everything we wanted to know, and we always had to sort of pull the information out of you, but you never lied to us. Through it all you always told us what we asked about, straight up. And that was not necessarily true of some officers more senior than you."

Mike O'Neill and I certainly had had times when we went at each other during the contra hearings, and he wasn't helpful in our efforts against the Sandinistas. The Boland Amendments had caused a great deal of grief at all levels of the Agency, but Mike was more straight than many on the Hill, and I respected him for that. Everyone from the Agency who was at that party nearly fell over when they saw him because he was the enemy, and the last person they expected to see.

Well, perhaps the second to last. William Webster wasn't invited. He came anyway.

CHAPTER 24

Crossing the Appalachians

Sometime in May during my last few weeks at the CTC, the phone rang at home. "I've got something very interesting to talk to you about," said a voice I didn't recognize. The caller refused to identify himself or give me any more information. Instead he directed me to a particular pay phone near my house. This was good tradecraft—especially if my home line was tapped by the people from Walsh's investigation, which I guess was a real possibility. Obviously, I was curious, so I followed his instructions.

I got in the car and drove about five blocks to the designated booth. Soon thereafter, the phone rang, and I picked it up The same voice directed me to another pay phone nearby. There the process was repeated. The time frame he gave me to get from one booth to the next was pretty short—too short for anyone to get a tap on the next phone. Whoever was conducting this operation was taking suitable precautions.

When I finally got to the last phone booth, the voice said, "You've been treated very badly by your government as a whole, and by the CIA in particular. You gave thirty years of your life to the Agency. Now you've been stabbed in the back. Don't you feel betrayed?"

I said, "What's your angle? What do you want?"

"You could really fuck the government, if you want to."

I said, "I'm not interested. Good-bye," and hung up.

But it wasn't good-bye. Another call came a few days later. The booth-to-booth telephone tactic was the same, but this time the phone booths I was sent to were different. This time they were long distances from my home. Although my first instinct had been to ignore the caller, I became interested in getting to the bottom of what was going on. I asked him what he thought I was in a position to do to hurt the U.S. government. The voice at the other end played it coy: "We'll let you know." I hung up on him again.

Then came a third call. I was tired of the phone-hopping game, but my curiosity got the best of me. I said, "Suppose I am angry about the way I've been treated. Then what?"

The caller finally got to his point: "Surely you recognize that you are privy to information that could dismantle a very key element of U.S. intelligence-collecting apparatus."

There it was. Someone wanted to use me to get at U.S. intelligence. I couldn't determine if he knew for a fact that I had this access, or if he merely surmised that I must have it, due to my position and my experience. I told him, "Let's say that I am privy to the information you think I have. Let's say that I do want to be vindictive. How do I do this?"

The answer came back quickly: "Look, you have access to a lot of publications abroad, or you can gain access through your contacts. You can have it all done abroad and no one will be the wiser." The matters they were interested in are so sensitive that I can't go into more detail, but they were suggesting that I publish highly classified U.S. intelligence secrets overseas. He—or possibly "they," as I had sensed that more than one person was behind the calls—insinuated that they wanted to use this either to destroy American intelligence-gathering capabilities and harm our relationships with other countries, or to blackmail the government into bringing the Iran-contra investigation to a halt.

I concluded that the caller was either seeking revenge against the government through me or a crank or someone who thought he was helping me. I dismissed the possibility that this was an approach by professionals from a foreign intelligence service, because they would be far more interested in recruiting me for what I knew, rather than exposing it to the public. Moreover, they had never hinted at a monetary return nor had they suggested a face-to-face meeting, which would have been a more likely scenario had it been a professional intelligence operation.

However, I decided that I should make a record of the event, so I told my lawyer, Bill McDaniel, about it. I also informed Barry Kelly at the NSC. Kelly had formerly been with the Agency and knew immediately what the sensitive information was that the caller was speaking about. He informed Colin Powell, who by this time was national security adviser. For the moment, I decided not to inform anyone in the Agency, although the NSC may have, for fear it was some well-intentioned but idiotic idea of someone there and my revelation would begin a witch-hunt, necessarily involving me just at the moment when I was retiring and had other things to do. In any event, there were no further calls, and that was the end of it.

At the end of the day on June 1, there was yet another party—this time, the final one. I said good-bye to everyone and headed downstairs. Sarah Clinger, my supersecretary as well as my friend, went with me. I ran my badge through the badge machine. As I turned around to hand it to her, I noticed tears in her eyes. There may have been some in mine as well, not because I was leaving the CIA, but because I would miss some of its inmates. I gave her my badge and walked out of Langley for the last time as a CIA officer.

When one thinks about a second career, one seeks to capitalize on what one has learned from the first. The whole question of economic intelligence had interested me for some time, and I thought seriously about pursuing this possibility.

Before I left the Agency, another option appeared on the horizon. Having learned of my imminent retirement, and being appalled at the reason for it, the general manager of the Electronics Division of General Dynamics, Mel Barlow, approached me about coming to work for him. I had met him at one of those sessions when we had invited industry leaders to the CIA to find technology that could help us to combat terrorism. Barlow, a fine gentleman in every respect, had a high regard for Agency officers and already had a capable former CIA intelligence analyst, Al Dendo, on his staff. I accepted Barlow's offer, even though it meant crossing the Appalachian Mountains. My father had always drummed into me the notion that anyone who crossed these mountains must, perforce, be a failure. It meant he couldn't make it on the eastern seaboard.

As Helga and I packed up that summer, everything was quiet on the Walsh front. I hadn't heard anything from the Office of Independent Counsel (OIC) in months, but I knew I was still a "subject" of their investigation. Although being a "subject" is more serious than being a "witness," it's not as serious as being a "target." Walsh was already going after his "targets." North and Poindexter had been indicted in March. On June 20, Joseph Fernandez, who had been CIA station chief in Costa Rica, was also indicted.

The charges against them had little if anything to do with whether they had actually done anything felonious in arranging arms shipments to Iran, violating the Boland Amendment, or even using the profits to fund the anti-Sandinista forces in Central America. Walsh was preoccupied with proving that these dastardly villains had, in his interpretation, "lied to Congress" and "withheld information."

At the heart of the matter was a dispute over foreign policy. The Democratic majority in Congress disapproved of the president's course of action with regard to both Iran and Central America. Was shipping missiles to Iran consistent with the president's declared policies regarding nonnegotiations with terrorists and the embargo of Iran? No, it wasn't, but these presidential policies were not legally binding. President Reagan was entitled to change his mind, either publicly or privately. What should have been a political tug-of-war between the executive and the legislative branches of government had been thrust into the courts, where it really didn't belong.

I have always believed that if political action had been brought to bear quickly, when the Iran-contra story first broke, the whole thing would have withered away. Where were the conservative spin doctors who could explain the importance of the opening to the Iranian moderates and elicit public empathy for the administration's agony over the fate of the hostages? For that matter, where was the president? If Casey had been at normal operating speed and had been able to get Reagan to stand up in November of 1986 and say, "I wanted this done. I sanctioned it. Impeach me," it would all have been over right then and there in forty-eight hours or less.

I thought that perhaps it was not too late to pull the problem at least partway back into the political arena. That July, at my instigation, there was a meeting at Williams & Connolly to consider the possibility of organizing some political action. I didn't have anything particular in mind, just the idea that perhaps it was time to mobilize public support. Brendan Sullivan was there, together with my lawyer, Bill McDaniel; Tom Wilson, who represented Joe Fernandez; and Poindexter's attorney, Richard Beckler. Although everyone agreed that political action might potentially be useful, the consensus of the meeting was to defer action until after the November elections. The group felt that Reagan might pardon everyone as he left office, and no one wanted to jeopardize that.

Helga, Tarik, and I left Washington on August 3, 1988, heading for our new home in San Diego, and my new job with General Dynamics, as director of international marketing for its Electronics Division. As time passed, the East Coast seemed to have fewer and fewer redeeming features. After a business trip back East, I couldn't wait to return to San Diego. Moreover, I finally had an opportunity to concentrate on some longtime personal interests. I resumed wood sculpturing—carving birds of prey and totem poles—added to various collections, and pursued my interest in Egyptian hieroglyphs.

Relations with my "other" family had stabilized. Ian graduated from college and was a role model for Tarik. Cassi and I have grown closer and closer in recent years. She married a fine, accomplished husband, Robert "Trow" Trowbridge. Organized, self-disciplined, and hardworking, Cassi can be tough when required. Probably as a result of her less-than-adequate early family life, she has chosen not to work regularly outside the home and is devoted to bringing up three children, Courtney, Kirk, and Cooper.

Early that fall I got in touch with former national security adviser Bill Clark. We talked about possible strategies for obtaining pardons for North, Poindexter, and the others. We decided to bide our time until after the November election and agreed on a course of action. Clark would speak to President Reagan, and I would try to find a way to enlist Mrs. Reagan's support.

I did not know Mrs. Reagan personally, but I knew Mr. and Mrs. Charles Wick were among her small circle of friends. Charlie Wick had been head of the United States Information Service during the Reagan administration and was a friend of Bill Casey's. I didn't know him. I called Sophia Casey and asked her to get in touch with Wick and tell him I wanted to talk to him.

As we had hoped, in November Vice President Bush was elected to succeed Reagan. Around Thanksgiving, Bill Clark told me that he was becoming increasingly concerned about the response he was getting from President Reagan about the pardons. He said that Reagan was quite equivocal. Worse, Clark was sensing that Mrs. Reagan was very much against them. She felt that her husband's place in history would be sullied by pardoning these men. Clark planned to have another conversation with Reagan in a few days, hoping for a better outcome.

Shortly thereafter I spoke with Wick. After some pleasantries I got to the point: "Look, there is the sense around town that Mrs. Reagan is advising the president not to issue the pardons."

Wick assured me up and down that this was incorrect: "The president will make up his own mind about the pardons. Mrs. Reagan has no position on the issue and nothing to do with the president's decision."

Clark reported that his second effort with Reagan about the pardons came to naught.

Ronald Reagan left office in January 1989 without pardoning anyone. Although he had done his best for his Nicaraguan freedom fighters, he had left his own officers who had carried out his directives wounded on the battlefield. About three years later, quite by coincidence I had a conversation with someone who had accompanied Mrs. Reagan, Mrs. Wick, and others on Air Force One in the waning days of Reagan's presidency. This person overheard a conversation between Mrs. Wick and the first lady. Mrs. Reagan sounded out her friend about pardoning figures in the Iran-contra affair. Mrs. Wick stated firmly that the president should do no such thing.

As I settled into my new routine in San Diego, the Walsh investigation continued in Washington. By the middle of 1991, just as it appeared as if Walsh would finally close up shop, former Central American Task Force chief Alan Fiers changed lawyers. Tony Lapham, his first attorney, had an excellent reputation, but when Fiers changed lawyers, he cut a deal with Walsh. In July 1991, Alan Fiers pleaded guilty to misdemeanor charges— lying to Congress, of course. In exchange for having more serious felony charges dropped, he agreed to cooperate with the Walsh investigation.

Why did he do it? I never spoke with Fiers personally about it, but in all likelihood it was business-related. When Fiers left the Agency, he went to work for W. R. Grace, a company with a lot of government contracts. He became their Washington representative, a lobbyist. As long as Walsh's investigation was ongoing and the threat of indictment was still pending, Fiers was tainted—it was difficult for him to be truly effective on Capitol Hill.

The timing of Fiers's action was also significant. Webster had resigned as DCI in May, and Bush had nominated Deputy National Security Adviser Bob Gates to succeed him. Because Gates had been deputy and then acting director of the CIA during Iran-contra, his confirmation would be tough. Hearings on his nomination would surely resurrect questions regarding the extent of his knowledge about Iran-contra.

To think that Gates knew as little of these events as he claimed was hard for many to swallow. The officer below Gates—Clair George— knew. The individual above him—Casey—knew. Sandwiched like that, how far out of the loop could he have been? But given Casey's management style, it was very possible.

Gates's Senate confirmation was hostage to guilt by association with Casey. Gates needed all the support he could get to win, and Fiers was in a great place to give him a boost. Fiers's "confession" cleared the way for him to become a powerful witness on behalf of Gates's nomination. During the confirmation hearings, Fiers gave a masterful performance.

What did W. R. Grace have to gain from this? They got Fiers scrubbed halfway clean so that he could be more effective for them on Capitol Hill. They also scored major points with the White House and with the new DCI, Gates. For a government contractor, that's not a bad trade-off.

I don't know what Fiers told Walsh, but whatever it was, it implicated Clair George. Walsh's probe began zeroing in on George, and suddenly I began to hear that they were heating up the situation on me. As a result, in August I was rewarded with a field promotion from Lawrence Walsh. In the view of the Office of Independent Counsel (OIC), I was no longer a "subject," I'd risen to become a "target," meaning that an indictment was much more likely. I found this puzzling, since Alan Fiers could have said nothing to Walsh that would have given them more cause to indict me than they already had.

Getting information out of government agencies is a popular sport in Washington, and Walsh's office had its own press operation to play the game. Walsh himself spoke with the press presumably to justify his actions and his expenditures to the public. Sources claim that others in the OIC leaked information to the various defense lawyers trying to level the playing field. I have no proof of this. I do know that sources with indirect access kept me fully informed of Walsh's plans for his court case against me, and when I read his "Final Report," there were *absolutely* no surprises. McDaniel soon learned that they were hoping to cut a deal with me in exchange for my information—probably on Clair George. Even if I'd been willing to betray him, I had no damaging information. I told them to get lost. Clair George was indicted on ten counts in September 1991.

I knew the stakes had been raised considerably, and that I might be next. Judging by what had happened to the others, the Office of Independent Counsel might indict me out of spite. With their deep pockets, they could drag me through the courts for a long time—and they knew it.

Walsh's office also began pursuing Vince Cannistraro. To my knowledge he was neither a "target" nor a "subject" of the investigation. There is no reason why he should have been. I have to assume that Vince was another of Walsh's stepping-stones—they were hoping to use him to get to me. When interrogated by the FBI in July 1991, Cannistraro recalled our meeting with Oliver North at Charley's Place in November of 1985.

The way Cannistraro remembered it, almost six years after the fact, the three of us had discussed North's struggle to send military equipment to Iran to free the hostages—not what we really talked about, which was North's problems shipping arms from Eastern Europe through Portugal to Honduras. According to Walsh's final report, Cannistraro also told the grand jury that Ollie had called Poindexter right from Charley's, seeking authorization to bring me into the missile-shipping operation. It never happened.

Cannistraro had made another bizarre claim about me during his testimony as a defense witness at Oliver North's trial in 1989. In what Walsh's final report characterizes as Cannistraro's "hearsay testimony," he describes a series of meetings in 1984 in which he said the "hand off" to North was accomplished. At one such meeting in June 1984 in Casey's office at which I was supposedly present, along with Casey, CIA Central American Task Force Officer Joe Fernandez, and contra leader Aldolfo Calero, Casey told Calero that North, who was not subject to Boland Amendment operational restrictions, "would be a principal point of reference." I can state unequivocally that I was not present at the meeting described by Cannistraro, and Fernandez tells me that neither was he. Interestingly, Cannistraro apparently also testified that Casey had discussed this with the President who purportedly agreed "this was how it should be handled." The footnote to this point in Walsh's report notes that "Independent Counsel was unable to corroborate Cannistraro's testimony."

In November of 1991, I had a chance meeting with Cannistraro in the terminal at Dulles International on my way into Washington from San Diego. It was like a scene from a Hitchcock movie. As I was going down the escalator, I saw Vince on the landing above me. He scurried down the stairs to meet me at the bottom and said, "They're going to indict you," and disappeared to meet an Italian movie producer whom we had both known in Rome.

Walsh had requested that my case not be assigned to a judge randomly selected as is the custom but instead assigned to a judge handpicked by the court. (Harold Greene, the judge I got, is perhaps best remembered as the one whose decision to dismantle AT&T took the United States from having the best telecommunications system in the world to having a third world one.) The OIC considered him sympathetic to their cause. Greene was indisposed on the day of my arraignment and another judge, Aubrey Robinson, stepped in to preside.

On November 26, 1991, Bill McDaniel and I waded through reporters in front of the Federal Court House in Washington and pleaded not guilty before Judge Robinson. Tom Wilson, Joe Fernandez's lawyer and a prince of a man, came down for moral support. I was indicted on seven counts of lying to Congress and the Tower Commission. The charges were based on the same information that was available in 1987—with the dubious addition of Cannistraro's version of our meeting with Oliver North at Charley's Place. The maximum penalty for each of my felonies was five years in prison and $250,000 in fines.

The accusation came at the eleventh hour. Most of the counts were based on statements I had made before SSCI, HPSCI, and the Tower Commission in early to mid-December 1986. The five-year statute of limitations would have expired on them within three weeks.

When entering my not-guilty plea, I wore a camouflage jacket that the British Twenty-second SAS (Special Air Service) Regiment had given me on a visit to their headquarters at Hereford. As we exited, one of the reporters asked me why I was wearing cammo. I said, "When you're at battle stations, you might as well be prepared for battle stations."

After giving the media their sound bite for the day, I was booked. Ordinarily, the Marshals' Service does this in the courthouse, but I was given special treatment. Taken to FBI Headquarters, I was fingerprinted and a mug shot was taken. This episode seemed to disturb my lawyer, Bill McDaniel, a lot more than it did me.

I've been a believer in the Stoic philosophy all my adult life, trying to live by many of its precepts. As a result, I was able to go through the indictment, arraignment, and booking with a mix of curiosity and detachment. As the Roman Stoic philosopher and statesman Lucius Seneca said in the first century A.D., "The thing that matters is not what you bear but how you bear it."

Soon after Clair George was indicted, a group of retired Agency officers—spearheaded by Amos Longstreet [F], John Waller, William Donnelly, and Samuel Halprin—began organizing the Legal Defense Fund.

Dick Stolz, whom Webster had brought in as DDO after Clair retired, was involved, at least at the outset.

Russell Bruemmer, who had written the one-sided report for DCI Webster in December 1987, and several other lawyers published a letter to the legal community, recommending contributions to the Legal Defense Fund. Maybe Bruemmer regretted his role in this affair, or perhaps he wanted to be sure that his fellow lawyers defending the Iran-contra defendants were paid.

When I was indicted, my superior, Terry Straeter, who was the new general manager of General Dynamics's Electronics Division, and his superior, Michael Keel, the General Dynamics group chief on the West Coast, discussed whether I should be put on leave with or without pay. Straeter recommended a paid leave on the basis that you are innocent until proven guilty, but Keel overruled him and put me on leave without pay.

I had a good rapport with Straeter, who is a real stand-up fellow. He called me in on the day before Thanksgiving to give me the bad news in person. "Dewey, I'm sorry this has happened," he said. "This was not my position. I argued against it, but this is where Keel is coming from and he's taken the decision out of my hands."

I didn't want to leave it at that, and I suspected that Keel had not consulted with corporate headquarters when he made his determination. I asked Terry, "Do you mind if I play hardball around you? I don't want you to get hurt in the process."

After Terry told me to go ahead, I called Rich Armitage, who I knew well from his days as assistant secretary of defense for international security affairs. Armitage has little time for spongy liberals. He has no patience with what is not morally or politically right and has a take-no-prisoners approach to life. Above all, he's my friend. I asked him to call Frank Carlucci, who was a member of the General Dynamics Board of Directors. I knew Carlucci well enough to call him myself, but I didn't want to put him on the spot.

I assumed that Carlucci would call Bill Anders, the former astronaut who was GD's chief executive officer, and discuss my situation with him. I was fairly confident that Anders was unaware of what had happened. At the same time, Mike Ledeen, a scholar and former consultant to the National Security Council whom I knew well, suggested that he had a link to the Crown family, who were major GD shareholders, owning about a quarter of the stock and calling the shots. This contact was made. The Crowns engaged through Harvey Kapnick, General Dynamics's deputy CEO.

I may never know the full saga of all the efforts made on my behalf, but they worked. I am grateful to all involved. Shortly thereafter, I was on paid leave, and within a couple of weeks I was back at work. Thankfully,

Terry Straeter suffered no repercussions when Keel's decision was reversed. Straeter went on to generously donate $10,000 (not tax-deductible) to the Legal Defense Fund.

I did what I could to help the Legal Defense Fund raise money, but it became apparent that the organizers mainly wanted to use me as a conduit to Ollie North. They were after his list of major contributors who underwrote the cost of Brendan Sullivan and his colleagues. There was nothing wrong with this, but as time passed, it became clear to me and others that the fund would be used primarily to defray Clair George's legal expenses. If he had not been in trouble, I doubt it would even have been established.

Oliver North did go to bat for the fund, writing a special letter, but it was largely unsuccessful. We simply weren't Ollie North. I forced the Legal Defense Fund to cough up $5,000 for Joe Fernandez in return for North's help with the letter. Up until then, Joe had not received a dime from the fund, which was supposedly for all CIA officers involved.

This was a heavy time for Helga. She was extremely worried about the future, my going to prison, and whether we faced financial ruin. I wanted to get on with the final act, and then out of the blue my trial was postponed because Walsh had decided to go after Caspar Weinberger. In June of 1992, the former secretary of defense was indicted on five felony counts of withholding evidence and lying to Congress and to the OIC.

Walsh had to know that he was really going to have a tough time prosecuting Weinberger. Here was a man who staunchly opposed the opening to the Iranian moderates and the shipment of missiles. Walsh's costs and productivity were coming under increasing scrutiny in the press. My suspicion is that as Walsh became apprehensive about his abominable track record in court, he decided he had to nail someone big in the administration to justify himself.

As my case started to make its way through the legal system, Bill McDaniel got some charges against me thrown out. Even Judge Greene had to agree that I'd been indicted for the same "lie" on two different counts. He slated my court date for March 15, 1993, and we started lining up our case.

Though I knew we'd mount a strong defense, I also knew that any trial in Washington, D.C., was a chancy proposition. The legal issues in Iran-contra had been fogged over by the media, and by Walsh himself. In the case of the CIA, those issues were quite complex. It was questionable whether any group of jurors could really grasp them.

In November of 1992, George Bush lost his bid for reelection. Almost immediately, friends began making overtures to him about the possibility of presidential pardons. Bush was being counseled by some advisers (including, I had heard, his national security adviser, Brent Scowcroft) to pardon Caspar Weinberger and let the rest of us hang out to dry—in other words, to leave the wounded on the battlefield, the way Reagan had. George Bush is not a leave-them-on-the-battlefield type.

I was of two minds when the offer of the pardon came through. I knew that by taking it I would be giving up a chance to clear my name in court and felt strongly that the acceptance would imply that I was guilty. Fortunately, John McGaffin, who was one of my colleagues at the Agency, had told me over dinner a couple of months earlier, "Don't be stupid. This thing started as a political event. It should end as a political event. You should take the pardon. Don't reject it out of pride."

I knew he was right. I also knew that for the sake of my family it was time to put an end to the struggle. Bush announced my pardon, along with those of Bud McFarlane, Elliott Abrams, Caspar Weinberger, Alan Fiers, and Clair George, on Christmas Eve, 1992.

It was over for me, but not for Lawrence Walsh, who imploded and made a fool of himself on national television. He angrily turned his sights on the president himself, declaring that Bush was now a "subject" of his never-ending investigation.

In early 1993, I went to Washington on business. I decided to ask Vince Cannistraro to lunch. Friends thought that after all the grief he had caused me, I was crazy to go anywhere near him—unless I was bringing my sawed-off shotgun. We chatted easily over lunch at a little restaurant in McLean, Virginia, called Cafe Oggi. When we got to the coffee, I finally asked, "Why did you do it, Vince?"

What had been a quiet conversation underwent a startling increase in decibels. "You know what those people are like!" he said, raising his voice and gesticulating wildly. Eyebrows were raised at the tables around us. By "those people" he obviously meant Walsh and his prosecutors.

"No, Vince," I said softly, "I only met one once. His name was Keker, and I had sort of a normal conversation with the guy. He was the only person I'd ever met from the OIC."

I had known Vince Cannistraro for almost twenty years. We had been friends and colleagues. When he'd been under me in Rome, I thought his performance was exemplary, and he had done me a great favor in tipping me off to the antics of my deputy at that time, who had been trying to stab me in the back. He'd done a good job as Central American Task Force chief as well. When he was to be reassigned from the Central American Task Force in 1984, I helped him first get a position at the NSC, and then later another in the Department of Defense.

I still wanted to know why he had turned state's evidence against me on that famous drink at Charley's Place. As I waited for an explanation, I recalled that some in the Agency called him a crybaby.

"They put terrible pressure on me," he said as his voice reached a crescendo. He waved his arms in the air. We had the attention of many in the restaurant. "You know what those people are like, and I didn't have any choice!"

Although I didn't take it as an admission that he hadn't told the truth, that was enough for me. I'd found out everything I needed to know. They had leaned hard on him and he had caved in.

I should have called out Cannistraro to seek satisfaction, but alas, this mind-focusing, soul-cleansing custom has fallen into disfavor these days. Pity.

Alan Wolfe's first law is, "In is in, and out is out." This means that when you are in the CIA, you are a part of the organization, with all that implies. When you leave the Agency, you should not lurk around its fringes. I agree with the dictum, but circumstances from one's past occasionally intrude. In reality you are never totally "out," no more than anyone can ever escape his past. These intrusions are sometimes painful, and others are bizarre in terms of time and space.

There is an Ottoman (Turkish) proverb, *Ölümle öç alinmaz.* This roughly translates as, "Revenge should not be taken by death." However, that is exactly what happened to my former Turkish colleague Hiram Abas. We had become good friends, almost like brothers, after our retirements from our respective agencies. He was brutally murdered on September 26, 1990, by cowardly members of the terrorist band known as the Kurdish Communist Party (PKK), or contracted out by the PKK to the Turkish leftist terrorist group Dev Sol. The PKK has long been supported by the Syrian government.

Hiram was unique. In his time, he was Turkey's finest intelligence officer. This view of Hiram was shared by all foreign intelligence officers who had the privilege of knowing him. Eventually, he became the deputy chief of the Turkish intelligence service, the only civilian ever to hold that office. In this position, he organized successful counterterrorist operations against the PKK; hence its motive for revenge.

Hiram had been retired for about two years in September 1990, but had information that he was still a target of terrorist groups. Consequently he took precautions. He was meticulous in varying his route and was an excellent shot with a handgun. On the morning of September 26, in his vehicle, he was caught in a crossfire from both sides of the street by the murderers, who were dressed as municipal workers. After the fusillade, one of the terrorists crossed the street, opened the car door, and put a final shot into Hiram's head. It was a professional killing.

A color photograph of Hiram's bloody body slumped in his car was placed on the cover of the magazine *Yüzyil*, known to be pro-PKK. In the way of the Middle East, the PKK was not content with killing him; they also had to destroy his reputation. Accompanying the picture was a story containing a great deal of nonsense about Hiram's supposed connections with the Turkish criminal "mafia."

On September 26, 1995, I had the sad privilege to attend at Hiram's grave site, together with his other friends, a ceremony commemorating the fifth anniversary of his murder. Hiram was not only a superb intelligence officer, he was a fine human being. What a tragic waste.

The crash of Itavia Flight 870, otherwise known as the Ustica Affair, occurred on June 27, 1980, while I was chief in Rome. Sometime in 1993, I received a telephone call from the U.S. Department of Justice. The Italian magistrate investigating this case, Judge Rosario Priore, whom I had known during my days with the CIA Counterterrorist Center, wanted to interview me about the event, and also the crash of a Libyan MiG-23 in Calabria that happened on or about July 18 of the same year.

On the night of June 27, 1980, Italian Itavia Flight 870 with eighty-one passengers and crew crashed into the Tyrrhenian Sea near the island of Ustica. The aircraft was on a flight from Bologna to Palermo and had been delayed leaving Bologna due to bad weather. Because of the terrorism fomented by the Red Brigades and occasionally by rightist groups, speculation was that a terrorist bomb aboard the plane caused its plunge into the sea. The Italian authorities quickly dismissed this possibility, based on analysis of the few telephone calls claiming responsibility. In the terrorist sense, it was a nonevent for the Rome CIA.

In mid-July 1980, the chief of Italian Air Force Intelligence, Brig. Gen. Zeno Tascio, phoned me and asked me to come to his headquarters. He told me that a Libyan MiG-23 had crashed in the province of Calabria and that the pilot had been killed, apparently while trying to defect to Italy. He asked if the CIA was interested in examining the wreckage. I said I thought so and would get back to him shortly. I queried Headquarters, which in coordination with U.S. Air Force Intelligence sent out a team to examine the aircraft. As anticipated, it was of little interest, since the aircraft was an export version of the MiG-23 and thus less sophisticated than mainline Soviet models. However, some useful data was obtained. After a few days, I submitted a report of our findings to General Tascio. End of story—not quite.

When Priore and I met in 1994 (and again in 1996), fourteen years had elapsed since the tragic Itavia 870 crash. Outside of Italy, the crash had from the beginning been treated as ho-hum. However, in Italy during these years, thousands and thousands of words about the tragedy had appeared in the media and elsewhere. The Italians, with their fine eye for a conspiracy, had concocted various theories about who was responsible, either accidentally or not. These included the Americans (their favorite suspects), because an American aircraft carrier was in Palermo at the time; the Italian Air Force, out of sheer ineptitude during a training mission; the French, by mistake, trying to shoot down a flight from Tripoli to Moscow that was supposed to be carrying Muammar Qaddafi; and the Libyans themselves, out to teach the Italians some lesson or other.

This is where the Libyan MiG-23 and Itavia Flight 870 were joined. The argument was advanced that the Italian Air Force had concealed the true date of the MiG's crash; that it had in fact gone down on June 27, the same date as the Itavia crash. The Italian Air Force had lied out of embarrassment that the Libyan MiG had penetrated Italian airspace unnoticed during a major NATO air defense exercise.

As years passed, the wreckage of Itavia Flight 870 was raised from some two thousand feet underwater and reassembled. Then in 1994, *Il Quinto Scenàrio,* "The Fifth Scenario," was published in Italian by the Italian journalist and author Claudio Gatti. Israel became the fifth possible perpetrator of the Itavia crash, with Gatti making a circumstantial case that the Israelis mistook Flight 870 for a French aircraft carrying nuclear fuel from Toulouse to Baghdad for Iraq's "experimental" reactor. Interestingly, despite the thoroughness of the author's investigation, the book was never published in English.

Priore's questioning of me appeared to be an effort to put the finishing touches on his investigation, during which every conceivable person on both sides of the Atlantic and elsewhere with possible knowledge of the events was queried. I confirmed to Priore that the crash of Itavia Flight 870 was of no interest to me in Rome from a professional point of view, and that to my knowledge none of my officers had participated in meetings in the U.S. defense attaché's office about the crash. Moreover, the MiG-23 episode was as straightforward as described above. Gatti's book was briefly touched on, for he had contacted me about the Libyan MiG-23 incident. And that was that, as far as I was concerned. Although the crash of Itavia Flight 870 remains unexplained, an air-to-air-missile expert who examined the retrieved fuselage maintains that the aircraft was hit by two "fire-and-forget" aircraft-launched missiles. The mystery is still out there awaiting final solution.

From a distance, with a mixture of alarm and sadness, I watch the steady disintegration of the CIA and particularly the Clandestine Services. This deterioration is aided and abetted by President Clinton, who fails to understand the need for an intelligence service producing "national or strategic intelligence." Even if this is not of interest to him, it may be for his successors.

CHAPTER 25

Whither
the Clandestine Services

(MY VIEWS CIRCA MARCH 1996)

In Robert Morley's small, witty volume *The Pleasures of Age* (Mercury House), he proposes that his grandson join him in a toast with Coca-Cola.

The grandson asks, "So, what is the toast to be, Grandpa?"

"To spies."

"Why spies particularly?"

"I always think they keep down the mischief."

Whether it was to "keep down the mischief" or to prevent another Pearl Harbor, the United States created after World War II a substantial intelligence-collection and -analysis system to provide "national or strategic" intelligence to the president and other policymakers. The military services retained their responsibility for providing themselves with "tactical or battlefield" intelligence and have jealously guarded this prerogative until they find themselves in trouble.

However, with the collapse of the Soviet empire, a number of politicians, members of the media, scholars, and officials of the executive branch began to recommend changes in the national intelligence system. The extremists sought its abolition or fragmentation, which would amount to the same thing. A more moderate and reasonable suggestion was that the system be rationalized and downsized for today's climate. The latter is certainly a legitimate position whence to start an examination of the issue, but interestingly, the primary focus of this debate was centered on the CIA, and more particularly the Clandestine Services within the CIA, despite the fact that the Clandestine Services' budget and personnel are minuscule. The Department of Defense spends approximately 85 percent of the intelligence budget. The CIA and several small departmental intelligence offices get what is left.

This debate became superheated during the Clinton administration because of the president's lack of interest in foreign intelligence. He was disinclined to support his "centurions" of the Clandestine Services, who, in any event, were not helping themselves by presenting him with messes such as the Aldrich Ames debacle and the French economic-spying case. The lack of presidential support was magnified with the appointment of John Deutch as DCI. Like William Webster before him, Deutch demonstrated no real interest in supporting the CIA and the Clandestine Services in particular. To the contrary, the more he attacked the Clandestine Services, the more the media and some in Congress applauded. Deutch was clearly using his time at the CIA and his attitude toward it to advance his own ambitions. He and Webster are unique among the CIA directors in this regard.

With no administration support for the CIA, Congress and the U.S. military have stepped in to take control of an agency that was historically managed and protected by the White House. The congressional intelligence oversight committees, particularly the Senate's, aided and abetted by Deutch, have moved to fulfill their long-sought goal of getting their hands on the president's "last centurions," the Clandestine Services, whose small budget defies control by power of the purse. This is being accomplished by endless investigations of alleged wrongdoings in the past by the Clandestine Services, which requires the rewriting of the previous understood rules of engagement to support the allegations. For example, CIA case officers have had to deal from time to time with unsavory or worse individuals—just as the FBI and the DEA deal with criminals to prosecute other criminals. Suddenly, it was retroactively unacceptable to deal with "bad" people. Officers who had had such relationships have been punished both to instill fear and an "understanding of the rules" in their compatriots within the Clandestine Services and to enable Deutch to demonstrate to Congress and the media that he was in charge.

The U.S. military's move into the CIA vacuum created by Clinton and Deutch is not so much aimed at the Clandestine Services, but rather at gathering the national intelligence system under its control in "support of the warfighter." But these technical and human collection systems were designed to provide long-term strategic information to the president and policymakers—not instant intelligence to the soldiers on the battlefield. The military insisted on providing its own tactical or battlefield intelligence and basically distrusted those national systems that were designed and controlled by civilians. The military had been afforded billions of dollars over the years to build a tactical capability for itself for the battlefield, with apparently less than sufficient results. The abysmal failure of the U.S. military to provide itself with tactical intelligence was underlined repeatedly during Grenada, Panama, Somalia, and the Gulf War.

During the latter, the U.S. military discovered the value of the national collection systems and now demands to have this intelligence for maintaining "dominant battlefield awareness" and to "aim" its smart weapons. Clearly, the military wants to control, if not own, all the national collection systems. That after-action reports during the Gulf War indicated that the military had much of the intelligence it needed from the CIA and other national systems, but was incapable of disseminating it properly to those who required the information, particularly at the lower echelons, has been largely ignored. Apparently, all the supposed attention paid to communications interoperability among our military services after their fiasco in Grenada was simply lip service. Worse still, there is evidence of hoarding of intelligence by higher echelons, particularly within the U.S. Air Force, during the Gulf War.

Of course, the military should have the best intelligence the American people can provide; it is one of the major force multipliers on the battlefield. However, by redirecting most of the nation's intelligence assets to "supporting the warfighter," the president and other policymakers risk not having a reasonable strategic intelligence system to assist them in their decisions about whether to go to war in the first place.

Meanwhile, the Clandestine Services (Directorate of Operations) is being destroyed in detail rather than in whole and continues a steady decline into something resembling the style, work ethic, and morale of the post office. The morale of the Clandestine Services is at rock bottom. Few serious operations are being undertaken; why take the risk of being accused in hindsight of wrongdoing by the next owners of the Agency? Lawyers abound, looking over everyone's shoulder, a sure inhibition to initiative, needless to say risk taking. The Clandestine Services cannot even meet its modest recruitment quota for entry-level case officers from outside; thus the deficiency is being made up from personnel already within the Agency. This begs the question of why they are not already case officers.

Does it matter whether the United States has an effective Clandestine Services capable of serious espionage and covert action operations? I submit that it does, if for nothing more than "keeping down the mischief." Is it possible to rebuild it into an effective organization, to improve it by learning from its past mistakes, and to anticipate that it will be able to meet effectively the challenges of the twenty-first century? Let's look at the key issues that impact the answer to that question: one, the Clandestine Services' mission; two, its personnel; and three, the overarching and essential requirement of political support for the institution in the White House, Congress, and elsewhere in the government.

When the Berlin Wall went down, various commentators immediately said that the Clandestine Services, in fact all intelligence-collection agencies, needed new missions or sets of requirements to justify their existence, given the supposed lack of a serious nation-state threat to the United States. Some suggested that it should go away, an anachronism of the Cold War. When nothing seemed changed from their vantage point, these same commentators began to claim that the Clandestine Services didn't know what to do in the post-Soviet world. All of this was absurd. The Clandestine Services, the spies, knew better than most that the world was still a dangerous place and perhaps even more dangerous with the demise of the Soviet empire. After all, it had been working on other threatening problems, such as terrorism and the proliferation of weapons of mass destruction, when the Soviets were still considered the main threat to world peace and certainly to our national security. What was required now was a change in priorities, something the Clandestine Services is used to, but in honesty has not always adjusted to as rapidly as it should have.

One does not have to be in the Clandestine Services to divine the new priorities. They certainly include proliferation of weapons of mass destruction and their delivery systems; ethnic and religious mayhem and strife; stability issues in the former colonies of the Soviet empire and Russia itself; terrorism; plans and policies of radical states such as Libya, Iran, North Korea, and Iraq; economic intelligence; narcotics/crime/human rights; counterintelligence; and the maintenance of a covert action capability.

This suggests that the Clandestine Services has a rather full plate even in today's world, and most of these requirements do not lend themselves to complete or even partial solution by the antiseptic technical means of satellites and the like. Instead, they require human sources—agents— who may occasionally not be acceptable family in-laws, but have the access, and sometimes the only access, to the critical, lifesaving information. Several of these requirements have and have always had certain special problems associated with them. Recently, some have been media and congressional events.

The Ames debacle has brought the whole counterintelligence issue to the forefront in the media and government. Over the years the Clandestine Services has not handled counterintelligence well for a number of reasons. First, there was a lack of what I would call "adult supervision." James Angleton was the first egregious example of those who were allowed by senior management to isolate themselves from the mainstream of the Clandestine Services in the name of security and carry on unfocused and often paranoid investigations that had little relevance to the Agency's ongoing operations and were often mindlessly destructive of positive efforts. Richard Helms should go to his grave deploring his lack of courage or misplaced loyalty in his failure to remove Angleton; at least William Colby rose to the occasion.

Other problems revolve around compartmentation. There is an absolutely legitimate reason to protect operations under the need-to-know and no-legacies principles; however, it is too frequently abused. For example, the counterintelligence/security crowd, those in the Clandestine Services involved in Soviet operations within the Soviet Union and the U.S. Air Force's former Los Angeles satellite warriors, have been notorious for using security and compartmentation to protect themselves from legitimate inquiries that might expose operational failures or uncover financial overruns or schedule slips. Knowledge is power, and thus for some, compartmentation serves this purpose. On the other hand, for the paranoid counterintelligence officer, nearly everyone is suspect, justifying his zeal with enforcing compartmentation.

The quality of the personnel engaged in counterintelligence is another issue. Even in the mid-1980s when there was a new focus on counterintelligence (well before Ames), senior management still basically ignored counterintelligence as a key discipline. Assignments to counterintelligence functions were not considered career enhancing, and most good officers avoided them. Thus the ranks of counterintelligence, like those of the Soviet Division, were filled to an unacceptable degree with mediocre case officers and those lacking interpersonal skills. (You could have a successful career in the Counterintelligence Staff or Soviet Division without ever recruiting anyone.) I am as guilty as anyone in this regard. When I realized in Ankara, Turkey, that Ames would never make it as a mainstream case officer in the Clandestine Services, what did I do? I basically recommended that he follow a career in counterintelligence!

Some believe that you need special, long-term officers to staff counterintelligence programs to maintain a continuity of knowledge. I support this notion, providing that it is rationally applied.

The Office of Security also shoulders no small degree of fault for the Ames debacle. This office has traditionally undertaken most of its investigative work with new hires and retirees from a variety of government agencies. Few of these were expert investigators. As a result the work was performed in a perfunctory manner and was further undermined by the reluctance of most CIA personnel to make derogatory comments about their fellow employees even when they suspected that things might not be "quite right." Now, of course, the pendulum will swing the other way, and there will be aggressive and intrusive investigations of all employees' bank accounts, stock holdings, and so on. The next Ames—and there will be one—is unlikely to be as stupid as Ames and will afford himself a foreign bank account beyond the view of the Office of Security. (I sympathize with Ames's KGB case officer. He must now be without a hair on his head, having uprooted them contending with Ames's diabolical, suicidal, and stupid lack of security in the way he flaunted his wealth.)

The polygraph is yet another issue closely associated with counter-intelligence. The device works best on individuals raised to feel guilt about lying. Those with no conscience and a different view of lying can "defeat" the polygraph, and one can be trained to beat it as well. That said, I admit to being a supporter of the polygraph, for I believe that it acts as a deterrent to traitorous and other aberrant behavior. This is its negative or defensive advantage. Its positive contribution is in authenticating and verifying an agent or case officer. However, it is only one of the tools that should be used to decide veracity.

Unfortunately, by the early 1980s, in agent operations the polygraph had become the dominant and often only element in determining their authenticity despite vigorous efforts by some of us to use a more complete approach. We largely failed. Paralleling this activity on agent operations was the reinvigoration during Casey's tenure as DCI of the reinvestigation of staff employees, which had been neglected for years. This included a background investigation prior to a polygraph. Given the number of personnel involved, new polygraph operators with little or no experience were hired in profusion to handle the cases. It was an unmitigated disaster and resulted in the situation that allowed the Office of Security to excuse "evidence" of deception by Ames on several polygraph examinations.

By mid-1985, I was spending considerable energy every day dealing with cases of staff personnel who were having problems with their polygraphs. Most of these individuals were irate about their treatment by the polygraph operators and their supervisors. The problems were obvious. First of all, polygraphy is hardly a science, but it isn't black magic either. It takes a sensitive operator with considerable experience to produce real results. Unfortunately, the operators were inexperienced and their tenuous results required constant adjudication by their supervisors, who were naturally loath to take too frequent exception to their juniors' readings of the polygraph charts. This was compounded by a new emphasis in the polygraph examination on "lifestyle" questions like "Are you screwing anyone besides or instead of your spouse?" I did not and do not disagree with any of this; the problem was that it was ineptly and insensitively carried out.

By 1988, when I left the Agency, and surely by 1990, the Office of Security and its polygraph division in particular were on the defensive because of their excessive earlier zeal, which had produced no real traitors, only the occasional pederast or sodomite. The pendulum was against them just at the time they needed momentum to confront Ames. Aberrant polygraph results such as those of Ames were now subjected to endless searches for rational explanations, the intellectual masturbation of "what ifs," and in these murky circumstances, Ames slipped through.

After Ames was discovered, Congress and the media questioned the competence of the counterintelligence and security elements of the Agency. Some of the Agency's senior management was crucified for its failures in connection with Ames; others, such as Jack Devine (aka Easter Island man), who had also supervised Ames, skated for seemingly inexplicable reasons, if supervision was in and of itself grounds for reprimand.

However, let's put the event in its true perspective. Ames is a monumental embarrassment to the Clandestine Services in particular and to one degree or another the rest of the U.S. government. It really is an ego issue for most insiders. In reality, however, it is a passing event, albeit unfortunate. The tragic heroes are those Russian agents compromised by Ames who went to the wall or the furnace for execution. Let's not make it complicated. Ames is simply a common murderer, who did so for money. He had no fig leaf of real or imagined ideological identification with the Soviet Union or Russia, unlike the Rosenbergs, Cohen, and others. Ames should have been executed not because he is a traitor, but because he is guilty of murder.

In the end, institutional security fixes will be put in place to detect another Ames more rapidly. But the bottom line is that intelligence agents are a renewable resource, like trees, particularly for a major world power. Human nature being what it is, the ranks of the agents murdered by Ames will be or have already been filled. Thus, let's stop the hand-wringing; let's fix the security problems that have been identified; let's get on with pursuing other possible traitors; and above all, let's put an undistracted Clandestine Services back to work.

Economic intelligence is another requirement for the Clandestine Services that is under public debate. Economic intelligence should be divided into two components. One is just that—economic intelligence, information that supports the federal government in trade negotiations with foreign powers, provides the Federal Reserve with advance information on rate changes by foreign central banks, ensures no surprise technological breakthroughs abroad, and the like. This information does not directly aid a particular U.S. industry or company; it supports policy-making by the federal government. In the past at least, the Clandestine Services could be proud of its success in this arena.

The second component is industrial espionage, which is the gathering of proprietary business information (contract negotiations, "trade secrets," manufacturing processes, and so on). Neither the CIA nor any other agency of the U.S. intelligence community engages in industrial espionage. Because the French, Israelis, Russians, Japanese, Chinese, and just about every other country with a serious technological base do, some argue that the Clandestine Services should also do so to support U.S. industry. The Clandestine Services has eschewed this activity largely for two reasons. One, some case officers argue that industrial espionage has no bearing on national security, and they are not prepared to take risks to assist General Motors in making greater profits. I would argue that the success of U.S. business abroad does affect national security as the global marketplace expands and economic security becomes a larger element of national security and well-being. Two, and this is the principal argument against engaging in industrial espionage, how can the information obtained be fairly and securely distributed to U.S. industry? An example perhaps best explains the dilemma. Let us say that the European Airbus consortium is competing with the U.S. aircraft manufacturers Boeing and McDonnell Douglas for a foreign aircraft purchase. The Clandestine Services acquires some useful information that would aid the U.S. companies in their winning of the contract. Arguably it would be better to give the information to only one of the U.S. companies, but given our society, it would probably leak and the CIA would find itself being sued in court by the company denied the data. Other countries have solved this dilemma. Their industries are used to receiving the advantages of industrial espionage on one occasion and not on another. They keep their mouths shut and stay out of court—their turn will come next. In some cases, the foreign industries are owned by their governments or are basically their creatures, and thus the handling of the data is simple. None of this works in our country, but here the problem can be solved by providing the information to all U.S. competitors, perhaps not the optimum solution but better than doing nothing. In many instances the information should be published overtly for the world to see. In this way the playing field is really leveled and offsets to some extent the effects of the bribery too often employed by some foreign firms. That the publication of this information could endanger sources and methods is a real concern, but not insurmountable in most instances, and should not be allowed to deflect a thorough and thoughtful examination of a successful solution of the matter.

No one seriously disputes that the Clandestine Services should collect secret intelligence on terrorism, proliferation of weapons of mass destruction, narcotics, and international crime. The issues here are the methods, and the largely ignored attitudes of the case officers and the serious limitations imposed by the U.S. legal system on the efficacy of a Clandestine Services effort against some of these requirements.

The perpetrators of the above activities are a collection of dangerous, wicked individuals, groups, and nation-states. The handwringers claim that by collecting information on these targets, one perforce becomes "one of the bad guys." This is absurd. But you do have to deal with undesirables to penetrate the organizations or states involved to obtain information. Mother Teresa, for all her wisdom, unfortunately doesn't have it. What is disturbing is the hypocrisy on this issue of some in Congress, the executive branch, the media, academia, and, most disgraceful of all, the current CIA leadership. The CIA is lambasted by these worthies for dealing with "scumbags" to acquire secret intelligence to protect American lives and property, whereas no such condemnation is leveled at the FBI, the DEA, and local law enforcement agencies, which deal routinely with criminals (called paid informers rather than agents) to capture and convict other criminals. Nor do these same dignitaries get up on their high horses to berate their special foreign friends and nations who engage in the same or worse to obtain the required intelligence. You can't have it both ways. If you want the protection that secret intelligence can provide, you cannot expect the Clandestine Services to deal only with Boy Scouts to obtain it. It must be afforded the same methods allowed the FBI and the others.

Besides being hung out to dry on the above issue, case officers are also reluctant to tackle the requirements of international crime, narcotics trafficking, and human rights violations because these are regarded as law enforcement matters. They joined the CIA to steal the secrets of Iraq, North Korea, and the like. Had they wanted to be involved in law enforcement, they would have joined the FBI or a police force. If the Clandestine Services is to pursue such requirements, I suggest that it begin hiring some personnel who are prepared to confront these issues. However, the problem is larger than the case officers and their attitudes.

The goals of law enforcement and intelligence collection conflict. Law enforcement agencies collect information solely to put criminals in prison—a onetime, short-term goal; pay the informant, make a bust, go to trial with the informer as witness. Espionage is conducted for the long-term production of intelligence: recruit the agent, collect the information, hopefully for years or decades. Moreover, intelligence gathered by CIA agents and case officers on law enforcement targets may be used in trials, and either the agent or case officer or both may be required to appear in court. If that happens, even with the use of fictitious names, the agent and case officer may lose their anonymity and be unable to continue to work. The Justice Department is rightly proud of its mitigation of this concern in actual cases, but the fear persists. I know that in the past the Clandestine Services abandoned some foreign narcotics-collection operations because of this fear and because these operations were likely to produce information on alleged criminal activity by American citizens, which is forbidden to the Agency. The problem may be insolvable in our society, but possible solutions need frank examination by Congress and the executive branch if they are really serious about propelling the Clandestine Services into intelligence gathering against law enforcement targets.

A final requirement that draws vigorous debate is covert action, which, sometimes under different names, has been undertaken by the government since the founding of the republic. The three basic types of covert action are perception management (historically known as propaganda), political action (influencing the actions of a foreign leader or government), and paramilitary operations (support to insurgents). The most recent argument has been that paramilitary activities should be turned over to the U.S. military because that is their area of expertise. That is a singularly bad idea. To begin with, the whole idea behind covert action is deniability by the U.S. government. It is hard to deny that the U.S. government is involved if uniformed U.S. military personnel are in the operation, and in many circumstances U.S. military personnel cannot by law "pretend" to be anything but that.

An equally important drawback to the use of the U.S. military is the number of personnel required to do a given task and the support troops that go with these for whatever reason. Gen. Paul Gorman told me once that it would have taken nearly three hundred soldiers to do what twenty to thirty CIA personnel accomplished with the Nicaraguan guerrillas. A more recent example is the ratio of support troops to peacekeepers in Bosnia— twenty thousand peacekeepers and probably triple this number in their support. This is not meant to knock the military; they simply have a different way of doing things and other requirements that do not lend themselves to minimal use of manpower even among the Special Forces units.

Moreover, the regular, the "straight-leg," U.S. Army has no interest in paramilitary operations; as was evident in Grenada, it doesn't like or want its own Special Forces units. The Army's attitude is not unique; neither the JCS nor the other services want a piece of the paramilitary requirement. Their legitimate fear is that, à la Vietnam, they will be fed piecemeal into smaller conflicts by the politicians, who will also circumscribe their actions, limiting their ability to close with the enemy to end the conflict in a clear-cut victory. Paramilitary activities compound this problem for our military because they are usually conducted indirectly in support of the insurgents. They aren't hands-on types of operations, are often politically contentious in Washington, and can lack American public support. These conditions are anathema to the military.

Does the Clandestine Services have the type of personnel and atmosphere to accomplish its tasks assuming someone seriously wants it to?

First, if the American people want an effective Clandestine Services willing to make the personal and other sacrifices inherent in the work, the organization has to feel that it is elite.

Second, the absolutely essential ingredient of the Clandestine Services is talented personnel capable of recruiting and skillfully handling their agents. Without that, you have nothing but a bunch of timeservers pretending to be spies. An effective Clandestine Services cannot mirror the gender and ethnicity of the American population as a whole. Like it or not, gender and ethnic quotas or diversity are no substitute for talent. Furthermore, the rest of the world (and some would say most of this country) retains its prejudices and cultural attitudes toward females and various ethnic groups. This presents serious problems and disadvantages for female and ethnic officers, particularly in recruitment. Most of the secret intelligence in the world is still in the hands of men. The development of an individual toward recruitment, even when subtly conducted, involves rather aggressive behavior. When a female case officer undertakes the development of a male target, the latter's reaction is often that this female is coming on to him for sex. His instinct is to try to jump her into bed, something the Clandestine Services will not countenance as a recruitment ploy. Thus, recruitment for the female case officer has inherent difficulties. American ethnic males and females also encounter prejudices that inhibit their ability to recruit and often even to handle agents not of their ethnic background. On the other hand, I have had agents tell me that their best handlers were females.

Because the Clandestine Services cannot control or even influence the world's various prejudices, we should allow it to deal with reality, seeking to recruit the most talented case officers possible with due attention to gender and ethnic diversity. Moreover, the Clandestine Services should seek to take positive advantage of gender and ethnicity where appropriate and to recognize people equally for the roles they play in accomplishing the organization's mission.

Until a number of months ago, I thought the Clandestine Services would emerge from all the current furor, right itself, clean up its act, and get on with the job. I've lost my optimism, largely because political support has failed to materialize. The opposite has happened. Deutch, instead of sorting out the Clandestine Services and then supporting it, simply drove a knife into its back.

What Washington, D.C., knows, but may not be taught in Cambridge, Massachusetts, is that history attests that what goes around, comes around. It is merely a matter of time.

The Clandestine Services was an easy mark for Deutch and his cronies on Capitol Hill. What Americans need to understand is that unlike all other U.S. government agencies and the U.S. military, the Clandestine Services cannot undertake its own public relations campaign, for if its successes are to be effective, they should remain secret. Because of this, the Clandestine Services has always been dependent on the support of its director, the president, and nowadays the congressional oversight committees. Sensing little support for the Clandestine Services on the Hill or in the White House and with his own greater ambition in the offering, Deutch toadied to Congress, particularly the Senate oversight committee, delivering the requested coup de grâce to the organization.

Therefore, I conclude that the Clandestine Services is finished as a really effective intelligence service. It will be reinvented or restored to competency only after some appalling catastrophe befalls us, such as the explosion of a nuclear device or a biological attack or the like by some rogue group or nation-state, and the following investigation demonstrates that the act was undetectable by our national technical means. Then, when it becomes apparent that only a human source, an agent, could have provided forewarning, someone will ask why we don't have any agents and the answer will force the issue. Unfortunately, this is the American way.

While mindful of the Clandestine Services' past and present follies, but also aware of its real successes, I am sad to witness its decline, if not in fact its demise. Aside from concerns about national security, my distress is for the many talented young people who will not have the opportunity and privilege to work for the vibrant organization that I knew and to serve their country. I had often thought during my career that I should have been paying the Agency for the privilege of serving in the Clandestine Services. Perhaps, even more to the point, never once during my thirty-three years at the CIA did I awake in the morning and not want to go to work; I couldn't wait to get there.

Index

Index

Index

Index

Dendo, Al, 389
Deogin, Padma, 88
Deogin, Sami, 88
Deutch, John, 402, 411–12
Dev Genc (Revolutionary Youth), 111
Devine, Jack, 206, 407
Dev Sol, 398
Dewey, Thomas E., 26
Diario Las Americas, 224
Dickinson, Angie, 84
Diego, Wycliffe, 236
Di Genova, Joe, 358, 359
Digital Equipment Corporation, 301–2
Directorate of Administration, 323
Directorate of General Intelligence
    (DGI), Iraqi, 15, 20
Directorate of Intelligence (DI), 41, 178,
    204, 229, 333
  counterterrorism analysis and, 322–23,
    327, 328
  "elite" reputation of, 303–4
  intelligence analysis problem in, 151–52
Directorate of Operations (DO), 41, 48,
    49, 51, 65, 105, 179, 204, 280,
    289–90, 309, 311, 312, 322, 333
  Ames debacle and, 120–21, 402, 404,
    405–6, 407
  Clinton administration and, 401–2
  compartmentation and, 405
  counterintelligence failure of, 404–5
  covert action role and, 410
  CTC opposed by, 323–24, 326
  culture of other directorates and,
    227–28
  deterioration of, 403–4, 411–12
  downsizing of, 165
  drug war and, 409–10
  economic intelligence and, 389, 407
  functions of, 42
  future terrorism and, 408–9
  industrial espionage and, 407–8
  law enforcement targets and, 409–10
  "no legacy" policy and, 300
  polygraph controversy and, 406–7
  post-Soviet era and, 401–2
  quality personnel recruitment and,
    410–11
  Turner's tenure and, 165
  U.S. military and, 402–3

Directorate of Science and Technology,
    227–28, 323
Distinguished Intelligence Medal, 293
Dominica, 250
Dominican Republic, 114, 226
"domino theory," 75
Donahue, Mick, 207, 321
Donnelly, William, 394
Dornan, Diane, 375
Doublecrossed (film), 287
Drug Enforcement Agency (DEA), 237,
    286–87, 326, 402, 408
  CIA and, 118–20
  Noriega episode and, 342–43, 344
Duarte, José Napoleón, 225
Dubček, Alexander, 123
Duffy, John, 326
Dulles, Allen, 65–66, 101, 110, 165
  Thapa's visit to, 73–74
Duncan, Monty, 268–69
Duval, Tom, 386
Duvalier, Papa Doc, 89

Earl, Robert, 324
economic intelligence, 389, 407
Ecuador, 342
Egypt, 114, 151, 152, 154, 162, 331
  Achille Lauro affair and, 16, 307–8
Eighty-second Airborne Division, U.S.,
    257
Eisenhower, Dwight D., 28
elections:
  of 1940, 24
  of 1944, 26
  of 1960, 84
  of 1968, 123
  of 1980, 179–80, 187
  of 1984, 255, 286–87, 292, 294
  of 1986, 363
  of 1988, 385, 390, 391
  of 1992, 396
Elephant Herd, Operation, 267
Enders, Rudy, 271
Enders, Thomas, 199, 201, 202–3,
    228–29, 240–41, 248, 271
Escobar, Pablo, 286
espionage:
  "gangplank" recruitment and, 77
  industrial, 407–8

418

Index

Index

Index

Index

Printed in the United States
16170LVS00008B/4

9 780743 245364